Fierce Angels

Fierce Angels

Living with a Legacy
from the Sacred Dark Feminine
to the Strong Black Woman

Sheri Parks, PhD
Foreword by Marcia Ann Gillespie

Lawrence Hill Books

Fierce Angels is a work of nonfiction. Some names and identifying details have been changed.

Copyright © 2013 by Sheri Parks
All rights reserved
Published by Chicago Review Press, Incorporated
814 North Franklin Street
Chicago, Illinois 60610
ISBN 978-1-61374-504-5

First edition published in the United States in 2010 by One World Books, an imprint of The Random House Publishing Group, a division of Random House, Inc., New York.

Library of Congress Cataloging-in-Publication Data
Is available from the Library of Congress.

Cover design: Rebecca Lown
Cover art: "Good Morning Lord" by Ernest Varner, varneroriginals@aol.com
Interior design: PerfecType, Nashville, TN

Printed in the United States of America
5 4 3 2 1

For Mama,
Helen Mashburn Parks,
My Fierce Angel

CONTENTS

FOREWORD

We Know Her

WE KNOW THAT WOMAN. She wears mighty big shoes! She's the fear-
less foremother: Harriet stealing back into the pit of slavery boldly leading us to
freedom; Sojourner the abolitionist refusing to be cowed, the feminist declaring
"Ain't I a Woman?," speaking truth to power. She's Mary Mcleod Bethune,
Nannie Burroughs, and a legion of activists, educators, leaders, and founders of
organizations dedicated to lifting us up. She's Ida B. Wells wielding her journalist's pen like a sword to denounce Jim Crow. She's Ella Baker and Diane Nash,
Daisy Bates and Rosa Parks spearheading the Movement. She's our Mississippi
queen Fannie Lou Hammer, ever valiant, never wavering in her quest for racial
and gender justice. She's Shirley C. claiming our right to the White House by
boldly running for the presidency, Barbara Jordan and Maxine Waters exercising their political clout. She's Sonia Sanchez and Nikki Giovanni, June Jordan
and Toni Cade Bambara, Toni Morrison and Alice Walker, Sapphire, Ntozake
Shange, and Lorraine Hansberry, giving us words that provoke and inspire, telling beautiful, sometimes painful truths about our lives. She's Maya, her long
arm raised, finger high pointing ever upward declaring "And Still I Rise."

Yes, indeed, we know her.

She's twined throughout the branches of our family trees. She's my fiercely
independent great-grandmother who remained undaunted by slavery and, later,
when she could no longer tolerate my successful great-grandfather's bad behavior gathered her large brood and walked away from the marriage, moved north,
and became a farmer. She's your grandmother whose love seemed boundless
and everlasting regardless of your slips or stumbles. She's that Mama men love

to brag about who sacrificed all for them. There's the tough mother ready to lay down the law at home and to raise hell with anybody who dares wronging one of her chicks. The do-it-all mother, always on-call, raising children, sustaining households, working both outside and inside the home, whose task lists and feats of juggling put those of most captains of industry to shame. She's that community mother the neighborhood comes to for advice and succor, looks to to take the lead; that church mother whose faith becomes the rock on which we stand. There's the hard-loving aunt who never minces her words and gives no tea for the fever, and that kick-butt cousin who lets the world know when she's mad as hell. She's the good wife and the stalwart girlfriend ever true no matter what. She's the determined sister who against all odds got that college degree, the super achiever sister navigating her way through the minefields in her workplace, the hardworking sister who scrimped and saved to stake her claim to the middle-class dream for herself or her children. She's our solemn-eyed kinswoman stoically bearing backbreaking burdens, the one who keeps hope alive in the midst of poverty, the keen-eyed one who remains constantly on guard trying to keep her children safe from drugs, gangs, and all the skulking predators and the less-than-color-blind law.

She's all around us. We pass her in the street; she sits next to us on the bus, beside us on the pew, across from us at work. She's the girlfriend you bare all with, the one you tell your troubles to. The sister-friend you know you can depend on to watch your back. The sister-stranger with whom you exchange that "do you believe this shit?" or "I don't think so" or "this is working my last nerve" look. She's the woman with that "don't mess with me" glint in her eye that signals she's ready for battle. She's part of our family lore passed from one generation to the next. She's a staple figure in the stories we tell and the fiction others create about us, the multidimensional woman we often lose sight of in the midst of all the stereotypes that swirl around her.

We've named her "Strong Black Woman" and as Sheri Parks so eloquently makes plain in this book, her roots extend farther back and way beyond the crucible of our American experience. Back to the Sacred Dark Feminine, the powerful giver of life and protection, whose wrath was as mighty as her love. Back to that fierce, loving, relentless, many-named Black She at the core of the earliest creation stories that thread the world; the great She who mothers the waters and births humankind; the mythic She that male-centered theologies sought to erase. The She, who like our African foremothers, got hijacked by Western culture to serve its own ends. But as Parks reminds us, in America, from the moment the first African woman stood on that auction block the hijacking of the Black female identity has been a constant. New myths and damaging stereotypes were created to advance the big lies. The guilty white lie that sought to portray us as willing participants in our oppression, the patriarchal lie that caged all women, the racist lie that slandered and demeaned our people and dumped a host of neurotic desires and beliefs about female sexuality, power, and womanhood on our backs. Time and again the needs of others have been superimposed on us. The need to believe that a black woman will love you come rain or come shine, that no matter how heavy the burden we can shoulder it, that we are naturally more resilient, that mothering and self-sacrifice are second nature to us, that we are called to be of service to others, that we will bear the shield. Strong Black Woman is the amalgam of all that and so much more. She's flesh and blood real, myth and fiction, fact and lie. The assumption that we African American females are inherently strong, as if it were woven into our mitochondrial DNA, is taken as gospel by our tribe as well as by others.

No matter whether we consciously seek to emulate her or not, Strong Black Woman is there. We've been schooled by the stories about her, seen her in action, witnessed her in our sisters. Sometimes we see her looking back at us in the mirror and smile; other times we shudder. Sometimes we call her forth, other times she rises up when we least expect her. Those times when we say exactly what we think. Times when the only somebody willing to do it—take a stand, stare the devil down, challenge the status quo, raise hell, love mightily, be generous of spirit, break new ground, be a fierce angel—is us.

Yes, we know her. I know her a hell of a lot better now after reading this book. In these pages Parks provides much needed, richly detailed historical context, deconstructs the stereotypes, strips many of the lies and wrong-headed assumptions bare, shares her own to-the-bone personal stories and those of others about how the mantel can box and liberate, curdle our souls and kindle our spirits. She urges us to cut through the one-dimensional scripted roles that have been ascribed to our sheroes as iconic symbols and see the whole women. She reminds us to beware the one-size-fits-all cookie-cutter model of the strong black woman. And she poses the question we Black women all need to ponder. Isn't it time for us to take charge of her? Take charge by embracing our power to change, not just our strength to bear. Take charge by claiming our right to take care of ourselves. Take charge by making our needs and those of our sisters a priority. Like those women who stand in our pantheon of heroes, take charge by refusing to be taken for granted or bound by someone else's script. Take charge

INTRODUCTION

JILL JENKINS CRIED OUT.

Outside, a young man walked up to her house. The father of Jill's children, Maurice Sr., dropped his cell phone midconversation and ran out of the house, in the direction that Jill was looking. She tried to catch him, to stop him, but he brushed her away. He caught the young man and began to beat him. Maurice Sr. was a big man who worked for the city, and he soon had the young man on the ground. Some neighbor men joined in with him, beating and kicking the man.

Jill ran out too, pushed through the small band of men, and threw herself on the man they were beating. She covered him with her whole body, cradled his head in her own hands. She yelled at the men and they stopped.

The night before, her son, Maurice Jr., had been shot dead on the stoop of a house a few steps from her door while hanging out with his teenage friends. A man, with his face covered, had walked up, shot him, and walked away. This young man, who had been there with Maurice Jr., was not shot. The family figured he had set up their son, had made sure Maurice Jr. was where he was when the murderer arrived there.

A reporter and a photographer from the *Baltimore Sun* were there, working on what was supposed to have been another routine story of a teenage black boy dead in the streets of Baltimore that summer. When the fight broke out, the two women left quickly, but not before they had gotten another, better story and clicked off some photographs.

Two days after Jill Jenkins's son was killed, the story ran in the *Baltimore Sun* accompanied by two photographs: one of Maurice Sr. and an unidentified man beating the young man, and another of Jill Jenkins crouched over the man she thought had helped kill her son. Later, the photo of the beating would win two national photojournalism prizes. But there were no prizes for the photograph of Jill Jenkins.

In an instant, the day after the sudden and violent death of her oldest child, her only son, Jill Jenkins broke through her grief with a compassion, a strength, that would seem to most people to be outside human capacity.

I am a black woman. And so I am supposed to be Jill Jenkins. All black women are.

As I shared Jill's story with other black women, a pattern emerged: They would finish the story before I did. "She stopped it, didn't she?" They *expected* it of her. They even provided her with a motivation. "Too much violence; enough already." What some people might see as an act of heroism, they saw as her doing what she was supposed to do, as her following a script that they all knew so well that each one could leap into action without a conscious thought. The circumstances provided Jill Jenkins with too little time or opportunity to make a considered choice. She was able to look past her family to help someone else, whether or not he deserved it.

I was raised to be strong and nurturing. As far back as I can see, so were all the women of my family. We never asked why. The survival of our family and of our race seemed enough. In black life, women are the fierce girlies, mamas, and grandmamas who hold together black families and neighborhoods through sheer determination. Folks consider them to be the "backbone" of their families and culture, with "back" being an important operative word. Black females in this country are born into the army of Fierce Angels, and they have no choice in the matter. Membership is required, and the expectations placed on them are completely universal; *all* black women are supposed to be strong and selfless. Generations of people—black, white, and just about everybody else—have been raised with the underlying assumption that black women will save them.

Training for the role starts at birth. Black people traditionally raise their daughters to be sensible and responsible and are often much harder on them than on their sons. As girls become women, they are expected to become wise, their connections to God personal and intimate. They are expected to become confident and worthy of their idealized assignment as the universal helpers. They often tend to take on responsibility for other people, even strangers.

In American popular culture, Strong Black Women stand like friendly sentinels—reliable, warm, selfless, feisty, funny—as saviors and fierce protectors, watching, waiting, wanting only to help. They're seen as the generous women who show up in the nick of time to save anybody who needs it, whether or not anyone asked them. And what an attractive idea—that random but interested dark women are watching over us, ready to pop in just when we are in deep, deep trouble and in need of advice or sanctuary. In the mainstream popular culture, black women are usually shown supporting and rescuing white people; those they know and those they don't. Sometimes those women are so extreme, so stereotyped, they are cringe-worthy.

Like all stereotypes, there is a grain of truth to this one. I know how wonderful it is to have these Strong Black Women—my mother, my aunts, my sister, my friends—in my life. They are wise, giving, selfless and self-effacing, fierce, nurturing, all at the same time. From the outside, it looks like a win-win arrangement to be so idealized and useful. But admiration of the Strong Black Woman comes with standards that are humanly impossible to sustain over a lifetime without huge sacrifices. Every day, black women pick up a load that is heavy and complicated. The role is overwhelming—it calls for incredible levels of emotional, spiritual, and intellectual energy, combined with a selflessness that is truly superhuman and wildly unrealistic. And nobody asked them if they wanted the job.

Fierce Angels is the story of the strong, compassionate black woman as she unfolded before me, the story of the women I've known, whom I've interviewed, whose faces I've seen in countless popular images from American life. It is also the story of my struggle to come to terms with the image in *my* life. My mother and the women I knew selflessly nurtured their own children and everyone else's, making sure everything would be all right. It was hard for them. Very hard.

Now here I am, like so many other black women with new lives, moving into places our elders could only imagine. Some of us are living in neighborhoods in which our grandmothers cleaned houses, making up the new parts as we go along, trying to decide what to keep of our old lives and what to leave behind. How could the old role fit into my own progressive, New Black Woman professional life? I am a feminist with a PhD, a university professor at one of the finest state schools on the East Coast. Why would I drag such an old stereotype with me as I moved into new spaces, broke new ground, and learned new roles? But I wasted my time even asking the question, because the Strong Black Woman came with me anyway, ushered on through by the expectations of other people.

Sometimes it was the little things. Years before my daughter was born, a young, tough-looking black man opened a door for me. "Happy Mother's Day," he said, smiling sweetly. "Thank you," I answered, "but I'm not a mother." His face clouded with confusion and rejection. Then he looked at me again, as if to ask, "Well, why not?" Exchanges like that kept happening every Mother's Day, and with time I learned to simply accept the happy wishes in the spirit they were given. "Thank you," I would say, smiling back, and the tough-looking young men would drop their street looks for a moment longer. I learned what they wanted from me and what they did not. They did not need me to be their mother but to remind them that someone knew they were somebody's child. Someone who, just for that instant, was neither frightened nor threatening. Who was safe.

It wasn't only young black men who expected something of me. I began to see the others: the white man in the market who walked past white women to ask me about mangoes; the white students who did not know me but passed by other supportive faculty members and expected me to take up their problems against the university; the black students who assumed that I would always go to the mat for them, even to the point of harming my own career; the group of Jewish mothers in New Jersey who were giving out my name and number to other college mothers as an advocate for their children.

Remember the painting in the Huxtables' living room in *The Cosby Show*, the one of the black woman holding up the world on her back? It feels like that.

Picture the following scene on a recent graduation day at the University of Maryland, where my job as a professor is to guide students into the next phase of their lives and graciously accept whatever gratitude might come my way.

I was sitting at my desk when a large white man—blond and ruddy faced—beamed at me from my office door. "I just want to meet you and thank you for getting my daughter through."

His daughter, who was receiving her master's degree that day, stuck her head in under his arm and smiled at me too. "My dad wanted to meet you," she said.

"I did," he told me again. "I wanted to meet the person who got her through." I demurred as I stood to meet him. The master's thesis was hers; she had done the work, I suggested. He shook his head as he pumped my hand up and down. "That may well be, but I know her. She wouldn't have gotten through without you." Then he said, "I told her to go find a black woman," as if there were a compliment in there somewhere. My smile froze. His daughter looked uncomfortable, but he shook my hand one last time and beamed his way down the hall.

His daughter returned later to explain. Another black woman had been central to their family's life and livelihood. She had started as a domestic worker, doing the work that the family's wife and mother had been unable to do. The black woman turned the family around, organizing them and giving them back a family life. They owned a small factory and she soon went to work there, too, organizing the business and turning it into a profitable venture. She had saved the family and made them wealthy. Since then, whenever anyone in the family was in trouble, their dad told them to go to a black woman. This time it was me, and I didn't even know it.

I was appalled. Images of Mammy danced in my head. Was I a walking stereotype? Was I just another helpful, smiling black woman but with an updated hairdo? Gradually I began to wonder: Was it the Strong Black Woman herself or her reason for being that disgusted me? Was it the actual history of real women or the stories that had been manufactured by other people to bring comfort to themselves? Because the stereotype, like most stereotypes, is just the tip of the iceberg.

In Gabriel García Márquez's novel *Love in the Time of Cholera*, the main character spends most of the novel chasing the elusive love of a Spanish woman. Near the end of his life, he turns to Leona Cassiani, an intelligent and capable friend and employee, a black woman whom he had originally mistaken for a prostitute. Over the years she has moved up in his company, vanquished his enemies, and made him wealthy. Finally, he sees her not as the prostitute he had mistaken her for, not as the helper, but as the woman of his life. He tells her that he knows she is "the lionlady" of his soul, but she replies that it's too late, that they will go on as they did before. I stopped cold when I read that passage. I knew that woman. I knew lots of black lionladies who had worked behind the scenes, advancing the careers and fortunes of other people. The question black women must ask for Leona and for themselves is, if they are so talented and useful, why have they remained so long in the supporting role?

Because somebody else has been writing the story. Both the lives and the images of black women have been steered to serve the needs of everybody else. Although there is a periodic fuss about the supportive roles of black women in the stories of white people, there is less rabble-rousing when they're depicted as supportive in the lives of black men and families too.

Strong Black Women routinely hide all that they are and that they have accomplished from black men, from one another, even from themselves. They know that they are expected to. And if they purposefully or inadvertently break what amounts to a cultural rule, the full brunt of the culture comes down on them. Indeed, the largest contradiction of black life, the elephant in the room that so many have tacitly agreed to ignore, is that for all the adoration, black women are under tight control, trapped in a cultural lockdown that offers few choices. There are requirements to being a Strong Black Woman that nobody says but everybody knows. They are allowed to be strong, but only for the good of others. And they conspire in their own invisibility by refusing to talk about their accomplishments.

There will be people upset with me for even saying this, but by almost every measure of success—from high school, college, and graduate degrees to employment rates, business starts, and longevity—black women have surpassed black men. No matter how much power black women have, they are never supposed to flaunt it, never supposed to keep any for themselves or enjoy it too much, for fear of upstaging black men. In an elaborate charade, black women pretend that the men are in control; they "build them up" and hurt themselves in the meantime. Black women are running to the back of the bus and plopping themselves down in that last seat, this time behind black men. The toll that the role is taking in the lives of black women is staggering.

Perhaps more than any other American ethnic group, black women are routinely on the front lines, because they go there and because their culture leaves them to it. Women were positioned on the front lines of the civil rights movement. Rosa Parks, Ruby Bridges, Fannie Lou Hamer, and Etta Baker were there because they were female and black. They worked behind the scenes, pushing the men to the front. They were supposed to be quiet and self-sacrificing.

A woman in Dallas once told me that she allowed her ex-husband to beat her after he lost his job "to let him feel like a man." They both knew that she was sacrificing her body for the sake of his ego, and they both were willing for her to suffer, at least for a while. When he got carried away and hit her too hard, she reminded him that she was really the better fighter.

If a young woman were abused or raped, she was supposed to be quiet about it, to take it, not like a man but like a black woman. One of those women was me. When I was sixteen, I survived being raped and almost murdered by the young man who was the next big hope, the next Martin Luther King. And as it was for too many young black women, members of the local black and white liberal middle class made it clear that my duty to my people was to shut up.

I was lucky; I am alive. Now women are facing up to the violence and crime in their neighborhoods, and they are suffering and dying for it. Angela Dawson and her family were firebombed in their sleep after she confronted young black men for selling drugs in front of her children. Other women, like Joan Hairston, have faced public retribution that came with upsetting older black ministers who were not helping black women find jobs to support their children because, the ministers said, the men should have them.

Many, many others are living stress-filled lives and dying the slow deaths of stress-related diseases. Black women pay with their health when they keep responsibility for all that is around them yet place themselves behind black men and so expose themselves to the most dangerous type of stress—that tied to responsibility without control. Stress and fatigue exact their tolls. The diseases that kill black women—diabetes, heart conditions, obesity, hypertension—are all connected to and worsened by stress. Even though on average black women take *more* preventive health measures than other women, they still get sick more often and die earlier. The women I spoke to had taken on overwhelming responsibilities, with the stress and fatigue that came with them, because they felt that they had to. They had not allowed themselves to stop long enough to think about it.

They are living the roles they feel they must. They are not fools; they know the costs and they live with the stress and the fatigue, the constant demands, the self-sacrifice because they feel they have no other choice. They know what it feels like to be burned out. They keep on anyway. Rest is a luxury many of them feel they cannot afford. If they don't do it, they say, nobody else will. So every day, from the grass roots of urban America to the halls of power, they get up and do what needs to be done. Until I asked, many of the women to whom I spoke never questioned why. Many of them said it was in their DNA.

Some critics have called the image of the Strong Black Women a lie, but it is not a lie to the women I interviewed. The image, or a closer version of it, is the truth of their lives. They told me that they feel they really are supposed to be strong and available to solve other people's problems, to sacrifice and to endure. They also think that they are to be humble and silent about the sheer volume of their contributions. They have been silent too long. How can they expect to help themselves if they don't tell their own stories?

Black women need to *understand* the assumptions that other people are carrying. Only then will they have the knowledge to make their own choices. The black women who said they felt they were born to be caring and fierce—what were they responding to? Do they know, deep in their bones, of the Mitochondrial Eve, the East African woman whose DNA is in the body of every subsequent human? Or is it the Great Dark Cosmic Goddess who gave birth to the earth and the heavens in so many mythological creation stories? Or the big black bang of energy that scientists believe jump-started the stars and the planets, the same dark matter that still makes up 96 percent of the known universe?

As I began to look differently at my life and the lives of other black women, I found more things I wanted to know and understand. I had to use a number of strategies and methods: interviews—both short- and long-term—media and literary analyses, and, finally, mythological investigation, all against the backdrop of historical and social developments. In the course of the work, changes came to my life that turned intellectual work into life work. First I gave birth to a daughter who seemed to have come out of the womb as a protective mother. Then my own mother died, leaving me to consider all that I had lost. Her community lost much too. At her memorial service, her friends, colleagues, and neighbors stood, one by one, and told how my mother had befriended them, protected them, fought for them. When Helen Parks took you under her wing, you won your battle, you laughed, and you were healed. I went from wanting to know to *needing* to know the story of black female power.

Eventually my search led me straight back to the Sacred Dark Feminine image, the black woman who appears in just about every religious tradition in the world. It was hard at first to follow. The tracks were well covered. It was like trying to find a needle that someone had *worked* to hide in the haystack. But after you know what to look for, you see her everywhere. It got easier. My husband, a rational sociologist, was skeptical at first. But after finding so many, he, too, sees them. Now when he is watching a movie and sees the protagonists in too much trouble to get out by themselves, he'll say, "I feel a Strong Black Woman coming." And she often does.

My daughter introduced me to the ones in her television shows. Students and former students found them and sent them in. Sometimes there was a direct connection to the sacred as oracles, wise women, angels, mystics, or as God Herself. Always they were strong, wise, and compassionate, with the capacity for ferocity when needed, and they are becoming increasingly present in the mainstream culture, where reverence for the Black Madonna has been resurging.

Since there have been stories, there have been stories of a big black female giving birth to the world. The oldest creation stories in the world, including many of the Western and African ones, begin that way. She is Everything, and so all by herself, she births the heavens and the earth. The Black First Mother is hidden within the traditions of every major religion on the planet, including Christianity. She was and still is used to represent transformations, and the transformative black female is present but underrecognized in Western cultures.

I had only just admitted that the Strong Black Woman was as familiar to me as my own breath; then I found that she had been leading a double life, that other people—entire countries and continents of them—had relationships with the strong and dark female as intimate as their own souls, relationships that could not be explained by romantic childhood memories or television. They appeal to the Dark Feminine in times of personal crisis. For them, she is a friend through the worst, the powerful and caring miracle-maker.

So there are two parallel stories involving black women: one that black women know intimately through their daily lives and another that uses images that look like them but are mostly without their participation or even knowledge. The resurging reverence for the Sacred Dark Feminine and the expectations placed on Strong Black Women in American daily life are two trains that started from the same station; they run along tracks that are parallel but just out of sight, always pacing but never meeting up again. Even when black women know of the sacred use of black femaleness, some are reluctant to put her at the same level as a male Jesus. Others have not been so reluctant. Across town, Sister Mary Aquin O'Neill of the Mount St. Agnes Theological Center for Women saw the same photo of Jill Jenkins saving the man who may have helped kill her son. She also saw the Sacred Dark Feminine, so she composed and held a loving prayer service that used religious and literary language to draw Jill into the long tradition of reverence for the Dark Feminine.

African and African-descendant women are being connected over and over to the Dark Feminine; the connection was made as soon as Europeans saw them, and that connection has continued for centuries. When Europeans enslaved Africans, they loaded their own mythological story lines onto the backs of the black women they kidnapped, bought, and sold. The Dark Feminine became the Mammy, a twisted, extreme aberration that Southerners used in their pro-slavery propaganda. The idea of Mammy was made to fulfill the wishes of white slave owners for happy, loving slaves; there are few historical instances of women like her. Yet the propaganda Mammy is still hurled at black women as a slur, especially if they succeed in mainstream society.

Fierce Angels explains the connections between the Sacred Dark Feminine, the propaganda Mammy—the slave ghost who still haunts black women, who is ridiculed, feared, and vilified, the cautionary tale used to keep black women from commanding their own images, from controlling where they go and what they do, in order to keep their energies within black culture—and the historical lives of black women who worked to use the role to the advantage of their families and communities.

Fierce Angels describes in detail those strong, feisty black women all over American popular culture—from the movies, television comedies, dramas, to ads and comic books—who keep showing up just in the nick of time to fix the problems of white folks.

Fierce Angels shines light on the Angry Black Woman—the black woman as a one-emotion Tasmanian she-devil—another aberration of the Strong Black Woman, brazenly used as a political weapon, even during the 2008 and 2012 presidential elections.

And *Fierce Angels* shows black women as they really live, embodying the entrepreneurial spirit to start businesses and grassroots organizations. Famous and powerful women who fight the status quo and engage in significant acts of charity and philanthropy. Political insiders who exercise their personal brands of strong love and fierce energy to foster social change. And everyday women, whose names have been changed to protect their privacy, as they share stories of quotidian survival and service. Some are still struggling to love themselves as well as they love others. Some have found a way to value themselves, to heal, to choose when and how to give of themselves.

Researching and writing *Fierce Angels* gave me a way to value myself and understand the legacy I have been given. The knowledge it gave me grew into the instrument of my own healing. After the publication of the hardback edition, women from all over the country contacted me and told me a similar story, that someone who loved them had presented them with a copy and said "You are my Fierce Angel," and that in reading it they had come to understand their lives in a new way, giving them what they needed to take control of their time and their energies. They might still be busy or tired but now it was *their* choice. I hope this edition does the same for many, many others.

The Sacred Dark Feminine

Before the Beginning, Darkness was everything and everywhere.
The Darkness was female, and while she had lain with no one,
she was pregnant with all the universe would become. When it was time,
she gave birth to the world.

THE STORY OF the Strong Black Woman starts at the beginning of the world as we know it. Ancient people observed the world around them; they saw the sea, the huge night sky, the dark soil from which plant life sprang, returning to die, decay, and grow again, and the womb from which their own lives began. They found ways to explain to themselves what they saw. They told stories and made statues of the cosmic Dark Mother, and they held her as sacred. Their stories have come down through the generations in many ways, in many forms. If black women are to have some power over their own stories now, they will need to know the ancient stories and how the images they carry have been woven into the collective memory, how they became so common that they are assumed.

The most ancient of myths and the most advanced of the sciences tell the same story—that the primordial darkness existed before anything else and contained within it all that the universe would eventually become. In the science of particle physics, the vast dark matter and energy exploded, giving rise to the planets. Researchers are still working to find out how, but they think that dark energy and matter still make up 96 percent of the universe.

The ancient myths—stories passed down, generation upon generation—have always had their own answer as to how. In them, the primordial darkness was female or androgynous. As there was nothing before her, she was the mother of herself. She was alone yet pregnant, and the world began when she spontaneously gave birth to it. For cultures in continents as far flung as Europe, Africa, the Americas, and Asia, she was the mother of everything that came after—the stars, the planets, and the gods and goddesses. She became the Sacred Dark Feminine, the Mother Goddess—Nana Buruku, the most powerful deity and Mother of the West African gods; the Hindu Kundalini; Tara, the name of the mother for both the European Druid gods and the Asian Buddhas—all dark, all powerful, and fiercely protective. Significantly, the Sacred Dark Feminine usually kept the underworld—the transforming place for death, regeneration, and rebirth—for herself.

Early cultures lived closely with the elements and rhythms of the natural world. Without artificial light, heat, or cooling, they were subject to the dangers and comforts of nature. Darkness—the rest and protection it provided and the danger it threatened—was central to their lives. Most mammals are born at night; after the womb, the night is a second protective darkness, providing quiet and cover from predators. So the stories describing the Sacred Dark Feminine are like the darkness, with both danger and protection at their core. Early cultures also associated the darkness with water. Mammals, including human ones, are borne into the world on a current of water, and to this day the Sacred Dark Feminine is tied to rivers and oceans.

Mortal women were goddesslike because they carried in them potential life and the power of birth. It matters who is godlike. The nature of the darkness, of the night sky, the ocean, the womb, was both holy and necessary. The myths awarded an ancient power to black women. The cosmic Dark Mother had a human parallel in the Mitochondrial Eve, the East African woman whose DNA is in every living human being.

Many ancient cultures saw life and death as part of an ever-running cycle, so that birth, death, and birth again were parts of one grand rhythm, like the growing year. The Sacred Dark Feminine was thought to facilitate these greatest of transformations and so, too, the many smaller transformations of life. Ancient mythologies accounted for the entirety of human existence, and the Sacred Dark Feminine reflected a worldview of life as both pleasant and terrible, with suffering as a part of life (something modern Western life has worked hard but unsuccessfully to suppress). The deities reflected that worldview and so were gentle when they could be and ruthless, even cruel, when they had to be. The Sacred Dark Feminine was fierce, violent, and angry yet also nourishing, gentle, and loving, because it was her job to give life and to protect it. Because her violence was usually protective, she was not "heroic" in the modern sense of the word, not concerned with achievement or superiority. Instead, she was concerned with the business of everyday life; the living, ripening, dying, renewal, and rebirth.

The history explains why the images of the Sacred Dark Feminine and the mortal Strong Black Woman have been so resistant to change. Creation stories are extremely important because they are the base stories from which other stories are built. The Sacred Dark Feminine is an archetype, a central image passed down the lines of generations in various forms. Carl Jung, one of the fathers of modern psychology, popularized the idea of the archetypes and thought the Sacred Dark Feminine to be the oldest archetype. He believed she was so commonly occurring that she was inherited into our collective consciousness—hardwired into our brain chemistry.

The old mythologies of the world met in the Americas. The Native Americans had their own ancient Sacred Dark Feminine, including the Laguna spider woman and the corn goddess of the American tribes of the Southwest, and all of the major ethnic groups that joined them brought theirs. The black slaves, mostly from West Africa, brought Nana Buruku and the powerful orishas, more local and personal deities that included Oya, the beautiful and fierce deity of rebirth, and Oshun, the deity of love, maternity, and respect for women. From North Africa there was the Egyptian Isis and the Jewish dark Wisdom, and from Europe the miracle-working Black Madonnas, who bore a striking resemblance to Isis and who came to be fused with the native goddesses of South and Central Americas. From India came Kali: the fearsome and loving Dark Mother of Hinduism, the Black Mother Time, who was related to the transitions of death and rebirth, sometimes wearing a black face. From other parts of Asia came the Chinese Matsu, goddess of the sea, and Kwan Yin, the black female Buddha and goddess of mercy and compassion. The most popular dark goddess of all is right under our feet—Mother Earth or Mother Nature—from aboriginal religions and folk myths from New Zealand to Ireland. If we are to understand why the stories about black women being strong, giving, fierce, and selfless have stayed so long in American culture, we must know their roots. So we must begin where they do, at the beginning.

The first statues that humans carved were of dark goddesses and were thought to have been used in ritualistic ceremonies. Ancient people fashioned figures and painted pictures on cave walls of god-women, dark like the stones or the earth from which they were made. The earliest examples date back to 30,000–25,000 BC. The oldest known written story lines began in Sumeria, sometimes called Mesopotamia (*circa* 3500–2350 BC), in roughly the area of present-day Iraq, where it was thought that the primordial Darkness contained the heavens, the earth, the gods, and the underworld. The being was Nammu, the sea—dark and explicitly female. There was no mention of the birth of the sea—she appeared to have always existed. She was everything, the original complete being. She symbolized the power of the forces that ultimately shaped all of life and death, of space, time, and matter. She was pregnant, full with chaotic potential—here "chaos" simply meant absence of categories—and when she gave birth, having lain with no one, the world as we know it began. She was the Mother of All, the mother of life itself and of every form that eventually arose—the heavens, the earth, the underworld, the gods, the good and the evil, the dark and the light, the beautiful and horrible. She was "the womb and the tomb of the world," the matrix of all life experience, of birth, death, and rebirth, at once ruthless and generous, terrible and wonderful.

Greek mythology is central to Western culture, and the ancient Greek story was much like the Sumerian. In pre-Homeric Greece, the Sacred Dark Feminine had a place of honor. Chaos, the pregnant darkness and the mother of the gods, was there first: "First of all, then, Khaos came to be." Like the Sumerian mother, she contained everything and delivered the world through a virgin birth. Then came Gaia (earth) and, later, Night. The Greeks, and the Romans who borrowed from them, saw the dark goddesses as transformative, generating order, which both cultures valued, from chaos. Night gave birth to the heavens and day. They retained the underworld function because it was the most pivotal, the most necessary place of transformation, but it was also seen as the most unruly.

By the time Hesiod wrote down the Greek creation story in his *Theogony*, Greece was already a fiercely patriarchal society; that he wrote of the divine world as female is a show of the myth's resilience. The Sacred Dark Feminine's position at the beginning of Western myth has made her a permanent fixture in Western life. The Feminine Darkness is still there in the Hebrew and Christian Genesis, in the primordial darkness that existed before the presumably male God did anything. As men gained more power in Western cultures, they changed the stories; many goddesses were killed or married off, their old powers absorbed by men or reduced to female "intuition" and folk belief. That which could not be erased or absorbed was relegated to the alien but permanent black woman.

The Greeks and Romans knew of Africa and something of African cultures, but there were few black women among them. They were free to imagine them any way they liked. Darkness and female power remained fused together, and light women were considered to have been weakened. The Greek and Roman goddess Night, the dark daughter of Chaos, absorbed all of the ruthless anarchy of the old Mother Gods, the concern with death, suffering, and the inevitability of fate. The power of the Sacred Feminine was relegated back to black women because the mythology made them the logical repository. It would have been difficult to see them any other way.

The early mythic Mothers were androgynous, encompassing traits we now consider "masculine" and "feminine," and they were more powerful for it. They were whole, and their wholeness encompassed other traits we now tend to see as separate: creation and destruction, warmth and violence, care and rejection. They combined nurture and suffering, life and death, not as opposites but as parts of one whole. They were balanced, fluid, beyond category. An idea that shows up in many cultures is that the whole is stronger than the split halves. To the extent that the Dark Feminine was considered to be without category, she was also assumed to be strong. As the mythology progressed, the Greeks further reduced the role of the Mother and completed the process of gender separation. "Civilization" included elevating certain elements at the expense of others. The Greeks had a decided preference for the elements of the day—light, order, and air—which they came to associate with maleness. Zeus, the male supergod concerned with order, control, and light, became the supreme ruler and god of the sky.

Night, though, still scared him. She was his ancestor, and Homer wrote in the *Iliad* that *every* god, including Zeus, was afraid to transgress upon Night or the children still under her protection. One challenged the dark goddess or those under her protection at one's own peril, because her mother anger was protective and horrible. But there was a catch, and it was a big one, one that would reverberate through the centuries—Night was respected but not widely worshipped. Few signs of temples or worship to her have been found. Fierce maternity was effectively shoved from center stage. After occupying an early and central role in the organization of the universe, after being described by Homer as so strong that no god would challenge her, Night and her mother, Chaos, were left largely undeveloped in Greek mythology. She became the necessary and functional fringe figure. She contributed to the appearance of control and order because she was seen as holding the mysteries, the parts of the world that could not be predicted or controlled: irrationality, the strongest and most uncomfortable of human emotions, and the chaos of death and the underworld. Night and Chaos stood away—strong, formidable, and alienated, a bank for all the untamable forces of the universe.

But myth is resilient, and established stories almost never die out. The primordial darkness and her formidable daughters survived. Physically dark or darkness-related goddesses still dotted the early mythology of Greece and Rome, later to be picked up by the masterworks of Western culture by writers such as Shakespeare and Milton and the pre-science of alchemy. Nature, night, and disorder—as fullness came to be defined—continued to be associated with femaleness. In Greek myth, Rhea, the mother of Zeus, was represented as a black stone. The Romans had dark Cybele, the mother of the gods. The Greek Gaia, or earth, infinitely wise and fierce, was black because she was simultaneously the physical soil.

The Romans borrowed much of the Sumerian-Greek mythology and carried it with them when they invaded the Germanic tribes, including the Celtic people of England, Ireland, Scotland, Wales, and other parts of Europe. There the stories met up with the Celts' mythology, which had its own dark and dark-related goddesses, who were later carried to America with the Irish. The Celts held an attitude toward religion that was still more tied to ordinary life rhythms and still very involved with the divine feminine and darkness. The Angles—the future English—worshipped Nerthus, Mother Earth, who was concerned with both war and peace. They believed that she took an interest in their affairs and rode among them. She and other female divinities were whole, capable of revenge, war, or generosity. The Germanic tribes believed that mortal women carried with them an element of the holiness and prophecy, and women were asked for advice. Plutarch wrote that Celtic women often acted as ambassadors in battles and rivalries between the Celtic tribes and sat on peace councils when disputes were discussed. The prophetesses often accompanied troops into battles, gave advice and strategies, and helped to broker peace.

The Celts' and other ancient goddesses could be violent, lethally so. But they continued a trend that would be carried by the Dark Feminine through the ages. They were usually violent only when necessary to protect their people or to avenge harm done to them or their people. Their rage was compassionate. Cerridwen (Cauldron, or Fortress of Wisdom) was a prominent goddess. She was physically black and gave birth to a son as black as a raven. Other Celtic goddesses sometimes hid themselves in darkened bodies. Celtic goddesses had the ability to shift shape and color, and it was common for them to turn into animals with black coloring. In another link that would become important in America, they would disguise themselves as old and poor women.

Fierceness was associated with blackness, and some Germanic goddesses turned black when they were angry. The Celtic mothers became blackbirds, ravens, crows, vultures, or cormorants when they had to be fiercely protective. Morrigan would take the form of a black battle crow, a raven or other large blackbird, or sometimes a long black eel. The Arthur legends that would travel around the world retained Morrigan as the whitened Morgan Le Fay or as the Lady of the Lake; she was usually depicted with dark hair and living underwater, keeping the relationship between darkness and water. As world religions changed and masculine images became more dominant, the Sacred Dark Feminine has remained continuously in some form.

Judeo-Christianity is particularly central to the mythology of the United States. It is commonly perceived, with cause, to be a patriarchal religion. But the dark and feminine are there. The Hebrews wrote expansively about the Sacred Dark Feminine, and many representations were carried into early Christianity. In the Hebrew Book of Wisdom, also now part of the Catholic Bible, Wisdom was not a trait but a being, a black feminine entity who shielded the Jews as they escaped slavery in Exodus. Hokhmah, translated as "Wisdom," was depicted in *In Praise of Wisdom* as God's female partner. "She enhances her noble birth by sharing God's life, for the Master of all has always loved her. Indeed she shares the secrets of God's knowledge and she chooses what he will do." Although she was beautiful, she was valued for more than beauty. She was radiant darkness. The author wrote, "I loved her more than health or beauty, preferred her to the light since her radiance never sleeps." She was valued more than light because she was stronger than light. "She is indeed more splendid than the sun. She outshines all the constellations. Compared with light, she takes first place, for light must yield to night."

Like the primordial darkness, she contained everything. Wisdom was the creative force, "the fashioner of all things." She encompassed the entire world. "She reaches mightily from one end of the earth to the other and she orders all things well."

The idea of the Sacred Dark Feminine as overseeing transformation had appeared again. She facilitated change, but she was constant. "Though she is but one, she can do all things, and while remaining in herself, she renews all things." She was "intelligent, holy, unique, manifold, subtle, mobile, incisive, unsullied, lucid, invulnerable, benevolent, shrewd, irresistible, beneficent, friendly to human beings, steadfast, dependable, unperturbed, almighty, all-surveying, penetrating all intelligent, pure and most subtle of spirits." She was a spirit friendly to humanity, but she would not let evil go unpunished.

There was nothing she could not do. "Although she is alone, she can do anything; herself unchanging, she renews the world." Wisdom taught Solomon temperance, thoughtfulness, justice, and strength. "She knows the past, she forecasts the future . . . and of the unfolding of the ages and the times." She protected, taught, and saved humans from the perils created by human foolishness and evil—Adam after the fall, Noah, Abraham, Jacob, and Joseph. She punished Cain by abandoning him.

Because she was dark, she could not be seen by ignorant or evil humans. "Wisdom is brilliant, she never fades. By those who love her, she is readily seen, by those who seek her she is readily found." She manifested herself in the accomplishments of humans; the technical skill of the artisan was the fruit of Wisdom. Like the primordial darkness, the Hebrew Sacred Dark Feminine figure defied category and so was still able to carry traits thought to be contradictory. She was dark but brilliant, a personified contradiction. "She is a reflection of the eternal light."

The first Christians were Hebrews, and the writings of the early Christian Church reveal belief in a personified Wisdom and in Sophia—the feminine faces of God—and in Mary of Magdala, or Magdalene, as a central figure in the life of Jesus. Early Christians, particularly the Gnostics, were able to temporarily continue the image of the androgynous mother through Sophia, the feminine aspect of God. She was "divine wisdom," another personification of the old dark Wisdom, the cocreator with the male God of the Christian universe, the force through which the male God became conscious of Himself. There were many other dark Hebrew mothers, all eventually driven underground. In the Christian Bible, the personified dark and feminine Wisdom became wisdom, a concept rather than a being.

The patriarchal God's ability to create the world by a method other than birth was a striking departure from previous mythologies. If Genesis was written, as some scholars believe, to persuade Hebrew followers away from their traditional Mother Gods, then the story of God and darkness takes on new significance. The Hebrew God had to usurp the primordial darkness before He could create the world, which may explain the many verses Genesis takes to describe it. Genesis referred to goddess earth: "In the sweat of your face, you shall eat bread, til you return to the ground, for out of it you were taken; you are dust and to dust you will return." The dust was the goddess earth, less her anthropomorphic features, retaining the function of giving and taking life.

The people who were least like the Sacred Dark Feminine—who were not female or dark—worked to suppress the Sacred Feminine in official Church doctrine. The Gnostic texts were relegated to the Apocrypha, meaning literally "left out" or "hidden," and so do not appear in most Bibles. (Some theologians have questioned whether the third member of the trinity, the Holy Ghost, is a vestige of the feminine god Wisdom.) That which could not be written off was co-opted. In 431 AD, Theodosius II summoned a council at Ephesus, the city that had been the chief temple site of Artemis, the Asian mother of the world and the ever-dying resurrected god. The council of bishops declared the Virgin Mother to be the mother of God. The *mother* rather than God herself. Yet again, mainstream representations of Christian female deities were reduced to the lighter representation of Mary, the mother of Christ: kind, gentle, passive. She inherited only one of the central functions of the old Sacred Feminine—until recently she was called upon by Catholics to intercede at the time of death.

Along with diminishment of the Sacred Feminine came the move to rationalism as the only way to *know* something and the idea that we could live in a world that was only ordered, only rational, and only based on what we can see. (We see vestiges of the recognized tie between women and nonrational ways of knowing when we speak of "women's intuition.") Women came to be seen as dangerous hindrances to the rationality associated with men.

There was one major exception: the imagined black woman. Her blackness changed femininity. Her femininity changed blackness. The same holy men who demonized the white women around them still sang the praises of the distant and imagined Dark Feminine. The process of stripping white women of power included pushing off the powerful attributes of the goddesses onto alien dark women, who were less central to the culture's idea of itself. As she had with the Greeks, the dark female became the repository of all that the old female goddesses had once been for the Christians. The histories and mythologies of the dark female and the white female have always been interrelated. Over the centuries, depictions of the black woman have remained the same: loving, fiercely protective, present at the most terrible of times and able to change them.

The Sacred Dark Feminine is stubborn. There are hundreds of Black Madonnas—brown and black versions of Mary—all over Europe, usually on the same sacred sites of the dark earth goddesses. Catholic reformers just built chapels on top of them. Many of the statues of Mary and Jesus are positioned exactly like those of the Egyptian goddess Isis holding her son Horus on her knee, both figures facing forward. Some scholars believe the Black Madonnas are the direct result of early matriarchal Africans traveling throughout the ancient world, spreading the pyramid technologies, the stone and clay arts, hieroglyphic scripts, and images of the Great Mother/Black Goddess. Other researchers concluded that "Black Madonnas are Christian borrowings from earlier pagan art forms that depicted Ceres, Demeter, Melaina, Diana, Isis, Cybele, Artemis, or Rhea as black, the color characteristic of goddesses of the earth's fertility."

Black Madonnas have long been revered in the folk practices of Catholics and are becoming more prominent. All of them share traits: They show rage and compassion, often at the same time; they face the terror as well as the comfort of life. They are creative forces; they can be destructive, but their destruction is part of the cycle of life rather than for conquest. They respond to the worst of problems. The statues of dark women in countries of white people have puzzled scholars. Some created elaborate theories for the darkness, attributing it to dust, soot, or fire damage—although the dust and soot somehow missed the statues' robes and often could not be washed away. Leonard Moss and Stephen Cappannari examined the perennial excuses for why the European Madonnas are black and wrote an essay entitled "In Quest of the Black Virgin: She Is Black Because She Is Black," using a quote from a local priest.

English colonists, many of them Protestant, also inherited a rich mythological concept of the black feminine, much of it related to maternity and deeply embedded in their religious and aesthetic lives. There was one image of the Dark Feminine that for centuries captured the imaginations of Western thinkers and writers like no other: Beloved, the dark bride of Solomon in the Song of Songs, one of the greatest love stories in the Bible. The song was written in richly romantic, sensual language and often taken to be symbolic of the love between Jesus and the Church. In it, the black female was unrevealed purity, and her story has run from ancient Hebrew myth through Christianity to secular literature.

The biblical Beloved described herself. The most familiar quote is this one: "I am black but comely, O ye daughters of Jerusalem . . . because the Sunne hath looked upon me." She was pretty despite being black. She was black because she had been out in the sun too long, which meant, of course, that she was not black to begin with. Western texts often spent a lot of time trying to explain or explain away blackness in their sacred women. However, the Ethiopian version read otherwise:

Black am I and fair above the daughters of Jerusalem.
Like the tabernacles of Kedar and the Tents of Solomon.
Do ye not look at me that I am black, that the sun has not seen
    me . . .
My own vineyard I kept not.

Her blackness was not from the sun but from the night. She had not been out in the vineyards and so had not been exposed to the sun. She was black because she was born that way. The dark bride was a reconciliation of paradox; she was dark and lovely, poor yet rich, without power but powerful in a larger sense. The text went on like a man in the present flirting with a pretty black woman: "Sunburnt and lean they call you; you're honey-brown to me." He then compared her to a dark violet.

Beloved was interpreted as a significant figure, standing in for some of the most important aspects of the lives of authors of different religious perspectives. According to Jewish scholar Rabbi Judah, the words "I am black but I am comely" refer to Israel itself, which was black because it was in captivity and comely because of the Torah and good works. Solomon's black bride has been interpreted as Israel in the Talmud and as the mother of Christ and the Protestant Church in Christianity. For others, the black bride symbolizes the human soul. She is beautiful because she has received God's light. Like an onyx, she is an example of dazzling darkness.

The bride was spoken of in religious services and publications throughout the medieval period. St. Bernard of Clairvaux (1090–1153), one of the period's principal theologians, was fascinated with the bride. His *Sermons on the Song of Songs* spanned a lifetime of writing and rewriting. He began them soon after becoming an abbot and wrote until he died, leaving number eighty-six unfinished at his death. For Bernard, the bride's blackness was a precondition to her comeliness and purity itself. "Blessed blackness! Which gives birth to whiteness of the mind; to light of knowledge; to purity of conscience!" Bernard wrote. "Who is the bride? . . . It is the soul thirsting for God."

She was also the human soul for sixteenth-century theologian St. John of the Cross, and he took the Song of Songs as the basis for much of his work. St. John's contemporaries, the English Jesuits, followed his and Bernard's idea that the bride was God's elect, afflicted and smirched by this life but blessed. But for many English Catholics of the Counter-Reformation, including John Brerelay, Henry Hawkins, John Hall, and Richard Crenshaw, the bride was also the mother of Christ. In Hawkins's *Partheneia Sacra*, the bride spoke: "Black I am but beautiful; as if she has said: I am outwardly black through humilitie, but inwardly beautiful in grace and majesty." For Hawkins, she became the Blessed Virgin of the Moon, as the black dove, and the traditional symbol of womanly fidelity, the heliotrope plant.

Filtered through Western culture, the bride's blackness made her different. Church fathers continued to regularly degrade the white feminine as dirty and evil while praising the bride. St. Augustine and St. Bernard, who praised her regularly, described women in their immediate families as excrement. She was seen as more like the men themselves than were lighter women. Rosemary Ruether argued that the only manifestation of the feminine that the fathers praised was the "bisexual" or the androgynous. The bride was androgynous; she worked in the fields, endured physical hardship, and spoke her mind, violating the standard definition of "feminine." She was praised because she was androgynous, distant, and alien. She was used not as a woman but as a metaphor.

The bride came to America as a favorite religious topic in sermons and commentaries. Linda Van Norden studied sixteen English and American commentaries of the black bride between 1549 and 1676. In all of them, the bridegroom was Christ or a Christlike figure and the bride was the Church. She was black from adversity, affliction, envy of the world, persecution, or remnants of original sin or corruption, with these concepts overlapping. She was comely through God's love and grace and her own goodness. Centuries later, African American Nobel Laureate Toni Morrison would give Beloved back to black women. She used the black bride and the Song of Songs in *Beloved*, her novel that examined the compassionate rage of black slave mothers, some of whom killed their children rather than see them suffer as slaves. It is important to establish the ongoing historical presence of the Sacred Dark Feminine in America—how she has been seen and revered—because the beliefs and practices form the basis by which black women continue to be interpreted.

The African slaves who were forcibly brought to the Americas came from areas with their own prominent goddesses. The area that comprises present-day Nigeria, Benin, Togo, and eastern Ghana was known as the "slave coast" from the seventeenth to nineteenth centuries because so many slaves were taken from there. Although due to colonialism the tribes do not correspond to national borders, a version of Nana Buruku as a hugely powerful goddess is revered by, roughly speaking, the Akan of what is now Ghana; the Igbo of Nigeria; the Fon, now in southern Benin and Togo; the Ewe of southern Togo; the Yoruba of Benin, Nigeria, and Togo; and the Diaspora. Nana Buruku, sometimes called by Nan Baruku or similar names, is often dressed with a scarf and long, wide skirts. She carries a staff that she uses to direct her power at people, and, with this staff, she or a woman who carries her spirit can be lethal. Like the other primordial images, Nana of West Africa and South and Central America was the first Mother—"the Mother of herself" and the grandmother of the other gods and of the heavens and the earth—but she was never hidden away and remains revered to the present day. Teresa Washington called Nana Buruku "transgeographic" because she appears in so many tribes in West Africa, where, Washington writes, her power is "phenomenal" and she "may well be the most influential Àjé in West Africa." In Igboland, she is called Olisabuluwa—literally "she who supports the world." For the Akan, Fon, and Ewe, she is Nana Burukyu or Nana Buluku, the "Mother of All Deities."

There are many other African goddesses. In Yoruba, Oya is the goddess of fire, wind, and thunder. When she is angry, she creates tornadoes and hurricanes. She is also the patron of change and the guardian of the gates of death. Oshun is the Yoruba goddess of love and pleasure, beauty and diplomacy, with associations to money. Oshun is considered to be very generous and benign to mankind and usually teaches people to overcome their troubles through kindness and negotiation. The African goddesses retain the tool of feminine rage. Oshun also possesses an extraordinary temper, which, once provoked, is difficult to assuage.

In South America and the Caribbean, the slaves were able to keep their goddesses in something like their original form—as was the case with the Vodou and Santeria goddesses—or they were merged into Mary. In his book *Our Lady of Class Struggle*, Haitian scholar Terry Rey details the combinations of Mary and African goddesses. Poorer Haitians combined Mary and Ezili, the Vodou spirit of love and sensuality, so thoroughly that it would be difficult to tell them apart. More-wealthy Haitians revere a more traditional Mary, but Rey found that some traits of Ezili have nevertheless slipped into their worship practices.

In the United States, however, slaveholding practices were psychologically more brutal. The form of slavery that was imposed upon the Africans included coerced Christianity. Many if not most of the slave owners worked to eventually eradicate the religions of black slaves and replace them with a form of Christianity that had already subjugated the Sacred Feminine. In Louisiana, though, with its Catholic culture, the African goddesses and orishas would be allowed to merge with Catholic saints, and the Madonna could appear in darker form.

Sacred mythology is often carried into other spheres of everyday life and the Sacred Dark Feminine appears in many popular forms. Many contemporary women, including Oprah Winfrey, collect black angel figurines. When Winfrey mentioned on her show that she collected black angels, she received so many that she donated more than six hundred of them to the Angel Museum in Beloit, Wisconsin.

Vestiges of the Sacred Dark Feminine remain in present-day black communities, reflected in folk practices and the mystical reverence for older black women and the mother worship common in black daily life. Mother worship and the power and status of Big Mamas are direct results of the role of the African Sacred Dark Feminine. More-recent immigration by Africans to the United States and international travel are reacquainting African Americans with the original goddesses. Black Americans traveling to the motherland or shopping in African American stores purchase statues of goddesses and work them into their homes and relationships. When my husband and I were trying to get pregnant, we received several statues of African goddesses of fertility from friends and family.

The Sacred Dark Feminine also came with white ethnics who arrived later, at the turn of the twentieth century. The strongest representation was with Italian Catholics, millions of whom brought with them to America a determined reverence for their own numerous Black Madonnas.

"The various aspects of the dark-skinned Virgin Mary are considered miraculously powerful and are credited with having protected believers from such afflictions as earthquakes, pestilence, and the attacks of invading armies," wrote Joseph Sciorra of the Italian American Institute of the City University of New York. Although the official Church did not approve, the Italian immigrants had street festivals on feast days anyway. September 8 was the feast day of the Black Madonna, with the Madonna del Tindari as the most prominent of several Italian Black Madonnas. She was first celebrated in 1905 in Manhattan's Lower East Side by immigrants from Sicily.

Tindari is part of the city of Patti in the province of Messina, in northeastern Sicily, founded by the Greeks in the fourth century BC. According to Joseph Sciorra, the original statue of the Black Madonna has been dated back to the Middle Ages. As was common, the sanctuary of the Madonna was built on the same site where a temple to the fertility goddess Cybele, also known as the "Great Mother," had been. According to a popular legend, a polychromed cedar statue was brought to Sicily in the eighth or ninth century to save it from destruction during the Iconoclastic Wars. Her African origins were well known at the time. In 1751, Abbot Spitaleri wrote of "the exceedingly miraculous image of the Most Holy Mary, who with marvelous portent came from Africa."

In New York in 1906, a congregation of Pattesi was established, and a statue of the Black Madonna was built with Italian sponsorship. The statue was offered to the church of the Salesian fathers on Twelfth Street, but the priests refused it because they saw the street festivals as outside the Church's doctrine. The nuns had other ideas. Because the Madonna was already associated with the feistiness of the nuns, they sewed a cloak for her. A chapel was eventually built with private donations in 1913.

The festivals continued throughout the Great Depression, and writers and researchers who worked for the Works Progress Administration Federal Writers' Project documented them in *The Italians of New York*, published in 1936. WPA writer I. J. Isola noted: "The New York Black Madonna is credited by believers with possessing the miraculous curative powers of the original, as is attested by the many votive offerings at her shrine . . . in semblance of cures received on different parts of the body, such as arms, legs, hands, breasts, etc." The writers described festivals with "innumerable" people and streets decorated with lights and banners. The Black Madonna of Tindari was paraded through the narrow streets and, from their windows, people tossed down dollar bills, which were pinned to a ribbon on the fifty-eighty-inch-tall statue. Stands sold food, and a solemn High Mass was held. Inside the chapel, the statue was surrounded by offerings and graces for cures. At some point in time, the Latin phrase *Nigra sum sed formosa* ("I am black but beautiful"), a reference to Beloved, was inscribed at the base of the statue. As Italians moved from the city, the statue was taken to the suburbs. In Hoboken, New Jersey, the Madonna is housed in a private chapel on Fifth Street by the Santa Febronia Catholic Society and processions are still held every few years.

In 1998, after changing hands several times, the chapel on East Thirteenth Street became the Phoenix Bar, and every year on her feast day there is a celebration of the Black Madonna. The group of mostly Italians is organized by Joseph Sciorra, the Italian culture researcher who sees the Black Madonnas as "symbols of feminine strength, racial harmony and spiritual power." Stephanie Romeo, who described herself as a postmodern Catholic, said that the Black Madonna connected her to her Sicilian peasant ancestors. To her, the icon represents "a tradition of spirituality rooted in folklore, empowered by female essence, distrustful of clergy and unafraid of racial difference. 'I look at her and I know that I am not alone.'" In 2004 Ernest Davis, mayor of Mt. Vernon, New York, opened an exhibition entitled "Evviva La Madonna Nera! Italian American Devotion to the Black Madonna" with a dinner to honor the origins of the centuries-old devotions and to recognize contemporary Italian American women's reclamation of the Black Madonna.

Other immigrant groups brought their own Black Madonnas as well, and the images dot the religious landscape of the United States. I bought a prayer card to the Polish Madonna in Chicago. A replica of the Polish Black Madonna Shrine of Czestochowa, popular with tourists, was built by Franciscan priests who emigrated from Poland to Eureka, Missouri, to establish a retirement home for men. The Polish brothers remembered the pilgrims who walked for days and slept by the road to visit the Black Madonna of Poland, often covering the last part on their knees. The Missouri shrine and the grotto have become popular tourist attractions.

The Church of Saint Ignatius Loyola on Park Avenue in the Upper East Side of New York is a magnificent nineteenth-century building, filled with art, marble walls, and granite columns. Elaborate and richly colored stained-glass windows depict important scenes in the life of the Christian and Catholic Churches. One, situated in one of the archways, depicts the turning point in the life of Saint Ignatius, the founder of the Jesuit order for whom the church is named. And before that window is a statue of the Black Madonna.

The statue of the Black Madonna is a replica; the original is a famous wooden sculpture in the Benedictine abbey of Montserrat, near Barcelona in the Catalonia region of Spain. The stained glass depicts the story of the young courtier Iñigo López de Loyola, who was born in 1491 and came to the Black Madonna of Montserrat. After a night of praying before her, he laid down his sword, renounced the violence and vanity of his life as a courtier, and embraced a life of poverty and penance. He would later be known as Saint Ignatius. Our Lady of Montserrat would be proclaimed patron saint of Catalonia by Pope Leo XIII in 1881. Like many Black Madonnas, Our Lady of Montserrat is considered to be a "miracle-working" statue and is one of the most celebrated images in Spain. Each year, millions visit the statue they call La Moreneta, "the dear dark one."

Latinos have brought the brown-skinned Virgin of Guadalupe, a replica of the dark Spanish Madonna of the same name. The Spanish Black Madonna of Guadalupe was recognized in Mexico in the sixteenth century and honored by popes as patroness and mother of the Americas since. (Sometimes the Black

Madonnas are lighter brown, like some images of the Virgin of Guadalupe, but any Madonna that is not white is considered a Black Madonna.)

Black women are finding the Black Madonnas. Bonnie Greer was raised as an African American Catholic in Chicago, with white Madonnas, before she moved to Greece as a "Reagan refugee." One day, she followed the sound of church bells and saw a large group huddled around a small altar with dozens of candles and a Black Madonna and child. She wrote of her reaction: "I was stunned. I had never seen anything like her in my life." Greer began her own pilgrimage to some of the hundreds of Black Madonna statues all over Eastern and Western Europe.

Although other African American Catholics have also come to accept the Black Madonna, that path has not always been smooth. Our Lady of Victory in the Bedford-Stuyvesant neighborhood of Brooklyn was founded in 1869. Integrated in the 1930s, it became a predominantly black parish but with no black priest until 1995. The first black priest was Father Martin Carter, who was concerned that the black parishioners no longer be asked to "leave their blackness outside." He sent a nun out to the front of the church with a can of black paint. On Father Martin's orders, the white nun painted the alabaster Virgin Mary's skin black.

Parishioner Evette Moreland recalled, "When I saw her painting the face black, I had to look at myself to make sure I wasn't dreaming. I remember asking her, 'Sister, what on earth are you doing?'" While some members appreciated the message that the Black Madonna was as legitimate as the White Madonna, many objected vehemently and argued that Father Carter had inserted race where it need not be.

"Oh, it was horrendous," said one member. "What's color got to do with being Catholic?" Carter responded by showing slides of Black Madonnas and African saints. Gradually, the congregation began to warm to the black icons. In 2004, Our Lady of Victory received a prestigious gift: the Madonna Della Pieta, a bust of the Virgin Mary cast from Michelangelo's *Pietà*, but cast for the first time in black patina.

The growing numbers of Catholics of color around the world led the liberal *National Catholic Reporter* to launch Jesus 2000, an international art competition for the "new face of Jesus." Editor Michael Farrell said, "As the millennium approached, scarcely anyone seemed to recall the whole point of it: its reference to the arrival among us of Jesus." Farrell said that *NCR* wanted a Jesus that called for a second look and one that reflected that Catholicism was growing most rapidly in Africa and South America. The competition drew 1,678 entries from 1,004 artists from nineteen countries. Sister Wendy Beckett, BBC art critic, selected the winner: *Jesus of the People*, by Janet McKenzie, a white woman living in New England. It was the image of a black woman. Sister Beckett described it this way: "This is a haunting image of a person Jesus—dark, thick lipped, looking out on us with ineffable dignity, with sadness and confidence." While both McKenzie and Beckett referred to the figure as "he," the model was a black woman who lived near the artist.

A reporter for the *National Catholic Reporter* wrote, "The resulting image is masculine, McKenzie said, but a man whose features reflect feminine elements . . . the pink in the background . . . is both a feminine reference as well as being the color of blood—hinting at both suffering and redemption."

McKenzie explained, "I realized that my nephew, a mixed race African American living in Los Angeles . . . would never be able to recognize himself in my work. I determined to be more varied, to make a racially inclusive statement. I decided I would use a female model to incorporate, once and for all, women, who had been so neglected and left out, into this image of Jesus." In 1998, an African American Madonna and child by the same artist was featured in *Christianity and the Arts* magazine. It was later purchased by Cardinal Francis George for the Chicago archdiocese. McKenzie and *Jesus of the People* 2000 toured the United States; while she met with some objections to a black androgynous Jesus, the response was largely positive.

Other African Americans found the Black Madonna through other avenues. One of the earliest was the Shrine of the Black Madonna, founded in the 1960s by Albert Cleage, father of the well-known author Pearl Cleage. He would later change his name to Jaramogi Abebe Agyeman. His church grew out of the Black Christian Nationalist Movement to recognize a black Jesus and to counter the myth of black inferiority. The mother church is in Detroit, with other congregations in Atlanta and Houston.

Powerful images of the Dark Feminine—the Mother Goddess; Sophia, the female face of the Christian God; Beloved; Mary, the mother of Jesus; and, most recently, Mary Magdalene—are being rediscovered and brought into mainstream American life.

Mary of Magdala, more often called Mary Magdalene, the woman in the Christian scriptures who found Jesus's tomb empty and to whom Jesus appeared in his resurrected form, has recently been identified by religious scholars both as more central to the Christ story and as a brown-skinned woman. Due to the rediscovery of an ancient text, *The Gospel of Mary of Magdala*, some biblical scholars now see Mary of Magdala as the female apostle of Jesus. When Karen King, Winn Professor of Ecclesiastical History at Harvard University Divinity School, translated *The Gospel of Mary of Magdala*, she presented two versions of the gospel: In one, dated to the second century and known but omitted from the Bible, Mary of Magdala was depicted as a disciple of Jesus and the one to whom he gave his final instructions. For the cover of her book, King chose an image of a brown Mary of Magdala painted by Franciscan brother Robert Lentz in keeping with the scholar's finding that Mary of Magdala was a woman of color.

The Da Vinci Code, one of the most-read novels in American history, picked up on the scholarship and featured a brown Mary of Magdala. The book stirred controversy when it also resurrected the controversial claim that Jesus had a wife and a bloodline and that his wife was Mary of Magdala. Fearing threatened boycotts by Catholics, the makers of the film adaptation downplayed this part of the story line.

Sometimes, meetings of the European and African versions of the Sacred Dark Feminine fuse seamlessly, as in Haiti, but other times there have been harsh cultural clashes, such as the one between the mayor of New York and a black artist exhibiting at the Brooklyn Museum of Art. The story of the mayor and the Madonna started with *The Holy Virgin Mary*, a painting of a Black Madonna by Chris Ofili, a Catholic British citizen of Nigerian parents. The painting, part of the "Sensation: Young British Artists from the Saatchi Collection" exhibit, had been shown before in London. The exhibit was controversial there but because of other paintings. When the exhibit came to New York, the Holy Virgin became the center of a public controversy and legal battle between the city of New York and the Brooklyn Museum of Art. The portrait, painted in 1996, showed an Afrocentric Black Madonna with flowing robes. There was elephant dung over one breast and at the base. Genitalia from erotic magazines seemed to float in the background. Sexuality has never been divorced from West African goddesses, and as a fusion of the white Mary and the African goddess, Ofili's painting incorporated it. Elephant dung was a well-regarded fertility symbol. The battle lines that were drawn over the Madonna identified bumps in the road to fusion of the African and European Sacred Dark Feminine in the United States.

The exhibit and the uproar marked a pivotal event in the public knowledge of the Sacred Dark Feminine in the United States. Well-known and mainstream European Americans strikingly announced that the dark image was

Mary and that they did not like what Ofili had done to her. The most central figure was Rudolph Giuliani, an Italian Catholic. Born in 1944, the mayor of New York from 1993 to 2001 was the grandson of Catholic Italian immigrants. The Madonna had personal importance to him. When the Brooklyn Museum of Art displayed the portrait, part Mary and part African goddess, Mayor Giuliani was so angry that he tried to rip the funding away from the museum, but *not* because she was black. He took her darkness as a given. It was the dung that bothered him. (He may also have been concerned about his Roman Catholic constituency during his senate campaign against Hillary Clinton.) Before he was done, he had talked a little-known figure into the mainstream of the American press and public.

Much of the early discussion swirling around *The Holy Virgin Mary* continued without the public seeing the image for themselves; the media did not show it for weeks. Finally, the *New York Times* ran a small color image. The story gathered enough steam that the image also appeared later that week on *Saturday Night Live*. But before many people saw the art piece, Giuliani interpreted it for them, although he had not seen the exhibit either. He said that the image was "splattered" with dung; he said it was blasphemy. In never-before-seen form, the nation heard the mayor, mainstream media, and major religious leaders describe the desecration of the Black Virgin Mother with the same fervor and reverence displayed by the Catholic Church hierarchy. As other newspapers picked up the story, they used the terms "Madonna" and "Virgin" without the modifier "black." The black one was equal to the white one. At the exhibit opening, Catholic activists handed out vomit bags, and a nun held up a sign reading, "Defend your Holy Mother against this porno and filth."

Giuliani said, "You don't have the right to government subsidy for desecrating somebody else's religion." He continued, "And, therefore, we will do everything we can do to remove funding for the Brooklyn Museum until the director comes to his senses and realizes that if you are a government-subsidized enterprise, then you can't do things that desecrate the most personal and deeply held views of people in society. I mean, this is an outrageous thing to do." The next day he said, "Last time I checked, I'm the mayor" and stepped up his attack.

The Brooklyn Museum was caught in the middle. The museum was publicly funded and depended heavily upon grants from the City of New York. When the mayor voiced angry disapproval of the exhibit after seeing only the catalog, the staff invited him to see the show. When the museum staff resisted his demands to stop the exhibit, the mayor ordered the cancelation of the next scheduled payment to the museum. He threatened to terminate its lease with the city and possibly even seize control of the museum unless it canceled the show. Although the mayor did not succeed in closing the museum, he did leave it and its staff badly shaken.

The mayor helped to make the painting a *cause célèbre*. His message was picked up by other religious leaders, and they entered the public debate to stop the exhibit. William Donohue, president of the Catholic League for Religious and Civil Rights, was reported by the *New York Times* as saying a review of the catalog turned his stomach, that "I think the whole city should picket the show." Bishop Thomas V. Daily of the diocese of Brooklyn said that city funds should not support the exhibit. Newark Archbishop Theodore McCarrick said that the painting "comes dangerously close to the mentality that produces hate crimes" and that the museum trustees had shown "colossal insensitivity" to Catholics.

Other religious groups joined the protest, including the president of the Orthodox Union, the largest association of Orthodox Jews. Political pundits and politicians weighed in. After viewing the exhibit, Patrick Buchanan said, "It is dispirited, degrading, disgusting, sacrilegious, blasphemous, and an insult to the mother of God." In the US Congress, both the House and the Senate passed nonbinding resolutions to rescind the funding.

It is very important to note what Giuliani did not say. He never said that the image was a *Black* Madonna or that the artist was black, a practicing Roman Catholic, and a former altar boy with an equal claim to the Madonna. The media were following Giuliani, and because he did not identify Ofili, the media originally did not either. Ofili, with a master's degree from the Royal College of Art in London, was a widely known and exhibited artist. Both his parents were Nigerian, and he said that his work often included clumps of elephant dung as a cultural reference to his African heritage, where it is seen as a fertility symbol and sacred, fitting to adorn a goddess. He specifically mentioned Yoruba influence. Ofili said that the genitalia were allusions to naked putti in Old Master paintings and were his commentary on the sexually charged images of the Virgin Mary in those paintings. Slowly, the art critics dropped the terms "smeared" and "splattered," using "adorned" or "decorated" as they came to understand the cultural clash. So Giuliani's characterization of the dung application did not stick with the press, but the acceptance of the black woman as the Virgin Mary did.

Meanwhile, the Sacred Dark Feminine was becoming more popular in other circles. American and European spiritual feminists became interested in the Sacred Dark Feminine in the 1990s. They were not originally attracted to the Black Madonna, seeing Mary as too familiar and too domesticated. They preferred the goddesses of Africa, Asia, and South America. Many disregarded the specific cultures from which they took the goddesses and combined them into one cross-cultural figure, which they called the Dark Goddess. Black women were, for the most part, uninvolved.

Usually, these women described their relationship with the Dark Goddess as an internalized one—the transformation was one of consciousness. China Galland published the first edition of *Longing for Darkness*, the account of her personal journey to discover "the female face of God" and heal herself, in 1990. The book reintroduced many Westerners to the Sacred Dark Feminine and gave a public voice to spiritual searchers. Other books followed. Karlyn M. Ward, Jungian therapist and author of a DVD called *Anchored in the Heart: Redeeming the Dark Feminine*, said that when she began investigating the Dark Goddess more than two decades earlier, it was difficult to find material. Now, she said, it was difficult to keep up.

For most of the movement, the Dark Goddess is a psychic or spiritual internal presence. Fred Gustafson, a graduate of the C. G. Jung Institute in Zurich, wrote *The Black Madonna* in 1990. Carl Jung was a contemporary of Freud and one of the fathers of psychology. According to Jungian therapy, the Sacred Dark Feminine, with the Black Madonna as only one representation, is one of the central human archetypes. Jungian therapy has become widely popular, growing so quickly that Thomas Kirsch, author of the book *The Jungians*, said it is impossible to estimate how many Jungian therapists there are at this point, but there are more than a thousand in the San Francisco area alone.

Jungian therapy holds that one can transcend traumatic circumstances only by facing them. An addict can be cured only after going into the darkness to bottom out. But, according to Jungian therapy, the person is not alone in the darkness, because the Dark Feminine is there with them. She represents endurance and the hope of transformation. She is the guide who will lead the sufferer out, the psychic presence necessary for transformation and a new personal beginning. Jungian therapists and writers routinely use the goddesses and Black Madonnas as references.

The popularized version of Jungian therapy is even more far-reaching: It is the basis for twelve-step programs and all the bestselling self-help books that build upon them. Americans believe in redemption. It is one of the culture's major narratives, and American authors borrow liberally from Jung, who believed that people were always developing and that they could grow out of their past problems; self-help programs and related books borrow directly from Jung to teach us how. Bill Wilson, who cofounded Alcoholics Anonymous, wrote Carl Jung a letter in 1961 to tell him of the organization based on Jungian principles. As the basis of AA and the twelve-step programs that followed, Jungian therapy has had a tremendous impact on Western culture. The Sacred Dark Feminine has directly or indirectly become part of the therapy and self-help of people across the country and around the world.

Jungian therapists are reporting increased appearances of the Sacred Dark Feminine in the dreams of their clients. The contemporary image of the Sacred Dark Feminine has emerged as the one who is with you in your "darkest hour," who loves you at your worst, who understands the danger before you, who faces disaster with you and embraces you with her strong, loving, and muscular arms. She who knows the darkness leads you out of it. To "live in the lap" of the Dark Goddess is to be in the embrace of the most complete love imaginable, to be safe, encouraged, transformed in miraculous ways.

But the idea of the Dark Feminine as a universal psychic phenomenon that has little or nothing to do with race or culture is in stark contrast to the Sacred Dark Feminine with whom women of color identify more directly. It is important that she looks like them. Black, Native American, and Latina women have argued that the individual goddesses also carry significant cultural characteristics and need to be recognized within their original cultural contexts.

The situation came to a head when a South African priestess moved to celebrate the Dark Goddess in a way that excluded black women. In 2007, I found a Web announcement for a conference of women to be held in Cape Town, South Africa, in the spring of the next year. It was billed as the first official international recognition of the Dark Goddess. The site featured painted images of brown-skinned women and the Dark Goddess. I was intrigued. South Africa was overwhelmingly black and was still experiencing the aftereffects of its brutal racial apartheid system. Black women in Nigeria and other African countries were beginning to reclaim the precolonial Dark Goddesses, using them as a successful inspiration for grassroots female leadership in opposition of colonially inspired Westernization and toward indigenously based models of female empowerment and national growth. It would be exciting to see and hear from the aboriginal black women in South Africa, whom I assumed would be central to the conference. I wrote the organizer with questions and she replied with an invitation to speak. I was overjoyed.

Then, over the Christmas holiday, my e-mail in-box lit up with a heated exchange between the organizer and an interracial group of women with powerful international credentials. I had assumed the presence of other black women—people in academic and journalistic circles would never dream of having a conference about blackness without black people—but I was wrong. I was the only black woman on the unpublished program, and I was not South African. The organizer had not intended it that way—she did not see the Dark Goddess as involving race or physical blackness at all, and she sent out what she perceived to be a color-blind Web announcement. As an active priestess, she said she put out the message and allowed the energies to work to bring people to the conference. But affluence was an unintended filter: In addition to Internet access, there were fees for registration, workshops, travel, and hotels.

The American and South African activists were kind but quite clear in their response: Black women and the Dark Goddess were connected. To allow black women to be excluded was to fall in line behind centuries of racist practice. The activists positioned themselves to protect a spot at the table for black women. Their messages demonstrated the growing recognition of the Sacred Dark Feminine as well as her political potential. Several discussed whether to take the case to a national commission. Sharon Stanton, a white South African attorney whose legal research had helped lead to the international recognition and legal redress of Rape Trauma Syndrome, wrote her message as a white woman to another white woman and spoke of the potential of goddess reverence to dismantle racist assumptions: "We cannot praise the Goddess without deeply processing and acknowledging that the spiritual too is and must be political. Racism does not disappear merely because a person has no intention of discriminating against others. . . . As white women who flow in the path of the Goddesses we need to honour inclusiveness in our practices. We cannot whole-heartedly participate if our worship excludes black and in particular indigenous people. In doing so we trample on the Goddesses as we worship from our own concerns and in our own interest and languages. Racism has been and is always part of patriarchy. If we remain separated in our worship of the Goddesses we remain slaves to patriarchy."

Max Dashu, a white American artist, teacher, and founder of the Suppressed Histories Archives, warned of the necessity to actively push back against the powerful status quo and called out the unspoken racial privilege embedded in "color-blindness." "Otherwise" she wrote, "gravity invariably settles around the most privileged groups, and so the speakers chosen, invitees, word of mouth, issues and agendas get set within that range of people, those who know each other or have heard of each other. . . . That is why allowing the energies to find one has failed in this case. There is a difference between opening to the divine flow, a sacred and right thing, and following along the easier track. . . . That is why color blindness does not work." Speaking as a white woman, she ended by stating flatly a direct tie between the Sacred Dark Feminine and black women, that "these are their Women's Power."

Bernedette Muthien, a South African woman of color, a co-convener of the International Peace Research Association's Global Political Economy Commission, and founder of Engender, a gender-related organization, suggested scholarships. The activists were not arguing to exclude nonblack women but to include black women because, they said, the Sacred Dark Feminine could not be divorced from black women.

But the organizer felt it was too late. Some speakers pulled out. I was unable to attend. The conflict yielded lessons that must be learned now. The Sacred Dark Feminine is becoming more popular, and what was once an obscure image in the West is now more widely recognized and revered. Many people already have emotional involvement without any consideration of race on their part, and they are embarking on movements with far-reaching implications for women and the planet. As more African descendant people also become involved, there are bound to be more repercussions. Rha Goddess, a black spiritual activist and artist who operates from the perspective of the Sacred Dark Feminine, said that she was met with hostile stares from white women who had been working with the Dark Goddess when she began to appear on the same panels at national conferences.

The stakes are high. To those who revere her, the Sacred Dark Feminine is as serious as life and death. Her power is seen as active and miraculous, and she has long been a powerful political symbol of social justice. People around the world appeal to her as the patroness of the threatened, the besieged, and the disenfranchised as a powerful tool of resistance. Pope John Paul II prayed to the Black Madonna and credited her with saving his life when he was shot. His reverence for her stretched back to his early life as a freedom fighter. Like most Poles, he had grown up revering the Polish version of the Black Madonna; Our Lady of Czestochowa, Queen of Peace and Mercy, was a national symbol, credited with repelling invading armies and stopping disease epidemics. She was the symbol for the Polish Nazi-resistance fighters, including the young man who would be pope. Throughout his papacy, John Paul's visits around the world included pilgrimages to Madonnas, and he left instructions for gifts to Our Lady of Czestochowa upon his death.

The political potency of the Black Madonna was visible in another Polish revolution. In 1980, Polish electrician-turned-organizer Lech Walesa walked through the shipyards of Gdansk, Poland, with the Black Madonna on his lapel to signal the other workers. The pin was a sign of resistance, subversion, and Polish nationalism. The workers named themselves the Solidarity Movement, and they would bring down the communist government of Poland, starting a domino effect that would eventually topple the Soviet Union. The Sacred Dark Feminine inspires believers to stand up to power and to confront injustice. The Black Madonna is still a vibrant image in Poland, where both conservatives and liberals use her image. In one advertisement, her image is used in an antiracism message.

Lucia Chiavola Birnbaum, who had been writing in Italian, published *Black Madonnas: Feminism, Religion & Politics in Italy* in English in 1993, linking feminist empowerment and the Sacred Dark Feminine. In Haiti, where the working classes have fused the Black Madonna and African goddesses, she has become a symbol of resistance to dictatorship and ruinous economic policy. Ninety percent of Haitians believe that the Virgin has answered their prayers, and the vast majority of them see her as *at least* as powerful as Jesus or God the Father. Many believe that she ousted the military junta and restored democracy to Haiti in 1994.

In South and Central America, the Virgin of Guadalupe, called La Morena (the dark one) or, more affectionately, La Morenita (little darkling), is seen as the mother of the dispossessed. From 1976 to 1983, the repressive military regime of Argentina kidnapped, tortured, and often killed activists who dared to resist them. Most were never heard from again—they were called *Desaparecidos* (the Disappeared). The mothers of the Disappeared risked their own lives to take to the streets, to gather in the Plaza de Mayo right in front of the Government House, to silently but bravely protest the disappearance of their children and other family members. They emboldened others to join them, day after day. They succeeded in drawing international attention and pressuring investigations into the crimes of the military government. They dressed in black, and the image they carried was of the Black Madonna. "Mary, Mother of the Disappeared" was a popular painting by Franciscan artist Robert Lentz; it depicted the brown-skinned Madonna with a painted smeared handprint at the bottom, like the white handprint used by the regime to mark a house and target a person inside for government-sponsored terrorism. The handprint on the Black Madonna addressed the terror and offered protection for the mothers as they gathered to protest.

Appeals to the Sacred Dark Feminine are quickening. Many who have felt that we are in a time of unprecedented crisis have looked to the ancient calendars of the Mayans and other cultures, which predicted a great transformation in which the Sacred Dark Feminine would be key. Most well known is author Daniel Pinchbeck, *New York Times Magazine* contributor and author of *2012: The Return of Quetzalcoatl*. While an apocalypse is commonly understood to be the end of the world, Pinchbeck and others suggest that the proper translation tells of a great transformation rather than the end and that the ancient cultures predicted a time when the Dark Feminine would again become powerful and help humans to save their planet. According to their predictions, that time is upon us.

Whether or not one chooses to believe the predictions, it is clear that spiritual and political movements are expounding upon the Sacred Dark Feminine, and women and some men around the world are working to reclaim her. The Sacred Dark Feminine has worldwide implications—for women, for countries, for the ways in which we approach the planet and the people on it—and a growing number of people are becoming interested. Environmentalist groups, which have long appealed in the name of Mother Earth, are now more often using the explicitly sacred, dark, and female representation of the earth in an effort to save it. For them, she represents an ideology of working *with* the planet rather than trying to dominate it, and her image is woven into a new form of spiritual environmentalism.

Oxford-trained activist Andrew Harvey is a bestselling author and spiritual speaker. In workshops such as "Sacred Activism: Hope in Darkness," he says that we can save the planet only if we return to the ways of the Sacred Dark Feminine, with all her rage, beauty, and wildness. Harvey writes that we are crying out to "Beloved to dwell in us, to come and transform us, to make us wise . . . to give us the power, the grace, the intensity" required of us in times of crisis; he is building a movement of Sacred Activists. Harvey and many other activists are spiritual people doing earnest work, but race is not on the table for them either. (Ironically, in the age of digital imagery, visual representation of the Sacred Dark Feminine can look a lot like the models in *Essence* magazine.)

Like the white South African priestess, many nonblack North American practitioners continue to see the Sacred Dark Feminine as a psychic presence that inspires an internal transformation toward higher consciousness and more-engaged living, and race is not a factor for them. The Sacred Dark Feminine also has been a source of transformation for black women, but it is a different process when the image looks like you—it is internal but also cultural. Luisah

Teish, a black priestess in the Yoruba tradition, has researched, written, and led workshops for women of various cultures in the Southern California bay area for more than twenty years. "Spirita" is a female-centered spirituality of protest and resistance for social justice by black and brown women who call upon the strength and love of the Sacred Dark Feminine to work for global cooperation and healing. Multicultural therapist Lillian Comas-Diaz has argued that La Morenita provides a spirituality based in the histories and cultures of women of color, including Sojourner Truth and Alice Walker.

The cultural manifestations of the Sacred Dark Feminine are similar but not interchangeable. That is not to say that people of different cultures cannot draw strength from one another's images, but that those images should not be emptied of their individual cultural meanings and histories. Working with the Sacred Dark Feminine calls for different paradigms and strategies. There has to be room at the table for women of color. The patterns of dominance and access are such that business as usual will leave brown and black women out of important events and conversations, even when well-meaning people from dominant groups do not intend for that to happen.

If black women are to have a say in the new movements, they will have to speak up now. Otherwise, they risk becoming inadvertently irrelevant as an increasing number of groups regularly use images that look like them. But even if they tried, black women would have difficulty treating the Sacred Dark Feminine as only a psychic presence, because the Sacred Dark Feminine has been the unrecognized major factor in the way they are seen and treated in both the black and dominant cultures for centuries. Black women can decide for themselves whether the Sacred Dark Feminine is a source of strength and energy for them too. But they will still have to recognize and wrestle with the subconscious connections between the Sacred Dark Feminine and the persistent stereotypes—both sacred and secular—of black women in the media and the culture.

In Western secular literature, the culturally consistent way for a fierce celebrated female presence to be exhibited would be in the form of a dark female outsider. Secular images with close ties to the sacred ones were woven into the everyday culture, in stories, stage plays, films, music, and television in both black and white cultures, so that the image of the Sacred Dark Feminine and images related to her are present throughout the culture. In America, the strong outsider who takes an interest in the problems of other people and leads them through to safety is very often portrayed by a black woman.

Black women automatically inherit the ancient myths of the Sacred Dark Feminine; the image touches their lives every day. The stories and the images set up assumptions that lead to expectations of how black women are. People see in black women what they expect to see. Many of the images in the stories have been boiled down to stereotype, oversimplified into a code of social shorthand. Black women came to represent strong mother love, and it is easy to see its appeal. It is everything you need—gentle and giving enough to calm your deepest fears, to feed your soul and make you safe at the same time, because the one who loves you is also the one who is strong and fierce enough to destroy your enemies. She is able to repel armies and turn back epidemics, to face and fix the most terrible aspects of life. And yet she is intensely interested in you and your problems. For millennia, that is how people have imagined the love of the Sacred Dark Feminine—the dark goddesses, angels, spirits, and oracles and the dark-god women who work for God, through God, and as God. And it is how many have seen the black women who look most like her.

The Alchemical Mistress
of the Dazzling Darkness

IN THE MIDDLE Ages, early scientists practiced alchemy, the forerunner of chemistry and medicine, equal parts science, mythology, and spiritualism. Their goal was to turn base metals into gold. The focus of their work was the nigredo, the darkness in which the transformation was supposed to occur. Learned people of the time were familiar with alchemy and references to it were common in art and literature. The most potent nigredo was portrayed as female.

As the central figure of the creation stories, the Sacred Dark Feminine went on to take a variety of forms in different cultures. Her primordial position as the first being in the first stories for cultures as different as the Sumerians, the Greeks, the Germanic tribes of Europe, and, in the depersonified darkness, the Hebrews, meant that she would and does continue to play a powerful role in the ways that Westerners consider darkness and dark people. As mythology scholar Mircea Eliade wrote, "Every mythical account of the origin of anything presupposes and continues the cosmogony."

Myth is flexible and resilient, finding its way into many varied and commonly used cultural forms. The archetype of the Sacred Dark Feminine was still quite familiar to Europeans on her own, particularly because of the ongoing fascination with Beloved but also because of her related roles in art, literature, and science. An archetype, according to Carl Jung, is a primordial image that has been passed down from generation to generation, embedded in the collective unconscious. The very concept of blackness itself was developed into a rich and deeply meaningful and embedded concept, threaded through science, literature, and even everyday sayings.

Mothers have always been important to mythology. Goethe called myth the realm of the Mothers. While Asian, African, and Latino cultures have retained their Mothers to a larger degree, the Western cultures have pushed theirs into the corners of the collective consciousness. Simultaneous to the advancement of patriarchy, Western cultures worked to master, to predict, to control the ultimately uncontrollable, to rework nature through domestication of land, animals, and eventually, women. Western culture moved humans to the center of the piece of the world that could be controlled, a human-centered order, which came to be increasingly associated with the visible world of the day. The rest—the unseen, the ununderstandable, the uncontrollable—was shoved to the edges of human society. Gradually, those elements that were too chaotic to be forced into an orderly configuration but nevertheless continued to impinge upon everyday lives were associated with the seemingly disordered world of the night and the underworld and symbolized by the dark and the feminine. The advancement of Western patriarchy did not cause the Mothers to die but to be changed; the Black Mother has received much of the mythic Mother roles. If her role in the public consciousness or history is diminished, her role in the collective unconsciousness or mythology is not.

The Sacred Dark Feminine had impact well beyond religion, on almost every aspect of Western life—art and literature, science, and everyday sayings. The characteristics of originality, strength, permanence, and, contradictorily, transformation, were used to define the color black itself. Writers and scientists paid serious attention to theories about color and the meaning of black was highly developed. It owed much to the older stories of the Sacred Dark Feminine.

Black and white were seen as two important extremes. Thoephrastus defined black and white as the only primary colors; heraldic authors, writing of knighthood, wrote that there were but two colors, black and white, and that all other colors descended from them. The European Renaissance developed a full secular conceptualization of black and darkness, borrowed heavily from the ancient writers and the story of the Sacred Dark Feminine. Throughout Western culture, black continued to be considered the first color and the most singular color, alone in its relationship to white and to other colors. Using the Christian Genesis story as a starting point, some writers, Sir John Ferne in *Blazon of Gentrie* and Gerard Legh in *The Accedens of Armorie* among others, considered black to be the first and most ancient of all colors. Newton would write in *Opticks* that black alone was not contained in white.

In the overlapping areas of early optical science and allegorical art, light denoted the soul while the body was denoted by color and shadow. The light needed the dark: "Light without shadow [is] life without body . . . but colour [is] a soulesse body." The color's seemingly paradoxical quality—of being the absence of light and color but still visible—also made it a useful metaphor in Western literature and science. The elaborate color conceptualizations were drawn partly from science but owed as much to the color lore of Renaissance heraldry of knights, where it was seen as singularly strong enough to accomplish impossibility itself. Black was considered unique among colors for its strength; while it could negate any color, it could not be negated. It was considered the most striking; to see black "was to receive a kind of blow." As the oldest and strongest color, it was also therefore a color to be co-opted or feared.

The color black embodied a paradox: It was at once the color of the beginning and the color of the end, of birth and death, the beginning and end now being two different things, rather than parts of the same cycle. It was a paradox that fascinated Europeans.

Because the Dark Feminine was the one figure still seen as whole, she could embody characteristics that were elsewhere seen as contradictory: femininity and strength, fierceness and compassion, birth and death. Yet she does not just sit at the junction of the contradictory traits, she moves. She transcends and resolves the contradiction. She of the darkness was the catalyst that made light possible. She worked miracles. She came to represent the impossible made possible, a wondrous transformation in human form. She was and continues to be present at transformations—really smaller beginnings—for she becomes the bridge-figure, the linkage between what has come to be a carefully constructed and controlled social world and the other, older, less artificial realities. The Sacred Dark Feminine lives at the convergence of three long and ongoing currents in Western thought: the rise of the paternal and the demise of the maternal, both at the level of the divine and the social; the growth in importance of order, category, and the rational with the subordination of chaos and other levels of consciousness; and the cultural construction of black.

The rich conceptualization of blackness echoed the characteristics of the ancient Black Mother for she was the personification that fed the abstraction. The color black as a large, grandiose nought, from before the beginning, has been an almost universally held concept in western culture since antiquity. It was the only color that could violate physical realities of space, time, and possibility. Before or outside of life, it was outside of consciousness, as in death or sleep. Minor Elizabethan poet Barnabe Barnes, author of Parthenophil and Parthenophe, wrote in Sonnet XXIX, "Let dreadfull Pluto blesse blacke Heben tree" to evoke the feeling of "passions [which] neuer (never) cease." As eternity, black was outside time. It was the impossible made possible. As silence, it was outside sound; it was the color of silence, of silence heard. As memory it was experience beyond the human power to relive.

For European writers, creation of the organized world began with the acceptance of light into darkness. Blackness's association with the depersonified primordial environment still carried many of the old meanings. Milton continued the Greek connection with chaos when he wrote, "The black, tartareous, cold, Infernal dregs / Adverse to life." Several writers connected the color with the divine. Milton and Crashaw recalled black's prepatriarchal role when they wrote of black as the blindness of our morality which, paradoxically, protected us from God's light.

The mystical poets, more concerned with darkness as an abstract, theoretical idea than with visual appearance, further developed the culturally held nature of black in ways that would eventually be linked back to black women. As with the Hebrew Wisdom, the color black could be brilliant. Seventeenth-century metaphysical poet Henry Vaughan described darkness in "The Night" as the "deep but dazzling darkness." Absolute blackness was where God could be most clearly seen by the wise person.

> There is in God (some say)
> A deep, but dazzling darkness; As men here
> Say it is late and dusky, because they
>   See not all clear;
> O for that night! where I in him.
>   Might live invisible and dim.

The "dazzling darkness" was a place in which God may be found, much like the Sumerian princess Inanna who had to go to the darkness and her dark sister Ereshkigal in order to be transformed into a queen of the lightness.

Various color lores of science and moral considerations coalesced in the later Renaissance. Black was the base, unevolved, original color out of which the other colors grew. The peacock, which had been a literary figure for hundreds of years, was by 1600 also a long-standing central figure in Western color lore. He was prideful, "But when he lookes downe to his base blacke Feete,/ He droopes, and is asham'd of thing vnmeete." Black was a settling force and abated the peacock's pride. The conceptualization of the color black moved between allegory and fact. To the poets, black was perceived as an absolute, more imagined than physical.

Western culture developed a richly developed, if inaccurate, conceptualization of dark people long before Westerners met Africans in any large number. Grace Beardsley wrote that the Ethiopians of the poets were mythical or partly mythical while writers of prose tried to describe and explain actual Africans. The Greeks knew of the existence of Africans, but they were mostly a rarity until late in that empire. That did not stop the Greeks, or the Europeans after them, from defining Africans anyway. They saw them as "black" and once they did, they applied the definitions of the color that already were culturally embedded. Between 700 BC and 1700 AD, their blackness was ascribed a range of features that would show up later in images of black people, including cowardice, arrogance, venery, continual serenity, strength, lustiness, and godlike permanence. Eventually, the negative aspects of blackness would be associated with the masculine and the positive aspects with the feminine.

Figures that were meant to portray more realistic Africans appeared in the early seventeenth century and were incorporated into the literature and colloquial language. Black was sometimes regarded in Shakespeare's time as having a special purity (as admitting no other hue) and as a form of divine light, but when personified in masculine form this constancy took on an increasingly alluring but potentially dangerous image. In "Love's Cure, or the Marital Maid" by Beaumont and Fletcher, the color black's permanence was transferred to black men when Siavedra asks the chaste Clara,

> Being so fair, my Clara,
> Why d'ye delight in Black-work?
>
> Clara: Oh White Sir,
> The fairest Ladies like the blackest men;
> I ever lov'd the colour: all black things
> Are least subject to change.
>
> Siavedra: Why I do love
> A black thing too. and the beauteous faces
> Have oftnest of them: as the blackest eyes,
> Jet arched brows, such hair.

"Black is a pearl in a woman's eye" became a proverb, capturing the allure and the danger that the darkness held for the foolish woman. The phrase had a complex double meaning, one part being that women were to value those traits in a man that would destroy them, and the other being that passion that might destroy a woman's self-sufficiency might, in a sense, also become her death. C. S. Lewis, writing on allegory, argued that English Renaissance drama changed the black pearl of the proverb from the "immaterial fact" of lust into a common interpretation of a visible person. Dramatists visualized the proverb, giving it more publication and cultural meaning. Shakespeare's Othello destroyed the white woman, despite his love for her or her love for him. Spenser's character Lechery is physically black—not a lecherous black man but black lechery personified. Black represented a devil that will destroy the white woman. He was considered deviant because he was lustful and dangerous; she because she was foolish. The theme was picked up by other writers and became a common item in an entire school of plays as chaste, noble white women were seduced or disastrously loved by blacks. Van Norden explained the connection, "Lust represents an extremity of pleasure not fully attained, nor ever quite perfectly remembered, nor ever had—for by its nature, Lust is always in excess of what it has. The pearl it requires is on the other side of black, the impossible." The juxtaposition of black and white represented impossibility, one that the black Feminine would make possible.

"Black is a pearl" was represented in visual art. Greek figurines and Janiform cups used black male and white feminine figures to form one design. The imagery connected with blackness was engendered, with black men shown as the most "base" manifestation of the color, and black females shown as transformative. Ovid's story of Phaeton the Ethiope and his daughters was translated by Golding, Brinsley, Sandys, and Hall and reprinted more often through the seventeenth century than other classic works. It would have been widely known between 1565 and 1660. In it, the Ethiopians were black-skinned because the blood was drawn to the skin surface by heat. Because of Phaeton's fall from grace, he and his descendants were all stigmatized by their blackness, which was outward and visible rather than abstract.

The color black and its meanings were developed in the world of knighthood or heraldry. Writers of the time such as Upton, Legh, Ferne, and Bolton differed as to whether or not black's status as an original color also meant that it was also the most "base" of colors, but the concept of primitivity stayed with the color nevertheless. In heraldry, blackness was considered strong but dangerous, since it could negate all other colors but could not itself be negated by any other color—or as Ferne wrote, "It can hardly be altered into any other show or colour than the same which of nature it is, whereas . . . it doth easily extinguish and blot out any other colour." The observation that black would bear no other hue became another proverb, invoking strong resistance or impossibility. Impossibility, wrote Van Norden, could have been pictured in the Renaissance only as blackness. Black's ability to negate or "kill" other colors was translated into a military metaphor as the tincture sable, which signified military prowess, glorious lineage and wealth, or the killing of one's enemies. Other, perhaps contradictory, virtues were also attributed to the color. Black's heraldic use also suggested compassion. According to Legh and Ferne, the stone proper to black was the diamond, with its virtue of constancy or steadfastness.

The idea of blackness as steadfast showed up in other literature. John Lyly wrote in his *Euphues: The Anatomy of Wit*, first published in 1579, "Do you not know that all men do affirm and know that black will take no other colour? . . . That fire cannot be forced downward? That Nature will have course after kind? Can the AEthiope change or alter his skin? Or the Leopard his hue? Is it possible to gather grapes of thorns, or figs of thistles? Or to cause anything to strive against Nature?" From the mid-sixteenth to mid-seventeenth centuries the proverb "to wash black white" also became personified in literature and visual art. Nicholas Breton in *Pray Be Not Angry* wrote, "Loose not thy paines to teach on Owle to speake, Nor striue to wash an Ethiopian white" [sic]. It became the rough equivalent of our "when hell freezes over." Philip Massinger's *The Bondman: An Antient Storie*, about the rebellion and resubmission of slaves, was first performed at court in 1623 and went on to become a popular and long-running play. Leosthenes, the principal slave, would never be free. "When he can wash an Æthiop white, Leosthenes may hope to free himself; But til then never."

The two concepts related to blackness—wholeness and impossibility—came together in science. Early scientists of the time were fascinated, as now, with making the impossible possible. And blackness played a central role. The Renaissance color concept of black as embodying paradox was also represented in the pre-science of alchemy, concerned with the transformation of the baser metals into gold or silver. The stem of alchemy, *chem*, means "black earth," and it was popularly associated with the Egyptians. In today's science, the "black box" is still where the unseen or unexplained chemical process occurs. Our black box stems from the original alchemical idea of chemical change, seen as black.

The alchemical transformation process, the melanosis or nigredo, was conceptualized as the color black. Black was the sign of chemical change, disintegration, reduction to the chaos that was before the Beginning, before creation or rebirth could occur.

The association of blackness with the original chaos, or unrecognized order, also came into play. Chaos allowed the absence of categories, which permitted paradox to be unconvoluted and emerge as change and order. In the black chaos that gave birth to order, the enigma of impossibility was resolved. The black chaos literally gave birth to order. Alchemists explained chemistry in gender related and sexual terms. The nigredo symbolized a love-death, in which union was so complete that any individual entity was killed. Destruction led to construction, like the ancient Sacred Dark Feminine's use of destruction in order to facilitate renewal. Chaos and creation of the world were analogous in alchemy. Also, like the Sacred Dark Feminine, it is the "terrible attraction" out of which came life. Out of the blackness came the rainbow of the peacock's tail—and eventually whiteness.

The nigredo was symbolized by many of the same images as were the dark Egyptian and Celtic goddesses who turned black—vultures, crows, ravens, black wolves, black clothing. The raven or vulture was one of the most common symbols of the nigredo. The vulture of the nigredo cries the otherwise impossible, "I am the white of the black!" While all of the nigredo figures, including that of the black man, signify the unknowable in nature, itself conceived as blackness which makes change possible, the symbols of nigredo were not interchangeable. The male and female versions had very different roles. The black male usually symbolized the impossibility of the process, the paradox left unresolved, the chaos left unorganized. The blackness of the alchemical man is a pearl; he is the paradox. "His deadliness produces life. And he expresses all the darkness of the human spirit in the pretense of extreme desire or death."

The black male retained the most extreme, most alienated definitions of the color black: Black as impossibility, the otherness that existed outside of the rational, tangible, and white human experience and which could not be brought closer. The alchemical negredo reprinted often in London in the sixteenth century grew more and more detailed, into a larger, more athletic-looking black man, with smaller, weaker-looking white men trying vainly to wash him white. A common symbol of the negredo was the black man in the presence of white women or an imprisoned black man near or on a white woman's head. They are opposites, impossibility personified.

The representations of the impossibility of blackness would continue to use black male figures, but transformation, the impossible made possible, would be represented by a dark female. In the negredo, the raven, associated with the feminine, symbolized the otherwise impossible, the successful transmutation process. As the alchemical representation was popularized by Renaissance drama, the impossible became possible, paradox and chaos became ordered and knowable—but not before the personified male nigredo symbol was exchanged for the personified black female symbol. Permanence, as female, became explicitly a virtue. She also was used to pick up other characteristics associated with black that had been largely absent in the black male representations. With her, black was also compassion and purity.

In Ben Jonson's Twelfth Night masques in 1605, with Blackness and its sequel, Beauty, the impossible was transformed: feminine blackness was transformed into feminine whiteness. The skin of twelve Ethiopian girls was washed in the sea. Their way was lit by their patron moon goddess, named AEthiopia, "whose person signified the intrinsic absolute white, the fleshly permanence and the almost divinity of the Ethiopian people." The women, who leave their blackness in the sea, were purer for having had the preservative of blackness covering their white goodness.

> Since Death herself . . .
> Can never alter their most faithful hue:
> All which are arguments to prove how far
> Their beauties conquer in great beauty's war;
> And more, how near divinity they be
> That stand from passion or decay so free.

The women were the impossible and the paradoxical personified, their blackness simply covered their inner whiteness, but humans were too weak to see the goodness overlaid with black. Rather than doomed by their blackness, the black females were saved by it.

Milton also wrote on this theme, of Prince Memnon's sister, "that starred Ethiope queen" in "Il Penseroso" whom he compared to:

> Melancholy
> Whose saintly visage is too bright
> To hit the sense of human sight,
> And therefore to our weaker view
> O'erlaid with black . . .

So in the areas of alchemy, religion, and public aesthetic forms, black women were regarded as a special case, combining the qualities of blackness and womanhood. Black was associated with naturalness, with the lack of artifice as in Shakespeare, who considered this to be a trait more pleasant than the artifice necessary to preserve the more delicate whiteness. Lyric and dramatic poet Thomas Randolph wrote in the poem "A Mask for Lydia" that Lydia's black controls her pride.

> Where's Lydia now? where shall I seek
> Her charming lip, her tempting cheek,
> That my affections bow'd
> So dark a sable hath eclips'd my fair,
> That durst not see the star.
>
> But yet (methinks) my thoughts begin
> To say there lies a white within,
> Through black her pride controule
> And what care I how black a face I see,
> So there be whitenesse in the soul?
> Still such an Ethiope be

In Thomas Randolph's play *The Conceited Peddler*, the peddler speaks of a alabaster doll in primarily sexual terms emphasizing her whiteness. Only when he describes a maternal function does he use the word "black."

> O, let me—or I shall ne'er rest—
> Suck the black bottles of thy breast.

Blackness became a useful alternative to fair maidens. In Randolph's play *Amyntas or the Impossible Dowry*, acted before the king and queen of Whitehall and printed in 1638, Damon remarks that he would rather kiss an Ethiopian than his fair maid Amaryllis: "I'll rather kiss An Ethiop's crisped lip; embrace a viper. Deformity itself to her is fair."

Perhaps the most famous examples are Shakespeare's sonnets 127–142 to the Dark Lady, who is beautiful because she is more natural than the artifice used by fair ladies:

> Then will I swear beauty herself is black,
> And all they foul that thy complexion lack.

And:

> In the old age black was not counted fair,
> Or if it were, it bore not beauty's name;
> But now is black beauty's successive heir,
> And beauty slandered with a bastard shame

Many English writers depended upon the works of ancient writers for descriptions of the black feminine. Ovid was a particular favorite of Renaissance writers; Chaucer, Gower, Spenser, Marlowe, Shakespeare, Donne, Milton, and Pope were among those he influenced. In Ovid's *Metamorphoses*, Nature was the beginning. His first metamorphosis was the evolution from chaos, and from darkness into light. In his *Fasti* the Great Mother of the gods was brought to Rome in a vessel of state during the night. In *Paradise Lost*, originally published in 1667, Milton used Ovid and other sources to create what is perhaps the most complete and complex imagery of the dark and the maternal and catapulted that imagery into the contemporary mind. Milton kept the original powers for female, or in hermaphroditic men who echoed her androgyny. Milton also kept the ancient names, if not the original genders, and gave Chaos a more central role in the narrative.

Milton furthered the development of the black feminine in his synthesis of the many ancient and contemporary works that he used as sources: Ovid, Virgil, Hesiod, alchemy, the Bible, and the Christian fathers. In his description of the black hermaphroditic and feminine, Milton relied heavily upon both alchemical and theological treatments of darkness. He moved the image from the fields of alchemical and theological debate into the slightly more accessible field of literature. The Bible and Hesiod were among the principal sources for the creation scene. The God presented in *Paradise Lost* reflected its sources in the Hermetic God and the God of the early Christian fathers.

When Milton described a God surrounded by light and a strong yet secondary set of gods surrounded by darkness, he set up a fine balance of color mythology that would continue indefinitely in Western mythology: The darkness remained powerful but was co-opted so that the strong dark was in the service of the light. This enabled the dark's power to remain a good thing even as it opposed the light.

Genesis provided the basis for the images of primordial darkness, and Hesiod provided the personification of darkness in the persons of Chaos and Night. Milton took the old role and qualities of Mother Chaos and spread her qualities among several characters—God and Chaos, both male but hermaphroditic, and a minor character, the female Demogorgon. God contained and transcended darkness as had the old female Chaos. The new male Chaos lived and ruled with his female consort "Old Night" in the region of unformed matter between Heaven and Hell which would, in time, become the world.

Both God and Chaos, as hermaphrodites, recalled the birthing functions of the old dark Mother. God, who like the primordial darkness he displaced, was present from the first and sat "dove-like . . . brooding on the vast abyss and made it pregnant," combining the traditional male and female roles. Chaos retained the essence of the old black Mother by having a womb. There is little doubt that Milton would have known how he was using and deviating from Hesiod. Elsewhere, Milton directly cited Hesiod's description of the beginning of the world, that "from Chaos sprang Erebus and black Night." As in Virgil, the female Erebus is Hell itself. The female-related imagery and birthing were still very much a part of creationism. Church fathers had already managed to reconcile the primordial being of Chaos with the Christian creation story. Milton editor Fowler wrote that chaos was often depicted as an egg-shaped mass in the visual art of the period.

Chaos and Night presided over a region that was the same as the old chaotic primordial ocean. "The secrets of the hoary deep, a dark illimitable ocean without bound, without dimension, where length, breadth, and highths and time are lost; where eldest Night and Chaos, ancestors of Nature, hold eternal anarchy amidst the noise of endless wars, and by confusion stand."

Hesiod and Boccaccio had similarly made Chaos and Night the ancestors of the more determinate powers of nature. Milton also recalled Ovid's account of the primordial Chaos where "cold things strove with hot, moist with dry, soft with hard, weighless with heavy."

Elsewhere in *Paradise Lost*, Night was described as the "eldest of things." Chambers argued that Night was a personification of prime matter. "The dreaded name of Demogorgon," who was among the beings stood by Chaos and Night, was "the ancestor of all the gods"—a reference to the goddess "the name whose knowing and whose speaking" the ghosts dread. She was identified by Statius as Demogorgon. The abyss over which Chaos and Night reigned owed much to the Sumerian primordial darkness pregnant with the potential matter of the world.

> Into this wild abyss,
> The womb of nature and perhaps her grave,
> Of neither sea, nor shore, nor air, nor fire,

But all of these in their pregnant causes mixed
Confusedly, and which thus might ever fight,
Unless the mighty maker them ordain
His dark materials to create more worlds.

The only difference was that in Milton, God controlled when the primordial mass went on to create more worlds. God did not directly create, but he ordains the abyss to create.

So in Milton, there was a distinction between the state of darkness and personification of darkness. Milton set forth and carried through to later writers the images of darkness as abstraction and personification as separate but related entities. The personified Chaos and Night are less bothersome beings than was the region they inhabit. Chaos and Night were not perverted, as Satan was when he first spoke to Chaos on his way through their region, nor evil, as Satan eventually became. Chaos and Night were just unpleasant and anarchic. By juxtaposing Chaos and Satan, Milton made Chaos more obviously benign. The eternal anarchy was a necessary legacy of the previous world that continued to coexist along with the ordered world. Chaos was located not far from the created order of the human world and, according to Fowler, "amplifies the fragility and delicacy of its created order." The threat of a powerful and eternal anarchy so near to the ordered artifice of human society played a role in keeping humans in line. It was not something humans chose, but they had to recognize and, in order for it to serve its full purpose, to fear it.

Milton was blind, which led to his rich contemplation of the darkness. Blinded when he was forty-four years old after years of intense study and activity, Milton lived twenty-two more years and went on to publish his greatest works, to engage in public debate, and to marry again. While his life was hardly easier for his blindness, the darkness in which he lived was neither evil nor debilitating.

Milton reaffirmed the interrelation of dark and light in his writing. God's skirts were so bright that they appeared "dark with excessive light." A bit of darkness actually made God more accessible to humans. The light around God was so bright that he was inaccessible until he shaded the "full blaze of [his] beams" and his skirts became visible. To be sure, Milton saw light as more sacred than darkness; the world was saved from eternal anarchy from light. Light came "from the walls of heaven" and was a sacred influence upon darkness. The moon kept the world, Night's "old possession," from being reclaimed by Night and life from being extinguished.

Although Milton added much to the cultural conceptualization of darkness and humans, the Western dark feminine was most fully developed in the religious treatments of the dark bride in the Song of Songs. She captured the imagination of writers for centuries. In the Song of Songs, the black female as unrevealed purity received a culturally significant treatment.

Connections developed between the religious and the secular interpretations, as in Zohar, the thirteenth-century classic of Jewish kabbalism, and the ninth-century Turba Philosophorum, a classic of medieval alchemy. For the alchemical work, the female blackness was the source of gold out of chaos. In the field of alchemical dream literature, Henry Medathanas wrote "The Golden Age Restored," a tract published early in the seventeenth century but purporting to be medieval, which moved the blackness from the woman's skin to her clothes, where they can be shed and light allowed to show through. "Her garments are old, defiled, and foul but I will purge them, and love her with all my heart. Let her be my sister, my spouse." The originality of the darkness was also retained. The alchemical bride was the orginal female, her light hidden under the darkness. The dark clothes were themselves virgin matter. The science and literary masterworks of European culture carried the miraculous Dark Feminine into everyday consciousness. Along with the religious sermons of Beloved, the secular idea of the Dark Feminine as able to transform impossibility came with colonists to the American shores.

A culturally held image of the black feminine, distinct from the white feminine and the black masculine, was firmly in place by the time African women were enslaved in colonial North America and the mythical image has since been used to define black women, to make them the nigredo in the baseness of slavery. When American colonists forcibly imported African women and brought them into their homes as midwives, nurses, cooks, and confidantes, they co-opted the archetypal image of the Sacred Dark Feminine and used it to romanticize human slavery in the land of the free. In England, the mythology of the Sacred Dark Feminine had been largely abstract, constructed in the relative absence of living black women. Although Africans were known in England and black slaves were held there, there was nothing of the scale and cultural impact of American slavery. In North America, British colonials would have to cope with an unprecedented level of black presence; African slaves were the largest single group of non-English-speaking people in colonial North America.

The white slaveholders used the image of the Black Mother to cover over the monstrosity of slavery, to sentimentalize the role of enslaved women in the white home, and to patch the incongruities of white society itself. The positioning of the Black Mother was a specific case of the general positioning of the black woman, whose movement between field and house led to ramifications for white culture that went far beyond those of a conveniently flexible labor source. The personal and public myths allowed slave owners to iron out many of the problematic contradictions inherent in the enslavement of black women and men. Slaves were sometimes seen as human, sometimes not. They were sometimes intimates, but that could change in an instant. Slave owners wrote of loving the people they owned. If we peep beneath the monstrous macro-level institution of slavery, we see individuals, neither all good nor all bad, trying to survive as emotional beings within the emotional vortex of human slavery. Mythology is the language of emotional survival.

When they imported and enslaved Africans, European colonists also brought among themselves people whom they necessarily saw as dangerous. Their fears were in part based upon the logical expectation of retribution for slavery and for the particularly brutal nature of the slavery they imposed. That the slaves they imported were black only added to the Europeans' fear.

So another paradox of North American slavery was set: white people needed and feared black people at the same time. Laws were passed to keep black proportions from becoming too large—owners could not expect slaves to remain docile under such conditions. Slaveholders were particularly afraid of the men. Gender became an important tool in the emotional contortions that allowed slave owners to live in the conditions they had made. Female blackness and male blackness had already been defined as related but strategically different. Both black maleness and black femaleness were defined as strong, but black maleness was permanent and dangerous. Black femaleness was protective and transformational. The images of the Sacred Dark Feminine were adapted to allay the fears of slave owners; black women were positioned at a functional fringe, between whites and other enslaved blacks, to supposedly protect whites from the retributions of the slaves they bought but feared.

The mythology of the Sacred Dark Feminine and her secular sister, the Strong Black Woman, became very useful in the ways in which slave owners lived in a world fraught with contradiction. Europeans saw African women in the way that their mythology led them to, as more physically and emotionally durable than white women and more compassionate and nurturing than black men, as well as miraculously transformative.

It does not excuse slavery to also investigate the micro-level relationships of those who lived within its grip, for it is only there that we may find how the whites managed to live with themselves and how black women managed to live at all: the personal and cultural myths of slave owners allowed black women small pockets of power. The myth of the Black Mother was instrumental to the emotional survival of slavery for blacks and whites. There existed a tension between what slave owners wanted from black women and what black women were. Some women were able to work the tension to some small advantages for themselves, their families, and their slave communities.

Although the South quickly became dependent upon coerced black labor, slavery was much more than an agricultural system. Slaveholders incorporated the status, the role, and the daily routine of slavery into their daily lives. Slavery gave them their identity. In an oration delivered on Independence Day in 1850, William Henry Trescott explained why the South would rather dissolve the union than give up slavery. Owning slaves made them who they were: "Slavery informs all our modes of life, all our habits of thought, lies at the basis of our social existence, and of our political faith." Historian Rosengarten, in his introduction to the diary of South Carolina slave owner Thomas Chaplin, identified the emotional dependency upon slavery: "Telling them was what he had to do; it was how he conceived of his vocation." Thomas Chaplin wrote in his journal on December, 27, 1848, during the three-day Christmas work break, "last days of the holidays & I am glad for then the Negroes will go to work & something for me to do." Chaplin looked forward to a time when he would only allow his slaves one day for Christmas for, as biographer Rosengarten wrote, "he lost his sense of himself when the Negroes were not working."

If slave owners incorporated slavery into their self-identities and were to continue to think highly of themselves, then they would have to redefine slavery into a humane institution of large, biracial families rather than a brutal life based on disenfranchisement and force. The Black Mother became a pivotal figure in their reconstruction of slavery into a family in which she was positioned to nurture her brood of white and black "children." The movement of black women into the position of Mother was aided by the mythology of slavery itself that slaveholders created. The Victorian period's emphasis upon family and idealized domestic life led to the reinterpretation of slaves as members of a large family with white parents and black children. By 1830 slavery had become a "domestic institution" which "came to mean slavery idealized, slavery translated into a fundamental and idealized Victorian institution, the family." Rather than always being treated as savages, slaves were often treated as eternal children, an emotionally safer and more comfortable concept for slaveholders. The Black

Mother was the exception that supported the rule: she was placed in a position of relative power and used as an authority figure over the "black children" as well as a maternal figure for white families. If a slave woman gained power, it was most often in the role of the Mammy. It was not unusual for the older black house slave woman to discipline and settle disputes among other house servants and to achieve a fragile position of dominance in the white home.

Myth plays a role in the emotional survival of individuals and entire cultures by allowing us to carry the messy and irrational aspects of our lives. Life is chaotic, ultimately uncontrollable, but Western culture, in particular, carries on as if everything were neat and rational. Myth allows us to do that by absorbing and altering the messy bits. History and myth coevolve in a reflexive relationship, each responding to changes in the other. Recorded history is a country's self-conscious representation of itself, carefully reworked for the following generations. It is the result of serious and officially sanctioned work. Unlike recorded history, popular mythology is "unashamed subjectivity"; it gathers up the pieces of events and emotion and arranges a script that "makes sense," a narrative that is reproduced for the generations.

Myth is of the public and of the private, always occurring at the two levels at once; it bridges the private experience and the public narrative. It plays off of "facts" and "truth" of experiential social reality, turning them into even more faithful depictions of the collective values and interpretations. If history is rational, logical, and inherently ordered, mythology is emotional and subjective, an attempt to render the world to our desires and needs. We live in a world that we do not always understand or control. Mythology is an attempt to accommodate the world to us. If slave owners could not coerce the slave women they wanted, they could imagine them so. They may not have had enough power to erase the social reality of what they had done, but they did have enough power to fashion mythology to their collective mother-fantasy.

The image of the black woman was put to use at a very specific era for the country and for specific women.

Slavery peaked during the Victorian era (1837–1901), a period full of paradox for white women and the world they lived in. The black woman was grafted onto a system in which ladies were not allowed to acquire female power, where the parts of a family operated symbiotically but carried out their separate tasks independently, where the more customary sexual, familial, and labor interplay between genders was proscribed by social fashion. The popular feminine idealization was of a woman of a particular type. The popular ideal set up extreme

social expectations that were contradictory: The white woman was to be physically attractive but was not be engaged in sexual intercourse except under strictly
defined circumstances. She was to remain delicate and infirm in a period when
domestic work was particularly difficult and often brutal. She was to be a loving
and patient mother when lack of reliable birth control led to too many children and too much work. Relationships between white males and females were
particularly distant and gender driven. The prescribed daily duties of men and
women were divided and defined by gender so that the genders developed different subcultures and daily routines.

The passive White Mother and the "cult of true womanhood" were unwork-
able, publicly held ideals that needed private props in order to exist. What was
to be a horrific experience for the slave woman was also useful for the Southern
society as a whole. The black woman moved between the boundaries of race,
gender, or class more than any of the other players. She moved more frequently
in the free world than did the unskilled black man; she moved more intimately
in the white female domestic world than did the white man; she moved more in
the male dominated field than did the white woman. Simply put, she filled in
the gaps of a divided society. Her presence allowed paradoxical gender situations
to remain standing for longer than might have otherwise been the case.

Early on, a clear distinction between black female slaves and white female
servants was made. Black women could work like men, "on the ground"; white
women could not. Labor codes were established to ensure the distinction. An
early example is provided by Franklin: "Sufficient distinction is also made
between the female Servants & Slaves: for a White woman is rarely or never put
in the Ground, if she be good for anything else, and to Discourage all Planters
from using Women so. Their Law imposes the heaviest Taxes upon Female-
Servants working in the Ground . . . Whereas on the other hand it is a common
thing to work a Woman Slave out of Doors; nor does the law make Distinction
in her Taxes, whether her Work be Abroad or at Home."

When American colonists forcibly imported African women and brought
them into their homes as midwives, nurses, cooks, and confidantes, they also
co-opted the archetypal image of the Sacred Dark Feminine and used it to
romanticize human slavery in the land of the free.

Slave owners immediately applied the label to the women who were forced
to work in and around their homes. The labor was coerced and the image
co-opted. The mythological slave woman was the maternity who was meant to
save white slave owners from the physical and emotional dangers they created

when they used slave labor. As the institution developed, the Black Mother would be reinterpreted as needed.

The Black Mother has become one of the most enduring figures in the popular culture of the United States. From early American folklore, popular theater, and almanacs through the introduction of film and television, she has played a particular role in the humor, drama, and commercial advertisement of the country. Sitting as she is, at the pivotal and socially explosive categorizations of race, gender, and class/caste, she plays a central role in both the cultural history and mythology of the country by crossing societally imposed and often dichotomized categorizations of American culture. Although she has occurred throughout the society's mythology, she has been most prominent during periods of economic and social unrest, when the status quo conceptualizations of class, gender, and race have been threatened as members of the disenfranchised groups pushed for change. Her popularity has peaked during the periods of the post–Civil War, the Depression, and the post-industrial age, when she has been used as the mythical figure of transformation and deliverance from chaos back to order.

Just as it had been thought of in religion, in early Western color-science and secular literature black was considered to be the first color and the beginning of the world to come. The Sacred Dark Feminine delivered the new, rational world out of the nether abyss but she remained chaotic. When a character fell back into the chaos of the other worlds, she delivered them again to the world of order, of patriarchal law, of the light. The stories and theories reflected Western attitudes toward women, caste/class, blackness, and fierce maternal figures. She has survived for centuries, saved by her wholeness. She is now one of the few whole women left in post-industrial Western mythology. To understand the Fierce Angel, we must understand the meanings attributed to femaleness and to darkness. She changes both: her darkness changes femininity and her femininity changes darkness.

It is important to tease out the difference between the mother fantasy and the lives of black women as they lived them, while keeping in mind the ways in which the myth affected the women's lives. Black women sometimes had power as nurses and midwives. Mammies technically existed only on large plantations, but on smaller plantations, nurses took on many of the same characteristics. The power Mammies, nurses, and maids gained came from the sentimental role they carried within the white household. When Mary Chestnut wrote of her mother's black maid, the image approached the myth of the wise, black woman.

Mary made clear the mother's love and dependence upon the black woman and the power the black woman derived from her position.

"She is my mother's factotum—has been her maid since she was bought from a Virginia speculator (her mother and all her children) at six years old. She is pampered until she is a rare old tyrant at times. She can do everything better than anyone else. And my mother leans on her heavily."

Besides her roles with food and children, the black woman also took on the roles of confidante and messenger. Black women and white women were involved in each other's romantic adventures. In her recollection of slavery thirty years later, Anne Laurie Broidrick of Mississippi wrote, "Many a romantic tale was confided by mistress and maid to each other during the hours the hair was being brushed and the soft wrapper donned." The white culture's cult of true womanhood demanded that love communication be carried out in secrecy, and some female house slaves became carriers of romantic messages. Slave women, carrying passes, had actually more mobility than did their mistresses and so had access to men on other plantations and knew their servants. The black women could provide information on the man's emotional life and private affairs and could be sent to his home. Since the black woman had more direct information about the male love-object, her advice was often sought.

Some white women also delighted in orchestrating the romantic events in the lives of the slaves. Thomas Chaplin's wife encouraged slave marriages, hosting the celebrations with a "grand supper" in her living room and, according to her husband's journal, using, "very foolishly, my crockery, tables, chairs, candlesticks & I suppose everything else they wanted" as well as his "good liquor" for the punch bowl.

Whites appeared to have been far more emotionally dependent upon black women than black women were upon them. Genovese wrote, "In the reciprocal dependency of slavery, especially in the Big House, the slaves needed masters and mistresses they could depend on; they did not need masters and mistresses to love them. But the whites needed their servants' love and trust. The slaves had the upper hand and many of them learned to use it."

Slave owners sometimes openly acknowledged their dependency upon a black maternal caretaker. Laura S. Tibbetts of Louisiana wrote to her sister-in-law in 1853, "We would not hesitate about coming to see you if I could bring my servants, but I could not bring my baby without assistance. She is a great deal fonder of her Mammy than she is of me."

Mammies managed to live in a relatively privileged and protected position. Although violence toward Mammies did occur, it was an occasion of different significance. Ma Eppes of Alabama reported the results of an overseer whipping a Mammy in the absence of the mistress:

> Miss Sarah went to Demopolis to visit with her sister, and whilest she were gone the overseer, what go by the name of Allen, whupped my mammy 'crost her back till the blood runned out. When Miss Sarah comed back and found it out she was the maddest white lady I seed. She sont for the overseer and she say: "Allen, what you mean by whipping Mammy? You know I don't allow you to touch my house servants." She jerk her dress down and stand there looking like a soldier with her white shoulders shining and she say: "I'd rather see them marks on my old shoulders than to see 'em on Mammy's. They wouldn't hurt me no worse." Then she say: "Allen, take your family and git offen my place. Don't you let sundown catch you here." So he left. He was nothing but white trash nohow.

Another overseer asked for permission to punish a Mammy and got this response: "What! What! Why I would as soon think of punishing my own mother! Why man you'd have four of the biggest men in Mississippi down on you if you even dare suggest a thing, and she knows it! All you can do is to knuckle down to Mammy." Some Mammies could also defend themselves from cruel treatment. Ellen Cragin of Mississippi's mother worked so long that she fell asleep at the loom, to be awakened by the blows of her master's young son. According to Cragin, "He beat my mother til she woke up. When she woke up, she took a pole out of the loom and beat him nearly to death with it. He hollered, 'Don't beat me no more, and I won't let them whip you.' She said, 'I'm going to kill you. These black titties sucked you and then you come her to beat me.' And when she left him, he wasn't able to walk."

While the myth suggests that the Mammy could do no wrong, there were definite limits to the degree that black women could violate slave codes. Ellen Cragin's mother left the plantation, riding off with a milk cow, to escape punishment, "because she knew they would kill her if she stayed." She would not see her daughter again until after Emancipation.

The death of a favorite Mammy was an occasion for emotional outpourings of grief and respect. Mandy Marrow, ex-slave and former cook of Governor Stephen Hogg of Texas, recalled, "Yes, suh, de Gov'nor am de good man. You knows, when he old nigger mammy die in Temple, him drap all he work and goes to de fun'ral and dat show him don't forgit de kindness."

Marrow's statement suggests a recognition that the slave gave Hogg something out of kindness rather than coercion. When Susan Dabney Smedes's Mammy died, her father did not allow a sermon, saying, "I do not know anybody good enough to preach a sermon over her" and led the funeral procession himself, followed by all his children (co-opting the mourning of her biological family). "He ordered out the whole plantation, every one who could walk, and every man, woman, and child carried a torch." Susan, out of grief, asked to be excused from the procession, "but the master seemed unapproachable in his grief, and I was afraid of incurring his displeasure if he should discover that I was unwilling to pay what he considered fitting respect to the memory of this trusted friend."

Judith Page Rives of Albemarle County, Virginia recalled a similar scene:

It was also the day of poor Mammy's interment. She was attacked monday [sic] the 1st. I am thankful to say that she apparently suffered little or no pain, and that in the brief intervals of lethargic but tranquil sleep that marked the progress of the fatal malady she was sufficiently conscious to join in the prayers of High at her bed side, and to express to me her firm faith in a savior's love and pardon. Every mark of respect was shown to this good and faithful servant, who I trust, has entered into joy of her lord. Mr. Boyden performed the service and we attended with the people of the neighboring farms and our own.

The energy of the Black Mother was co-opted for the use of white families, and these families assumed that the African woman worked in the interests of the white family. Susan Dabney Smedes, daughter of a prominent planter, assumed that "in no hands was the dignity of the family so safe as with the negro slaves." The Smedes household had two Mammies: Granny Harriet, whose memories were the basis of Smedes's book, and a younger Mammy, Mammy Maria, who while old enough to have raised Mrs. Smedes's mother actually did the housework. Susan remembered that Maria "had come to love the white family better than her own blood and race." What would become a central mythological role of the enslaved Mother also showed up in the relationship of the Smedes-Dabney family and their Mammy, that of spiritual redemption for the wrong of slavery. When Mr. Dabney died, one of his daughters asked Mammy if the father needed to be afraid to meet any of his former slaves at God's judgment bar. Mrs. Smedes ended her book with the black woman's assurances that her old, good, master had nothing to fear "while tears ran down her venerable black face." The old woman then died of grief, her role as Mammy and spiritual redeemer complete.

The myth at its extreme depicts women who returned the level of devotion displayed by these white families, women who, upon seeing white people, dropped everything, lost all sense of self, family, tribe, or color to pick up the concerns of the people who, despite their affection, kidnapped her, enslaved her, bought, sold, and worked her as if she were one of so many head of cattle. Olmsted argued that many black women preferred their white children to their black children. To be sure, there were some Mammies who did live to serve, like Adeline Johnson of South Carolina.

> I hope and prays to git to heben. Whether I's white or black when I git dere, I'll be satisfied to see my Savior dat my old marster worshipped and my husband preached 'bout. I wants to be in hevven wid all my white folks, just to wait on them and love them and serve them, sorta lak I did in slavery time. Dat will be enough for Adeline."

However, a body of evidence to support the image of the black mother neglecting her own family for her white family does not exist. Genovese argued "willful neglect of or indifference to their own children cannot be deduced from their behavior. In particular the idea that the Mammies actually loved the white children more than their own rests on nothing more than wishful white perceptions." Actually, it was not unusual for black mothers to fight in defense of their children. Fannie Moore of Asheville, North Carolina, recalled:

> My mammy she work in de field all day and piece and quilt all night. Den she have to spin enough thread to make four cuts for de white folks every night. . . . I never see how my mammy stand such hard work. She stand up for her chillen though. De old overseer he hate my mammy, 'cause she fought him for beatin' her chillen. Why she get more whippin' for dat dan anythin' else.

Another contradiction within the myth itself becomes apparent. If one carries the myth's line of sentiment to its logical conclusion, it would follow that these women who forsook themselves and their people were stupid or amoral enough to miss the truth of their enslavement. But according to both history and the myth, these are the same women who, like this woman, were competent enough to control inventory, run households, and oversee the lives of future masters: "Cause I was really only ole Mis' housekeeper; kept house, took care of her money and everything; she was one o' these kinds of women that couldn't keep up with nothing, and I just handled her money like it was mine almost."

The women selected for these duties were neither stupid nor amoral. To the contrary, the Mammy for Susan Bradford Eppes's family was selected for her "worth and reliability." Mothers were selected out of pools of black women, and while it would be likely that a master or mistress selected one of the least hostile slave women, it is also clear that many and perhaps most Mammies did not forget the well-being of themselves, their families, or the slave community. Indeed their maternity of black children may have acted to decrease "disloyal" acts such as escape and increase "loyal" acts designed to encourage favorable treatment of the slave children. On the more numerous small and medium-sized plantations, the maternal black woman would be more likely to work in the field as well as the house and have a somewhat closer relationship with the field slaves than the myth posits. Some women welcomed the change of job and the opportunity to socialize when they had to help the field hands. One well-treated cook commented on the relative freedom of outdoor work away from the family. "We could talk and do anything we wanted to, just so we picked the cotton; we used to sing and have lots of fun."

White families relied on the Black Mother enough that they needed to be able to assume her loyalty whether the assumption was based upon solid evidence or not. Susan Dabney Smedes reported events on the Dabney plantation after the mistress died and her daughters tried to run the household: "Those were days of trial and perplexity for the young mistresses. The old house servants, though having at heart an affection for them, considered or pretended to consider them too young to know what they wanted. Besides, had they not known these young ladies ever since they were born? And did they not call them mammy or aunt in consideration of superior age?"

The young women eventually established their authority when the elder Mammy threw them her support and helped discipline the others. For reasons that probably went to the grave with Mammy Harriet, she did not throw her support behind the young Smedes women immediately, restoring order only after it was abundantly clear to everyone who was really in charge. That Mammy Harriet accomplished this by seeming to place herself in the subordinate position to the young women was not lost upon Susan Smedes.

The sentimental role of the Black Mother was also used in relationships between white women. A white mother admonished her daughter by invoking the displeasure of the daughter's old Mammy. "I *should not* offer my services to walk out with you to Mrs. A's any more and I do not 'spect your old nurse will be anxious to go with you again. She said she was very sorry you behaved as you did."

The role of the Mammy in white American culture has led to much vilification of her in black American popular culture, but it is important to separate out, as much as one can, what black women did from the myths about what they did. Black women managed to offer their individual power to black people and to sometimes violate the patriarchal order. While her maternal position was seen by dependent whites as a reinforcement of their order, it also allowed an essential vehicle for black and female power. There is a great difference between co-opting the role and co-opting the person, and black women often acted in ways contradictory to their assigned role. Slavery produced strange circumstances, and people did what they needed to survive, physically and emotionally. Slave owners and slaves lived with contradiction, like the driver who insisted he loved his master and mistress and admitted to planning a bloody insurrection, and who, while being hanged for his plotting, trusted his master to look after his allegedly innocent wife. Some black women cared for and nurtured some white people while also being willing to forsake them for their race. Human beings are perfectly capable of holding contradictory emotions, and if slave women loved their masters and mistresses as individuals, they could not escape the subsuming condition of enslavement. If whites loved their blacks, they still enslaved them. Molly, the favorite slave of Mary Chestnut, seemed to care for Mary but she did not remain her maid after the war. The two women operated an egg business together.

Rather than a willing pawn for the white patriarchal order, the black maternal slave woman was an example of survivalism. In Sir Charles Lyell's *Second Visit*, he noticed that many slaves exhibited a sense of self, a merged consciousness that acknowledged their political disenfranchisement while not giving in to it. Black slaves did not necessarily absorb the consciousness of white slave owners. "The Negroes here have certainly not the manners of an oppressed race," and while displaying admirable courtesy, they knew how to stand their ground when they chose. Genovese's own concept of reciprocal obligation between slaves and slavers becomes useful here. If slave women had completely accepted their position as selfless slaves who lived for white families, they would have expected nothing in return and would seek no power for themselves. Instead, slaves spoke of "their" white folks, seemingly fully aware of the power statement inherent in the possessive term. Lyell asked a black woman in Georgia if she belonged to a white family, and she replied, "Yes, I belong to them and they belong to me." Slave women did not magically fall in love with white families or children. Like the white families who came to care for women who were kind to their children, black women became fond of families who were kind to them. Genia Woodbury, a former South Carolina Mammy, noted that when white folks treated her kindly, she developed kind feelings toward their children.

While there is evidence that white families believed that the loyalties of many black women lay with them, there is also evidence that black women used their position of privilege to benefit their own black families and friends. Mammies quickly translated their position into power, and it was common for Mammies to not have to worry often about being sold—or their husbands or children being sold. Many used their influence to better condition for field slaves. The Smedeses' slaves did. While Susan remembered, "Our childish associations with Grannie Harriet were delightful. She petted and spoiled us to our heart's content, and could not bear any fault found in us," Granny Harriet also used her privilege to elevate other blacks. While the slaves usually used more affiliative titles for one another, on formal occasions they addressed each other in keeping with the formality but in violation of an otherwise strictly held social convention. Hearing "faithful" Mammy Maria formally address her brother, Susan questioned the practice and was made immediately to regret it.

> On formal occasions they were [Mister and Missus]. Ignorance of this led me into sad disgrace one night with my usually indulgent Mammy Maria. She had taken me to see her brother married. I heard her address him as Mr. Ferguson, and at once asked, "Mammy, what makes you call Henry Mr. Ferguson?" "Do you think 'cause we are black we cyarn't have no names?" was Mammy's indignant reply.

Looking at slavery from the outside, it would at first appear that slaves would have little opportunity for the exercise of power. But they did and slave owners knew it. The balance of power had much to do with fear of black slaves and how much advantage slaves chose to take. During Nat Turner's rebellion, a Mrs. Nathaniel hid in a closet, hearing the cries of whites who were being murdered in her house. While her slaves knew where she was hiding and she feared they would reveal her hiding place, they did not. They did, however, divide up her clothes. Knowledge gained by intimacy gave slaves power. Proximity created opportunity to use that power.

The black maternal figure was in a unique position to know secrets and there is ample evidence that she often became a confidante, the best type of confidante for the powerful since her power to make use of secrets was limited. Nevertheless, even untold secrets have their power; Thomas Chaplin considered "the old cooks and maumas" to be dangerously knowledgeable about domestic and political events. The black traditional role of older women as healers and midwives also became useful to white families and gave the Mammy some level of influence. Intimacy also invited fear created by opportunity: Black women, using the same skills used for cooking and healing, were especially adept at poisoning their masters in the early years of slavery. Poisoning of food by cooks, while infrequent, made enslavers nervous.

In his own rather sentimental argument Genovese wrote of the balancing act performed by the Black Mother:

> The place that she made for herself was one that would, in a character less sure and strong, have brought on herself the hatred and distrust of her race. But they knew her to be just, one who never assailed the innocent, and with so warm and compassionate a heart in real trouble that none were afraid to come to her. From being a confidential servant she grew into being a kind of prime minister, and it was well known that if she espoused a cause and took it to the master it was sure to be attended to at once, and according to her advice.

The Smedeses saw the slave woman Maria's role as the household's "prime minister" to be amusing and romantic, but under the conditions of enslavement, her intervention would have been pivotal for other slaves. A talk with the elder Granny Harriet was a daily evening ritual for Smedes's father, who also consulted her on important plantation decisions and usually followed her advice. Granny Harriet was in a position to save lives and families and to improve working and living conditions.

Regardless of gender, there were constant tensions between slave and slave owner, who did not have absolute power. Black women lived in the middle of this tension and often, when presented with an opportunity to test the limits, took it. They commonly overrode the opinions of white women, and what could have been interpreted as insubordination was reinterpreted as loyalty and wisdom. Virginia Tunstall Clay, wife of a Confederate senator from Alabama, reported an argument she had with her maid that she interpreted as a charming example of her maid's loyalty and wisdom. Under the circumstances of slavery, the maid was committing an act of insubordination.

The personal journal of Mary Chestnut is perhaps the best known of the Civil War–era journals left by women. Mary was a prominent Southern lady, the wife of a South Carolina senator and brigadier general in the Confederate army. The relationship between the slave Molly and Mary Chestnut affords a close examination of the particular nature of the emotional dependency that made Molly so valuable to Mary that she allowed the slave woman to repeatedly violate the usually strict prescriptions for slave behavior, and of the tension between intimacy and racial alienation between the black and white women. In a conversation with Molly that Mary recorded in her journal, Molly possesses the voice of a woman who had a strong sense of self and family, making it clear that she knew her worth to the Chestnut household and that she would continue to use her position to ensure that her own children would not go hungry. While she was clearly looking after Mary, it was also clear that her first allegiance was with her own family. When Molly uses the term "we," she is making a general statement about slaves and her slave husband, Laurence. In the conversation, Mary had heard of another plantation where all the food has been stolen. Molly told her that the slaves probably stole it but that

> "You needn't look that scared. You sleep in your bed—easy. Why should we takes 'em in de bulk? We takes 'em as we wants 'em. Don't I make things last better than you ever did? Tell you why. We ain't going to the Yankees, and we keeps you keys, and we is going home to our husband and chillun when you go home."
>
> "But why do my things last? You forget to tell me that?"
>
> "Because we only want what we can eat ourselves. At home there's the children. If any woman tells you she won't give her children anything good to eat if they hangs around her and begs for it, don't you believe it. Dey gets a little of all dat's going."

The tone Molly used here was one that she used commonly. Mary insulted her, and Molly made it clear that she would not stand for it. Mary needed Molly and both women knew it. Mary allowed Molly and her other servants to mother her, to scold her, to order her to bed, and she obeyed. Molly's "fussiness" exhibits her distance from Mary and may have worked to maintain a delicate balancing job in the face of a contradiction that was to Molly's advantage: she could benefit from a position of relative privilege without being completely co-opted by an institution designed to dehumanize her and her people.

The relationship between Mary Chestnut and Molly presents a picture very different from that of the myth. Like many of the slave women, Molly seems to have genuinely cared about the white woman who owned her—to a point.

Rather than having the selfless, cheerful, mythological Mammy, Mary lived with a woman who constantly violated the prescribed slave behavior to her own advantage, and Mary put up with it because Molly did many things Mary could not do for herself. Mary seemed to understand the balance of Molly's life, that she looked after Mary and she looked after her own family but that the family came first. During the war, as Mary traveled with her husband, Molly left her several times to take care of her own children. The emotional tone of these reports say much. During one, Mary was unsure of Molly's loyalty and she asked Molly for reassurance. Molly gave Mary a dramatic response of loyalty while simultaneously making it clear to Mary that her own children came first: "Molly all in tears because I asked her if she were going to turn against me. No she would follow me to the ends of the earth—that is, she would if it warn't for her children. But this is the reason she was out."

Molly also disobeyed Mary when she felt it necessary. Despite Mary's request, when one of Molly's older daughters neglected Molly's infant, causing the child's death, Molly was filled with motherly rage for her younger child and beat the older child. Mary wrote, "I begged Molly to keep everything dead still," but Mary's request meant little to Molly. It is significant that as Molly moved away from Mary, Mary reminded herself of her own race status:

> Then when I was so tired yesterday: Molly looking more like an enraged lioness than anything else, roaring that her baby's neck was broken. Howling cries of vengeance. And the poor little careless nurse's dark face had an ashen tinge of grey terror, and she was crouching near the ground, like an animal trying to hide, and her mother striking at her as she rolled away. All this was my welcome as I entered the gate. It takes these half-Africans but a moment to go back to their naked, savage animal nature.

Molly exhibited her own race consciousness and separated her personal relationship with Mary from other whites, just as Mary separated out Molly from other blacks. When Molly spoke of "our own people," she meant her people, black slaves. Molly also openly worried about her fellow slaves, even when it meant criticizing a white man. When she rightly suspected their basket of food had been stolen by men traveling in the same vehicle, Molly raged, "White mens, which of you stole my chicken?" In associating herself with black people, separating herself from white people, Molly went so far as to assume airs of superiority when a white person violated her personal code of ethics.

Mary had clearly selected Molly as a woman whose company she enjoyed. On a train trip, Molly and Mary witnessed a man and a woman being affectionate in a way that violated the etiquette of the day. Later Molly and Mary met the same woman in the hall. As the white women talked, Molly interrupted, "You had better go yonder ma'am where your husband is calling you." When the woman explained that she was a widow and the man was a cousin, Molly displayed her anger and asserted her moral superiority to the woman. "After all that gwine on in the [train] cars! Oh, Lord—I should a'let it go—'twas my husband and me! nigger as I am."

As the war progressed, Mary's emotional dependence upon Molly increased. Although the myth insists that there were many faithful slaves to serve distressed whites, the slaves' responses to the war varied widely and would have to be forced to fit into a simplistic formula (which is what nostalgic Southern whites eventually did). Molly was not always present when Mary needed her. After hearing a woman giggle in her presence, the aging and ailing Mary wrote, "I felt uncomfortable and wondered if there was anything amiss with me. I dressed in the dusk of the evening. Generally I hold Molly responsible that I shall not be a figure of fun. This afternoon she was not at home."

Later she traveled only with Molly and took comfort from Molly's presence.

Molly stayed with Mary during the winter of 1863 working as "housekeeper, cook, anything and everything, as the time required. This was her spirit." Molly became a truly maternal figure as Mary became more helpless, looking after the small and large aspects of her life and showing concern for Mary and the potential humiliation of having her journal published in Northern newspapers. But Molly never lapsed into the role of the selfless servant.

Molly's company gave Mary courage and strength. She considered them not as a black woman slave and a white woman mistress but as "we poor women." The two took a trip to see Mary's ill mother, a trip which Mary's husband had forbidden. "On that lonely riverside Molly and I remained—dismal swamps on every side, immense plantations, white people few or none."

James Boykin, whom they had met by chance, had promised to send back a carriage to fetch them but it had not come. As the trip progressed, Molly kept up the fires and provided hot cups of coffee on cold nights. As the women traveled on alone, they stopped at a small riverside inn, without light. Molly kept up a fire of pine knots for light and reassurance.

Mary became frightened by a white drunken guest and Molly reassured her, stating that she would not hesitate to defend Mary; that the man's race, with its explicit power, was less important to her than her relationship with Mary. Her relationship with an individual, rather than the love of an entire white race, guided her actions. In the role of defender, Molly took on a more traditionally white male stance than Mary ever could have, and Mary knew this. "I am sure Molly believes herself my bodyguard as well as my servant."

Molly continued to stand her ground against Mary and other white people. In this potentially explosive incident, Mary seemed more concerned with the harm and humiliation to Molly than to the white woman.

Shall I ever forget the headache of that night and the fright? My temples throbbed with dumb misery. I sat upon a chair—Molly on the floor, with her head resting against my chair. She was as near as she could get to me, and I kept my hand on her. "Missis, now I believe you are scared, scared of that poor drunken thing, If he was sober I could whip him—fair fight— and drunk as he is, I kin throw him over the bannister—ef he so much as teches you. I don't value him a button!" Taking heart from such brave words, I laughed.

Mary knew that her private relationship with Molly was fashioned more by personal feeling than class privilege. She knew that Molly's allegiance did not extend to every other white person; that for all Molly's skill, her generosity was limited.

Molly had more mobility than a white woman, so she was able to bring news of other families and street life to Mary. Molly called it "perusing the street." In return, Molly assumed and used Mary's authority when Mary's social status prevented her from asserting authority herself. Once while traveling Molly took it upon herself to scold a white man. "I felt Molly give me a gentle shake. 'Listen, Missis, how loud Mars Adam Team is talking. And all about old Marster and our business to stranger. It's a shame. . . . I'm going to tell him to stop.' Up stalked Molly. 'Mars Adam, Missis say please don't talk so loud. When people travel they don't do thataway.'" It is important to note here that Molly was in truth less concerned that Mary should be awakened than with her personal sense of propriety.

Later as Sherman's army approached and economic times grew still worse, Molly helped the family save face by skillfully fashioning food for company to hide its paltriness—she piled fried oysters on top of a bird whose breast had been eaten so company would not know they were being served leftover food. As keeper of the food and considering the dire straits of the family, Molly demanded some consideration in her duties. After hearing that there would be guests for the evening meal, the Chestnuts decided to eat less chicken in order to have more for the guests' meal but also decided that a cake was needed. The picture that emerges is one of a white family too concerned with social status and appearances and a black woman all too aware of the economic and political realities around them.

> We sent for Molly to order some cake. She came to the dining-room door with a fiery face, which she wiped with her apron. "Name o' God! Why don't dey ax you dere? It is cook, cook in dis house, from daylight till dark. Yo' time is come to be axed somewhere." She spoke at the top of her voice.
>
> "Molly, you forget yourself," I said in a low tone. Sally G.'s little maid standing open-mouth, all eyeballs and white teeth.
>
> "Blige to talk dis here way. You'll soon have nothing left for yo'self to eat."

As soon as Molly and most black women could, they changed their behavior toward white families entirely and many left domestic service altogether. One of the Chestnut nurses, Myrtilla, formerly described as a "black angel," ran away to the Yankees. Others like Molly asserted new "insolence" until they could leave.

After the end of the Civil War and slavery, with the collapse of the Southern way of life and the identities that it had supported, the increasingly fantastical belief in strong black women who had loved them would become more important than ever before. In what they saw as a fight for their personal, emotional and cultural lives, Southerners used every weapon in their arsenal, including the mythic ones. The image of the miraculous, transformational Dark Feminine was their nigredo, which they would use to rescue them, to change the awful social reality of slavery and the war into a romantic, noble story of love and honor. The stories they presented during and after the Civil War would pale in comparison to the high tales they concocted in the years to come.

3

She Made It Paradise

IN 1916, THE Jerome Remick & Company publishing house of New York and Detroit issued a song, "They Made It Twice as Nice as Paradise and They Called It Dixieland," with lyrics by Raymond Egan and music by Richard A. Whiting. The song sheet, which was also copyrighted in Canada and Mexico, carried a painted cover with a large-breasted dark woman; her straightened white hair was covered with a red-and-white kerchief, and she smiled and spoke to an attentive white child of ambiguous gender dressed for bed who sat happily on her lap. The child was held so she or he could still look directly into the black woman's eyes. One of the woman's hands was around the child, the other raised in song or story. The Mammy and child were obviously very close friends. Behind them was a wide vista of crops growing in the field, lush trees, and a peaceful home. The music told of a slave Mammy, sentimentally remembered by the singer as wise, dear, and so old that she might have been present at the creation of Dixieland:

Verse One:
 I used to have a dear old Mammy
In the days of old Black Joe.
She used to cuddle me up on her knee
And tell me tales of long ago.
She said the angels built old Dixie,
And I know that's not a fib.
For to me it looks like heaven
And I'll tell you what the angels did.
 Chorus:
 They built a little garden rose
And they called it Dixieland,

They built a summer breeze to keep the snows
Far away from Dixieland,
They built the finest place I've known
When they built my home sweet home,
Nothing was forgotten in the land of cotton,
From the clover to the honey-comb.
And then they took an angel from the skies
And they gave her heart to me.
She had a bit of heaven in her eyes.
Just as blue as blue can be.
They put some fine spring chickens in the land
And taught my Mammy how to use a frying pan,
They made it twice as nice as Paradise,
And they called it Dixieland

Verse Two:
    My dear old Mammy never told me
Where she learned this mystery.
And if I seem'd surpris'd
she'd look so wise
And say "Ma chile, that's history!"
But she liv'd so long in Dixie,
She was old enough to know,
And I think she might have been there,
When the land was built, so long ago.

Like the goddess, the Mammy was so old that she may have been present at the Creation, so wise that she was not to be questioned, and so reassuring that the singer did not want to question her. She knew the mysteries and had all the answers, and to the white post-Reconstruction singer, they were very pleasant answers because they were all for him. The very angels gave her a frying pan and taught her how to use it. Slavery gave slave masters the power to capture the old archetype and to use it to try to convince themselves and others that the strong dark women they needed also loved and supported them.

The slave Mammy remains one of the most controversial figures in American life. She is the slave ghost who haunts black women and still charms nonblack audiences. The 1939 film *Gone with the Wind*, with its feisty and wise slave Mammy, is still one of the country's favorite stories. The lives of black slave women have been co-opted, turned into a form of wish fulfillment, in an attempt to scratch the emotional itches of the dominant culture. Every era has its own itches—its traumas, longings, and dreams—and the reassuring image of strong and loving black women has been used as an effective balm.

It is no cultural accident that the image of the Sacred Dark Feminine is very much like that of the stereotypical slave Mammy since Europeans put the Sacred Dark Feminine onto the backs of black women as soon as they met them. Characteristics that deeply trouble contemporary African Americans are rooted in the sacred images and in the earth goddesses; in them we can see traits that would later be turned against black women. The black goddesses were big and threatening, with the strength and power to create and to destroy. That image would be taken to extremes and appropriated by slave owners for pro-slavery propaganda. The propagandistic happy slave Mammy was big because Mother Earth Gaia was huge, "broad breasted," and "monstrous" before her, shiny because she represented the "dazzling darkness."

There were historical black women who were called Mammy by black and white people, but there is considerable distance between them and the mythical Mammy, who was created as a piece of nostalgic propaganda to reconstruct the slaveholding South into a peaceful, loving place with contented slaves and wise Mammies who loved white children more than anything or anyone else. The mythical stories built around her were used to transform slavery and more: Her wisdom and comfort would help the country through the social and economic upheavals of the Great Depression. The myth grew so familiar that it left little room to see the lives that slave women actually lived. And to a large extent, black people have bought the image, too, handing their own mothers over to the myth.

Mammy is the American crone, the older woman who holds the redemptive wisdom. The crone—the old wise woman—was a powerful but common fixture in older cultures. The goddess might appear as a young woman, a woman in her prime, or an old woman; as the oldest manifestation of the goddess, crones took over transitions, death, and catastrophes. They were often represented by the color black. If one picks up the story of the crone in the later Arthurian stories, she is already a weakened, shriveled old witch, but in the earlier European stories and in other cultures, the crones were healers, teachers, "way showers," and spiritual midwives. They knew the mysteries, were bearers of sacred wisdom and mediators between the spirit realm and social reality; they cared for the dying and were the link between death and rebirth. They were the most potent form of feminine wisdom and power. As in other aspects of the European Feminine, Celtic mythology has retained crones most like their original form—big and robust women, associated with sows and darkness.

The Mammy filled in the gaps left by the image of white women. By the time of slavery, young affluent white women had been so thoroughly idealized as to be rendered almost helpless. Just as the fierce goddess Night hovered at the margins of Greek society, keeping the useful but "unfeminine" traits, the strong slave Mammy fulfilled the functions left out by the white feminine ideal. The propaganda Mammy image had more to do with the needs of the times than with how actual women behaved. The popular image of the Mammy was mostly fiction, created as a defense of slavery and a way for slave owners to convince themselves that it was safe to forcefully enslave women and then bring them into their houses. Owning other human beings called forth the need for Herculean acts of self-delusion: "I keep them here by force, *but they love me.*" An observer writing in *The Atlantic Monthly*, a Northern magazine, noticed that whites were "sentimentally attached" to their Mammies, more than to other slaves; that "every white man loves his old 'mauma,'" and that the black woman was similarly attached to the family "with whom, perhaps, [she] has always stayed."

Slave owners had so convinced themselves that *their* slaves were loyal to them that many never questioned their relationships with them. Henry Watson Jr., explained that most slaveholders felt "an attachment for the servants similar, in some respects, to that we feel for our children. We feed them, clothe them, nurse them when sick and in all things provide for them. How can we do this and not love them?" He thought that the slaves returned his sense of affection. "They too feel an affection for their master, his wife and children, and they are proud of his and their success." Slaves were thought to "look upon and to their master with the same feeling that a child looks to his father. It is a lovely trait in them. This being the case, how can we fear them?" By necessity, the greatest delusions often happened with the slaves who were kept closest to the families.

Despite the powerlessness enforced by their captors, *some* slaves possessed *some* control in *some* realms. Black women were in positions to know secrets, and with secrets came some power. Thomas Chaplin thought "the old cooks and maumas" to be dangerously knowledgeable about domestic and political events. As cooks and caregivers, black women had opportunities to do harm to white families. Some did. Using the same skills as for cooking and healing, black women were especially adept at poisoning their masters in the early years of slavery. Poisoning of food by cooks was not routine, but it happened often enough that slave owners were nervous about it. The stories traveled from farm to farm and engendered fear. But because their whole way of life rested on slaves and the "proper" planter domesticity required them as servants, slave owners had to convince themselves that the women loved them and would forgive them in their enslavement. Slave owners wrote that they were sure *their* Mammy loved *them*, would always care for them, and was happy.

Men such as John C. Calhoun and, later, George Fitzhugh fashioned the argument that slavery was beneficial for whites and for slaves, a line of thought that was contradicted by the social and class realities of everyday life. Historian James Roark wrote:

> The proslavery ideology was itself internally contradictory—planters, for example, often indiscriminately adopted clashing race and class arguments in slavery's defense. And it also contradicted the reality of their everyday lives—where, for instance, paternalistic sympathies warred with crass exploitation of labor. Like most ideologies, therefore, it was inconsistent, contradictory, and self-serving. And yet, for planters it sufficed. It provided justification for the master–slave relationship with which they had grown to maturity, and it told them there was virtue in their lives and social system.

In addition to the conservative planters who hoped to protect Southern society as it existed in 1861, there were others who hoped to recoup the past. Alfred Huger wrote in 1858 that the South was not great for "What we *have*, but for being what we have *been* [emphasis his]." Mammy was a part of their efforts. Southerners called the post-Reconstruction era the "Redemption"; Mammy would be the redeemer.

So there were two "Mammies": the actual slave women who were mothers and working women, whose own black children may have called them "Mammy," and the image of the slave mother, who may have also been called "aunt" or "mauma" as "South Carolinian" did, and who came to be used as propaganda for the slave South before, during, and after the Civil War. The image that we have come to call Mammy is an extreme caricature, kidnapped and enslaved for the purpose of rewriting the social history of a region. The propaganda Mammy is usually defined as a large (and therefore assumed to be ugly), dark (and therefore assumed to be uglier) woman who was happy in her role as a domestic slave or servant. It has been extended into the present to describe black women who spend too much of their energy to help white people. The recorded behavior of black women during that time and even the responsible journalistic and literary treatments show very different women. As time passed and memories of actual women gave way to the longing of nostalgia, the simple, patient woman whose loyalties lay completely with the slave owners was created. The image that draws the most ire is Aunt Jemima, and for many, she *is* the Mammy. But Aunt Jemima is an example of a specific use of the Mammy image. She is the commercialized version of the pro-slavery propagandistic Mammy.

Still, the first propagandistic Mammies were not quite of the Aunt Jemima variety. *Black Diamonds Gathered in the Darkey Homes of the South* was a collection of sentimental letters written by E. A. Pollard to a friend in the North and then published as a book in 1859. The central figure was "Aunt Debby," who was "fond of usurping the authority of her mistress," enjoyed a good joke at the expense of white people, and often got her own way. But Pollard's audience was not looking for slave women who mocked their masters. What he and his enthusiastic audiences looked for and found was a star of their own sentimentality, who stood for home and bygone youth. According to Pollard, Aunt Debby was full of an irrepressible *joie de vivre*, so tickled was she to be a slave. He thought that she existed only for her white folks. When he mourned her, he mourned his own past. "At this moment my eyes are tenderly filled with tears when I look back through the mists of long years upon the image of that dear old slave and recollect how she loved me in her simple manner; how when chided even by my mother, she would protect and humor me; and how, in the long days of summer, I have wept out my boyish passion on her grave."

Aunt Debby was loved by the white family while she lived and mourned by them when she died (conveniently before the war and freedom could tempt her loyalty). It was the fictionalized Aunt Debbys that a defeated South would openly mourn into the next century. She was the faithful Mammy *of their dreams*, rather than one of the many women who left them after the war finally made their freedom and their allegiances indisputable.

Horace Greeley, editor of the *New York Tribune*, wrote of the "heartfulness" of *Black Diamonds*. A New Orleans *Delta* editorial called it "appreciative, tender and sympathetic" and continued, "The negro nature he especially knows, profoundly, intimately; knows it, not through the cold light of ethnographical science only, but most of all, through the warm, enkindling recollections of boyhood and youth."

The popular image of the Mammy had more to do with what whites needed than what black women did. Whites systematically reconstructed symbols to their own needs. For instance, the head kerchief worn by slave women and later made famous in post-slavery popular cultural depictions of Aunt Jemima came to be perceived as a symbol of subservience. But the head cloth was an African vestige, like the Yoruba head tie, and black slave women wore it as a symbol of status. Women in fields wore them whenever they could. Carol Tulloch argued that the head tie was the one piece of apparel that could be traced back to British and American slaves' African heritage. The practice and some of its meaning of revolutionary resistance were retained in areas with the strongest African cultural retention. In some areas it was a symbol of a married woman. However, on Aunt Jemima's head, the kerchief was translated through the prism of nostalgia as a symbol of servility, and the idea that the black woman might be expressing her own history or status was lost on mainstream audiences.

The pictures of tranquil slaves on large, prosperous, and peaceful plantations covered over the turmoil of the slave South. The planters feared the very slaves upon whom they relied. Alfred Huger wrote, "I am utterly dependent as to property & as to the safety of my family for peace and tranquility among our Negroes." Rumors of slave insurrections spread. By 1862, Catherine Ann Edmonston was praying, "Keep us from internal as well as external foes." They had other reasons to fear. In addition to an economy built upon coerced labor, Southerners had a fragile white class structure. White people who did not own slaves were at a labor disadvantage, and class resentment was a problem. The South was not a well-educated culture. Even members of the planter class had slight formal education. For the most part, they were simply working farmers, made wealthier than their neighbors by the fact that they could afford to purchase slaves. If they lost their slaves, little beyond manners and memories divided them from their poorer neighbors.

The Civil War was the "critical moment" in the culture of the South, when the by-then-familiar relationships and institutions were turned on their heads. Confederate wealth declined as much as 43 percent in the first four years of war, excluding the value of slaves. After the war, when they lost their slaves, the former slave owners were in trouble and they knew it.

The journals and letters of planters show their emotional distress. Ella Clanton Thomas of Georgia said that a "life of emotion, quick rapid succession of startling events" was wearing upon "the constitution and weakened the physical nature." Her "nervous organization" was "so completely disorganized" that she needed perfect quiet. "I feel as if I did not have energy to raise my head," she wrote. "My mind is sluggish and my will is weak and undecided. I lack energy . . . spiritually, intellectually & physically. I have been . . . dull, inert and desponding. . . . The human mind is so constituted that it cannot stand a constant pressure." She read pro-slavery books to try to convince herself that slavery had been right, but she failed. The Clantons still had their land but lost much of their wealth and experienced foreclosures in the twenty-five years after the war. Thomas wrote that she did not mind the loss of wealth so much as the "loss of Faith, of confidence," bemoaning "our season of humiliation." When she was forced to take her oldest son out of school so he could work in the fields, she worried that he was "engaged in work which any Negro could have done as well." She wrote in 1860, *Oh it is humiliating. I am tired mind, body and soul."*

David Gaven wrote, "I have plenty of provisions and yet I am sick, dull and low spirited . . . sick, sick, heart, soul, mind, body and spirit." Henry L. Graves wrote, "These are strange times. One does not know what to believe or what to think; things have got into a sort of whirlwind, and are whirling and kicking & jumping around at such a rate that, half the time, a man hardly knows whether he is standing on his head or his feet. He does not know whether to laugh or cry." Catherine Edmonston said, "I feel as tho I held in my hand only broken threads, thwarted plants. My time seems like the fragment of a broken mirror."

White people were confused, scared, and impoverished, and they very much wanted black people to make it right again for them. Without slaves, they could not be masters. If they could not be masters, they did not know who they were or could be. In the behavior of blacks, they said, lay the future of the South.

Many, if not most, responded by resisting the changes that were upon them. They could not imagine anything else. Changes in values often lag behind social reality. A culture holds on to its beliefs and its mythologies for generations, only ever so slowly adapting a bit here and there. People do not alter their worldview quickly, and men and women work to hold on even if it means self-delusion. The privileged classes, the keepers of slave-related mythology, met the advent of war with a great amount of denial. Rather than changing their customs and beliefs, they responded to the threat of impending change by digging in their heels, insisting that their ways were both permanent and ideal and would eventually be proven so. If anything, the war magnified essential values. As James Roark wrote, they were *Masters without Slaves*, the title of his work on the cultural impact of the war and Reconstruction upon the planter class.

At the end of the war, most slave owners considered themselves as still owning "their" slaves. Many Southerners emerged from the war not guilt ridden over slavery but convinced that they had been right all along. C. D. Whittle wrote, "All those people who say they would not take back their slaves if they could are near of kin to Baron Munchausen [a character who told outrageously tall tales]. I am no kith & want mine."

In 1867 William H. Heyward, of a once-wealthy South Carolina family, was "not prepared for the great change" and wrote that "When I go to my rest at night, my wish and great desire is that I may not open my eyes another day." He and his friends had "always been accustomed to obedience to every order to be now subject to the humour of the Negro." He gave up farming and lived in a hotel but eventually stopped eating in the main dining room because he could not stand the "insolence" of the black steward. He gave up all his servants and cooked his own meals in his hotel room. Major Joseph Abney, a former slave owner, said it "is enough to drive any people into despair and desperation. There is no earthly power that can interpose to save us and our children." Abney thought the solution was to leave the country, and he became the president of a company that helped to evacuate planters.

When they could, former planters forced former slaves back to work on terms that we now know were close to slavery. Some mounted trains and pulled off freed people at gunpoint, forcing them back to the fields and houses. House servants were usually the first to leave. Later, they would be the last to return. The quick withdrawal of black women as laborers and domestics, including the refusal of black female domestics to "live in," was difficult for white families to accept. Black women and families were so resistant to the women being returned to work as domestics that some states refused to let the man work unless his wife did too. Louisiana and Texas mandated that work contracts "shall embrace the labor of all members of the family able to work." Black women were ridiculed for acting like ladies.

The nostalgic mythology became particularly important. After the upheaval of war, the need for restoration of the previously prevailing mythology was great. Southern mythology was much more flexible than the South's physical reality or the more physically bound elements of social reality. It was easier and more expedient for the planters to use myth as the first line of defense of their position of power. As privileged whites lost control of the social environment, they worked to control what they could and created a mythical South better (for them) than the old one, which had none of the tensions, contradictions, or dangers. As long as the essential points were preserved, Southerners could alter mythologies to suit their purposes. The imagery surrounding the Black Mother was an important tool in the white South's cultural response to the war and Reconstruction. Just as the archetype had been altered and used during slavery to give a human face to an inhumane institution, the Black Mother's image was returned to duty in defense of newer forms of racial, class, and gender subjugation.

The Black Mother was used to meet mythological needs created by the planters' fears of vengeful black men, angry poor white farmers, and "uppity" white women. Mythology also supported the effort to reposition a new "free" black laborer class and to restore to the South something that looked very much like the old slavery. The cultural myth worked to return white women to a protected and unprivileged position as well, by making the black woman society's man–woman again, placing her, as she was during slavery, between the two genders. Most of all, postwar culture used the Black Mother mythology to nurture the defeated South, to heal its wounded pride, and to restore the status quo upon which that pride rested.

By contrast, the North had a very different image of the black woman before and during the war. A poignant example of this was the melodramatic antislavery argument "Aunt Sally," a story told from the viewpoint of a slave child whose mother, Aunt Sally, was being sold away. He visited her for the last time in the slave pen. He sobbed.

The story, used in Northern Sunday school lessons, asked, "Can you imagine a scene like this? Can you think of your mother, who, dear as she is, is no dearer to you than Isaac's was to him, torn by brute force from her home, shut up in a narrow ward like a wild animal in a cage, her every look and tear watched by her purchaser, who walks about, whip in hand, to quell any who may be refractory, and her last agonized words of affection spoken to you through a crack in the fence which guards the enclosure? Yet all this the poor boy had to suffer, and his heart was as tender as yours.

"What would you do? Would you become almost frantic in your grief, and rave wildly at the master, and strive to break down the bars and release your mother from so terrible a captivity? Would you? Then you would be guilty of treason and rebellion in the eyes of the law, and her owner would be justified in imprisoning you—nay, in taking your life as he deemed expedient. Merciful Father! Pity those whom no man pities, and by thine own power elevate those on whom the world and the world's law tramples!"

Aunt Sally was to be pitied rather than admired. The story included a pen sketch of her, a thin, dark woman whose eyes were heavy and vacant with pain. She was dressed not in the coarse dress of a slave but in the same dress of white women of the period; her hands even appear to have gloves. The entire sketch is styled in such a way that the Northern white child could easily insert his or her mother into the picture and identify with the sorrow of "poor" Isaac.

Southerners, on the other hand, focused on their own needs. The nostalgic mythology became particularly important. In their stories, they were loved and cared for by wonderful black women. Slavery was reconstituted into a humane institution, full of love and warmth. Thomas Nelson Page was primarily responsible for the rise of the plantation myth after the war and for the particular direction that the myth took; he thought that a society of courage, hospitality, magnanimity, affection, and honor had disappeared with the South's defeat.

During the war, the North had appeared to become more interested in the people and culture of the South. Southern writers who could observe and explain the South found willing Northern publishers and an appreciative national audience. As early as 1866, Northern magazines began to carry stories of the Old South with romantic images of the slave mother. Magazines such as *Scribner's*, *Lippincott's Monthly*, *The Atlantic Monthly*, and *Harper's Monthly* reflected a growing fascination with the South. The postwar Black Mother became a national symbol of warmth, strength, and forgiveness. The propagandistic image of the Mammy spread quickly. The stories romanticized the Old South, with the now archetypal Black Mother becoming a literary staple. She was a strong but pleasant woman, "a guardian angel" who protected white children from harm and received respect for it. She bathed wounds that others were afraid to touch, listened to stories too horrible for others to hear; she was a friend during the worst. She was the most prominent image of the Black Mother of the time, fulfilling the cultural function of the crone; teaching wisdom, mediating transformations, facing the horrible parts of life and death.

For a time after the war, she could be realistically human. While she was sometimes large and jolly, she was also sometimes thin, pretty, and aware of the political reality of her position. Based on actual individuals within immediate memory and tempered by the antislavery sentiments of the North, the postwar Mammies often were full characters, with their own voices within the narrative. Unlike the post-Reconstruction and Depression Black Mother, the post-slavery Black Mother was a main character in the reports and fiction of the major magazines. Northern writers often simply reported what they saw with little of the emotion of Southern writers. In "Letters from a Hospital," written to Mary Lawrence in 1864 and published in the *Atlantic Monthly* in May 1876, a Northern woman told her sister about a visit to freed black women who were working in a laundry. She wrote, "The women seemed very much pleased to see us. One of the old women was very excited and talked very earnestly, throwing up her arms as she spoke." However familiar the warmth of the black woman may have been to Southern readers, the story the black woman told would not have been particularly endearing. She was excited because she had seen a Union victory and used the opportunity to escape.

Southerners were more sentimental. In the June 1877 *Atlantic Monthly* article "South Carolina Society," a "South Carolinian" described the elevated position and closeness of Mammy with emotion, recalling that, while other slaves were called by their Christian names, the Mammy was called by "Aunty" or "Mauma." "South Carolinian" emphasized the intimacy of the black woman with the white family, that "it was not thought wrong for a white baby to be suckled by its colored nurse and that many black women slept on the floor of their mistresses' bedroom." In another *Atlantic Monthly* article, "South Carolina Morals," a "South Carolinian" wrote that whites were more "sentimentally attached" to the old house servants "but towards other negroes their conduct is more sullen and reckless; and for the rights of the race at large they have no consideration whatever, save what springs from compulsion." The "old relations have not been forgotten" because "every white man loves his old 'mauma'" and the black woman was thought to be similarly attached to the family, "with whom, perhaps [she] has always stayed."

Magazine fiction allowed the freedom to lean more toward type. Although there was an occasional mulatto with "affected airs," black women were for the most part written as highly spirited, strong women who knew much, spoke their minds, violated the social rules of gender and class, and fussed distressed whites into surviving and going on.

In "Queen's Good Work," a short story in *Harper's* from May 1866, Maum Rina, "with her glistening black face and spotted turban, and her queer shapeless figure waddling . . . over the way," saved a family from tragedy. The Virginia family was trying to outlast the Civil War. With the master gone to war, Maum Rina was left in charge of the house—a source of humor since Maum Rina was a secret sympathizer of the Union, "'heart and soul with 'Linkum's army.'" She openly criticized the Confederacy, quipping, "'De Federate sojers are as plenty as de Federate bonds round yere jes now, an as wuthless.'"

She and the adolescent girl, Queen, helped a Yankee captain. Rina, fulfilling the crone function, was the only person willing to face his wounds, installing him in a bedroom and nursing him back to consciousness with beef tea, calling for a Union doctor, and offering general "spiritual comfort." She nurtured the soldier—body and soul—singing him spirituals. "It came to the sick man's ears with a simple power and pathos of its own." He realized how close he had been to death and "a prayer of thanksgiving shaped itself in his heart." But Rina also provided strategic military assistance; she had her son, Sip, run the captain's dispatches back to the Union army.

With Queen's abusive father at war and her delicate white mother taken to her bed, the adolescent Queen looked to Rina for love. "Some sudden hunger for the affection she had never received from father or mother made her cry out, 'Do *you* love me, Maum Rina?'" This story was written in 1866, just after the war, and the character Rina did something that the black female figure would not be depicted as doing twenty years later. She did not rush to comfort the child; instead, she gave her a candid and heartfelt answer, which showed full recognition of the inhumanity of slavery and the contradiction of black maternity toward the master's children. Her answer suggested the delicate emotional balance that black women maintained during slavery.

> "Sakes alive!" said Rina, in a startled kind of way; "I nussed yer, an it stans to nature dat I tinks a heap on yer. But lovin! Ya see, chile, I'se been de mudder ob six chilen, an ebbery one ob dem cept Sip been done stole away from me. God didn't took em, Miss Queen. Je gin em to me; He lef em in my hans—but Marse Bevil wanted money. I tell ye, honey, ebbery one dat was took gin me a blow—a blow right on de heart, chile—so dat now dis poor old heart hain't got no life in it; 'twaint gwine to set itself on yethly tings agin. Tank de Lord, it's sot on Him, what can't be sole or took away."

Rina refused to disguise the greedy cruelty of Queen's father or the effect it had upon her life. Queen turned away, "comfortless." Rina did not desert the all-but-orphaned Queen, but she did not lie to her. When the young woman's father came home, drunk and angry at the rumors of his household harboring a Yankee, he threw Queen into the dark, cold night, a melodramatic chaos from which Rina would save her.

How horrible it all was! Some terrible dream, perhaps, from which she could wake herself in her own snug little bed. But that wonder was real enough, and made her cower to the very ground; and the flash of lightning that followed showed her the trees all dripping and shining with the rain, the path turned to brooks, and a night full of black shadows and solitude. She looked up to a sky that was all darkness, save when it was rent with angry flame, for some helper in time of need, and some of old Rina's verses came to her: "Though I pass through the deep waters."

Queen took comfort and went on until she could go no more. Miraculously, she awoke in her own bed, attended by the patient Rina, who had searched for her in the storm and brought her home. A few days later, the evil father conveniently died in battle, announced so by Rina and mourned slightly by the otherwise almost-invisible white mother. The Union had taken their area and "'We's free colored folks now,' continued Rina, with an important air." Although Rina decided that she was too old to work anywhere else, it was clearly not her first choice for her son. When Queen was alarmed that the family would be without servants or money, Rina did not rush to comfort her.

"'Oh, Sip, he's free, ye know, an has a right to hisself.'" But Rina managed an arrangement that would give Sip his freedom and bring some money into the white household. Sip would continue to live with the family and contribute to the cost of the house given that Rina "put principles" in him. As it turned out, Sip and Rina would be looking out only for the delicate white mother, for Queen had fallen in love with the Union captain. The story ended as Queen made plans with him to leave for the North and Rina sang, "The Lord Makes a Way."

As the Black Mother took on a larger mythological role, the image also gradually attained more-mythic characteristics, even in Northern stories. The September 1872 issue of the *Atlantic Monthly* carried a story by Olive Wadsworth entitled "Aunt Rosy's Chest." Aunt Rosy was a slave mother who captured in one person all of the mythological traits of the Black Mother. "She was the idol of the nursery . . . we all united to worship at her shrine." She was huge with muscle rather than fat, strong and ancient, having been in the house for years. "She was nurse of the old place for more than thirty years, and two generations of babies had been cradled on her wide lap, tossed in her strong arms and hushed to sleep under the eaves of her turban." She was whole, encompassing everything. She was soft but gentle, her round body carried squarely. "Her great cushioned feet came down with elephantine weight and softness silent as a cat's, but shaking the earth," in a rolling gait that appeared unsteady but always landed softly, "as if she had scrubbing brushes strapped to her soles."

She seemed to have magical powers with children. "Cross babies became serene under her conciliatory cooing; staring wakeful little eyes were seduced into sleep with her slumberous hushaby; stubborn stomach-aches were charmed away with her soft patting and peppermint tea combined; cruel hidden pins that pierced tender flesh her knowing fingers would find and draw out as with a magnet; and first and last, and black and white, seventeen babies have cut their teeth on the soft, tough forefinger of Aunt Rosy's left hand."

She had status in the house because she was perfect, her needlework exquisite, her cooking divine. "In fact, there was hardly anything about a house that she could not do admirably; so good and so skillful was she that every one looked up to her and loved her, from the head of the house down." She managed to work all day, entertaining the children as she worked, and still help out the other servants who fell behind. She was a complete parent—mother and father, nurturing and strong—and the relationship between her and the family was close and physically intimate in the ways of a mother and child. She was a wealth of sensual delights and created ecstasy just by holding a child. In hindsight, she was remarkable for what she was *not*—not grotesque, not the object of ridicule.

"As for the woes of older children, it paid well to be thwarted, for the exquisite comfort of throwing yourself on her broad, pacific bosom, and feeling her arms around you as she swayed to and fro and crooned to you; while her long ear-ring dangled against your cheek all the time and her big boxing-glove of a hand went pat, pat, pat, on the middle of your back, til you felt as if heaven, and love, and all things dear, had found their home within the folds of Aunt Rosy's blue jean gown and red and yellow bandana."

The chest mentioned in the title was a wonderful thing, full of mysterious bits and pieces. It was the only thing in Aunt Rosy's life that was allowed to stay in a state of chaos, because the children played in it, and it was the only thing she never got around to, making it the more interesting. It had a mysterious smell, a mixture of wood, peppermint, and age.

For all of her gentleness, she was also proud and fierce. A Christian, she reserved her wrath for sinners, exercising a "muscular Christianity" that was "ponderous and pious" and "a terror to evil doers." She did not hesitate to physically remove black men who violated her sense of honor or religion. This is an important distinction—Rosy defended herself rather than her white masters.

"More than once it happened that when one of the men in the kitchen had infringed Rosy's rights, or used his tongue too freely in her presence, she had quietly but remorselessly shouldered him like a bag of meal, and marching out of the kitchen door, tossed him into the middle of the duck pond. 'Let 'em mind their manner,' she would say loftily, 'or Aunt Rosy'll give 'em another chance to larn.'"

The use of angelic language to describe slave women was common. In the short story "My Debut" in an 1868 edition of *Harper's*, the author, Susan P. King, was a white debutante with a "guardian angel" in the role of Aunt Polly, the family's cook, analyst, and charmer. Mary Chestnut described one of her family's nurses, Myrtilla, as a "black angel" (before she ran away to the Yankees).

Thomas Nelson Page overtly linked slave Mammies to divinity, eternity, and myth: "Who may picture a mother? . . . The Eternal verity stands forth like the eternal verity of the Holy Mother, outside our conception, only to be apprehended in our highest moments, and never to be truly pictured by pen or pencil. So, no one can describe what the Mammy was, and only those who can apprehend her who were rocked on her generous bosom, slept on her bed, fed at her table, were directed and controlled by her, watched by her unsleeping eye, and led by her precept in the way of truth, justice and humanity. She was far more than a servant. She was a member of the family in high standing."

Page concluded that it was impossible to reproduce the real Mammy, that his and other descriptions were inadequate, an interesting admission given that he is largely credited with the invention of the lovely Southern mythology. It was created largely as a piece of propaganda, to convince Southerners and other Americans that the South had been a noble, superior culture before the war destroyed it, part of a successful effort to regain Southern power on the national political stage. (Page's book was published by Scribner's, a New York publishing house.) That this passage was included in a book about the *problems* that Negroes presented is telling. The Mammy, of course, was not the problem, as Page saw it; the black man was.

The propaganda Mammy was an image stripped of any allegiance to her own race or family so the white audience could imagine her devotion to them. She was the perfect maternal figure—generous of bosom and spirit; fiercely, unsleepingly watchful; wise in the ways of truth, justice, and humanity—and a magnificent stereotype.

Walter Lippmann took the term "stereotype" from the language of the printing trade, meaning a piece of type that had been standardized so that each *A* or *P* looked like every other one. He applied it to the ways we perceive groups of people and defined it as "an oversimplified image." The Mammy stereotype drains away the individual detail; the stripped-down version resembles no woman in particular but keeps the useful bits.

Often the stereotype *adds* features: elderliness and fat. Photographs of actual slave women show that they, of course, ranged in age, body type, and facial expressions. Most often they were not smiling, in keeping with photography fashion of the time. Yet, even in photographs that showed slender or younger women, the descriptions spoke of them as if they were large, and in fact they were often described by white male writers in terms of ampleness. The ample body part that they most appreciated was the bosom.

Age and ampleness play at least two roles here. There was considerable physical interaction between white men and families with black women. The rape of young black girls is now so well documented as to be a foregone conclusion, but at the time it was an open secret. Polite conversation did not admit to the horrific danger of everyday Southern life for a black girl. Sexual dictates of the time meant that "good" white women were to be bedded only for reproductive purposes, leaving a sexual hunger that was too often satisfied with the bodies of the young black women whose lives the men controlled. (In the North, young white immigrant working girls were misused in a similar way.) Although we often speak of them as if they were different people, Mammy was the young girl grown old. The older white male writers would describe women with whom they could and sometimes did have sex. Mary Chestnut wrote of white men having sex with slave women, and the former slave woman Harriet Jacobs described the traumatic sexual advances and escaping a feared rape in *Incidents in the Life of a Slave Girl*.

Like the wonderful breasts of Rosy or the woman who rocked Thomas Nelson Page on her generous bosom, white children grew up in intimate contact with black women's bodies. One black woman could be a wet nurse for multiple generations of a family. To describe women who were not old, large, or *ugly* hid the sensuality lurking just beneath the surface. The combination of maternal and sensual figures is rare in American culture, *except* with black women.

A relief in the Confederate section of Arlington Cemetery shows a Confederate soldier leaving for the war. There to see him off is his Mammy, instead of his wife, surrounded by children. They are caught in an embrace. The Mammy is voluptuous rather than obese, and the posture of the man and woman is sensually affectionate. The only aspects that prevent the scene from being interpreted as sexual are race and social position. Age, weight, and supposed ugliness moved the black woman closer to a mythological figure.

In November 1874, the *Atlantic* ran "Miss Georgine's Husband," a ghost story narrated by a black woman who described herself in standard English as a "very old" ex-slave. Although the audience was assured that the narrative was faithful to the black woman's version, a white woman was listed as the author. Here the North recollected its own slave institution with a slave story set in New York. The woman recalled that she was born in Maryland but that she was a slave in New York, where she was the death nurse for a husband and then his wife—"poor unlucky children"—whom she had known all of their adult lives. For all of her grief, the black woman was humorously candid in her description of the uncomfortably dead wife.

> She wasn't a pleasant corpse to look at. Those same purple spots were on her cheeks, and a dark frown on her forehead; but worst was that her eyes wouldn't shut. I had tried every way to close them, and the doctor had tried, but they wouldn't stay shut!

But the black woman saw more than did the attending physician. She saw the already dead man looking into his dead wife's coffin and witnessed her soul finding peace after reconciliation with her husband. The spots faded, the eyes closed, and a look of peace came upon the dead woman's face.

> The doctor, he talked learnedly about contraction of muscles and what not, but doctors don't know everything, and he hadn't seen what I had. My own opinion is that she wasn't free to go till it was made up, and that they made it up then.

An endnote by the editor, Lucy Ellen Guernsey, read:

> This story rests upon a better foundation than most such legends. The ghostly part of the story was told to me by the ghost-seer, a very intelligent and good woman, and I have adhered as closely to her narration as propriety would allow.

Guernsey used the persona of the black woman to lend credibility to the ghost story. It was common practice for a slave woman to sit with the dying and the dead while family mourning took place elsewhere. The image of the Black Mother as wise and very spiritual was used to the story's advantage: If anyone was in a position to see spirits, it was the Black Mother. Often depicted as being closer to the workings of God, she had special knowledge. Her intimacy with the characters would have also added to her credibility.

The Black Mother as spiritual guide through emotional chaos was developed fully in an unsigned *Harper's* story entitled "Derrick Halsey." Derrick, an adult male, was an orphan. Margy, "best and most faithful of servants," the possessor of a "black, comely face," was the closest person he had to functional family; the rest were dead or near dead. The near dead was his sister, Susan, who was the victim of an alcoholic husband, herself an alcoholic, and mentally and physically wasted. Margy, her keeper, witnessed the worst of her fits. The servant was so worn that she wondered if she could stand it and suggested an asylum for Susan. The Reconstruction Black Mother was not self-sacrificing. But she was kind. When Derrick began to sob, she relented and continued to care for his sister. At that point Margy's persona took over the narrative, changing the story from objective to subjective.

> "That nigh broke me down," said Margy months later, as she was relating the story to a compassionate listener. "I hadn't the heart to say more after that; so I left him goin' on in that awful way, and went back to that bloated, raving crittur we tended atween us. Ef our keepin' her could comfort the master any, she should be kept."

Derrick became the primary patient, but even Margy could not save him immediately.

> But the sore festered too deeply for faithful Margy's healing. She could not allay Derrick's heart-sickness and desolation. . . . He craved human sympathy. In all the vast world of humanity did no heart but poor, black Margy's beat pityingly and kindly for him?

> Margy tried to rally him. "'You don't 'preciate life as you out ter,' said Margy one day, squaring her sturdy shoulders and scanning Derrick shrewdly, yet kindly, with her bright eyes. 'Remember this, Master Derrick. The Lord is good to all, and his tender mercies are over all his works.'" Derrick questioned whether she really thought that to be true.

> "Yes, I do b'lieve—it's Divine. We must all hev our crosses to bear; but if we love and trust the One who sends 'em, we can't despair. And if our poor little lives ain't jist as we want them to be, we must remember He direct 'em, and that we hev our duties jist the same. We don't none of us live to ourselves." Derrick did not answer, but turned away and went slowly out of doors. A wild voice [his sister] called his name

from a barred upper window; an insane glee of laughter smote upon his ears. . . . "Margy is right," he said simply. "I don't believe my life is more of a benefit to my fellow-creatures than that thistle growing yonder. . . . It's so hard—so hard!"

As Derrick contemplated, he heard Margy's voice. His sister had escaped the "vigilant eye of her keeper" and fallen into a dry well and died. He fell down beside Susan and almost died himself. When he recovered, Margy prayed her thanks and found it difficult to leave him. "When he awoke again it was morning, bright and beautiful, and close at his side stood faithful Margy with a basin of cool water, with which she laved his face and hands" and fed him. His sister was relieved of her misery, and Derrick was cured.

Paule Marshall wrote, "The use of the Negro woman as an embodiment of myth and fantasies that have little to do with her and much to do with the troubled and repressed conscience of the country . . . has reached so far down in the national psyche that not even the best of the white writers have escaped it."

The Mammy figure had become popular during Reconstruction but went on to play a larger role in post-Reconstruction. Rayford Logan called post-Reconstruction the nadir of the black in American life and thought. Southerners and Northerners had wearied of the racial struggle, and there was little social movement to improve the status of blacks. Whites took the opportunity, in what they called Redemption, to reassume control of every aspect of daily life. Social Darwinists argued that the caste position of blacks was due to their natural place in society. Magazines carried stories of blacks as ignorant, immoral, lazy, and criminal. Thomas Dixon's novels, *The Clansman* and *The Leopard's Spots* carried the same message. The exception was the Black Mother.

During the cultural debate that followed Reconstruction, the Black Mother was used by friends and enemies of African Americans. Lewis H. Blair, who had been born into the Virginia planter aristocracy, argued in 1889 for the "elevation" and inclusion of black people into the same schools and other institutions as whites by invoking memories of the black women who cared for, taught, and protected white children.

Most of us above thirty years of age had our mammy, and generally she was the first to receive us from the doctor's hands, and was the first to proclaim, with heart bursting with pride, the arrival of a fine baby. Up to the age of ten we saw as much of the mammy as of the mother, perhaps more, and we loved her quite as well. The mammy first taught us to lisp and to walk, played with us and told us wonderful stories, taught us who made us and who redeemed us, dried our tears and soothed our bursting hearts, and saved us many a well-deserved whipping.

The Black Mother became the "good slave" and the voice of the Old South as exemplified by *Mammy's Reminiscences and Other Sketches*, written by a Southern woman, Martha S. Gielow of Alabama, and published in the North by A. S. Barnes and Company of New York in 1898. The stories were those of Gielow's own Mammy and were an attempt to counteract the "grossly exaggerated and caricatured" characters of the minstrel shows who were so distorted "as to be almost unrecognizable by those who knew and loved them." Gielow admitted that she had "gleaned the material of these sketches from actual happenings related to me by my own black Mammy" and seemed to mean her volume as a tribute to her Mammy. But the woman remained nameless, and there is no indication that she or her heirs received any benefit of publication. Gielow wrote in the foreword, "Her immortality is due to her devotion and loyalty, under circumstances which never before tried human hearts, and her memory will become a more and more precious legacy as time advances."

The book took a familiar strategy, that of the adult returning home to visit the Mammy and hearing the white family's history told. This Mammy was overjoyed to see the grown woman, whom she had not seen for years. When the young white woman spoke of her upcoming marriage, the Mammy sat her down for some advice. She warned about love, that "You know young folks is mighty foolish, Miss Ferginia, when dey's makin' love," told her to put off her marriage as long as she could because "Dis gittin' mar'ied is er mighty resky thing, dat 'tis." She warned her about men in general: "I done tole you befo', that men's, dey is de Debble, of de Lawd did make 'em. I ses ergin *dey* is." Then she went on to tell a story called "Ca'line's Weddin" to illustrate her warning.

As the book progressed, the stories went further into the past, and the next-to-last and most sentimental section of the book was a "Plantation Nursery Scene," in which the fierceness and gentleness of the archetypal Black Mother was more fully depicted. She was both threatening, to her black helpers, and affectionate, to the small white child.

Cum 'long now an' let Mammy rock you ter sleep, you done play'd in dat bowl of sud long 'nuff—le' Mammy wipe yo' li'l' han's and button

yo' li'l' gown, an' you, Cindy! What dat you doin' settin' dar eatin' up
dat sweet soap! Ain' you got no better sense den dat? Git up frum dar
an' pick dat chile's close up an' hang 'em on de back uv de cheer. Now
look at you! Done upsot de pan uv water all over de flo; you go 'long ter
de quarters, gal, whar you berlongs 'fo I wring yu' nake, an' sen' Mandy
hyar fer ter wipe up dat water while I git dis chile ter sleep.

She was still fierce, but her fierceness was reserved for black people. When
things were to her liking, she was gentle. "Cum long ter Mammy, dat's er good
baby—Mammy gwine git her ole tuckey tail fan ter blow de skeeters offen you.
Sing 'Li'l' Breezes'?—dat I will—. lay yo' head down now an' shet your eye, dat's
de way—now I gwine sing." She sang "Blow, Li'l' Breezes Blow: A Plantation
Lullaby," as the child requested. "Lyrics and music by Martha Gielow" included:

> Mammy's baby's white es snow,
> Blow, li'l' breezes blow,
> Hyar cum baby's coach an' fo',
> Blow, li'l' breezes blow.
> Fo' white horse fer er fac',
> Golden wheels an' golden trac',
> Blow, li'l' breezes blow.
>   Mammy's baby gwine ter ride,
> Blow, li'l' breezes blow;
> Ole black Mammy by 'er side,
> Blow, li'l' breezes blow.
> Ober all dem mountains high
> Whar de chimbly swallers fly,
> Way up yander in de sky!
> Blow li'l' breezes blow . . .

The song ended with the child going to sleep on the Mammy's breast as the
angels came down to see her. A watercolor that accompanied the music depicted
a serenely smiling Black Mother holding a happy white child as they looked out
the window of a fine and elaborately embellished coach. The next and last section of the book, "Evening in the Quarters," depicted the Mammy going home
to her own black family, with whom she was somewhat less fierce than she was
with the black workers.

Only in these "realistic" representations, usually based on the true stories of
particular women, did the Black Mother go home at all. In later depictions of

the Mammy, particularly during the Depression, she would have no home other than with her white children.

Mrs. Gielow's book was apparently well received. Before its publication, she performed readings in Boston, Brooklyn, and Greensboro, North Carolina, and was praised in the March 17, 1897, issue of the *New York Herald* for her ability to use "the Negro dialect," showing "a delicate humor and pathos" that "completely captured her audience." That her work was original was considered a "great merit." She read before the Southern Society of Brooklyn, whose president mentioned in a letter included in the book that she had become a great success in Brooklyn and New York: "To have made the position, the reputation, the success which you have made in less than one year in this great metropolis . . . speaks volumes for the ability which has demanded your presence before most of the most prominent clubs and churches and literary bodies." The rector of Christ Church in Brooklyn wrote:

> She touches the dreamy old plantation twilight with the wand of genius. The word of the "mammy"—a word so dear to some of us—comes again over life's horizon, and enchains our hearts. The portraiture is so unaffected, so unstrained, so simple and true, that it ravishes one with memories and half-forgotten pictures. . . . Her rendition of "Mammy's Li'l' Boy" makes one of the most delicately pathetic and winsome things I have ever heard.

The *Greensboro Beacon* reported that "We have heard nothing sweeter in many years than her cradle song." The minister of the South Congregational Church in Boston wrote, "It reproduces the indefinable charm of the negro's cabin speech—its melody, its quaintness, its touch of the grotesque, its underlying tone of pathos."

In 1894, the Bow-Knot Publishing Company of Chicago published William Lightfoot Visscher's *Harp of the South*, which contained nostalgic images of the Mammy. In the intendedly humorous poem "Sorry for the Lord," she was religious and particularly hard on black people, apologizing to God for their asking for things that they could work for. The illustrations that accompany the poem, however, are of a realistic black woman rather than a caricature. Nostalgia for the Mammy is more overtly conveyed in the song "Chrismus in de Ole Time," when "More love shines in black mammy's face; More joy pervades the old home place," and everything was sweeter, softer, and in the "happy days of long ago." The singer remembers the songs that the Mammy sang and how, on

Christmas morning, she herded the "whooping youngsters, white and black," to receive their gifts. She returned the white singer, who had traveled to "the western sea," back to the mythological South of slavery, when supposedly everyone was one big multiracial family. Filtered through myth, "All the happiness and glee, are borne on memory's wing to me." She also redeemed him of the sins of slavery when she blessed the white family in song: "Dar's ole Marster, good en true . . . Ole Mistess, she is dat way, too . . . Young Jim en sweet Miss Sue . . . Lawd bless all ole Marster's crew."

In 1897, Visscher published a somewhat more elaborately illustrated book, *Black Mammy: A Southern Romance*, through the H. C. Smith Publishing Company of Chicago. The gilt-laced book carried illustrations by Thomas Nicholl depicting a specific, rather dignified black woman of moderate body size, with spectacles and a white kerchief. Although she was pleasant looking, the grin that would later become familiar was not there. She was often depicted in her own slave home rather than the home of the white boy she nurtured. In the title poem, Mammy told of a "sacred" and "sweet" South of the past, of which the black woman was emblematic. She was not mentioned in the body of this poem; the title was used instead to invoke a feeling of sweet nostalgia. The Mammy character developed in the rest of the poems did have a name, Sis Tabb, which gave her a stronger than usual individuality. Sis Tabb was depicted as a member of a black family—although her husband was defined through her, as "Black Mammy's good old man"—and of the slave community, although she clearly had status and kept the other slaves in line, reminding them to work hard and not to sin. She was in better health than her husband and helped him do his work.

According to the myth, the post-Reconstruction Black Mother was a joy to be around. In "The Spinning Wheel," the singer remembered the joy of just seeing and hearing her work.

> Music my heart can feel
> I hear as before,
> In days of yore
> Black mammy's spinning wheel
>   It brings me joy, as when a boy.
> I sat in her cabin door.
> And heard her sing to the spindle's ring,
> As she paced the 'puncheon' floor;
> From the dawn to the gloam.

In the old South home.
A mammy, true, black and leal [*sic*, perhaps "real"]
She trudged to and fro,
In the long ago,
And wrought her spinning wheel.

The remainder of the song mourned the passing of the South and its symbol, the spinning wheel, as still and old. This theme was further developed in "A Memory," as the singer related a tale to his own daughter:

Come, sit beside me, daughter mine;
Where vines of honey-suckle twine,
And in a simple way I'll tell,
With rhyme and music, how befell
The story of a grandame who
Now rests beneath a Southern yew.
Her blood was from dark Afric's race,
And black her good and kindly face;
    Her heart was pure and strong and free,
And she it was who swaddled me;
An infant on her breast I lay,
And at her knee I learned to say
That "now I lay me down to sleep
I pray the Lord my soul to keep"
A foster mother—Mammy dear—
And loving as your Mother here.

An illustration later in the book depicted a firelit hearth and a young white boy saying his prayers on his knees before the seated Mammy, his folded hands and head praying directly into her lap. She rested a hand upon his head. The Mammy looked after white and black children, a position that gave some level of power, but, unlike many other mythological Mammies, she treated the children with equal fierceness.

In great authority she's grown,
Since children, white, beside her own,
Have been consigned to her command
And learned her slipper and her hand.

"A Memory" also described the war that destroyed the land of "bloom and sun" and the sight of slaves coming from the fields, "their darkey patois, queer and strong." Another poem, "The Stranger," further developed the destruction of war and the creation of wounds that did not heal until the singer returned to the plantation to see his Mammy. At first he listened to her voice from a distance and watched her as a kitten slept in the lap he remembered so well. Her story helped him recapture the Old South. Another poem, "Mammy's Story," is really the history of the Old South and his family. Having nursed three generations, she was the keeper of the cultural history, she was the only one who was old enough and remembered well enough to tell it. Her relationships with the three generations of children were so intimate that she remembered all of their personal histories.

> I'd nussed Marse Luther and Miss Sue,
> An' den I tuck Marse Luther's two;
> Now bless yo' life, Miss Gerry
> Has got six; and when dey's here
> They makes ole mammy jump, s'vere.
> En keeps me in a hurry.

As were the slave women in Victorian America, Sis Tabb was intimately involved in the white family's life from birth to death. Her character recalled the role of black slave women who waited with the dying person while the family mourned outside, as well as the Black Mother-Crone's ancient role as the conveyor of death. Sis Tabb monitored the deaths and near deaths of the plantation. In "Mammy's Story," she told of the death angel almost claiming a family member as she watched. The Mammy character was uncommonly intuitive and wise, able to size up a person upon sight. She noticed detail, remembered who did what to whom and the emotional reactions of all the actors. "Mammy's Story" is full of small mishaps, holidays, and routines that she remembered. Closely involved in Old Southern life from birth to death, she became the mythological voice of the South, speaking of the old and, to Southerners, ordered and simple times and helping the white son to remember.

In "A Picture," the homecoming is complete when the son reconciles with Sis Tabb. He is home again. She has made his past live again:

> Bright boyhood time—its holidays and toys;
> Its sorrows great, as seen through youthful eyes

Its earnest plans, sweet and satiate joys;
Ah! dulcet season! how it flies,
And then embalmed in memory lies.
　　"Black Mammy" held its picture up to me—
An etching traced in lines of living light . . . `
I caught the dear old soul within my arms,
Embraced her with an ecstasy of joy,
As lover would a mistress rich in charms;
She wondered, then exclaimed, "My boy!"
God bless us! you is Master Roy!

When he presented himself to her, she remembered and recognized him. She cried tears of joy and reintroduced him to the place and the people, giving him context. Sis Tabb accomplished the impossible: She brought the past into the present, invoked the orderly past into the chaos of the South.

As time passed, uses of the Mammy version of the Black Mother became even more sentimental and less individualized. In 1922, in a conciliatory move supported by the Daughters of the Confederacy, the US Senate voted to devote capital parkland for a monument to the "faithful mammies of the South." The monument was never built due to African American protests.

Perhaps the most popular image of the post-Reconstruction Black Mother, Aunt Jemima, was used to sell middle-class white women the idea that a pancake mix could taste good. If Aunt Jemima said it was good, then it was good. An entire myth was created for the fictional personality, including a slavery experience. An advertisement that appeared in women's magazines of the 1920s was entitled "When the *Rob't E. Lee* stopped at Aunt Jemima's cabin," and a subhead read, "This, they say, is how her pancakes became famous." The painting in an ad, by N. C. Wyeth of the Wyeth artist family, depicted three prosperous white men, one of them Robert E. Lee, stepping off a large and opulent steamboat named for the Confederate general. The painting itself had the head "For twenty long years he had remembered." The story, which took three columns and fifteen inches of copy, began with "Higbee's Landing! To most of the passengers on the *Rob't E. Lee* it meant simply a stop. To the old Confederate General aboard, it meant the goal of a twenty year purpose." He tells his story to two fellow passengers: "Back in '64 when things wuh hot in this section, Ah happened heah . . . In one of those sudden tuhrns in the tide of battle Ah found mahself separated from mah men. Just mah awderly was with me. An we sho' wuh in a fix." So the two men "played possum" in a thicket until nightfall, when they could move a few miles. At daylight, they again pretended to be dead, listening to the sounds of battle. The Confederacy, which had been losing, was gaining back ground, but Lee knew he was behind the enemy line. By the third day, after another night of dangerous movement, "the lack of food was tellin' on ouah strength. Just at the break o' day when we thought we'd drop from tiahrness, we came across a little path from the rivah. It led to that cabin, gentlemen." He pointed it out on the Louisiana shore. The orderly guessed that the cabin might be friendly and,

> "Gentlemen, Ah can't express mah feelings of that mawnin' when out o' that cabin came the sound of a mammy's voice and we heard 'er say something about huh 'chilluns havin' an evah-lastin' appetite fo' pan-cakes.' We could hardly believe ouah eahrs; it seemed too good to be true. But we wuh no time gettin' to that doahway."

The slave woman was so kind, so full of the spirit of giving, that she helped the general of the army fighting to keep her a slave. She had the power to remove the head of the Confederate army and she did not use it. She was as wise as she was kind and figured out their story without being told. She fed them from her meager food supply.

> That mammy seemed to guess oyah story and hahrdly befoah we knew it she had us down at the table with big stacks o' pancakes in front of us. Just pancakes—that's all she had—but such pancakes they wuh! Nevah befoah had I tasted theah equal—and nevah since.

He learned later that the Mammy was Aunt Jemima, the cook of wealthy plantation owner Colonel Higbee. Aunt Jemima was known all over the South for her cooking, particularly her pancakes. And now the general was return-ing "to pay mah respects to that kind mammy," having planned his journey to include a stop. He worried that she might be dead. The general and his two newfound friends were the first off the boat. "Sure enough, Aunt Jemima was still living in the little old cabin and she willingly, at the old General's request, whisked up a batch of her pancakes," for which he paid her in golden coins.

> Later, as the story goes, one of the party, a representative of a large Missouri flour mill, returned. He persuaded the mammy to sell him the recipe, and it was agreed that she should go to the mill and oversee its

preparation in a ready-mixed form. Thus, according to the records, were Aunt Jemima's Pancakes made known to the North.

The advertisement does not include an image of her in her new business role.

The pancake mix needed only to have water added and reportedly did not approach scratch pancakes in quality, but home cooks were assured, "And they're so fine-flavored, so rich, so wholesome and good—*always* that. Try them tomorrow—and you'll know why the old General remembered them all those years."

A smaller painting, apparently also by Wyeth, depicted the moderate-size woman serving a tall stack of cakes to the three men. At the end of the ad, which also carried a 1920 copyright and a premium offer for a "funny Aunt Jemima rag doll," is a picture of the box, which featured her face and a stack of pancakes. The logo above the box says, "I's in town, Honey!"

Actually, the product was created in Saint Louis in 1889 by Chris L. Rutt, a newspaper man, who came up with the idea of a self-rising pancake mix after he heard a cakewalk song. The song, entitled "Aunt Jemima," was performed by the vaudeville team of Baker and Farrell in Saint Louis that year. The R. T. Davis Milling Company bought the business from Rutt, kept the product name, and launched it at the 1893 Columbian Exposition in Chicago with a booth in the agricultural hall. The company hired Nancy Green, a black cook from Kentucky, to play the role. The exhibit proved very popular, and she cooked more than one million pancakes at the fair. A 1921 advertisement portrayed her as "a sensation at the World's Fair in 1893," where, with her "mulatto helper," she said, "Lawzee, we ain't never gwine be able to make enuf pancakes fo' all dem white folks."

> It seemed that *everybody* at the Fair wanted to taste those golden-brown pancakes, so many that guards were brought in. But she was up to the challenge, and over the mammy's ebon face spread that wonderful greeting smile which we today can see only in pictures. And thousands—some folks that perhaps you know—smiled back.

Green went on to portray Aunt Jemima in promotions until her death in 1923. In 1925 the product was sold to the Quaker Oats Company, a division of the American Cereal Company, which hired actress and singer Edith Wilson to portray the Mammy. By then Wilson was fifty-three and had been a regular on the *Amos 'n' Andy* radio and television shows. She portrayed Aunt Jemima for eighteen years and continues to be the most familiar face of the image.

A large array of premiums, advertising novelties, and advertisements remain. Ads from circa 1905 and 1949 offer Aunt Jemima and an entire black rag doll family, including her husband, Uncle Mose, and her children, Diana and Wade. In the 1949 version, a realistic image of the actress is depicted as saying, "Chilluns! Get yo' Aunt Jemima Rag Doll Family." The dolls were of "gay colors, washable plastic, ready to stuff with cotton or rags." Aunt Jemima and Uncle Mose cost twenty-five cents each and the children were twenty-five a pair, when accompanied with one box or sack top, or one could have all four for seventy-five cents and three tops. The 1905 advertisement also offered a climbing Aunt Jemima doll. There were pancake-club pins, cookie jars, needle books, sewing kits, Aunt Jemima sugar bowls and Uncle Mose creamers, masks, recipe books, recipe card sets, and metal pancake molds. In the late forties and early fifties, spice racks were available in copperplate and plastic, the copperplate version with a steamboat scene painted on the shelf back.

By 1951, the Old South was part of the advertising name; a magazine advertisement for "My Aunt Jemima Old South Recipe" had the woman assuring cooks that these were "the *lightest* pancakes you can bake!" The main selling point was always a combination of ease and history, "just the same as it was made years ago," with less trouble. The "I's in town, Honey," quote referred to personal appearances and demonstrations where pancakes were cooked on portable griddles and offered on paper plates decorated with Aunt Jemima's picture. By the late 1940s, she spoke standard English, offering a set of circa 1948 recipe cards: "a few of my favorite ways to serve Pancakes and Waffles." More recently, Quaker updated the Aunt Jemima portrait, slimming her face and removing her kerchief. Although black civil rights groups have petitioned for it, the company has refused to completely change the persona or the portrait, stating that she is "too valuable" to change.

Aunt Jemima was not a singular phenomenon. From post-Reconstruction on to the 1950s, the smiling faces of Mammies were on products such as Luzianne coffee, Mammy's Favorite Brand Coffee, Fun-to-Wash Washing Powder, Snowdrift shortening's recipe book, advertisements for Rumford Yeast Powder, Mammy's Delicious Drumstix ("Sho Am Good"), Down South luggage finish, Mammy brand fruit, the menu of the Old Dixie restaurant in Los Angeles, and a host of domestic decorations, memo pads, spice racks, serving utensils, dish towels, canisters, games, paper dolls, rag dolls, clocks, paperweights and doorstops, banks, pincushions, flyswatters, dinner and tea bells, candlesticks, brushes, spoon rests, teapots, wall pockets, scouring-pad holders, planters, egg timers, laundry bags, match holders, toaster covers, linen tablecloths, pot-holder covers, and grocery reminder boards with logos such as "We Needs" and "I Hasta Have." There were also a number of trade cookbooks, including *Fine Old Dixie Recipes: The Southern Cook Book*, copyrighted by Lillie Lustig, Claire Sondheim, and Sarah Rensel in 1939. Others included *Dixie Dishes*, published in 1941 by Hale, Cushman & Flint of Boston, and *Plantation Recipes*, copyrighted in 1959 by the granddaughter of a slave cook but published by Robert Speller & Sons of New York.

The Mammy myth was central to the nostalgia for a grand Old South, which Southern whites used to return to the delusions that made slavery palatable to them in the first place. The myth fulfilled their need to redefine themselves as a once great and powerful people, loved and cared for by wonderful black women. It reassured poorer whites that they had shared in the glorious past of the Old South, although they had really been hurt by the competition with slave labor. The myth also positioned the black woman as the protector from the more "savage" black man. The docile, happy male slave, according to the myth, became dangerous and angry when freed. Many believed that blacks were physically stronger than whites and that black men could not be assimilated. At the same time, many whites thought that black women were already assimilated.

The black woman was often seen as more intelligent, durable, determined—and more assimilated—than the black man. The rhetoric positioned the image of the black woman between the black man and white people. The myth reassured Southerners of the freed slave women's loyalties; conveniently, slave owners believed the black woman could protect "her" white people. Mary Chestnut expected the slave woman Molly to protect her from other black slaves even after Molly told her that she would continue to feed other slave women's children out the back door.

The images of the loving Mammy and the dangerous black man existed side by side. South Carolina Senator Ben "Pitchfork" Tillman told the New York Press Club that he was "born on a slave plantation and nursed by a Negro woman" but that he considered lynching black men without benefit of trial as the only recourse if the men bothered white women.

The fifteenth amendment technically gave the vote to black men, raising a debate over the relative qualities of black men and black women. Although not allowed to vote, black women were active in political mobilization, taking part in rallies and parades during the 1868 campaign. Both friends and enemies of black people voiced their assumptions about the relative merits of black men and women. Elizabeth Botume lamented, "We cannot help wishing that so much of the work was done by the colored women . . . they might also hold some of the offices held by the men." She said that the black women would vote and go home to work, rather than standing around talking. The same image of the black woman seemed to have been held by at least one black male leader. W. E. B. Du Bois wrote, "You can bribe some pauperized Negro leaders with a few dollars at election time, but you cannot bribe a Negro woman."

Although black men were being regularly described as "fiends," some opponents of black enfranchisement considered black women to be more politically dangerous for the same traits that others found admirable: They thought her to be more intelligent and fiercer in advancing the race. As he considered the black vote, Mississippi Senator James Vardaman said, "The negro woman will be more offensive, more difficult to handle at the polls than the negro man." South Carolina Senator Ben "Pitchfork" Tillman wrote to the editor of the *Maryland Suffrage News* that it would be dangerous to give black women the vote, that "a moment's thought will show you that if women were given the ballot, the negro woman would vote as well as the white woman. . . . Experience has taught us that negro women are much more aggressive in asserting the 'right of the race' than the negro men are. In other words, they have always urged the negro men on in the conflicts we have had in the past between the two races for supremacy." If the black woman was seen as stronger and more aggressive than the black man, she, too, would have to be somehow disarmed. Reconstruction-era writers remade the black slave woman into the Mammy with a smile in order to render her harmless and loyal to white people.

Most of all, postwar Southern culture used the mythology to nurse its defeats, to heal its wounded pride, and to restore the status quo upon which that pride rested. The post–Civil War Black Mother was the product of a region crying not for black people or even black women but for itself. She was an exercise of redemption rather than repentance. Over and over again, she absolved Southerners of the sins of slavery. She forgave Confederates who would have kept her a slave—she welcomed them home, sang them songs, told them stories, cooked them pancakes, and held them in her large, strong arms, close to her ample bosom. There was no overt mention of forgiveness—these slave owners had seemingly done nothing wrong—and she assured them that they would go to heaven upon their deaths. She who remembered the entirety of white history was portrayed as having forgotten the central political fact of her own life: slavery.

The South and, eventually, the North wanted to forget the social realities of slavery, and they needed her permission. The co-opted Black Mother displayed the Southerners' hope that they were still loved. Like the abandoned child who insists upon the love of the mother who left them, the South needed to know that the women who raised them and nursed them—and then were among the first to leave with Emancipation—were, at some level, still there with them. The Mammy-Crone was an instrument of repair—of the South after the Civil War, of national reconciliation into the twentieth century. She was a figure that both the North and South could appreciate because she was very far removed from the suffering and emotions of slavery, loss, and war.

The propaganda Mammy, the co-opted Sacred Dark Feminine, would serve the collective emotional needs of the country well past slavery into the twentieth century. The fictional slave woman and the freed maid would continue to solve problems and offer comfort, forgiveness, and transformation to and through the next season of economic and social upheaval—the Great Depression.

Pop Goddesses

THE MYTHIC STORY of a black woman leading other people through the darkness to the light is the basic plot for hundreds of fictional and realistic stories and movies. In them, the black woman is not only born from darkness, she is able to transcend it. She is the social worker, the rape counselor, the interested stranger who shows up just when things are at their worst. Entertainment and even news shows often reframe stories in alignment with mythologies so black women appear as strong, resilient, and interested in the problems of other people. Even when she is the person with a problem, she may be characterized as ready and able to help somebody else.

Take as an example a story that started out as a basic weeklong small-business makeover segment on the CBS *Early Show*. The business was Big Mama's House of Soul restaurant, one of the first African American–owned businesses in a black area of Pittsburgh called the Strip. Big Mama was owner Brenda Franklin's grandmother, and Brenda was using Big Mama's secret hundred-year-old family recipes "passed down through good and bad times." Big Mama cooked the way that many people do at home: by feel, without measuring ingredients. People would always say she "put her foot in that food," a popular euphemism in the black community to describe particularly delicious fare, implying that the cook's personal touch surpassed some standard recipe. The food and the restaurant were spirit-filled, and Big Mama's essence became the dominant force behind the news piece.

The first segment started with the voice of one of the white male hosts saying, "A remarkable woman who makes food from the soul," over a background vocalist singing, "I've had some heartaches . . ." The male narrator continued,

"Brenda Franklin begins each day long before the sun comes up, always starts with prayer. . . . Each day is filled with grace and praise."

Brenda Franklin, a pleasant-looking woman, explained her close relationship to the food and the restaurant: "This food goes all the way down to the heart. Every tribulation, every heartache, every hurt I've had is in this food. . . . Everywhere I've been in my life, there was a purpose why God put me here. Every struggle I've been through, there was a purpose."

Franklin graduated from the "school of hard knocks," and the CBS hosts loved her from the beginning. The food was reportedly fantastic and her customers loved her, but CBS decided to bring in a "mentor team" from the Ruth's Chris Steak House chain to help Franklin. The team included Jim Cannon, the National Vice President of Culinary, along with one of their national public relations people and a regional vice president. Cannon said they would help to make her restaurant more profitable, to "monetize" it by standardizing her recipes "without losing the magic that makes her food special." One host was skeptical: "Can that [standardization of recipes] be applied to soul food? It's all from the heart." Cannon assured them that it could.

Franklin called the consultants "her babies," and the team of white culinary professionals warmed to her like hungry infants. By the end of the first segment, Franklin was singing. The others joined in, and everyone hugged, sang, danced, and cried together on camera. Cannon said, "Her food is fantastic, but her singing, her ability to entertain, that's her sizzle."

Something was going on here, something more than just a feel-good news story. The television viewers wanted in, and before the end of the week, some were calling Franklin directly at the restaurant. She seemed a bit bewildered by the turn of events. "[The makeover] already has changed my life. People are calling for prayer. I answer the phone at Big Mama's House of Soul and they're saying, 'Big Mama, I need prayer today,' or 'Would you sing me a song?' The camera crew is standing there and I'm on the phone with this man called Hollywood Cowboy, singing."

At the end of the week, the live outside audience got to eat her food. The male host glowingly said that it was the "the biggest crowd we have had in a while today, [because] we have Big Mama's food," and playfully bickered with another male host about which one of them Franklin liked the best.

Brenda Franklin was clearly a wonderful woman whose food and presence brought more meaning than CBS could have manufactured on its own. CBS helped her and she was grateful. They brought in restaurant-quality equipment, found a new location, and sent her for training with the Ruth's Chris management team. (One regular patron sadly noted that the food tasted different afterward.) But perhaps even more interesting was what CBS did *not* include in its story, omissions that made Franklin seem more pitiable than she was. According to the local media, Franklin was a well-known singer, with more acclaim than the segment admitted. Her restaurant had been glowingly reviewed by several food critics, and members of the Pittsburgh Steelers professional football team were some of her most loyal customers. She was a pastor. And even she noticed that the segments were different from her perception of herself.

After seeing one, she said, "Oh, my God, that poor lady."

Franklin renamed her restaurant Big Mama's House of Southern Cuisine and moved into her a space in downtown Pittsburgh, but the business struggled due to higher rents and parking problems. The restaurant closed in 2010.

Brenda Franklin was part of a media trend. Producers of media often work to stay at the forefront of social change, picking up new trends and evangelizing them to a wider audience, so we often think of media as being on the cutting edge. But the media cannot afford to get too far ahead of its audience, and new ideas are often folded in with familiar ones. The segment on Brenda Franklin combined the concept of her as a modern black businesswoman with the culturally ensconced image of her as needy but very spiritually powerful. That allowed the hosts and the audience members to respond to her in ways that were evidently emotionally gratifying for them.

There is a long trail of images of the Sacred Dark Feminine and the more secular Strong Black Woman in American media. Over time the images have proven to be extremely comforting and healing for the culture as a whole. They have been most prominent when the culture needed them the most: during the post–Civil War era, the Great Depression, the large-scale social changes of the late 1960s and 1970s, and the economic recession that began in 2007 and marked the decline of the large middle class. In all these periods of economic and social upheaval, the poorer classes, women and minorities, advocated for change and upset the status quo. When in the service of the status quo, black women are figures of reconciliation and repair. And when working against it, they are figures of social justice and revolution.

The usefulness of the images to the larger culture has contributed to their longevity in the popular culture. Whoever controls the images of the Dark Feminine has a powerful weapon, and, as with the South African goddess conference discussed in chapter 1, black women themselves are often *not* the ones shaping that image. Rather, the dominant culture seems to pull those strings, leaving black women to decide whether to work with or against what the mainstream purports about them and the Dark Feminine. Often they have done both at the same time, going along a little to survive and resisting as much as they can get away with. The most pronounced venues for this conflict are the theater, the cinema, the radio, and the television screen. Together, they are the culture's center stage, the source of both private pleasures and national cultural attitudes. Black women and their mythically influenced roles have been staples in all of them.

By the Way, Meet Vera Stark is a play by Pulitzer Prize–winning playwright Lynn Nottage that explores the choices black actresses have had to make in order to practice their art, to work. The two main characters are actresses separated by talent and skin color. The title character, Vera Stark, is a gifted, light-skinned black actress who came to Hollywood determined to find refined acting roles, only to find those roles to be too few and far apart to live on. She takes a job as a housekeeper and drama coach for a less talented and less intelligent blond actress. The white actress comes to specialize in the roles of sweet and fragile girls, but as she ages those parts get scarce. There is a lot of buzz about a big new movie, a Civil War–era *Gone with the Wind* type, the kind of movie that America loves. The white actress is preparing to read for a part. After too many years and too little acting work, Vera decides to try for a role in the film too: the role of a slave woman, exactly the type of role that she had vowed never to take. It is a matter of her survival—both physically and professionally.

Vera tells her friends and herself that she will pump enough dignity and grace into the role that Hollywood will see her talent and give her other, better roles. They are skeptical; they, too, are intelligent black female actors who are trying to survive. One, a brown-skinned woman, is a classically trained actress—a good one—who survives by doing piecework, sewing labels into shirts. The other, a light-skinned woman, has to consider passing. Vera wins the Mammy role, the movie is a hit, and she becomes a star for a playing a slave. Throughout the rest of her life and the play, we see her wrestle with the choices she has made, at turns vilified and honored by others.

I sat with Nottage during the first public reading of her play at Center Stage in Baltimore, and we talked about the difficulty of her message. As a writer, she wanted to show the artistry and intellect of women in that era who found that the only roles for them in Hollywood required an apron and a smile. The casting of Tracie Thoms, familiar to audiences for her supporting roles in *The Devil Wears Prada, Rent,* and CBS's *Cold Case,* forced the audience to see a contemporary face asking hard questions about black women and Hollywood roles. Black Hollywood actors still say that they too often have to choose between their art and their dignity, to act in roles that make us all wince or not to act at all. The old questions are still with us: Why is the subordinated black female figure so enduring? Why does she show up so often in American stories? Why does the mainstream culture seem to love her so much?

Black women and white women are often depicted against each other. Many plays and films celebrate white women as soft and sweet, while contrastingly celebrating the black woman as fierce and resourceful—despite the fact that all women can be by turns soft and fierce. Ferocity was not imposed on the black woman; it was taken away from white women. The story of the black woman's ferocity and her willingness to use it for the benefit of white women and families filled a vacuum left by the subjugation of white women. Western mythology dictated that the vacuum be filled by a representative of the Dark Feminine. Like the Greeks who took away the mythical fierceness of the goddesses and loaded it onto black Night, American patriarchy—the dreams of men captured and exaggerated by Hollywood—created soft, idealized women and gave them strong black female sidekicks who would stay with them and protect them.

Historical slave Mammies worked as midwives, nurses, and nannies to both white and black children, bringing them into close proximity with slave-owner families. Historical Mammies were a varied lot, but the fictional Mammy was distilled down to one type and defined against the white female lead character as larger, darker, stronger, more outspoken, and wiser than the white woman. She was fierce, willing and able to fight for "her" white people because, according to the myth, her loyalty lay completely with them. Southerners used the Mammy character to help themselves through hardship and social upheavals both in antebellum times and following the Civil War. Later, the Mammy was a comforting old friend and stabilizing force to national audiences when the Great Depression hit. Mammy became a fixture in American pop culture, especially when times called for the assurance and love of a fierce woman. In the stories produced by Hollywood, these characters gave the support, advice, ideas, and recipes that led to economic and personal salvation. African Americans then and now have found the roles to be demeaning, often dismissing them and the women who played them. But actresses like Hattie McDaniel, Louise Beavers, and Ethel Waters have appeared in some of the most prominent stories of American culture, and to overlook them is to miss an important piece of the story.

Gone with the Wind—the 1939 movie about the Civil War–era Southern O'Hara family, based on Margaret Mitchell's novel of the same name—is one of the seminal works in American culture, and its images loom large in the country's impression of the time period. A 2008 survey found that, except among African Americans, *Gone with the Wind* is still the most popular film of all time, and the book is second only to the Bible.

In one scene depicting the weary end days of the Civil War, Confederate soldiers slowly dragged their way home to the O'Hara family plantation, Tara, in defeat—ragged, dirty, and lice-ridden. And Mammy, the de facto head of the household, was angry, disgusted at their disheveled garb and downtrodden spirits. At the end of the war, Mammy would have been legally free, but many slaves in the South still lived as slaves. In the film, Mammy was unfazed and unchanged by the shifting political scene around her; the narrative did not pause to even consider the slave woman's personal circumstances.

Instead, she got to work, forcing the men to take off their clothes so she could boil them to get rid of the lice. She ordered them to "Come on and give them pants. . . . Come on. Now you scrub yourself with that strong lye soap fore I'll come there and scrub you myself! I'm gwine put these breeches in the boiling pot." Mammy marched off, fussing to herself, "The whole Confederate army's got the same trouble—crawling clothes and dysentery."

Suellen O'Hara (Scarlett's sister), whose family owned Mammy, was in love with one of the soldiers and unhappy at Mammy's insolence. "I think it's humiliating the way you're treating Mr. Kennedy." Mammy, face-to-face with Suellen, said, "You'd be a sight more humiliated if Mr. Kennedy's lice gets on ya." Suellen's mouth dropped open in surprise. Mammy marched off again, having put the white woman in her place, and went on about her business.

Mammy carried herself proudly and knew she possessed the respect of not only Suellen and Scarlett but Rhett Butler, who called her "A smart old soul and one of the few people I know whose respect I'd like to have." (In *Scarlett*, the sequel to *Gone with the Wind*, Rhett returned to visit the ailing Mammy rather than to see Scarlett.) Mammy provided the moral structure of *Gone with the Wind*, and her moral judgments of Scarlett and Rhett led the audience.

Hattie McDaniel considered herself to be a comic, yet the scene from *Gone with the Wind* that was widely regarded to be the one that won her the Academy Award was a dramatic one, where she tearfully sympathized with a heartbroken and suffering father while still meting out the discipline and task work required for a decent burial of his child. The script made use of the audiences' expectations of her wisdom and concern for the affairs of white people to advance the plot. McDaniel was the first African American even to be nominated, much less to win an Oscar, and she beat out her costar Olivia de Havilland (Melanie) for the Best Supporting Actress award, despite de Havilland's prominent and dramatic death scene.

Hattie McDaniel is best known for her roles as Mammy, and it is often assumed that she must not have cared or understood the roles she played. But she skewered the stereotype when she was in control of the production. Although the Oscar was an important milestone in McDaniel's life and in black culture, she maintained higher artistic aspirations as a performer.

McDaniel and many black performers of her time worked in black theater, which they and their audiences used to comment upon the social conditions in which they lived. Sometimes the theater was dramatic, but often it was hilariously and scathingly funny. Before she became a mainstream film star, McDaniel and her work were already well regarded in black circles. In 1915, the all-female McDaniel Sisters Company troupe staged a fund-raiser for the Denver Sojourner Truth Club, a black women's organization. The women were well dressed, in narrow black skirts, black jackets, white shirtwaists, white gaiters, and bright red ties, in a performance that the *Colorado Statesman* said was "carried out very successfully with energy and taste." And, notably, the actresses wore blackface and, in doing so, participated in a very sophisticated joke.

White performers used minstrelsy to laugh at black people. After the Civil War, in black venues, however, black performers sometimes turned the joke upside down and used blackface to laugh at the inept imitations of white minstrels—they imitated the imitation. When in front of black audiences, McDaniel really parodied Mammy, taking the image to extremes in order to mock it and to suggest that the character and her stereotypical image were mere figments of white imaginations. But, like other performers, McDaniel would later find that when her performances crossed over to dominant culture audiences in the 1930s, she would lose much of the control and subversive potential she had come to enjoy.

In what would have been her most innovative and subversive role with the troupe, in March of 1915, McDaniel planned to perform in *whiteface*, completely upsetting the most humiliating aspects of minstrelsy that played to white audiences. Unfortunately, her husband, Howard Hickman, contracted pneumonia and died the day before the show was set to start. The recital was canceled, and McDaniel had to postpone the portrayal of her white characters—a

British nobleman, a German immigrant, two unemployed drifters, and a tango dancer—until the next year, when she revived versions of them in the play *Spirella Johnson*, a less ambitious two-act benefit for the Denver African American Masonic Lodge.

McDaniel's stage performances combined comedy and sensuality. She was also a singer, and she sang, bantered, and performed physical humor with the Morrison Orchestra for the pleasure of black and white audiences. She was a large and attractive woman, robust rather than fat, and physically agile. In the style of her contemporary black female singers Gertrude "Ma" Rainey, Bessie Smith, Trixie Smith, Alberta Hunter, and Sippie Wallace, McDaniel spoke openly about sex, pain, and power. Angela Davis wrote that the black female blues singer was a historically important example of female power and speech, and McDaniel used it that way. She recorded songs where she spoke squarely as a black woman, often combining the parodied Mammy with the sexy gender-speak of black women's blues in the same performance. In "I Thought I'd Do It," she sang, "This frame was made for loving, so you won't do for me." In "Just One Sorrowing Heart," she told the story of a young woman who allowed a man to make her his love slave, then took revenge and killed him.

When McDaniel arrived in Hollywood, she found a town that was more socially liberal than many other places but still artistically conservative. She could hold and attend racially integrated parties, but her work was confined to racially prescribed roles. Systemic forces kept black actors out of fuller roles. In an effort to preempt outside censorship, the film studios created the Motion Picture Producers and Distributors of America office, commonly known as the Hays Office after its president, Will H. Hays. The Hays Office created and enforced a production code to protect the industry from outside social criticism and controversy. While the Hays Office's control of sexual content is well known—their code is the reason so many film couples slept in twin beds—the office also controlled racial content, enforcing the studios' reluctance to show subversive or transgressive black roles and prohibiting black and white social relations. The code prohibited *any* interracial social interaction, not just sexual relations, in which the actors were portrayed as equals. African American actors were relegated to the roles of servants. Over time, the pressure to play the popular stereotypes hardened rather than softened.

With her ample figure and dark skin, McDaniel found her employment playing maids, the same figures she had earlier lampooned. Although her acting jobs were steadier than those of many other actors, they were still sporadic enough that she took what she could get. Hattie McDaniel said that she would rather play a maid than *be* one. It was more than just a flip statement, because she *had* been a maid. Employment opportunities for African American women were severely limited, and black actresses often worked as maids between acting gigs in order to survive. Ethel Waters, the first African American to be nominated for an Emmy Award, worked as a maid before she began on the vaudeville circuit. As a child, McDaniel had lived a life of extreme poverty that made her deeply afraid of not working. She *had* to work.

The actors worked to alter the roles they could get. McDaniel still tried to carry some of her old subversive material into her films by infusing her characters with disrespect and insolence. It was a sophisticated move, stretching the role by suggesting more equality between her and the white woman than the written script suggested. If a proper maid marked a white woman as a lady, a disrespectful maid suggested that the woman was no lady. McDaniel's Mammies resisted their positions' subservience by talking back. They were angry, sarcastic, snide, and disgusted. They fussed and fumed and criticized or opposed the decisions of their employers.

Using humor to its fullest extent, McDaniel, the comic innovator, had personal trademarks that were subversive, including direct and challenging looks, expressions of disdain and disgust, and shouting her lines, violating the submissive presence expected of good servants. She may be a maid, but she was a bad maid. Any servant would be fired for the behavior she portrayed, but the employer characters took it. They needed her because she often knew better than they did. They respected her. Just as slave women had in the Post-Reconstruction era, the black maid peaked again during the Great Depression, when the social fabric was again tattered by economic and social distress. Such women were a cinematic comfort to a desperate country that wanted to see films where somebody knew the answers and cared about them. But a maid who was wiser than the white people for whom she worked also undermined their social station.

In *Blonde Venus* (1932), McDaniel accepted the part of Cora, a character who was a particularly degraded Mammy—raggedly dressed, unkempt, speaking in dialect, and unquestionably loyal to Marlene Dietrich, a woman down on her luck. But director Josef von Sternberg deliberately created Cora as a maid who stepped further out of her traditional place than in previous films. When Cora confronted a white man who was stalking the two women, her attitude indicated intelligence, suspicion, and disdain all at the same time. In *Boiling Point* (1932), McDaniel's Mammy repeatedly called a white man "boy." In *Fate's*

Fathead (1934), a comedy produced by Hal Roach, McDaniel in the role of Mandy the maid pointed a shotgun at her white employer. In one of her films, *Alice Adams* (1935), she was so bossy and disrespectful to Katharine Hepburn that Southern audiences objected.

In *Shopworn Angel* (1938), every time McDaniel's employer yelled for her, she yelled back. In *The Mad Miss Manton* (1938), Barbara Stanwyck played a socialite and McDaniel played Hilda, her maid friend. Their relationship was familiar enough that Joseph Breen of the Hays Office warned that "The characterization of Hilda, the colored maid, may be found objectionable in the South, where the showing of Negroes on terms of familiarity and social equality is resented." The writers toned down the part, but McDaniel still delivered her lines to convey social power. Her Hilda was rude, telling a guest that the kitchen was closed. Her employer objected mildly, saying, "She's our guest." Hilda snapped, "I didn't invite her." When Stanwyck's character told her to, McDaniel as Hilda threw a pitcher of water in a white man's face.

The movies' black Mammy was one of a few images of a good woman speaking so frankly in American popular culture at the time. Having already broken the norms of genteel womanhood, bad white women—like the persona of Mae West and the character Scarlett O'Hara—could speak and act boldly but not with virtue. Mammy could be bold and virtuous because of her reduced social position. The same slave subservience that offended so many allowed her to be a safe acting-out woman.

Much has been made of the appearance of McDaniel and other film Mammies. They were large women. If the actresses inadvertently lost weight, they were padded so as to appear appropriately fat. One obvious reason was that large women would not be seen as competition for the younger, thinner white female leads. But there was more to Mammy's appearance. Her wide skirts and her scarf, which American audiences learned to read as the mark of a slave woman, were also the dress of a goddess. Images of Nana Buruku in Brazil and Cuba are dressed in a remarkably similar way. Mammy was also shiny black; products were applied to her skin to make it darker and shinier. Perhaps she was the visual embodiment of the dazzling darkness where God could be found.

Like the goddesses, McDaniel's Mammy was not as asexual as is now commonly assumed. In *Saratoga* (1937), with Jean Harlow and Clark Gable, McDaniel played Rosetta, a character who gave the Mammy sidekick a bit of sensuality by finding Clark Gable attractive. She said, "If he was only the right color, I'd marry him." Two years later, in *Gone with the Wind*, Rhett, also played by Gable, caught a glimpse of a red petticoat he had bought Mammy as a gift and demanded to see it. Mammy raised her skirts and teased, "My goodness, Mr. Butler, you is bad." Outside the studio, Gable and McDaniel were friends, which may have explained why he was willing to help her tug at the racial restrictions in films. He also acted as her advocate in the film industry and came to her integrated house parties.

The response of the black community to McDaniel's success was mixed. The black press celebrated McDaniel's procurement of a costarring role in such an important film as *Gone with the Wind*, regularly reported on the film's progress, and crowed about her Oscar. But reporters like Earl Morris of the *Pittsburgh Courier* and race activists like Walter White of the NAACP argued against the perpetuation of film slave roles. Led by White, organizations and the black press tried to encourage black actors to stop playing such stereotypical roles. Black actors countered that acting was their job. Who would support them if they quit? The NAACP and other organizations were working from the position of the audience; they were interested mainly in the images and their social consequences. The actors were operating from the inside, as workers concerned with more control of scripts, better wages, credits, dressing rooms, and other equal treatment. McDaniel and her longtime friend Clarence Muse worked to organize black actors, encouraging them to join the new Screen Actors Guild, a risky move at the time, to push for better working conditions and roles. The two groups vied for control of the conversation between black people and a largely white Hollywood.

McDaniel continued to mount stage performances where she would re-create the boldest and most subversive scenes from *Gone with the Wind*, including the petticoat scene and one in which she angrily confronted Scarlett for chasing a married man. McDaniel tried to bring humanity to the fictionally co-opted Mammy, but for most black people, the idea of Mammy had been complicated by an ambivalence that played out in both social life and popular culture.

Americans continued to go to the movies during the Great Depression to escape their worries, and the films they saw included black women who were strong, wise, and loyal, who were interested when nobody else was, and who often saved the day. Working Americans had much reason to lose faith in the power structure of the country and the maid, who had not grown powerful and rich, still could save them with her wit. And McDaniel was not the only one. There were hundreds of Mammy roles during and after the Depression—most of them uncredited. Louise Beavers saved a single white mother and daughter from poverty with her pancake recipe in *Imitation of Life*.

Imitation of Life (1934), a melodramatic woman's film, featured the first dramatic starring role created by a white studio for a black actress. Louise Beavers, whose film persona was softer than McDaniel's, got the part. The story line resembled the familiar Aunt Jemima story. Bea Pullman was a white widow who sold pancake syrup to try to support her daughter. Beavers played Delilah Johnson, another single mother, who came to Bea's door looking for work and moved in with her own daughter in exchange for room and board. Delilah's daughter, Peola, was light skinned because, as the film carefully explained, her father was a very light-skinned man. Delilah made delicious pancakes and, when Bea was desperate for money, offered the recipe to Bea to market. Delilah's recipe was a huge success, making Bea wealthy. She shared some of the proceeds with Delilah, but the black woman continued as her housekeeper. Delilah and her daughter still lived in the basement, where they listened to Bea's fancy parties above their heads. Bea offered Delilah a bigger share of the proceeds, enough to buy her own house. Delilah answered no, saying she preferred to stay on with Bea. What, she wondered, would she ever do with her own house? But the frustrated Peola started passing for white and eventually left. Her devoted mother died of a broken heart.

Named by *Time* as one of the top twenty-five films about race, the film was nominated for Best Picture in 1934 and has since been remade into at least three subsequent versions. Again, black audiences and critics were mixed in their reactions. Some felt that it forged new cinematic ground, others that it retained the old stereotypes. Both were right. Although it made use of an old stereotype, the movie altered it when it gave the Mammy figure dramatic scenes and concern for her own child. Change has always come slowly in Hollywood, and black female actors have continued to be caught up in the same dilemma, working hard for slow and steady improvements within the industry while facing demands for more dramatic progress from race advocates.

Historically, all slaves were forced into their jobs and roles, but the fictional Mammy is vilified because she seems to have submitted willingly to her oppressors. The popular, propagandistic Mammy image rested on the idea that black women somehow overlooked their legal condition as slaves, despite evidence to the contrary. In *Post Traumatic Slave Syndrome: America's Legacy of Enduring Injury and Healing*, Joy Degruy Leary explained that African Americans still suffer unresolved trauma from slavery and that black men are particularly still injured by their inability to protect black women. Anger at a fictional character may be a symptom.

The fictional Mammies, who spoke up and moved around as they needed, overshadowed the historical Mammies like Molly. As with minstrelsy, magazine fiction, and music, cinematic Mammies had more to do with the needs of the audience and less to do with how historical black women actually behaved. As media began to grow and expand into platforms such as radio and television, so did the roles for black female actors. Radio continued the portrayal of sassy servant women on the racially controversial *Amos 'n' Andy* and *Beulah*, both popular shows that moved onto television. On radio, both black characters were played by white actors, but on television they had to be played by black actors.

The Dark Mother, in the form of the caricatured Mammy-Crone, had been a vital part of the national persistence after the Civil War and the Great Depression. Although her role was less extreme after that, it was no less strategic. With the nationwide affluence following World War II, the dynamics of the white American family began to change—and large populations of white teenagers especially, experiencing new freedoms and new cultural identities, began to discover the "wild women of blues" on radio.

Ruth Brown's song "Mama (He Treats Your Daughter Mean)" was number one on the black R&B chart and number twenty-three on the white pop chart in 1953. Brown and singers like her presented a very different feminine ideal from the buttoned-down housewives of the time, perfect for an emerging age group that was biologically adult but protected from adult responsibilities by the new affluence. The black girl groups of the 1960s, whose music drew from a variety of blues traditions, were the first black groups to appear in mainstream white venues such as *The Ed Sullivan Show*. The music and the sexually free dancing that went with it were a great way to shock white middle-class parents. The leisure time, the rebellion, the attention to new ideas, behavior, and social relationships of the era would provide an entry point for massive social changes.

Television was a critical component in the new modern America. Instead of the high art and educational programs that would come to fill the television sets of Japan, Israel, or much of Europe, American television quickly came to be used for entertainment. However, by the late 1960s, the United States was rocked by a series of social upheavals that collectively matched the disruption of the Civil War or the Depression—and these watershed moments were captured on television. For most of the country, the African American civil rights movement was a televised news event. It was one of the first demonstrations of how the medium could provoke large-scale shifts in longstanding public opinion. News brought race to the forefront, but entertainment television would be left to address the questions that had been raised.

African Americans, women, sexual and gender minorities, and youth all agitated, rebelled, marched, and rallied. And in these revolutionary times, the mythology of the Black Feminine as crossing over social boundaries would come in handy. Women were iconic images of the black civil rights movement, from Rosa Parks to the four girls killed in the Birmingham church bombing to Elizabeth Eckford of the Little Rock Nine who integrated Arkansas's Little Rock Central High School in 1957. Norman Rockwell famously painted Ruby Bridges, the six-year-old who integrated the William Frantz Public School in New Orleans in 1960. With her head up and back straight, the little girl is escorted by four US marshals to protect her from the angry racist crowd. The word "nigger" is scrawled on the wall; a tomato has been hurled at the immaculately dressed young child. The painting is entitled *The Problem We All Live With.* Although men were the acknowledged leaders of the movement, many of the racially sympathetic public images were female.

Entertainment television provided commentary on the social changes. In 1968, *Julia,* starring Diahann Carroll, was the first modern black female show. As a picture-perfect nurse raising her son alone after the death of her husband in Vietnam, Julia was the female answer to the "exceptional Negro," the black person who was so smart, so beautiful, so ideal in every way, that no one could come up with a reason, other than race, to reject her. She was strong, stoic, and a little bland. She was to television what Sidney Poitier was to film, so perfect as to be beyond reproach or stereotype, a necessary first step toward a new image.

Television situation comedy is a quintessential American art form that closely follows American tastes and sensibilities. In the wake of the black civil rights movement, television sitcoms began to take on issues of race, social class, and gender with irreverent humor. As Hattie McDaniel demonstrated in her performances, humor is especially well suited to address issues of inequality and power, because the humor allows the introduction of otherwise dangerous ideas. Weekly television series required the audiences to develop ongoing relationships with the characters, a more intimate arrangement than the stage or film. The familiarity with and affection for characters allowed more and more frank cross-racial social interaction than had ever been the case in American culture.

Even as they took more cultural chances, television shows were still full of strong black women. The famously controversial federal Moynihan Report, issued in 1965, decried the number of black female households and suggested that the absence of fathers would hinder economic and social progress, but you couldn't tell by television. Given the considerable backlash to the report, it's no surprise that by the mid-1970s *more* shows with working-class black families headed by wise and heavyset black women began to appear. *That's My Mama* (1974–1975) starred Theresa Merritt as Eloise "Mama" Curtis, who was obsessed with finding a wife for her barber son. *What's Happening* (1976–1979), loosely based on the 1975 movie *Cooley High*, costarred Mabel King as Mabel "Mama" Thomas and Shirley Hemphill as Shirley Wilson, the friendly woman who ran the local snack shop and helped look after the neighborhood friends Raj, Rerun, Dwayne, and little sister Dee. By the sequel, *What's Happening Now!* (1985–1988), the mother was gone, but the show featured Shirley Hemphill's Shirley Wilson and Roger's new wife, Nadine, a college-educated social worker. The shows were new because they depicted black people as fully intelligent and sensitive, complex humans, but familiar because they were full of Strong Black Women.

Good Times (1974–1979) was a spin-off of another show, *Maude*—mother Florida Evans had been Maude's maid. The Evanses were a close-knit family with hardworking parents and intelligent, talented children, all living in the South Side of Chicago. They made living in the projects look cozy. The message was that no matter how hard the times, they had one another and their friends. *Good Times* starred Esther Rolle as Florida Evans, along with BernNadette Stanis as the fiery, intelligent, and independent-minded daughter Thelma, and Ja'net DuBois as the neighbor Willona. *Good Times* had a father in the family but only because Rolle fought for one; according to Stanis, the show's producers wanted the show to have a single mother, but after Rolle's protests, they hired John Amos, a former professional football player.

By 1974, the pivotal television event was *The Autobiography of Miss Jane Pittman*, a made-for-TV movie starring Cicely Tyson. The story of a 110-year-old good and wise woman who had witnessed and critiqued a century of American and black history was a shift in focus and tone. The situation comedies had introduced controversial material with humor as a way of easing the cultural shock. Miss Jane Pittman carried herself with a serious dignity that was far less familiar to television audiences but closer to the social role of the revered older women in African American culture.

Writers and actors continued to push for more variety, and the strong working-class women were followed by strong upwardly mobile black women. Racial housing integration came to the screen when *The Jeffersons* (1975–1985) moved on up, with Isabel Sanford as Louise Jefferson, Roxie Roker as neighbor Helen Willis, Zara Cully as Mother Jefferson, and Marla Gibbs as their own feisty black maid, Florence Johnston. The Jeffersons had been Edith and Archie Bunker's next-door neighbors in *All in the Family*. The story line featured George, who had become a successful dry cleaner, and his family—wife Louise and son Lionel—as they moved to a more affluent high-rise apartment. There the friendly neighbors included Tom and Helen Willis, who may have been television's first interracial couple.

Robert Thompson of Syracuse University wrote that the 1980s and early 1990s were the golden age for television, in large part because of the situation comedies that created a new kind of diversity and shared national culture. They also depicted new levels of interracial intimacy of social equals. *Gimme a Break!* (1981–1987) starred Nell Carter, after her Tony Award–winning stint on Broadway for *Ain't Misbehavin'*, a revue of the works of composer Fats Waller. Carter played Nell Harper. When Nell's white friend died, she was asked to take over as caregiver of the friend's family, including four children and husband Police Chief Carl Kanisky. When Dolph Sweet, the actor who played Chief Kanisky, died, Nell took over as mother of the children. In *Night Court* (1984–1992), Marsha Warfield starred as Roz, the sarcastic court bailiff and resident wise woman among the familylike cast, and she later starred in *The Marsha Warfield Show* (1990–1991).

The situation comedies of the period depicted black families with Strong Black Women in them as average families with whom mainstream audiences could identify. JoMarie Payton was Harriette Winslow, the elevator operator in *Perfect Strangers* (1986–1993) who solved the problems of two younger white men. Her character was spun off into the hit *Family Matters* (1989–1998), where she was joined by Rosetta LeNoire as energetic Estelle "Mother" Winslow, Kellie Shanygne Williams as the intelligent and sensible Laura, and Telma Hopkins as the glamorous Rachel.

Television shows began to employ black writers and producers, who seized the opportunity to create richer characters in black cultural situations. Marla Gibbs moved on up to her own show with *227* (1985–1990) to deliver a more realistic view of a functional black family and their working-class-neighborhood life. The plot revolved around Mary Jenkins; her husband Lester, played by Hal Williams; daughter Brenda, played by Regina King; and Mary's friends Pearl, played by Helen Martin; Rose Lee, played by Alaina Reed-Hall; and Sandra, played by Jackée Harry. The show remains one of television's fullest expressions of working-class urban black family and neighborhood life. In *Amen* (1986–1991), Sherman Hemsley starred as Deacon Ernest Frye and Clifton Davis as Reuben Gregory, the quieter, more cerebral pastor. But the women who ran these men's lives were Hemsley's daughter, Thelma, played by Anna Maria Horsford, and the church ladies, Amelia and Casietta Hetebrink, played by Roz Ryan and Barbara Montgomery.

The crown jewel of the era was *The Cosby Show* (1984–1992), the story of Cliff and Clair Huxtable and their intelligent, attractive children. A generation of American children grew up with the show, and it came to occupy a central role in the culture. Although the family operated as a black family with lots of cultural cues—food, music, language, art, and an *End Apartheid* sign in son Theo's room—white audiences identified strongly with the program and the family.

Although the show was a star vehicle for Bill Cosby, Phylicia Rashad as Clair was the wise center of the family who managed the household, disciplined the children, and kept Cliff out of trouble. Clair brought glamour and sensuality to the role. *The Cosby Show*, along with *The Jeffersons*, featured women who were smarter and had more power than their husbands, a reversal of the pattern for white middle-class television families. In early television shows, such as *Father Knows Best* or *Leave It to Beaver*, the father was unequivocally in control. Later shows depicted white middle-class parents with equal control between them but gave much more control to the children. For instance, *Family Ties* (1982–1989), which aired right after *The Cosby Show* from 1984 to 1987, included parents who were equally intelligent and shared the power they had. Their children, led by Michael J. Fox, had even more.

White working-class men, such as those in *The Honeymooners, All in the Family, Married with Children*, or *The Simpsons*, were often depicted as less intelligent than their wives, and the action and dialogue often suggested that the family's reduced financial status was due to the father's ineptitude. Although the men got into all sorts of predicaments, the audience was comforted that the more sensible wife would keep the family together. The racial difference was that middle-class black fathers were depicted differently than middle-class white fathers, in ways that were more like the working-class white father, more childlike and the object of humor. Cliff Huxtable was a successful doctor, trusted by families and hospitals to deliver babies, but he could not fix the plumbing or the doorbell and his wife had veto power over anything that had to do with the children or the house. American cultural mythology has always characterized black men as strong, fierce, and dangerous—unless they can be contained. On television they are contained by an organization or a uniform, such as the police or the military—or by a black woman.

The Cosby Show taught networks and advertisers that audiences could be enthusiastic about a black family, and it led the way for other black family sitcoms such as *Family Matters* (1989–1998), *My Wife and Kids* (2001–2005), *The Hughleys* (1998–2002), *The Bernie Mac Show* (2001–2006), and *Everybody Hates Chris* (2005–2009). By 1999, the percentage of African Americans on television actually slightly surpassed the percentage in the population.

In Hollywood, it is widely held that the most powerful people work behind the camera, and African American women gained power there during the 1980s and 1990s. Such writers and producers included Winifred Hervey, who started out writing for *Mork & Mindy* and *Laverne & Shirley* in the 1980s and went on to form Winifred Hervey Productions and write and produce *The Cosby Show*; *The Golden Girls* (1985–1989); *The Fresh Prince of Bel Air*, starring Will Smith (1991–1993); *In the House*, starring LL Cool J (1995–1999); and *The Steve Harvey Show* (1996–2002). Suzanne De Passe started out at Motown as a creative assistant to Berry Gordy and rose to be the president of Motown Productions. She cowrote the film *Lady Sings the Blues* (1972) and won Emmy Awards in 1983 for *Motown 25* and in 1985 for *Motown Returns to the Apollo* before leaving to produce shows such as the miniseries *Lonesome Dove* (1989) and the series *Sister, Sister* (1994–1999). As president of De Passe Entertainment, she was named Producer of the Year by the American Film Institute in 1995 and identified by *Variety* as perhaps second only to Oprah Winfrey as the most prominent African American woman working in television. Their shows reflected the Hollywood trend of favoring black male stars, but they also featured stronger, more-intelligent black women than ever before, women such as *Sister, Sister*'s Mowry twins and *The Cosby Show*'s Clair Huxtable.

Meanwhile, black women were getting their books published, creating a gold mine of literary voices. A wealth of richly written black women's fiction appeared, showcasing African American female characters who were strong in a wider variety of ways. Gloria Naylor wrote *The Women of Brewster Place*, about a community of working-class women who created a rich and powerful sisterhood. Alice Walker created Meridian Hill, the young, nonviolent race worker who worked harder and stayed longer than others, in *Meridian*; in *The Color Purple* she wrote of Celie, the woman who finally freed herself from her cruel husband, and Shug, the independent woman who helped her. Toni Morrison won the Nobel Prize for Literature for her black women fighting a society meant to crush them. These included Sula, who outrageously flouted the prudish social customs of her segregated Southern black community in *Sula*; Pilate, the strong and wise but outcast aunt in *Song of Solomon*; and Sethe, the slave mother who loved her child so much she killed her rather than have her live as a slave in *Beloved*. Toni Cade Bambara wrote *The Salt Eaters*, about a group of Southern women who are faith healers in the African sacred tradition. Terry McMillan wrote in her first book, *Mama*, of a poor, proud woman who worked hard for her children before she wrote of more-affluent, strong, independent women in *Waiting to Exhale* and *How Stella Got Her Groove Back*.

Essence magazine, the first mainstream magazine for black women, became a critical and commercial success during the same period, adding more writers and stories to the wealth of black literature. Begun in May 1970 with a circulation of fifty thousand and a promise to "delight and celebrate the beauty, pride, strength, uniqueness of all Black women," its circulation reached more than one million in 1994 and five million by 1997. The magazine presented a new voice for and by black women and reflected the ways in which black women's lives were different from those of other women. It offered career advice before some other women's magazines did and included articles on the criminal justice system, political crimes, and sexual issues, in frank language from writers such as Nikki Giovanni, Ntozake Shange, Toni Morrison, Gloria Naylor, and Alice Walker. Models sported strong Afrocentric features and bodies.

Essence also maintained the link between black women and spirituality. Maya Angelou said that she did not know any other nonreligious magazine that addressed spiritual health as *Essence* did. In 1995, editor in chief Susan Taylor said that the magazine's mission was to "inspire, inform, and uplift black women, to help our sisters move their lives forward so that they can spread the word and thereby hopefully uplift our race."

The 1990s promised real change, with black women front and center in print, on air, and in Hollywood—a striking difference between these new roles and those played by Hattie McDaniel and Louise Beavers. More starring roles began to crop up for black women, with carefully produced, intelligent, and emotionally evocative films for or about them that violated the stereotype.

Julie Dash's lovely masterpiece, *Daughters of the Dust* (1992), told the evocative story of a large family off the coast of South Carolina struggling with tensions between the old and the new. *Poetic Justice* (1993), with Khandi Alexander, Maya Angelou, and Janet Jackson, gave black girls their own coming-of-age story. Angela Bassett starred in the female manifesto *Waiting to Exhale* (1995) as well as *What's Love Got to Do with It* (1993), based on Tina Turner's life. Lynn Whitfield starred in *Eve's Bayou* (1997) as the wife of an adulterous husband, with Meagan Good and Jurnee Smollett as her daughters and Debbi Morgan as the psychic Aunt Mozelle. Both movies suggested that black women could be concerned with their own problems. *Set It Off* (1996), written and coproduced by Takashi Bufford, costarred Jada Pinkett Smith, Queen Latifah, Vivica A. Fox, and Kimberly Elise in a black female action movie about a morally complex band of bank robbers; the film opened up a whole new story line for black women.

Despite these strides, black industry insiders complained that Hollywood producers still too often assumed that black audiences did not want complexity and that white audiences would not watch black casts. But two books that made it to the big screen, Alice Walker's *The Color Purple* (1985) and Terry McMillan's *Waiting to Exhale* (1995), with the screenplay also by Terry McMillan, were crossover hits. *The Color Purple* went on to Broadway, thanks to the powerful entertainment maven Oprah Winfrey, who starred in the film and produced the Broadway musical. Oprah also used her power to bring Gloria Naylor's *The Women of Brewster Place* (1989), *Before Women Had Wings* (1997), Dorothy West's *The Wedding* (1998), and, later, Zora Neale Hurston's *Their Eyes Were Watching God* (2005) to mainstream television screens.

Whoopi Goldberg was for a time the highest-paid female actor in Hollywood. She took historically traditional roles and pushed at the edges, expanding them from stereotype to fuller, more complex women. In *The Color Purple* (1985), she was the abused woman who learned to defy an abusive man. In *Jumpin' Jack Flash* (1986), she played a woman who only reluctantly helped a stranger. In *Clara's Heart* (1988), she was a housekeeper who took a white child home to *her* world to heal him. In *Sister Act* (1992) and *Sister Act 2: Back in the Habit* (1993), she again only reluctantly saved a convent and the students and nuns there. In *Corrina, Corrina* (1994), she was the college-educated domestic servant who stepped out of the kitchen and into a romance with the white single father. In *The Long Walk Home* (1990), she joined the Birmingham bus boycott and emboldened the white woman for whom she worked to follow her personal convictions and to defy her husband and community to support the boycott. In *Sarafina!* (1992), she used her star status to bring attention to the story of children in South Africa.

Goldberg won an Academy Award for Best Supporting Actress in *Ghost* (1990), making her only the second black woman, after Hattie McDaniel, to win the award. She portrayed scam mystic Oda Mae, who reluctantly helped

Demi Moore communicate with her recently deceased love, Patrick Swayze, only to later realize that she really did possess mystical power. The casting directors for *Ghost* said that, although the role did not call for a black woman, they heard the voice of Whoopi Goldberg from the moment they read the script. In one of the most poignant scenes, Whoopi channeled Swayze so that Demi Moore could dance with him through her. Goldberg also held Moore in her arms as the villain approached—the white woman hiding her face in the black woman's chest—while she looked toward the advancing danger in a protective position. The scene was used for the promotional poster of the DVD. When it was time, Goldberg told Swayze that heaven was ready for him.

Whoopi Goldberg's direct representation of the mystical Dark Feminine did not stop with *Ghost*. She was the voice of the earth, of "Gaia," in the original cartoon *Captain Planet and the Planeteers* from 1990 to 1992. According to the show's official website, Gaia was the "spirit of the earth, protector of the planet." The animated character with Whoopi's voice was brown-skinned. She was "the source of wisdom and advice. Gaia is the archetypal mother. She loves earth's children unconditionally. . . . Gaia represents all cultures and is protector of all life on the planet. Her health is connected to the health of the planet. She feels anguish whenever damage is done to the planet, its seas, atmosphere or any living creatures."

Goldberg went into space as a very powerful woman when she played Guinan, the more-than-six-hundred-year-old humanoid counselor and hostess of the ship's bar in *Star Trek: The Next Generation* (1988–1993) and in two *Star Trek* films. Guinan was a member of an ancient race and a friend and confidante to the crew (particularly their captain), helping them to cope with the stresses and dangers of their space mission. She could sense when the time continuum had been disrupted and made sure that the crew did not disturb history. Goldberg starred in sitcoms such as *Bagdad Cafe* (1990–1991), running a desert hotel with Jean Stapleton as her best friend, and *Whoopi* (2003–2004), as ex-diva Mavis. She also starred in a talk show before settling in as moderator on *The View* and making guest appearances on shows such as *Glee*, where her formidable diva with a heart, Carmen Tibideaux, terrified aspiring performers, joining the cast that included Amber Riley as the big-hearted Mercedes.

Queen Latifah took up the mantle of the prominently archetypal black female comedic star and continued to stretch the traditional roles. The girlfriend comedy *Living Single* (1993–1998) established her as the sensible maternal friend, but for black people, with friends played by Kim Coles, Erika Alexander, and

Kim Fields. In the film *Bringing Down the House* (2003), she played a wrongly convicted woman who convinced Steve Martin to help her prove her innocence. In return, she taught his son to read, saved his daughter from a dangerous boy, and showed Martin how to romance his ex-wife with sensuality and attitude. Latifah played singers with attitude in *Living Out Loud* (1998), *Chicago* (2002), and *Hairspray* (2007). In *Last Holiday* (2006), she played a woman who decided to do something for herself for once after she was diagnosed with a terminal illness. She traveled to an elite European resort to be pampered, but once she was there, the chef and the patrons were drawn to her warmth, down-to-earth advice, and her knowledge of gourmet food. In her more recent films, Queen Latifah stretched and updated the image of the strong woman with a heart. In *Just Wright* (2010) she fell in love with Common, playing an injured NBA player who came to her for physical therapy, and in *Joyful Noise* (2012) she went toe to toe with a fierce white woman, played by Dolly Parton.

Meanwhile, daytime television shows were using black female characters in some of the most overtly archetypal roles as strong women, mystics, angels, and oracles with special connections to God. On *All My Children*, the love story of Jesse and Angie was the first to feature a black soap supercouple (1982–2008). The character Angie grew up to become a physician and, as Dr. Angela Hubbard, Debbi Morgan migrated to other soaps, returning intermittently to *All My Children*. On *The Young and the Restless*, from 1980 to 2004 and periodically afterward, Mamie Johnson was the housekeeper and nanny to the lead Abbott family. Several actors played Mamie, the last being Veronica Redd. Although Mamie was nominally a servant, she was much more. As her name suggested, she raised the Abbott children, who thought of her as their mother—but there was a twist to the usual servant-as-mother story. Mamie and Mr. Abbott fell in love, only to be thwarted in true soap opera fashion by his scheming almost-ex-wife. Mamie left town, newly wealthy, returning occasionally as a guest in the home she formerly cleaned.

In children's television, black women are magic—they are the ladies who walk through magic doors or float in on their magic rugs to solve the problems of children and their TV friends. *Barney & Friends* featured Phyllis Cicero as Stella the Storyteller, who arrived via a magic door when the children had a question or a dilemma. Although she traveled, she seemed to know what the children needed. A door would appear in the middle of the set, and Stella would walk through it to tell a story that answered the question that was posed before she got there.

The Big Comfy Couch was the story of a clown family. Most of the family was white, but Auntie Macassar, played by Taborah Johnson, was African American. The script took pains to show that she was a family member rather than a throwback to the slave aunties. She was also a traveler who provided answers to the main characters, but she actually anticipated their problems and questions. When a character had a dilemma, a postcard or a present would arrive from Auntie Macassar with a solution already on it. In *Bear in the Big Blue House*, Lynne Thigpen gave her voice to the moon, whom Bear consulted each night for advice and a song.

Disney Channel's *Hannah Montana* had a mother surrogate and bodyguard in Roxy, played by Frances Callier. In one episode, Hannah wanted to leave show business, and Roxie appeared in her dreams as an angel who showed Hannah the logical but negative outcomes of that decision.

When black men are present in children's programming, they are often quite different from the women. In *Happily Ever After: Fairy Tales for Every Child* (2000), a retelling of Aesop's fables narrated by Robert Guillaume, the layabout grasshopper was a black man; the industrious ants were black women who wore scarves. Even as insects, black females were the backbone of the community.

Due to rising costs and worker strikes, in 2007 the television industry began to replace scripted prime-time programs with reality shows. Although black women were not so numerous in these shows, there were some standout figures, such as Rapping Granny, a finalist on *America's Got Talent*, or Fat Momma (Nell Wilson) of *Who Wants to Be a Superhero?* In 2006, Fat Momma won the children's vote and the overall audience vote. (Comic-book mogul and final judge Stan Lee selected a white male as the superhero.) Omarosa Manigault–Stallworth became *The Apprentice* contestant whom Americans loved to hate. She first appeared on the show in 2004. In 2005 and again in 2008, she was voted as *TV Guide*'s number-one villain, and she also went on to appear on *Fear Factor*, *The Surreal Life*, and *Battle of the Network Reality Stars*. The maven of Style Network's *Clean House* show was Niecy Nash, who did not clean houses. She had a crew for that, and together they helped families to stop what she called their "foolishness" and addressed their "hot messes." Nash usually also threw in a free counseling session. Tempestt Bledsoe took over as host in 2011.

An offshoot of the reality-show trend included black men and women serving as judges in court TV. Black actors had already been regularly cast as judges in dramatic prime-time shows, but the reality-show trend made them stars who presided over their own courtroom shows. Judge Mablean Ephriam presided over the resurrected *Divorce Court*, and Judge Hatchett had a show that carried her name.

As television shifted from family sitcoms to ensemble shows, the lineups included some black ensemble shows, creating more opportunity for variety within one program. When UPN ran the show *Girlfriends* (2000–2008), the cast included Tracee Ellis Ross, Golden Brooks, Persia White, Keesha Sharp, and Jill Marie Jones, all of whom portrayed black female personalities who were strong in one way or another. Yet, as an ensemble, they had to be strong in different ways.

The cast rosters of integrated dramatic ensemble shows often included black female characters, but—as is often the case with television—the shows took two steps forward and one step back. The black female actors depicted supporting characters who were attractive, intelligent, and resourceful. As a rule, the women were strong-willed yet sensitive and caring. They were observant, and so they knew things that the other characters did not. Often, however, they played the lieutenant, the second in command, with a moral authority that exceeded their job titles. *ER*, begun in 1994 and set in a Chicago hospital emergency room, included Lynn Henderson as EMT Pam Olbes and Gloria Reuben as the physician's assistant Jeanie Boulet (1995–2008), who became the only HIV-positive prime-time television survivor. S. Epatha Merkerson joined *Law & Order* in 1991, a year after its premiere, to play Lt. Anita Van Buren. She then took the Van Buren role to the other *Law & Order* franchises: *Law & Order: Criminal Intent*; *Law & Order: Trial by Jury*; and the television movie *Exiled: A Law & Order Movie*. In 2000, Tamara Tunie joined *Law & Order: Special Victims Unit* as Dr. Melinda Warner. Merkerson left the series in 2010 after sixteen years.

Like the black female actors before them, many of these women made money on their second-in-command roles, which enabled them to take other roles to stretch their acting muscles. S. Epatha Merkerson won an Emmy, a Golden Globe, a Gracie, and an Image Award in 2006 for her lead role as the kind owner of a boarding house in the televised *Lackawanna Blues*; a 2006 Obie for her strong, warm, but slightly addled Birdie in the play *Birdie Blue*; and a 2007 Tony nomination for her role as a faded beauty queen in *Come Back, Little Sheba*. In 2006 she played Angela, the love interest in the artistically ambitious movie *Black Snake Moan*, and in 2012 she hosted TV One's series *Find Our Missing*, addressing the media's neglect of missing black women.

The black woman-in-charge got a promotion in *Grey's Anatomy*, the TV series about surgical interns and their supervisors created in 2005 by Shonda

Rhimes, an African American. Chandra Wilson played Miranda Bailey, chief resident. If roles like these were limiting, the actresses made the most of them, with a combination of beauty, authority, power, compassion, instinct, and intellect that was otherwise rare in female media roles. These roles also provided a variety of body types seldom seen in Hollywood productions: The women were short, tall, light, dark, solid-bodied, or dancer-slim.

Also like the actresses who came before them, African American actresses still have to counter criticism about the roles they play. Critics have noticed the transformational images of black women and some black men, and they don't like it. Filmmaker Spike Lee parodied black stereotypes in his film *Bamboozled* and argued that new images were nothing but updates of the old minstrels. In several talks to college students, he called the sidekick transformative black characters "super-duper magical Negroes." Although black people can and do use the word "Negro" more playfully, here it was meant to be a pejorative term, to say that the image is a throwback to slavery and the minstrel figures that arose from it.

Many newer roles have been lumped together as "best black friends," or BBFs, for leading white characters. Greg Braxton of the *Los Angeles Times* wrote that actresses such as Tracie Thoms, Nia Long, Brandy, Regina King, and Lisa Nicole Carson were BBFs. The buddy pairs included Alicia Keys with Scarlett Johansson in *The Nanny Diaries* and Tracie Thoms with Anne Hathaway in *The Devil Wears Prada*. Merrin Dungey costarred as Francie, best friend of secret agent Jennifer Garner, in *Alias*. Dungey went on to play Dr. Naomi Bennett, friend to Kate Walsh's Dr. Addison Montgomery, in the *Grey's Anatomy* spin-off *Private Practice*. Audra McDonald later took over the role.

It was as if saving their white friends was to be their highest calling. Black blogger A Belle in Brooklyn wrote: "It's not only insulting to Black folk to keep presenting saving white people as our best offering to society-at-large, it's insulting to competent white people everywhere too. White people have to be as sick of being portrayed as causing death and drama everywhere they go as I am of watching them cause it. In defense of all Black people who aren't Magical Negroes and self-sufficient White people, stop it already. Please."

But these characters were different from Mammy in some important ways. Mammy was wise due to her age and, sometimes, her instinct. The new women were wise, too, but they were also educated, with sharp intellects that could command a room. The black women were beautiful and talented in their own right. They were unequivocally the social equal of their white colleagues. But the scripts kept them in the supporting role, ready to listen, to talk, or to rescue their white friends. The *Los Angeles Times* quoted one African American actress who said that she and her actress friends teased one another about forming a support group for their characters, who had to help their "woefully helpless white girls." It is a dilemma that's too familiar to the black women in their audiences: being smart and competent enough to train the new white recruits, only to see them promoted ahead.

Some actresses resisted being grouped with others under the BBF umbrella, saying that it erased the distinct features of their performances or that the roles they played had been originally created for white actresses. Some of the roles were quite nuanced. Wanda Sykes played Barb, the best friend of Julia Louis-Dreyfus, in *The New Adventures of Old Christine*, which premiered in 2006. In the fall of 2008, in the midst of the gay-marriage controversy, Barb and Christine got married in order to keep Barb in the country. Soon after, Wanda Sykes came out to the public as a lesbian. She told a Las Vegas rally, "I'm proud to be a woman. I'm proud to be a black woman, and I'm proud to be gay."

Starting in 2006, a surge of feisty black women appeared in advertisements. The Pine-Sol lady levitated and proclaimed, "That's the power of Pine-Sol, honey." A Comcast advertisement called a black office worker "the miracle worker." The appearances were followed by critics who thought they saw Mammies. In a *New York Times* article, marketers and media scholars worried that the "sassy" black women showing up in television advertisements were "a return to a disturbing past." One quoted black man said that the images were "perpetuating a stereotype that black women are strong, aggressive, controlling people. I don't think you want to do that." Why not? When white men are strong, aggressive, and controlling, they are called heroes. There was only one black female audience member quoted in the *Times* article. She said that she liked the images, but the article rushed past her, never to return.

One of the most popular trends was the return of overtly sacred black female characters. *The Stand*, released as a book in 1978 and as a miniseries in 1994, is considered to be the most popular book by Stephen King and the most popular miniseries of all time. In it, a manmade flu virus wiped out 99.44 percent of the world's population. The survivors represented the larger forces of good and evil. Mother Abigail Freemantle, the old black wise woman, played by Ruby Dee in the miniseries, was the oracle who delivered the word of God to a band of survivors after the plague killed just about everybody else.

A show about angels included one of the most prominent starring roles for a black woman in television history. *Touched by an Angel* (original air dates

1994–2003, but airing continuously since) starred Della Reese as head angel Tess, and Roma Downey as angel Monica, both of whom were sent to earth to intercede for humans. Tess relayed the assignments from God and stayed around to guide Monica. Tess kept some of the hardest work for herself, telling bad news or getting people to tell the truth, usually a truth that would bring about a transformation.

Gloria Foster played the Oracle in *The Matrix* (1999) and *The Matrix Reloaded* (2003) films. After Foster died, she was replaced with Mary Alice, another well-known black female actor, for the role of the Oracle in *The Matrix Revolutions* (2003). The Oracle characters were wise black women who had supernatural vision and delivered key information—the postmodern version of the godly oracles—and the narrative turned on the information they gave to the humans fighting for survival against machines in a postapocalyptic universe. Both Mother Abigail and the Matrix Oracle were answering a higher calling and so were more interested in others than in themselves and allowed harm to come to them or their families. Mother Abigail left her family to help the others, and in the last of the three *Matrix* movies, the Oracle did not move to defend herself from the evil ones.

Writer and critic Nnedi Okorafor-Mbachu wrote that she wished the characters could be more self-interested and harness their power for themselves, moving the stories in a different direction. She wrote a short story called "The Magical Negro," which appeared in *Dark Matter: Reading the Bones*. She described it as a parody of the self-sacrificing Magical Negro; the protagonist in her story changes his mind and decides to save himself and go with his own life instead of helping the white character. Speaking about *The Stand*, Okorafor-Mbachu wondered, "What would have happened in *The Stand* if Mother Abigail had been more concerned with helping her own folks make it to a better place than the ragtag group that came along? What would all these stories have been if these characters' destinies weren't so tied to someone outside of themselves? If they hadn't been written that way? The answer: the stories would have been more complex, the characters more human, less lapdog."

Okorafor-Mbachu worried what it meant for a writer she admired to create a character like Mother Abigail. She concluded that King was not a racist but that he nevertheless benefited from the character because "Magical Negroes are always interesting, being magical and mysterious, and they make things happen. When a magical Negro pops up, the story crackles and pops."

Although the label "magical, mystical Negro" emphasizes magic and mysticism, both Spike Lee and Nnedi Okorafor-Mbachu use elements of magic, mysticism, and "magical realism" in their own art. Lee's famous tracking shot that makes the character appear to float toward or away from the audience is a type of visual magical realism. Okorafor-Mbachu is a respected and award-winning fantasy author whose first novel, *Zahrah the Windseeker*, featured "a magical forest and children with superhuman abilities." She has noted that there are similar black Sanskrit deities, and in an interview about her second novel, *The Shadow Speaker*, she wrote, "The foods, the spirituality, historical and mythical elements, culture, it's all woven into the story." Her short story "How Inyang Got Her Wings" is the story of a young Efik girl in Southeastern Nigeria who has, according to her website, "amazing" powers. In her prizewinning children's story "Long Juju Man," a Nigerian girl encounters a ghost. Since Okorafor-Mbachu creates magical characters, it cannot be really the magic or mysticism that is the problem but that the women are usually written so their power is used for the benefit of white people.

Black sacred women have become very powerful in some stories, even when they appear in the familiar role of the maid. In *Ivan and Adolf: The Last Man in Hell*, a play set in the present day by Stephen Vicchio, there are only two men left in hell: Adolf Hitler and Ivan Karamazov of the novel *The Brothers Karamazov* by nineteenth-century Russian author Fyodor Dostoevsky. There is also a black woman there. Her name is Sophie. Sophie describes herself as their maid. She does not live in but comes to care for them and then goes home. She brings their groceries from the company store, cooks, and straightens up. Vicchio addresses the stereotype head on; Sophie is dressed in a housecoat and apron, but she is really their counselor, truth teller, adviser, and keeper of the history. She complains that Genghis Khan wanted her to wait on him hand and foot, but as he leaves hell, she tells him to watch his temper, that he might be the first person to make a round trip. She sends people to heaven carrying a box lunch.

She knows what the company management wants and explains over and over to each man the reasons that he is still there. She watches them. She disapproves. With a look, she makes Hitler say grace before he eats. She sees through their self-delusions. She says to Ivan, "God is not the God of the Philosophers." Little by little there are hints about her real identity. She goes home every day to heaven, and she does not come in on Sundays.

Hitler is fond of her, and he is surprisingly affectionate. He busses her on the cheek. He tells her, "I have you, Sophie," but she rebuffs him: "This is not about me, and you know it." She tells him, "You need to stop running from yourself. You run so fast, you look like Jesse Owens," referring to the African

American runner who embarrassed Hitler and refuted his theory of Aryan superiority by winning four gold medals at the 1936 Olympics in Berlin. Hitler starts to listen, eventually asking questions about forgiveness. She tells him he has to take responsibility, to give God something to work with, but that it is possible for anyone to be forgiven. Then she wraps her arms around him from behind. Her hug is the moment of transformation, and Adolf Hitler is changed.

He later says that he is a worm, that he dreams of the dead babies at night, that he wishes for mercy but will accept justice. When Ivan asks Hitler about the changes, he answers, "It was mostly Sophie . . . the constant attention . . . her selflessness. After decades and decades it began to sink in. She has helped me to construct a self that does not spend all its time thinking about itself." When he finally has permission to leave, he is no longer wearing his military uniform.

Ivan, the rationalist, has rejected God. Sophie schools him that God is the God of love, or mercy and forgiveness, by saying, "Forgiveness happens when the violet lends sweet fragrance to the heel that crushes it." Ivan slowly begins to wonder about her—a good sign, she thinks, because it has taken him thousands of years to ask about her. When she tells him that she goes home to heaven, it dawns on him who she really is. "'Sophie' is not your real name, is it?" he asks. "Yes, it is," she responds, "but I am known by many different names, as well." Ivan asks, "Why would you come to Hell?" She tells him, "If the Devil can go to Heaven, why can't God help out a little bit in Hell . . . If you were God and all your creation was in Heaven but two lonely, fearful men who so often seem bent on their own eternal destruction, even after they already live in Hell, where would you be? Besides, they do fine up there without me." Sophie's name is a familiar form of Sophia, the feminine face of God, whose story has been left out of official modern Christian literature. The Gnostic works *The Sophia of Jesus Christ* and *Pistis Sophia* flourished in the first century AD of the Roman Empire.

Playwright Stephen Vicchio is also a philosophy professor (Sophie's line about God not being the God of philosophers is a joke at his own expense). I asked him about his audiences' responses to Sophie as God. He told me a story about a performance of *Ivan and Adolf* that he attended at DePauw University. "There was a very old man, ninety years old, maybe a hundred. Very dark, very black man. He raised his hand and stood up. 'Can you tell me why you made God a black woman?' I answered him, 'Why not?' He started clapping. 'That's the right answer,' he said, and sat down." The rest of the audience joined him in clapping. I asked again for a small but important detail: "Did you say he smiled at you?" He answered, "Yes, he smiled a very big smile."

In the popular novel *The Shack*, by William P. Young, God is also a black woman. Young wrote the Christian novel to explain his faith to his children and grandchildren. The first edition was published privately, but it went on to sell more than twelve million copies, becoming a *New York Times* trade paperback bestseller for more than two years, a year of that as number one. The main character, Mack, gets a note from God—or Papa, as his wife calls God—who wants him to return to the shack where his small daughter was murdered. Papa has invited him over to talk about love and pain. When he arrives, the shack has been transformed into a lovely cottage surrounded by flowers. There is a Jewish man, a diaphanous Asian woman, and a hearty black woman with a "questionable sense of humor," who cooks the most delicious food and likes to walk around in her bare feet. She is Papa. The Jewish man is Jesus, and the Asian woman is the Holy Spirit. Mack is confused, but as the weekend progresses he learns about himself, his own abusive father, and the nature of God's love. He leaves enlightened and healed.

On his website, Young imagines his own conversation with Papa, in which she explains the role of mystery and pain in his life: "I again finally nod as I submit to Papa's love and hug. I hadn't even heard her approach. 'Anyway,' she whispers, wrapping me up in her tender but firm embrace, 'the presence of pain doesn't indicate the absence of love. Often pain is present because of love. I also don't remember promising anyone that there would be no crosses to bear. But don't let that concern you either. I'm good with crosses. Together we can do this.'" *The Shack* met with both enthusiasm and dismay for deviating from orthodoxy, and it stayed on hardback and paperback bestselling lists for months.

In 1996, *The Divine Secrets of the Ya-Ya Sisterhood*, a novel set Louisiana, featured a black Madonna. When the father brought back a "gorgeous colored lady" Madonna from Cuba, the mother was appalled. "The Blessed Virgin is not a Negro," she said, and she made the girls scrub off the paint with turpentine. During the night the girls put makeup on the statue to make her black again, because as one them said, the Virgin probably didn't like getting her face scrubbed off like that. In the morning the mother declared it a miracle and made a bountiful offering of flowers. A 2002 movie adapted from the book starred Sandra Bullock and Ashley Judd.

The movie adaptation of *The Secret Life of Bees*, a novel by Sue Monk Kidd, brought the Black Madonna into even more theaters of Main Street, USA. It is the story of four black women and Lily, a young girl whose mother has died. They all live in South Carolina in 1964, nine years after Rosa Parks refused to sit in the back of the bus but before the changes of the Civil Rights Movement had taken hold in much of the South.

Kidd was a religious journalist who studied seriously the classics of Western spirituality, philosophy, depth psychology, and mythology, including the writings of Thomas Merton and C. G. Jung. "For a number of years I studied archetypal feminine images of the divine. . . . I inadvertently stumbled upon an array of mysterious black-skinned Madonnas. They captivated me immediately." Statues of the Black Madonnas inspired Sue Monk Kidd to write *The Secret Life of Bees*.

The story is told from the perspective of a young white girl, Lily, whose mother's death has left her with a father who is by turns negligent and abusive. The only thing she has left of her mother is a tin with the picture of a Black Madonna, and the only person on her side is her black nanny, Rosaleen. Rosaleen is not a smiling Mammy—she cares for Lily but she is often cross. She has her own agenda to exercise her right to vote—when she tries, she is attacked by white men. Rosaleen and Lily save each other—they leave town together. With nowhere to go, they decide to find the town whose name is printed on the Black Madonna tin.

Kidd said, "I knew Lily would have to find an undreamed of strength, and that she would do it the same way powerful black women around her did—through the empowerment of a divine feminine presence, in this case a Black Mary."

The two women find the town and a household of black women beekeepers who have a large statue of the Black Madonna and hold worship services at their home.

"I felt that any image of Mary in the novel would have to be black," said Kidd, "not only because the women who revered her were black, but because historical *Black* Madonnas have often been at the root of insurgence. . . . It was a revelation to me that hundreds of very old Black Madonnas exist in Europe and elsewhere, and that their darkness is a legacy of ancient black goddesses. I think of the Black Madonna as the White Madonna *before* the church scrubbed the really interesting stuff out of her." Kidd researched the Black Madonna by traveling to European pilgrimage sites, especially in France, where she found "images of startling strength and authority. Their stories reveal rebellious, even defiant sides. . . . I decided the Black Madonna had to make an appearance in my novel."

She found stories that regarded the Black Madonna as a symbol of revolution in Poland and South and Central America and as defiant in the face of oppression, and she decided to create a Madonna who had existed during the

period of slavery in the United States, "to be a symbol of freedom and conso-
lation." Kidd thought at first that it would be a "small statue, sitting quietly
in the corner," but the part grew. During a visit to a Trappist monastery, she
saw a masthead that had washed up onto the shores of a Caribbean island and
was purchased and consecrated as Mary. Kidd said that she fell in love with it
and began to imagine something similar in her book. "I imagined a masthead
washed up on the shore of Charleston during slavery" who "would be a mother
to the slaves, bringing comfort and inspiring them to freedom."

In 1993, Kidd traveled to Crete and visited a Greek Orthodox convent
where she saw a twelfth-century icon of a dark-skinned Mary draped in chains.
A nun told her that years before, the icon had been captured by the Turks and
taken away to Turkey, but the icon soon miraculously returned to the church.
The Turks came back and captured it a second time, this time chaining it up.
The icon returned to the church again, still wearing chains. The Turks gave up.
The convent left the chains around it as a reminder. So Kidd's Black Madonna
would have chains.

There are three levels of the Dark Feminine in *The Secret Life of Bees:* the
Black Madonna, the black holy women, and Rosaleen, the Mammy-Crone. (In
the film, however, young actress-singer Jennifer Hudson plays Lily's nanny.) The
three black sisters are the three faces of the goddess—the childlike May, the
sensuous and artistic June, and the wise and kind August. The months of their
names trace the progression of the year and of a woman's life.

Kidd pictured the beekeepers and their Black Madonna in a pink house.
"I pictured fabulous black women in grand hats dancing around her, coming
to touch their hands to her ear. I understood in that moment that here was
Lily's mother, a powerful symbolic essence that could take up residence inside
of her and become a catalyst in her transformation. Just like that, the Black
Madonna became a full-blown character in the novel." Before she started writing the novel, Kidd created a collage of a pink house, a trio of African American
women, and a wailing wall.

Kidd grew up in the small-town South of Sylvester, Georgia, where African
American women prominently populated her childhood and where she had a
black nanny. "As I wrote about Rosaleen, I could hear my own nanny's voice
in my head. She had a colorful way with words, and some of her sayings found
their way into Rosaleen's mouth." The three beekeeping sisters are drawn from
memories of other black women. "As for August, May, June, and the Daughters
of Mary, I'm sure I drew on amorphous memories of growing up around a lot

of wonderful Southern, African American women. As a child, I loved to listen
to their stories. But I wasn't thinking of any particular one of them as I wrote."
She recalled a scene in which she witnessed strength in an older black woman.
"I remember, for instance, when the Ku Klux Klan came to my hometown one
Saturday wearing robes and hoods, streaming into the stores along Front Street,
and how everyone scattered, both black and white, except for me and my friends,
who got trapped behind a table with an elderly black woman who lifted her chin
and rolled out her lip in a picture of defiance and challenge."

The black sisters became real to her. "The inspiration for August came mostly
from a vision I carry inside, of feminine wisdom, compassion and strength. I just
kept trying to imagine the woman I would've wanted to find if I'd been in Lily's
complicated situation." And unlike the countless supporting black women who
drop in just long enough to save the main character, Lily and Rosaleen come
to live with the women. Kidd said, "I had a dream in which August came to
me, complaining about my idea for an ending. 'You must let Lily stay with her
"mothers,"' she told me. I woke a little awed and a lot relieved. I knew immediately that I would take August's advice. It was what I'd really wanted all along."

The Boatwright sisters are the most cultured women Lily has ever seen.
They worship a Black Madonna and keep bees that produce a healing honey.
Although Lily is surrounded by black women, some reviewers did not notice.
The *New York Times* still described the book as a coming-of-age story, with-
out saying that she comes of age with the help and guidance of black women:
"In South Carolina in 1964, a teenage girl tries to discover the secret to her
mother's past."

The Secret Life of Bees sold more than 4.5 million copies, spent more than
eighty weeks on the *New York Times* bestseller list, and was published in more
than twenty languages. The book won national and international awards, including the Boeke Prize in South Africa and the Orange Prize in England, before
being adapted into a movie. Filming began in eastern North Carolina in January
2008. Reportedly Queen Latifah and Whoopi Goldberg had been considered
for the role of Rosaleen, but the younger Jennifer Hudson was cast, maybe to
avoid the controversy that had already begun to build about a "Mammy movie."
Alicia Keys, Sophie Okonedo, and Queen Latifah were cast as the sisters, and
Dakota Fanning was Lily. North Carolina native David Gordon Green was
originally reported to be the director, but Gina Prince-Bythewood, who had
previously written and directed *Love & Basketball* (2000) and had written the
screenplay for *Drumline*, eventually directed *Bees* from a screenplay she wrote.

The film adaptation emphasized the healing power of the love of the black sisters. Queen Latifah, as August, is the beekeeping sister whose wisdom and warmth makes her the spiritual soul of the movie. As danger approaches, Lily worries that she has brought the outside world into their haven. August tells the frightened white child, "You listen to me now. There's love all around you," a quote that was used in the promotional film trailer. The song "It's Alright" figured prominently in the promotion of the film. August tells Lily, "Don't ever be afraid. *We* are enough."

With the black Boatwright sisters, Rosaleen and Lily find women whose love is warm but tough, giving them the ability to create a safe haven in a racist world. Lily is safer with them than she was with her own father. They give her the protection and nurturing that her own mother could not. The book and film rejoin the black woman and the Sacred Dark Feminine. The women draw their strength and their joy from their relationship with the Madonna.

The sisters also heal the younger and diminished Rosaleen, the character who loses the most in the transition from book to film because Mammy—or any character who can be confused with Mammy—remains the most controversial face of the Strong Black Feminine. That confusion, between the fictional slave-ghost Mammy and actual black women, has haunted black people and blunted their ideas about black female strength for centuries. Rita Williams wrote that when she first heard of the movie, she wondered what was new about black women saving white people. She interviewed Sue Monk Kidd and asked her why she wrote about black women. Kidd told her that "I feel they are like hidden royalty dwelling among us, and we need to rupture our old assumptions and develop the willingness to see them as they are."

Oprah Winfrey is recognized television royalty. The Associated Press called her the most powerful woman in show business. *Forbes* magazine put her at the top of the Celebrity 100 list of the most powerful celebrities in 2007 and 2008, based on earnings, press mentions, Internet hits, and magazine-cover appearances. But, more to the point, she has been probably the most important spiritual guide in American culture.

Oprah started as a young journalist and television host. In 1984 she moved from Baltimore to Chicago to host *AM Chicago*, which became the number-one talk show, surpassing *The Phil Donohue Show* in its first month. WLS-TV expanded the show to an hour and renamed it *The Oprah Winfrey Show*. The next year, the show was syndicated and quickly became the highest-rated talk show in television history. In 1988, Oprah started Harpo Studios, making her the third woman in the American entertainment industry (after Mary Pickford and Lucille Ball) to own her own studio. *The Oprah Winfrey Show* remained the number-one talk show for twenty-one consecutive seasons, was seen by an estimated forty-six million viewers a week in the United States, and was broadcast internationally in 134 countries. Oprah.com averages ninety-two million page views and more than six million users per month and has more than 1.8 million newsletter subscribers. In its first year, Oprah's Book Club grew to be the largest book club in the world, with approximately 1.8 million members. Now the Oprah experience includes the OWN television network, *O* magazine, XM radio, and a website with interactive multimedia workshops. Twelve million people follow her on Twitter.

There is no figure in American culture with more popular influence. When Oprah mentioned that she was eating less beef, the sale of beef fell so much that the industry sued her, unsuccessfully. When she endorsed KFC's grilled chicken on her show and website, so many fans responded that KFC could not keep up with the demand. An industry expert said, "The combination of free food and Oprah is a tsunami. Clearly KFC wasn't ready."

When her Chicago senator ran for president, she endorsed a candidate for the first time and told an Iowa audience, "He is the one. He is the one." It was a turning point in Barack Obama's campaign, in terms of fund-raising and votes. A study at the University of Maryland estimated that Winfrey was responsible for one million votes.

No one becomes so popular without fulfilling a cultural need, and the audience's response to Oprah Winfrey is very emotional. *Access Hollywood* dubbed her "The most beloved woman in America." When Roseanne Barr attacked Oprah on her blog, fans crashed her site and she reversed her attack. Oprah has inspired black women in a way that no modern image has. The Why Black Women Are Angry website proclaimed that it seeks to "encourage, empower, motivate and uplift in the spirit of Oprah." Even conservative Fox News praised her. Guest Deborah King said, "Oprah . . . stands more than anyone I can think of for the protection and welfare of women around the world" and called her "the spiritual mother of the girls in Africa." As Josh, the Oprah-obsessed character of the *Drake & Josh* show, exclaimed, "Oprah can do anything!"

Oprah is a secular representation of the Sacred Dark Feminine. The central point of her popularity has always been transformation after trauma. Her audience is well aware that she has known trouble personally and has still gotten to the other side; most days on her show, she is guiding someone else to the other side. Sometimes the transformation has large social implications, such as when it concerns African children or puppy mills, or sometimes the meaning is more intimate and personal as it was for the woman who was a compulsive shopper and hoarder whose house was almost uninhabitable due to clutter. Some are as small and personal as finding the right bra. Facing trauma is part of the mythical transformational process, and there is no popular figure who represents facing trauma as powerfully as Oprah Winfrey. She has pushed American audiences to dig beneath their calm facades and explore the emotions that previous generations kept hidden. There is now an entirely new emotional role in American public life. Critics have called it the "Oprahfication" of American culture.

There were moments on the Oprah show when friends spoke directly to her role in American public emotion. Lisa Marie Presley called her "Moses," and Ruby Dee took both of Oprah's hands in hers and said to her, "The angels gave us you."

Some new-old Hollywood images of the Sacred Dark Feminine are breaking into the public consciousness. They are new to Hollywood but as old as mythology itself. The popular *Pirates of the Caribbean* movie trilogy featured a black goddess of the old, pre-Mammy variety. In the last film, *Pirates of the Caribbean: At World's End* (2007), the sea goddess Calypso stands on the deck of the *Black Pearl*. She is huge, standing many times taller than the mostly male, mostly white crew members, who bow fearfully before her. She is fierce, able to whip the sea into a violently turbulent whirlpool powerful enough to suck an entire ship beneath it. It is not coincidental that Calypso is black—sea goddesses usually are. But in media portrayals the Sacred Dark Feminine has usually been less fierce, more benign, than the ancient versions. This one is not without compassion, but she belongs to herself. She is also sensuous. The goddess was played by the very attractive black Anglo-Jamaican actress Naomie Harris. Even in the heavy makeup worn by all the magical characters it is clear that she is desirable, and the pirate Davy Jones is in love with her. Calypso's popularity is a big step toward freeing dark goddesses from their servitude.

In the apocalyptic film *Children of Men* (2006), humans have lost the ability to reproduce. A young pregnant woman is discovered—she is black—and the entire future of the human race is growing in her womb. Screenwriter and director Alfonso Cuarón consulted with scientists because he wanted the film to refer back to the First Mother, the Mitochondrial Eve, the East African woman whose DNA is in all humans. These new-old images—Calypso, the First Mother—are promising because they skip back around the Mammy image and call up the Sacred Dark Feminine and the primordial mother before slavery. But for now, and probably for a long time to come, many Hollywood images of the Sacred Dark Feminine and the Strong Black Woman will hark back to the more subordinated image. There are still many, many people who love her.

A brave student once told me that when he came to the university and faced taking care of himself for the first time, he went to the grocery store. Alone and homesick, he was overwhelmed by all the choices. "I'm sorry, Dr. Parks, there was Aunt Jemima, smiling, looking at me." He bought the whole sugary line—pancake mix, syrup, everything with that face—and took her home. Of course, the Aunt Jemima he knew *did* look more like me than the one before. She'd lost her kerchief and some weight, gotten some new earrings.

It was the "I'm sorry" that should have caught more of my attention. Why apologize if he did not see the lady on the box as having anything to do with me? Just because I could understand why my students would want a Mammy did not mean that I was happy to be one. They taught me how little control I had over how people saw me, that Mammy is a *perception* and that they did not need to ask my permission to see me in the Mammy light.

Author Kathryn Stockett resurrected the narrative of the loving black maid with her novel *The Help*, in which a young, white, female aspiring journalist returns to her Mississippi hometown and, in an attempt to capture the attention a New York publisher, decides to write the stories of the black maids who work for her friends. Janet Maslin of the *New York Times* praised the book saying: "The two principal maid characters, the lovingly maternal Aibileen and the angry, scrappy Minny, leap off the page in all their warm, three-dimensional glory. Book groups armed with hankies will talk and talk. . . . [A] winning novel."

By the time the film opened in theatres, the book had already been published in thirty-five countries and sold more than five million copies, putting it on the *New York Times* bestseller list for more than one hundred weeks. Starring Viola Davis as Aibileen Clark and Octavia Spencer as Minny Jackson, the film necessarily condensed the book's storyline. In doing so, it omitted much of the violent racial terrorism of the white women's husbands, allowing the racism of the wives to appear more comical than part of a brutally enforced caste system. Just before the movie opened, I was a guest on WNYC-NPR's Brian Lehrer show, along with David Edelstein, film critic for *New York* magazine and NPR's *Fresh Air*, who commented that *The Help* was a "white movie, a white woman's vision . . . a real workout for white people but [for black people] false on that level." A white female caller said that she found the movie enlightening, that she had never thought about the everyday life of black maids.

The film was an immediate hit, making 25.5 million dollars in its first weekend. But there was controversy from the start. CNN asked "Is *The Help* heroic or stereotyping?" The response of African Americans to the film was mixed. Some response was much like that around the performances of Hattie McDaniel, proud of the performances and worried about the stereotypical roles. Some saw it as a useful airing of an honorable role. On *Midday with Dan Rodricks*, where I am a cultural critic, a young professional woman called in to say that she had taken her mother, aunts, and grandmother to the film, making an event of it, because they had worked as maids, using the money to send her to college and graduate school.

Actor Wendell Pierce, who played detective Bunk Moreland in the hit HBO series *The Wire* and plays trombonist Antoine Baptiste in *Treme*, described the film as "passive segregation lite that was painful to watch."

Pierce took his mother, a former elementary school teacher, to see the film and later posted on Twitter that his mother told him for the first time that she had worked as a maid. "My mother told me for the first time that she was 'The Help,' I never knew my mother had raised white children until we saw this movie. I was shocked. She was hurt by the film. She thought it was an insult."

In a series of tweets, he elaborated: "The Help was well done but was a passive version of the terror of Jim Crow South. My mother told me how she wasn't allowed in the kitchen. She couldn't eat during a 12-hour shift . . . She couldn't drink water from the kitchen but had to go to the faucet outdoors . . . Watching the film in Uptown New Orleans to the sniffles of elderly white people while my 80-year-old mother was seething, made clear distinction . . . the story was a sentimental primer of a palatable segregation history that is Jim Crow light."

When I asked the young black woman working at the box office of a local theatre if black women were coming to the film, she said yes, but that they often came during the day and alone.

Octavia Spencer won best supporting actress awards from the US and British film academies and the Hollywood Foreign Press. While the lead, Viola Davis, was nominated for many awards, she did not win the way that Spencer did. I believe it was because the audience was more comfortable with the fight-back, funny maid who got even than with the tragic one.

For all the publicity, it is interesting that *The Help* did not generate any widespread discussion of the continued exploitation of domestic workers in American homes now. Union activists tried but the discussion did not get much traction. I received some insight as to why when I was discussing the ideas on a radio show. I was speaking with midday film critic Linda DeLibero, who is also associate director of film and media studies at Johns Hopkins University; Hollis Robbins, associate research scholar at the Center for Africana Studies at Johns Hopkins and coauthor with Henry Louis Gates Jr. of *The Annotated Uncle Tom's Cabin* (2006); and host Dan Rodricks on the air, noting the distortions. Several callers were annoyed with us, suggesting that we were disrupting their enjoyment of the story. Their pleasure trumped history.

The popular culture has sustained that particular reading of black women who embody the legacies of the Sacred Dark Feminine and the Strong Black Woman. The media teaches others what to expect from black women, and black women either embrace or resist the images they see. It has taken me a while to come to the conclusion that the Sacred Dark Feminine, the Strong Black Woman, and the on-screen Mammy are versions of the same woman put to different uses, by different people, and that, like it or not, Mammy has something to do with me.

5

"You Say 'Angry Black Woman' Like It's a Bad Thing"

IN THE MYTHOLOGIES, one angers the Dark Feminine at the risk of extreme peril. Her anger is usually compassionate, protective, and retributive—you have to do something to her or those under her protection first—but once she *is* angry, offenders need to get out of her way. In other words, the Dark Feminine does not start fights, but she *does* finish them. Her anger is not out of control; it is strategic. Some black women are able to use the image to their advantage. A very wise woman who taught me about surviving in professional America told me that no one attacked her without getting themselves seriously wounded. Even the *fear* of making a black woman angry can be formidable.

Anger is an emotion that is more commonly attributed to men—an angry woman is acting outside traditional Western gender roles and is still, even today, often painted as unfeminine and unattractive. Male anger is often admired as a change agent—it starts revolutions and wars. Female anger is less storied and less admired and, like female strengths, appears to be often relegated to black women. There is a positive version—when it is used to protect other people—and a negative version. The negative version of the Angry Black Woman image is of a woman who is permanently furious and dangerously ready to act out her anger on innocent—read white—people. Some black women long to be done with the whole image of the Angry Black Woman. Black women may be the only women on earth who are fighting for the freedom to be *more* traditionally feminine.

In 2008, when it became clear that Barack Obama could actually become president and, with him, Michelle Obama the First Lady, supporters of the opposition took direct aim at her to portray her as an Angry Black Woman. The story of why they chose that strategy and how they went about it says much about the heat and the power of the Angry Black Woman image. The responses of African American women to Michelle Obama and the charges against her brought into the open a conversation about black feminine strength and anger and the positive and negative consequences of the Angry Black Woman image.

There was no evidence that Michelle Obama ever displayed anything more than the energy and fortitude it takes to help a spouse run an active presidential campaign, but the opposition press and bloggers took what they could find and ran with it. Michelle Obama was an attractive figure. Her background was right out of the American Dream storybook: She grew up in the working-class South Side of Chicago with two devoted and hardworking parents, went on to graduate from Princeton and Harvard Law School. She gave up a lucrative law career to take on a string of lower-paying public-service jobs until she was named vice president of community and external affairs at the University of Chicago Hospitals.

The profile that began to emerge was of a strong, attractive woman who worked hard for social justice. As reporters followed her, they began to write about her strength and its role in the campaign. *Newsweek* magazine used the title "Barack's Rock" to describe her. Michelle Obama seemed comfortable and confident. She was not intimidated by the campaign or the prospect of being the First Lady. She appeared strong enough to find humor in both. She gave casual talks without notes, keeping a "running deadpan dialogue about the tribulations of ordinary domestic life under extraordinary national circumstances." She liked to call her husband a "biracial, idealistic lawyer with a funny name." Richard Wolffe of *Newsweek* wrote that "Part of Michelle Obama's appeal . . . is that she comes across as so *normal*." But some writers did not like normal. When Michelle Obama told audiences that her husband didn't put the butter away when he made toast and that he was "snore-y and stinky" when he woke up in the morning, Maureen Dowd of the *New York Times* accused her of infantilizing and emasculating her husband.

Dowd's criticism may have been just the first hint in the mainstream press that Michelle Obama's strength would become an issue. Judy Keen wrote in *USA Today:* "Spend a few minutes with Michelle Obama and it quickly becomes clear that nobody tells her what to say." What Michelle said to her was, "Do you think I would ever hold my tongue?" Several commentators suggested that her particular type of humor, which depended on tone and inflection to show that

Maurice Gordon-Bey Sr. (back right) and an unidentified man beat a young man they suspect may be associated with murder of Gordon-Bey's fifteen-year-old son, Maurice Gordon.

Moments later, Jill Jenkins uses her own body to protect that of the young man.

Many cultures have representations of the Sacred Dark Feminine, including some of the Asian Buddhas. Head of Buddha: Thailand, Mon style, late eighth to ninth century, stucco.

Some theologians and art historians have found that images of Mary changed from that of a humble woman to a queen-like figure to more closely resemble Isis. Statuette of Isis and Horus: Egyptian, Third Intermediate Period, Dynasty 21–25, 1070–656 BC.

St. Mary Magdalene. Powerful images of the Dark Feminine are being rediscovered and brought into mainstream American life, including Mary Magdalene.

Nana Buruku, the most powerful deity and Mother of the West African gods. She has been brought to the Americas with immigration.

Madonna del Tindari was the most prominent of several Italian Black
Madonnas. She was first celebrated in 1905 in Manhattan's Lower East Side
by immigrants from Sicily. Members of the Societá di Mutuo Soccorso Santa
Febronia Patti e Circondario. East Thirteenth Street, Manhattan, circa 1940.

Italian Black Madonna in a private New York Home, 1938.

Pope John Paul II kneeling before the Polish Black Madonna. Our Lady of Czestochowa, Jasna Gora, Poland, June 17, 1999.

Jesus of the People by artist Janet McKenzie, selected to be the face of Jesus 2000 by the *National Catholic Reporter*. The model was an African American woman.

A monument in the Confederate section of Arlington Cemetery includes a relief of a Confederate soldier leaving for war. The Mammy, rather than the wife, and his children say good-bye.

Close-up of the relief on the Confederate monument, dedicated in 1914 by the Daughters of the Confederacy.

Amanda Waller with Batman. Amanda Waller was the first African American and the first mortal woman to run a superhero squad without support from a male. Here she is shown on the cover of DC Comic's *Suicide Squad*, issue 10.

Donna Brazile (right) talking with Representative Robert Wexler during a lunch break of the closed-door Democratic National Party Rules and Bylaws committee to decide what to do with delegates from Florida and Michigan to determine the party's nominee for president of the United States, May 31, 2008.

Poet and professor Nikki Giovanni at the end of convocation the day after the massacre at Virginia Polytechnic Institute and State University.

Joan Hairston (sixth from left); Governor Joe Manchin of West Virginia (fourth from left), and members of Hairston's Logan High School mentoring group after the young women presented the governor with a copy of their book, *Welcome to Our World*, 2005.

From left: Dominque Stevenson with volunteer Bashi Rose and Ronald Thomas-Bey, who helped develop a mentoring program at the Maryland Correctional Training Center in Hagerstown, Maryland.

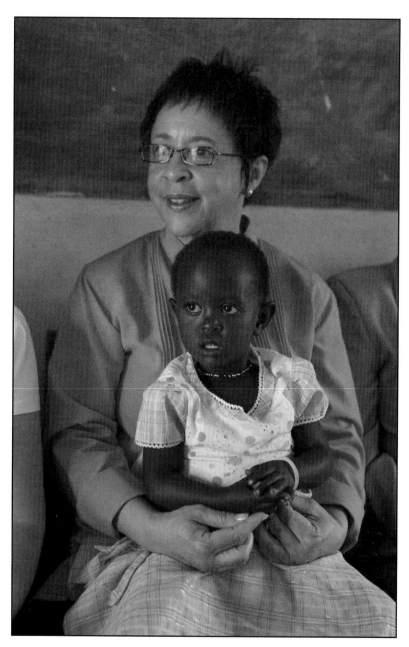

Sheila Johnson with a child in Rwanda.

Artist and activist Rha Goddess in her one-woman show, *Low*.

Mayor Abraham Beame of New York City swears in Eleanor Holmes Norton as chairman of the Human Rights Commission. Watching are Coretta Scott King (far left) and Representative Shirley Chisholm (far right), 1974.

she meant to be funny, might not always translate well in print. And they began to write about her in ways that invoked images of the Strong Black Woman. She was the Best Black Friend: "She is vivid, engaging, part therapist, part professor, part girlfriend who comes over for coffee and tells you hard truths about the stupid mistakes you're making." She was the Truth Teller: "If his loftiness can set him apart from the crowd, her bluntness draws them in." Sometimes the images were harder. A *Time* reporter wrote of her "gritty realism," and a writer for *Newsweek* wrote, "She can be tough, and even a little steely."

Her centrality to the real work of the campaign became increasingly clear. Aides called her "the Closer" because she'd get more commitment cards signed than her husband did at his rallies. After the surprise loss in New Hampshire, *she* delivered the necessary pep talk to aides. Opponents paid attention and began to look for opportunities to discredit her wherever they saw them. They seized one when Michelle Obama said that "for the first time in my adult lifetime I'm really proud of my country." It was not clear if she misspoke, meaning to say that she was proud of her country as never before, but it came out in a way that reflected the actual feelings of many: pride that America was finally able to seriously consider a black man for president. Although Michelle Obama had been joyful when she said it, she was interpreted as being angry. It was an opportunity.

Conservative host Bill O'Reilly asked, "Does Michelle Obama dislike America?" Compared to what was to come, O'Reilly was gentle—and prophetic: "I don't believe Michelle Obama dislikes her country. I sincerely hope she does not, but this is a big deal. It is not going away. And the Obama campaign should understand that."

O'Reilly may have known what was already brewing on the right. One blogger put it plainly: "Michelle Obama: Angry Black Woman." Conservatives discounted the look on her face and the joy in her voice and took her statement as suggesting that she had never been proud of her country. They mounted a scathing round of criticism. One blogger wrote, "Michelle evinces a typical characteristic of many black women in America: fixed intense anger as the *organizing force* of her personality [emphasis blogger's]." According to the blogger, Michelle was angry, the typical black woman was angry, and it was the organizing force of their personalities, the central core of their beings. The conservative blogger also wrote of her "unceasing anger at America, her unchanging emotional negativity. . . . Even in her 'pride,' she still projected bitterness and a sense of grievance."

If opponents could define her as angry, then they had justifications for going after her. By May, *Time* magazine ran the title "The War Over Michelle Obama."

She had become a favorite target, it said, and conservatives were attacking her full out, "with an exuberance that suggests there are not taboos anymore." John Hendren of ABC News warned, "Michelle Obama in for 'Very Ugly Stuff'" and that "She's the New Woman Conservatives Love to Hate." He quoted a Democratic strategist who warned that the complaints had turned into a strategy, that Republicans would try to depict her as "angry."

A commentator quoted by *Time* noted her accomplishments but called her "the bitter anti-American, ungrateful, rude, crude, ghetto, angry Michelle Obama." (Evidently, African American women can be elite and ghetto at the same time.) The conservative site VDARE ran the title "Michelle Obama and the Rage of a Privileged Class" and wrote that she felt "a deep racial anger" and was "not terribly good at hiding it." The *National Review* ran a photograph of her glowering on its April 2008 cover and called her "Mrs. Grievance." Maureen Dowd called it "Round two of the sulfurous national game of Kill the Witch" and quoted another political observer who used a military combat term to say that the "strong and opinionated" Michelle Obama was a "target rich environment." Barack went on the national media and told people to "lay off my wife."

Lee Walker, senior fellow of the Heartland Institute, a libertarian think tank, said, "Never in history has a candidate's wife been attacked like this." Even media commentators could not keep themselves from dipping into stale race jokes. Fox News erroneously called her Barack Obama's "baby mama."

Ironically, while Michele Obama was being attacked, disappointed Hillary Clinton supporters were carrying out one of the most dramatic demonstrations of female anger of our time. Black women began to ask about the slow and tepid response of white feminists to the attacks on Michelle Obama. Mary Curtis, columnist for the *Charlotte Observer*, wrote that "this black woman is wondering: Where are Obama's feminist defenders? . . . I want to know: What does Gloria Steinem think?" Mary Curtis echoed the sentiments of other black feminist writers when she wrote that "the campaign against Michelle Obama . . . has not caused a rift between black and white women so much as it has exposed it. . . . Okay, I get it: Your candidate lost. You're angry. But frankly, I'm getting a little peeved myself."

Third-wave feminists, in the same generation of voters that went heavily for Obama, began to sound out. As the language intensified, FighttheSmears.com and MichelleObamaWatch.com websites were set up to counter the rumors and smears. MichelleObamaWatch.com was set up by young white feminists.

Finally, the National Organization for Women weighed in with support for her, but some other groups remained silent.

Then, on June 16, 2008, a group of panelists was discussing strategies in the presidential election, and Jane Hall, a professor at American University, was explaining that the Republicans were trying to marginalize Barack Obama. She was speaking about the creation of a *fictional* image:

> I think one way that people who are trying to beat Obama are going to try is to somehow prove he's Other. He's not one of us. If they can't prove he's a Muslim, then let's prove his wife is an angry black woman. It's going to get ugly. I don't think McCain will sanction it . . . I think that it is the only and ugliest way to go after Obama and people are going to use it.

Then Cal Thomas, a syndicated columnist for Fox News, instantaneously did exactly what Professor Hall had predicted:

> I want to pick up on something that Jane said about the angry black woman. Look at the image of angry black women on television. Politically you have Maxine Waters of California, liberal Democrat. She's always angry every time she gets on television. Cynthia McKinney, another angry black woman. And who are the black women you see on the local news at night in cities all over the country? They're usually angry about something. They've had a son who has been shot in a drive-by shooting. They are angry at Bush. So you don't really have a profile of non-angry black women.

In unison, several of the panelists said, "Oprah Winfrey." Then Thomas said, "Oprah Winfrey. Yes, there you go, Oprah Winfrey."

So it was not just Michelle Obama. It was all black women, except Oprah Winfrey. It was Cynthia McKinney, the congresswoman who has been called "the most courageous member of Congress" because in 2001 she stood alone to question Secretary of Defense Donald Rumsfeld, on the record, about military war games carried out on the morning of the attack on the World Trade Center. McKinney ran as the 2008 Green Party candidate for US president. It was Maxine Waters, the longtime congresswoman from California, who has been called "the most effective woman in the US Congress" and is well respected for her ability to cut through political pontification. She represents Watts and South

Central Los Angeles, where she is widely respected by constituents, politicians, and gang leaders.

Democratic political consultant Donna Brazile described Maxine Waters: "This is a woman who can walk into any ghetto in America and force both sides to stop the violence. Her reputation as a tough, take-no-prisoners, abrasive, strong, and demanding diva has always made me blush. Maxine is a walking bottle of Tabasco sauce—spicy hot but smooth."

Anger is in the eye of the beholder. Barack Obama quipped, "I've got a feisty wife." Donna Brazile and Cal Thomas looked at the same woman, Maxine Waters, yet saw someone very different. Thomas saw the same anger in every black female face, even those of women grieving their sons. What were women whose sons had been killed supposed to do? They were supposed to smile, always smile, because the image says that anger is the black female default emotion, and anytime a black woman is not smiling, she must be angry. The only negative emotion he could imagine for them, even in grief, was anger. And angry meant dangerous. It explains why the smiling Mammy was so important; her smile was a disarmament, a signal that the black woman was safe.

The unanimous omission of Oprah is another indication that anger is as much perception as expression. Oprah Winfrey *does* become angry when the occasion calls for it. Her wrath is both formidable and effective. But audiences know her well enough to see that she has other emotions too.

The Dangerous and Angry Black Woman campaign was so over the top that the editors of the *New Yorker* magazine ran a parody of it with a cover cartoon that depicted Michelle and Barack Obama in the Oval Office. Barack was dressed in a traditional Arabic style and stood before a picture of Osama bin Laden. Michelle was dressed in what many critics came to call an Angela Davis style, with medium-size Afro, an AK-47, and a rack of ammunition slung over her shoulder. An American flag was burning in the fireplace. The two figures were facing each other, bumping their fists together, a reference to a fist bump the two had exchanged just before he accepted the Democratic nomination. (African Americans do not call it a fist bump—it is one of several in-culture ways of "giving dap" or supportive recognition.) It was a playful, affectionate gesture, significant in that it was just one more of a hundred small ways that the mere presence of African Americans changed the popular landscape. Barack later told NBC's Brian Williams that the gesture "captured what I love about my wife—there's irreverence about her and sense that for all the hoopla, I'm her husband, and sometimes we do silly things." Critics of the Obamas saw only fists and suggested that it was a terrorist sign.

The *New Yorker* editors thought that the uproar about anger and fists was ridiculous, and they meant the cover to convey that. The cartoon was supposed to be a parody of the attacks coming from the right. According to the magazine's press release, artist Barry Blitt gave it the title "The Politics of Fear" and used it to satirize the use of scare tactics and misinformation in the presidential election to derail Barack Obama's campaign. (The title did not run with the image, leaving the interpretation up to the reader.) Editor David Remnick said that he ran the cover "to hold up a mirror to the prejudice and dark imaginings about Barack Obama's—both Obamas'—past and their politics." It was meant to *address* "the distortions and misconceptions and prejudice." But parody works only with distance, and the cover was too close to the bone. The polls suggested that many Americans believed the messages that the cover parodied—that Barack was a Muslim and Michelle was a dangerously Angry Black Woman. Their supposed connections to terrorism would become a centerpiece of the Republican campaign. If the *New Yorker* cover had been seen only by its own segmented, well-educated, and sophisticated print readership, the joke would have been understood and contained. But the image exploded onto television and the Internet. When so many people still believed the distortions, Obama supporters said, it was dangerous for a prestigious magazine to repeat them.

The "Angry Black Michelle Obama" campaign threatened to disable a style that many black women use every day—taking their justified anger and shaking it and shaking it until it is empty and dead and then flattening it, like some political steamroller, into a caricature, to be pulled out and flung as a slur at women whenever necessary. It was the same thing that had been done with the word "liberal." Michelle made it clear that she saw her husband and herself as bold. "We need to be here now, while we're still fresh and open and fearless and bold," she told *Vanity Fair*. "Even if it's inconvenient," Michelle Obama said in *Salon*, "we have to be bold."

The image of the Angry Black Woman described by Cal Thomas and others is an insult that seeks to rob black women of emotional nuance and intelligence. It does not admit that anger could very well be a reasonable response to certain conditions. Mary Mitchell of the *Chicago Sun-Times* told her readers to stop playing around with the term, that she knew what a real Angry Black Woman was angry about, when she wrote:

Michelle Obama bitter? Not likely

　　She's got a great husband, beautiful daughters, loving mom.

　　Michelle Obama an angry black woman?

　　Please.

　　Michelle Obama bitter?

　　Give me a break . . .

　　No. This is angry:

　　The black woman who is stuck in a slum building in an unsafe neighborhood, she's angry.

　　The black woman who is dragging her baby's daddy to court once a month trying to get child support, she's angry.

　　The black woman who has to rob Peter to pay Paul and still can't pay the gas bill, she's angry.

　　Successful black women don't have to walk around grinning all the time to assure white people that they are happy they aren't on food stamps. . . . Asking her to skin and grin is too much.

Other black writers began to write back in a conversation about black women and the difference between strength and anger. A blogger called That Black Girl wrote:

Without realizing it, Michelle Obama is going to take the angry black woman discussion global. I don't believe that Michelle is an angry black woman. In fact, she is like many of us, confident, strong and opinion-ated and she isn't about to apologize for who she is. But I have noticed that the world doesn't know what to make of a strong black woman. If we speak too directly, we are immediately labeled as angry, tough or as a woman with an "attitude." And if we don't feel like smiling, well forget about it! (Yeah, I know, sometimes we do have an attitude but doesn't everybody?)

　　I am rooting for Michelle because she isn't about to back down. She is taking the world to school about a different kind of African American woman. She's smart, educated, grounded and fiercely protective of her family. She will get angry if necessary but anger is not what fuels her life. . . . She is showing herself and her passion in a very real way. The world may never look at a strong black woman the same way again. . . . Why do you think that strong = angry when it comes to us?

The last question is important. Sometimes black women do not perform the self-disarming signals that other women do. It is common for women of other racial groups to weaken their speech with disclaimers—"I think . . . " or "I don't mean to . . ."—or they may end a statement with the up-tone sound of a question. They may avoid looking the person to whom they are speaking directly in the eye. Often, black women do not do any of these things—I never had to learn to smile when I did not mean it—so black women are often perceived as "angry" when they are not. Communication researchers have documented the cultural differences in black and white speech and found that whites often misunderstand black speech patterns as conflictive.

An example from my classroom: A black female graduate student from New York was a walking illustration of the communications research. She was a perfectly cheerful person; she did not attack other students, but she would state her piece and defend it if necessary. I began to notice that two white women who often sat behind her looked uncomfortable every time she spoke, even when she was not speaking to them. Finally, they stayed after class and asked me to shut down the black woman. "She is aggressive," they said. I agreed that her speech style and tone may have been more assertive than that of some others, but she was being civil and addressing the points being discussed. They were surprised that I refused to shut down another student. I suggested that they get to know the black woman. I also suggested to the black woman that she get to know the other students better. By the end of the semester, the white women had become comfortable with the black woman's speech.

After I gave a speech to an affluent "ladies who lunch" women's club, one woman said she wished that she could be strong like black women. I asked if she had children and whether she had ever acted as a strong advocate for them. She said she had, but she sighed and said that she knew she was not supposed to be like that. In the context of women whose justified anger is inhibited, black women seem particularly angry.

Like the grieving black mothers who looked angry to the Fox commentator, the circumstances of black women's lives may lead others to assume them to be angry. The culturally defined strength of the Strong Black Woman has its unhappy side, but nobody is angry all the time. That is what black women resist: the characterization that angry is all they get to be, that they have one emotion and that is anger—a cold, humorless, dangerous anger. People and anger are more complicated, more flexible than the popular negative image of the Angry Black Woman allows. What is labeled as anger could easily be another emotion.

If we replace the word "anger" with "indignation" or even "determination," it is easier to see the complexities.

The perception of anger begets anger, and the public animosity toward Angry Black Women can be truly awful. Piers Morgan, the British tabloid editor and talk show host, clashed with Omarosa Manigault-Stallworth, a black woman, on Donald Trump's *Celebrity Apprentice* show. Omarosa had appeared on the first season of Donald Trump's *The Apprentice* reality show and was voted the most-hated reality star of all time. Fighting with her rehabilitated Morgan's mass popularity. "I'm a national hero. I killed Omarosa." Somehow discounting the untold number of prime-time TV murderers, he said, "Her only claim to fame is that she is the most unpleasant creature ever unleashed on American TV."

Of course, winning changed much for Michelle Obama. After the election she became a media darling. Beauty magazines inspected her hair, her dresses, her body (particularly her muscular arms), and they approved. Comments about anger changed into comments about strength and "grace"—another term that suggested resilience under difficult circumstances. As a black woman, Michelle Obama had been hit with the double whammy of prejudices—racism and sexism. Maureen Dowd suggested that the anger accusations grew out of an inability to see a black woman as First Lady, a title that had been associated with sweetness and docility. Republican strategists complained that it was difficult to attack Barack without appearing racist. But gender changes race, and they were already warmed up from attacking Hillary Clinton. Mary Curtis of the *Charlotte Observer* offered another reason: "In America, there's seldom a cost for disrespecting black women."

The Angry Black Woman label surfaced again early in the 2012 presidential campaign with the publication of *The Obamas: A Mission, A Marriage*, a portrait of the lives of the Obamas as a couple. While some saw the book as largely sympathetic, it did contain some stories of friction with White House aides. Mrs. Obama told CBS *This Morning* cohost Gayle King that some have tried to portray her as an "angry black woman" since Mr. Obama first announced he was seeking the presidency.

The accusation of anger is a type of push back designed to control black women who step out of their assigned spots; the image of out-of-control anger is dangerous to black women. During a discussion after a talk I gave to educators, a high school administrator asked me about a black female student who had physically attacked a white female student. The attack seemed to the administrator to have come out of nowhere. She followed school policy and brought the black student to her office. What perplexed her was that the young black woman kept asking, "Why am I the only one here? Why is she not in here too?" The administrator responded that the white woman had not done anything, but the black student continued to ask, and the administrator wondered why.

I asked about the young black woman—had she ever shown any signs of psychosis or had any previous violent episodes? The administrator said no. Then I asked her if the white student could have said something—something particularly offensive, perhaps? The administrator had not considered that the black woman was trying to tell her that. It seemed plausible to her that black women just went off in that way. The crazy-angry black woman scenario rendered the student as unthinking, as dangerous, and got her suspended.

Another version of the Angry Black Woman is the "harsh" black woman. Some black men have used the term to say that black women are too aggressive, not "feminine" or submissive enough. In 2006, first-time filmmaker Tim Alexander gained attention and rekindled an old controversy as he promoted his film, *Diary of a Tired Black Man*. He described black women's anger as centered around black men and as a disease he named "angry black woman syndrome." His film asserted that some black men prefer white women because black women are too angry. As the discussion about the film grew, some black men indicated that one person's "self-sufficient and independent" was another person's "angry." When Alexander appeared on *Keeping It Real*, Al Sharpton's syndicated radio show, a male caller said, "When we come home, we don't need that loud-mouth, self-sufficient, independent, macho woman disagreeing with everything we say. We need kind women."

Self-sufficiency is a necessary trait for black women, so if independence and self-sufficiency are the same as anger, then black women are angry. They have to be independent in order to survive, and the images around them are changing to reflect the realization that they have to be in control of their lives.

Black women were never required to give up anger, but anger is still controversial for white women, even after three waves of feminism. Anger can sometimes be justified and instrumental, and black women, like men, have used anger as a tool in very intelligent ways, as a useful emotional platform from which to provoke change.

Many African American women have embraced the Angry Black Woman label, using it like a sword for empowerment and social justice. Patricia Williams, Columbia University law professor, writes a column for the *Nation* magazine called "Diary of a Mad Law Professor." Williams is elegant and offhandedly patrician—the opposite of the stereotypical Angry Black Woman—but she uses the label to regularly and scathingly speak truth to power. Williams is making full use of both meanings of the word "mad." Psychosis is always nearby when speaking of Angry Black Women—the fear is that they will lose control and erupt.

Other black women have been using their fierceness and occasional anger to get important things done in Washington, DC, during the exact same period as the attacks on Michelle Obama. Congresswoman Maxine Waters sits on the House Judiciary Committee and called in representatives of the oil companies for hearings on the rising price of oil. Sometimes hearings such as these are just political theater to make constituents feel better, but Maxine Waters wanted answers. According to the *New York Times*, "In one of the more pointed exchanges, Representative Maxine Waters . . . seized on the record $40.6 billion profit of ExxonMobil in 2007. She pounded on the company's senior vice president . . . demanding to know if gas prices could be lower if the company earned a few billion dollars less."

Waters "brazenly" suggested that perhaps the oil industry should be nationalized. She said she recognized it was an "extreme step" but one that might become necessary if exorbitant prices continued to produce outsize profits. When she thanked the executives for coming, she added, "If you feel a little bit beaten up on, we all feel beaten up on, so share the pain. We get our behinds kicked every day in our districts about what is going on."

During the same time period, also in the same city, political strategist Donna Brazile was using strong language and taking strong stances. Her image of strength mixed with humor and compassion became much admired during the presidential election. Brazile already had a reputation as a strong fighter, but that reputation had always been tempered by her concern for a reasonable outcome. She worked on Dick Gephardt's 1988 presidential campaign, which started out well but soon began to run out of money. After he won the Iowa caucuses, she deployed some of "her troops" to New Hampshire and the Super Tuesday states and drove the rest home for the Presidents' Day holiday. "I told the kids to sleep, and I drove nonstop all the way from Des Moines to Pittsburgh. . . . When [an aide] told me that he would not pay the kids for the holidays, I challenged him to go downstairs so I could kick his ass." The kids got paid.

When Brazile worked on Michael Dukakis's presidential campaign later that same year, she was relegated to the smallest office on a floor away from the other senior aides. She and a small group of other black women commandeered a conference room on the appropriate floor. They called it the "Sojourner Truth, Harriet Tubman, Ida B. Wells Room"—also known as the "colored girls room—we shall not be moved."

Over time, Brazile learned that she did not have to fight battles by herself. She had help from friends, allies, sometimes from the press. Working for her close friend Eleanor Holmes Norton on Norton's first congressional campaign, Brazile learned to build coalitions. She learned how to be what she calls "a fixer" and how to take down people who attacked her candidate. "If our opponents were willing to take us on, I was ready to destroy them before they could strike again. . . . I don't need to be called when a friend is in trouble. They just need to make room for me, because I'll be there, especially when the person is being unfairly attacked and maligned in the media."

Brazile was an important figure in the 2008 campaign talk. As a superdelegate, a regular commentator on CNN, and a member of the DNC rules panel, she was well positioned. In the bitter partisan primary-season fights between the Clinton and Obama campaigns, she argued to preserve the party, which meant she had to take on former allies in the Clinton camp. The blogosphere called their confrontations "smackdowns," and the media covered them like prize-fights. First came what *Salon* called the "Brazile–Begala Smackdown" on CNN. Brazile, an uncommitted superdelegate, had said that Obama was building a new coalition so that he might be able to win without working-class whites or Latinos. Paul Begala, a Clinton supporter, came on and fired back, saying that she was suggesting a new coalition of "eggheads and African Americans." She called him "baby," which should have been a sign that she did not see him as a threat, but he charged on.

She responded: "First of all, Paul, you didn't hear me right. Maybe I should come and cook you something, because you've got a little hearing problem." She told him that she knew the demographic numbers as well as he did, but that was not the issue. "Just don't divide me and tell me I cannot stand in Hillary's camp because I'm black, and I can't stand in Obama's camp because I'm female. Because I'm both. And I'm wealthy, so I might go with McCain and sit with Bill Bennett, Paul." Begala said that was funny, but he wasn't laughing. Brazile continued. She called him "baby" again and reminded him that she had participated in presidential campaigns, as had he. "Don't start with me, baby. . . . And, Paul, I was there with you. I was there. It's our party, Paul."

Lanny Davis, an unhappy Clinton supporter, took issue with the panel of CNN commentators who said that the primary race was settled. He perceived them as all anti-Clinton. Brazile said, "You know, Lanny, I wish you would have been with us last August when we avoided this train wreck. I was there, Lanny, I was there. I said on May thirty-first that the Democratic Party will work with Senator Obama and Senator Clinton to come up with a resolution, Lanny. Now, if you want to keep fighting, let's fight. But let's you and I go in the green room and fight, and not keep this up." Davis said, "I'm not fighting with you, Donna." Someone off-mike warned Davis, "Don't go there." Davis agreed and said, "I'd lose that one."

Websites cheered. One read, "Donna Brazile ripped Paul Begala a new one" and provided video of the exchange. Brazile was becoming a star, and the media and audience followed closely as she mixed her fabled ferocity with warmth and humor. CNN's Anderson Cooper asked to be her boo, while trying to get details of a private conversation between Brazile and Obama. "Boo" is an African American slang term for a favorite romantic friend. He teased, "I think he hasn't told anyone else, just you." Brazile smiled coyly and said, "Anderson, you're not my boo," perhaps referring to an earlier reference to CNN's Lou Dobbs as her boo. Cooper said, "I want to be your boo." Brazile playfully looked at her watch and said, "Are we still on TV? I think I better watch my words." Cooper admitted he was not sure what being her boo meant, but the exchange sparked a flurry of inquiries. A T-shirt with the phrase "Anderson Cooper, 'You're Not My Boo'" became CNN's second-top seller.

By the time the media covered the meeting of the DNC rules panel where members met to figure out how to split contested delegates between the Clinton and Obama campaigns, Brazile was one of the most recognizable people in the room. What the media did not report were all the personal relationships and histories also in the room that would allow her to mix strength with strategy. Brazile had helped to win the black vote that was important to both of Bill Clinton's presidential elections; she and Clinton senior adviser Harold Ickes (and Begala) had worked on the campaigns together. During Clinton's impeachment, it was Brazile who helped get him onto black radio, where support for him and for Hillary poured in.

The woman presiding over the DNC rules panel, to whom Ickes and the gallery of Hillary Clinton supporters directed their fire, was Alexis Herman, who had been named the first African American secretary of labor during Bill Clinton's administration. During the nomination process, Herman had been attacked by opponents; Brazile had orchestrated her defense. This was a fight among familiars.

Brazile was fighting to keep her party in one piece. When former Michigan governor Jim Blanchard argued that Clinton should get more than half of the delegates despite violating party rules, Brazile talked about her mama.

"My mama taught me to play by the rules and respect those rules. My mother taught me, and I'm sure your mother taught you, that when you decide to change the rules, middle of the game, end of the game, that is referred to as cheating." MSNBC made it the quote of the day.

In her book, *Cooking with Grease*, Brazile explained her motivations. "The struggle for inclusion is hard, but the prizes are great. They are the ideals of this nation: freedom, liberty, equality and justice for all Americans. As long as I have breath in my body, I will continue to work toward them. I was raised to stir pots, and I'm not stopping now."

Brazile presented the Angry Black Woman and the lack of a smile in perspective. "It's hard to get a smile out of me," she wrote. But when she traveled to war-torn Somalia, a woman about her age, clearly starving, begged her for food. Brazile held the woman's hand and emptied her purse to her: "My American gum, candy and every dollar I had in my purse. I couldn't help but cry."

That is what a whole black woman looks like. She gets to be strong, angry even, *and* compassionate. Anger does not negate the potential for humor or intelligent thinking. Other black women are using the image. In the wake of the Michelle Obama attacks, the Angry Black Woman blog playfully challenged the negative interpretation of black female anger with the title "You say 'Angry Black Woman' like it's a bad thing." The blogger had taken the term and used it as a political stance. In correspondence, she and I agreed that when she used Angry Black Woman and I used Strong Black Woman, we were really talking about the same image. She just liked the edgier sound of "angry." Other black women who are taking the term and using it are the blogger on Theangryblackwoman.com website, for instance, and radio host Sunny James, who posts an Internet version of her show on the website.

Three African American women who were magazine editors—Denene Millner of *Parenting* magazine, Angela Burt-Murray of *Teen People*, and Mitzi Miller at *Jane* magazine—got together to write *The Angry Black Woman's Guide to Life*. It was dedicated, in part, to "ABWs everywhere, who love hard, dance with abandon and don't hesitate to put 'em in their place."

The authors explain that many important racial moments have happened when a black woman got angry, and they offer brief histories of black women whose anger has changed the world: Sojourner Truth, Harriet Tubman, Angela

Davis, Winnie Mandela, Shirley Chisholm, and Anita Hill. They explain that "It wasn't until Rosa Parks got angry about the lynching of Emmett Till that she decided not to move from her bus seat—an angry black woman's strike that ushered in the civil rights movement. . . . Simply put, anger spurs progress." *The Angry Black Woman's Guide to Life* offered anger as a strategy, suggesting the use of a subtler, professional version in office situations, for example.

In an interview, social activist Dominque Stevenson told me she was angry. "I am still angry about slavery and the disenfranchisement of black people," she said. But she described her anger as a "slow burn" that led her to work for social justice. Another way to think of the anger she and *The Angry Black Woman's Guide* described is as a fierce energy, an indignant intolerance for the status quo, which propels black women forward and makes them so effective. It is a strategy *and* a style, a modus operandi used to spark change. It is also a link back to the fierce and compassionate Dark Feminine.

Many black children grow up feeling protected because of their mother's freedom to anger when necessary. The day my daughter was born, the first thing my mother asked was, "Did you ever think that you could love someone this much? That you would kill or die for?" Tamara Nikuradse wrote of an exquisite feeling of security that black mothers can provide: "If anyone should dare mess with us, they will deal with the wrath of our mothers—what an awful surprise for the uninitiated!" I attended a dinner party of black professionals where everyone present had at least one story of their mother's anger saving them at school. The most popular story was of a mother going up to her child's school for a face-off with a school administrator after the child was wrongly placed in vocational classes or special education. Some mothers simply sat and refused to leave until the child's record was pulled and examined. Others argued and cursed if they had to. One mother followed the principal as he fled down the hall. Another man said he had been absolutely sure that he and his mother were going to hell because she cornered a nun in the hallway. One man, now a corporate director, said, "Where would we be today if they had not done that?"

Others outside her family have witnessed and welcomed the defenses of the Angry Black Woman. The Anchored Nomad is a blog by *portuguesa nova*, who describes herself as a skinny white woman. She posted a celebration of three Angry Black Women who rescued her and other passengers as they traveled around Chicago by train. The stories are true. She gave her blog trilogy the title "God Bless You, Large, Angry Black Woman" and posted a painting of a black angel.

> Tonight I was rescued from a long, annoying commute by who I consider to be the guardian angel of Chicago Transit Authority: the Large, Angry Black Woman who doesn't take shit from anyone.
>
> This is not the first time The Large, Angry Black Woman has unknowingly rescued me. I am eternally grateful and eternally guilty, for each time it has happened I am, for some reason, unable to express my gratitude.
>
> I will list all three instances below, the most recent first.
>
> **Episode #1: Where the Angry, Large Black Woman Saves the Entire Car from Having to Listen to a Crazy Preaching Man on the Express Train**
>
> The train preacher is a very tall man in his late 60s with a ZZ Top beard. He speaks with the heaviest Hebrew accent (is Hebrew an accent?) you have ever heard. Every vowel is pronounced as a guttural sound. Phlegm flies everywhere as he speaks. He is wearing a blue snow suit. The preaching is already in session as I, and several others, get on the train at the Davis stop in Evanston. Dismayed looks abound as we realize that there is a perfectly good reason why this train car is nearly empty, while the others are standing room only, and now it is too late to move:
>
> *Crazy Preacher Man:* "If you study the Torah, you will learn that that [sic] there is in fact a planet made of *DIAMONDS*! In fact, scientists say there are many planets made of *DIAMONDS*! But the one I speak of specifically has fish with eyes of *DIAMONDS*! The people drive *DIAMOND SPACE CARS*! If you study the Torah for 40 days you will learn about this planet. You can even put these *DIAMONDS* straight into the *MICROWAVE*! For reasons I have not studied, the *DIAMONDS* will not melt and will not ruin your *MICROWAVE*! But you must study the Torah."
>
> *Large, Angry Black Woman:* "Man, why don't you shut your crazy ass mouth? You think any one here cares about your diamond planet? I just got done with ten hours of work. My feet hurt, I've got a headache, I'm tired and I still gotta go home and feed my kids, my husband and

my grandkids. So why don't you get in your diamond space car and get the hell outta here?!"

I want to clap, but find it is not necessary when a few other people on the train beat me to it. Besides, the woman has a headache, she said so herself.

Episode #2: Where the Large, Angry Black Woman Saves Me and at Least One Other Person from Having to Deal with an Unassuming Pervert (I think)

Disguised Crazy Man is about 20 years old, well dressed, and wearing sterling white tennies. He is also carrying a notebook. Looks completely normal. I assume he is headed to school. He enters the train at Howard and tries to sit down next to a large and soon-to-be angry black woman behind me.

Large, Angry Black Woman: "I want you to get up and keep walkin', cuz you ain't sittin' by me. And don't think you can sit behind me, and don't think you [can sit] in front of me (aka next to yours truly), because you're ten kindsa' crazy and I don't need it right now."

Disguised Crazy Man: "W-W-W-What'd you j-j-j-just s-s-say?"

Large, Angry Black Woman: "I said KEEP WALKING and find a new place to sit."

Disguised Crazy Man goes to the end of the train car and sits down next to an innocent middle-aged female passenger. He opens the notebook, thrusts it in innocent middle-aged female passenger's face: "N-n-n-now what you see h-h-h-here is what I-I-I-I'd like to do to you."

I have no clue what he is showing her in his notebook, but middle-aged female passenger's face turns bright red.

Disguised Crazy Man: "You c-c-c-come over to my p-p-p-place, and we can d-d-d-do this. And I got a f-f-f-friend, and he'll w-w-w-watch."

Innocent middle-aged female passenger immediately gets up and moves to the most logical seat, right next to the Large and Angry Black Woman.

I desperately want to ask the woman how she knew the guy was crazy. I'd like to grab her by the shoulders, shake her and scream, "Tell me your secrets!"

He had me fooled. But I just couldn't ask. I didn't want to attract any attention. Moreover, I probably didn't want to hear her answer, since I'm guessing I am blissfully ignorant to a lot of people who are ten kindsa' crazy who cross my path each and every day. I'd rather not know. I'll take my chances.

Episode #3: Where the Large, Angry Black Woman Saves an Undetermined Number of People from God Only Knows What

It is May and I find myself, yet again, headed to the ultimate breeding ground for lunatics: the Howard stop. It is a beautiful morning and the temperature is warm. The train is crowded. A large, soon-to-be-angry black woman and I do not have a seat and are standing across from one another by the door.

I take off my suit jacket. It is that nice out.

Train stops at Howard. The door opens. The large, soon-to-be angry black woman and I are standing face to face with a man wearing khaki pants, a red t-shirt and a ski mask.

For some reason, my instinct immediately tells me that he is not about to highjack the train, nor is he going to try to take anyone's money. Though probably highjacking or robbery would be preferable to his no doubt uncontrollably insane, but completely non-violent presence. He is just a raving lunatic wearing a ski mask on a crowded El train in May, and that's good enough for me. He takes a step to get on the train.

"Oh, *HELL* No!" says large, angry black woman.

"What?!" this man dares reply, as though there is some question about the source of her concern.

"If I gotta' tell you why you aren't getting on this train, then you got more problems than wearing a damn ski mask in the summer. Take a step back and wait for the next train. We ain't traveling to crazy land."

"Ding-dong. Doors closing." Says the recording on the train.

"What?!" he says again, trying to get on the train.

Large, angry black woman basically clothes-lines him just as the doors close on his face.

I should be kissing her feet. Instead, nose still in my book, I pretend not to have seen anything.

When I wrote to her, *portuguesa nova* said that she was happy to honor the women. So were her readers, who wrote in comments of admiration and wistfulness:

Great post, girly :)) looks like She is one of those with an in-built shit-detector. You got yourself the perfect guardian angel on that train!

It sounds like I need to make sure I'm situated near large, able-to-be-angry black women when I'm taking public transit :)

i too attract freaks on trains . . . i need to find me a large angry black woman to travel with . . . lol

I'm very jealous of you being in the vicinity of large, angry black women at opportune times.

Some told stories of other Angry Black Women who had rescued them or their loved ones:

I met my own Large Angry Black Woman a few weeks back. She yelled at some big kids who were bullying my little kids. . . . I wouldn't have had the guts to do that myself.

My god. I haven't lived in Chicago for 6 years, and yet I remember my encounter with St. Large Angry Black Woman clearly—it was, naturally enough, on the red line. . . . She could easily be the patron saint of the CTA. . . . I'd nominate her.

Others just went straight into praise mode:

All Hail the Large Angry Black Woman!
niiice! i'll be adding her to my list of favorite large angry deities.

Still others wished they could be more like her or learn from her:

I wish I could *be* the large, angry black woman. Or be more like her.

I wish I could pull off Angry Black Woman. Unfortunately, I am just skinny-white-programmer-chick.

I think there should be self-empowerment/assertiveness classes held along the lines of "Embrace the Large, Angry, Black Woman Within." I'd sign-up.

One woman said,

People like that are a godsend. You need to carry a little gift for her in your purse, and the next time you see her, give it to her (and explain why. Or give her a printout of this post). People like that need to be rewarded and encouraged.

The black women were riding the train, just trying to get someplace. One said she had worked ten hours, her feet hurt, and she had a headache. They were not looking for trouble, but when trouble found them, they responded protectively, for themselves *and* the other people on the train. They were indeed angry, but briefly and with reason. To *portuguesa nova*, they were prescient, generous, and able to instantly and correctly appraise the situation and defuse it. The famous redemptive worth of the black woman is in part due to wisdom but also to style and attitude. Strong Black Women seem to specialize in up-close, personal combat, and they can be hard and humorous at the same time. They were described as large because these particular women were large, but maybe they were more noticeable, more formidable because they were large. I wondered what the Angry Black Women said about their train rides when they got home to their families. If they are like the women I know and love, I can imagine them laughing.

A study of black female classroom teachers found them to be culturally traditional "warm demanders," meaning that they were "tough minded, no-nonsense teachers"—stricter, more authoritarian, and requiring more discipline from their students than the national standards called for—but that they *simultaneously* joked and spoke affectionately to them. The study also found that the teachers were motivated by a sense of urgency and that black and Latino students responded favorably and achieved more than with other styles of teaching.

The most prominent contemporary Angry Black Woman in American life is Madea, created by Tyler Perry and adored by audiences of black women. Madea is a large, loud, older black woman who moves through plays, movies, and books, giving out her own brand of outrageous but useful advice. She is portrayed in drag by Perry, who is more than six feet tall. Madea really is larger than life; she reaches mythical proportions. Her symbolism is not missed. When she talks, people listen. She moves with an authority that is based in social reality but expands to just short of parody.

Madea is a product of black nostalgia. Perry told *Booklist* that Madea sprang from recollections of growing up in a black community in the South and growing wise through tribulations, and that he lamented the absence of Madea from communities where children are now left unattended by adults. Perry may have orchestrated the reclamation of Mammy—taking the image back from white culture and reinserting it into black communities, where older black women still carry authority. One older woman in Baltimore told me that she routinely walked up to black children in the streets and admonished them.

According to her backstory, Madea Mabel Simmons was born in Greens-berg, Louisiana, and carried her homespun ways to the city. The politics of drag mean that the audience can laugh because they know that there is a man in the dress. The Mammy look is abstracted just enough to make it palatable. Madea is God-fearing, but hers is an assertive Christianity. She carries a gun in her purse. "I got more weapons in here than the US dropped on the Taliban," she shouts. *"You don't want to mess with me."* In *Diary of a Mad Black Woman*, her middle-class daughter prepares to confront the woman who stole her husband. Madea intervenes, saying, "No, you gonna deal with her like a white woman. *I'm gonna deal with her like a black woman.*" Images such as Madea change the direction of control. Critics who cringe at Madea may need to see her through the lens of her original core audience—middle and working class black women. She is speaking to and for them in larger-than-life terms. The audience is not laughing at her; they are feeling with the woman. When the audience identifies with the Angry Black Woman, the traditional Hollywood relationship is upended.

The Angry Black Woman and the fear she engenders have been used recently in advertising. In a Dairy Queen commercial, a passenger is distracted by someone else eating his Dairy Queen Blizzard and repeatedly drops his lug-gage on an African American woman, who gasps irritably. In order for the ad to work, we have to project our own fear that she is about to hurt him, to know that it is within her power to hurt him. But the audience is invited to identify with her rather than the silly-looking man. Who among us would not be annoyed?

One of the bloggers on TheAngryBlackWoman.com said it this way in her introductory post: "It's true that the Angry Black Woman is a negative stereo-type. Black men don't like us, white people fear us, and non-angry black women wish we would stop being so loud. Anger isn't going to solve all of the world's problems, true. Anger is sometimes an unhealthy emotion. However, anger can be used for good. We sometimes need to get angry to propel us toward positive change or to stop injustice and oppression. We can't stop being angry until the fight is over. And the fight is far from over, kids. So this is me embracing the anger, the black, and the woman. Condemn me if you will, but just try living for a week and tell me there isn't reason to be angry. I'll be calm, peaceful, and chill once racism, sexism and queerism is gone. I feel I may never be chill. Prove me wrong."

At the Angry Black Bitch website ("Practicing the Fine Art of Bitchitude") blogger Pamela Merritt reacted to cuts in benefits for the disabled, including her brother who had been forced to stop working to keep his Medicaid, only to have his food assistance cut. "I don't get to dwell on my disgust. All I get to do in this situation is fight."

A fictional character allows us to look behind the formidable facade to what the Angry Black Woman means to the culture, to see why a creator would write an Angry Black Woman and how an audience receives her. Created in the late 1980s by John Ostrander and John Byrne, Amanda Waller is one of the strongest characters in comic books. She was a mortal, with no special powers, but was mentally stronger than her allies or her enemies. She was the first African American and the first mortal woman to run a superhero squad without support from a male. Comic scholar Michael Robinson said that it was rare for any humans to operate at the same level as superheroes, much less to lead them. Amanda was the leader of the "Suicide Squad," a band of superheroes who all had suffered psychotic episodes and were being kept in a psychiatric prison. The administration considered them to be damaged goods and therefore expendable.

In a genre not traditionally diverse with women or minorities as artists, editors, or characters, the makers of comics have no outstanding reason to create black female characters unless they want to. John Ostrander wanted a black woman.

Ostrander wrote in an email, "The story demanded a tough, no nonsense, take charge person with a lot of attitude. I have met several African American women who fit that description and each had reasons—backgrounds—as to why that should be so. I specifically wanted her black because there were no black characters running a superpowered team at the time, insofar as I remember. And I very much wanted her to have NO superpowers—everything came from who she was. I felt that would make her formidable and unique—and I think it did."

He gave Waller a good reason to be angry. Her husband and one of her daughters were murdered in the Chicago Cabrini Green housing projects. Deciding that she had to do something about the conditions that led to their murders, she left the projects, earned a PhD in political science, and became a congressional aid. Her education and accomplishments did not mollify her anger; instead, her anger fueled the slow burn that propelled her forward. Waller was not out of control. Her anger did not interfere with her intellect—if anything, her anger had a clarifying effect, giving her a type of tunnel vision that focused relentlessly on the greater good. She was brilliant *and* angry, strategically emotional. She demonstrated why masculine culture would perceive such a woman as a threat to the status quo. She faced terrible situations without hesitation. Her anger gave her courage to go into places and make decisions that would frighten anyone else. Her prosocial motives were unassailable, so even when she appeared to be doing bad, she was doing good. In a culture that tends to see good and bad as distant opposites, she worked in the necessary middle. She would associate with villains in order to get close enough to destroy them. She controlled with her intelligence and willpower. Comic scholar Michael Robinson described her as "a tough-as-nails lady making tough choices, still the ultimate organizer."

She operated at the highest levels, working with and sometimes against presidents, and was assigned by the United Nations as Checkmate's White Queen, a member of its senior policy-making board. A fan wrote, "White Queen of Checkmate? Amanda Waller is the Queen of the DC Universe as far as I'm concerned."

Waller could be ruthless, and she had a mouth. According to critic Pedro Tejeda in the comic book literary forum *Funnybook Babylon*, "With the right words, she could do more damage than Superman's heat vision, escape situations that would tax Mr. Miracle and his motherbox, and save the day better than Wonder Woman could." These were not the out-of-control, neck-snapping tirades that Hollywood is so fond of but well-placed, penetrating words. She had a mouth like a sailor but a brain like a steel trap. She could outtalk, outcurse, outthink the best or the worst figures in the world. And she was willing to go into the most dangerous of situations and do the most difficult of assignments. She was unafraid and unflinching. Her fans called her "The Wall."

Comic-book women are often drawn in highly sexualized ways, but Waller did not *look* like anyone else either: She was short and round at five foot one inches and two hundred pounds. She was neither obese nor terribly muscular; she was just round. Ostrander wrote that he based her body type on a woman he knew who was short and stocky, but who in personality was quite unlike Amanda Waller.

Tejeda wrote, "What makes everyone fearful of her is that she didn't receive a magic wishing ring or powers from a bolt of lightning. Instead, she worked herself from nothing, which has made every one of her accomplishments defined by what she is willing to do. It's this drive to do better that also makes her a sympathetic character to me." A white male hero, Rick Flagg, was supposed to run the Suicide Squad, but Waller overshadowed him. Comic scholar Robinson described her as a realistic hero, one we could imagine among us: "Waller has a strong sense of realism. . . . It takes a certain amount of work to imagine a 'real' Batman. While she wouldn't have supervillains and heroes to manipulate,

I don't think it's hard at all to imagine a real Waller." She was only stronger than anyone else around her.

The Suicide Squad has been disbanded at times, but Waller has not been out of a job. She has made drop-in appearances on other comic-book heroes to organize them and has traveled to television and film, voiced by C. C. H. Pounder, to lead the Justice League. In 2011, Angela Bassett played Dr. Waller in the *Green Lantern* movie. As tough as she was, she also had a heart—she was fighting to save the world from the bad guys and trying to save her superheroes from themselves. "All my people come back," she said, and they did. She developed a habit of defying her superiors in order to achieve her goals. She would go up against presidents to save "her" people, but she would go up against her own people, too, if she had to.

Despite what the DC Database website called her "dominant and threatening personality," Amanda grew close to her operatives, going with them on field missions. "Most of the team's criminal members didn't really take to Waller's methods and even the team's heroes were often at odds with Waller. . . . Nonetheless, the team remained loyal to her, often choosing to side with her instead of the government."

Amanda Waller was a healer. She could take supervillains and convince them to change their ways. She dug into their psychoses, making them relive the most traumatic episodes of their lives in the name of healing. Most of her relationships could be described as love/hate, and one of the most prominent of those was with Batman. Characters who move back and forth between comic books and movies must have some inter-text continuity—the characters in the books and films have to resemble one another. Comic-book fans make up the earliest and innermost core audiences for comic-book-based films. Their approval is important to the perceived integrity of the film, and they have been vocal in their disapproval of film figures who are inconsistent with their comic-book versions. Prior to the series of Batman movies, the Dark Knight had a particularly sinister run in the comic books, making him a little too shady for film audiences. If he were to be a better person, the rehabilitation would have to come in the pages of the comic book first. Amanda Waller was his rehabilitator. Batman had opposed the formation of a Suicide Squad made up of villains he had helped to put away, but he and Amanda came to an uneasy understanding. On one cover of *The Suicide Squad*, Waller had the much bigger Batman backed up against a wall, her finger in his chest. Later, he would see the necessity of the squad and help to re-form it.

Comic book critic Jamaal Thomas wrote:

> I still remember one of the first comics I read starring her, when she
> faced down Batman. At that time in my life, I didn't really question the
> essential rightness of superheroes. They righted wrongs and brought vil-
> lains to justice. But in that issue, I saw Batman in a way that I would've
> seen him if he was an actual person, rather than a two dimensional
> character. . . . There was a scene . . . where she gave him a look of utter
> contempt for his imperiousness, his conviction that he was always right.
> For that moment, I understood. She (and we) had been far more than he
> could ever imagine. And while he played his games, she was engaged in
> the ugly work that's needed to make the world a better place.

Amanda was ruthless and appeared to be "morally ambiguous." She was
definitely a "by any means necessary" leader. "If you were to ask her why she goes
to the extremes that she does, she would tell you that someone with the resolve
has to go out there and do the awful things to keep the world safe," wrote Tejeda.

Batman asked Waller to deprogram superhero Blue Beetle after he had been
mentally programmed. Blue Beetle went into a trance and tried to kill her. A
reader commented, "Waller's response? Slug the bejeezus out of him. . . . I didn't
leave that scene thinking that Blue Beetle got punked by a woman. I just left it
thinking that, holy shit, Waller rules." Another reader wrote, "That's Amanda
Waller for you. She's the toughest lady in the DCU, and 100 percent woman.
Watch out or she'll kick your ass."

The country was safe because Amanda Waller was on the case. Waller could
use dubious methods because her audience trusted that she was working for the
right purpose. She bested the strongest, the most brilliant, and the most evil of
adversaries. She could call on psychological strength in her operatives that they
did not know they had. She seemed to notice, and know how to use, everything.
Every now and then there would be a break in her demeanor. After she rescued
a baby—a by-product rather than the focus of her mission—she cuddled it.

The 4thletter! blog named her its 2008 Black History Month figure and
called her "one of the single best black characters in comics." Guest columnist
Pedro Tejeda wrote:

> Not only was this Amanda Waller character black and female, but she
> was the toughest person among an entire room of politicians, soldiers,
> villains, and heroes. Shit, Ronald Reagan, who was in nearly a quarter

of these Giffen League comics, was in awe and a bit frightened of her. . . . You could tell that she was assigned to work with the villains because she was the only person tough enough to keep them in line. They were afraid to cross her because she seemed to have the resolve and determination to make them pay. . . . I saw the Wall at what she does best, politically outmaneuvering everyone else in the room in search of what was best for the American people.

It was an interesting choice, very different from the perfected figures of most African American celebrations. Waller got dirty and said and did things that would keep her out of the NAACP Image Awards, but she illustrated the role of the Dark Goddess in her willingness to face the terrible and in her ability to transport her charges out of the chaos back to ordinary life. In complete opposition to the political strategists who tried to paint a supposedly black female anger as simplistic and crude, Waller was used to demonstrate nuance and emotional complexity. Wrote Tejeda:

When Waller is done right, she's one of the most complicated and nuanced characters in all of comics. She's neither villain or hero and does very little to benefit herself. Shit, one time in the cartoon, Brainiac showed up out of nowhere. What did Waller do, did she run away? No, she whipped out her gun and helped the same heroes that she had been working against all series long fight this common threat. Sometimes a character like her can be too much for the simpleness that people want in their superhero comics, but to me, comics are in a better place because of characters like her. . . . Sure, she was ruthless, did things that only benefited the United States, and worked with the worst of the worst. And yet, I couldn't help loving her as she did it all, because she was so different than everyone else I had read before.

Although she looked very different from other women in comic books, Amanda was not asexual. When drawn by African American artists, she was given a more feminine traditional face, a less muscular body. One scene opened with the appearance of a sexual teaser, with Amanda taking a morning shower. As she stepped out, Batman handed her a towel and said, "We need to talk." It turned out that he was trying to intimidate her. It did not work. Even naked, Amanda was The Wall.

Waller was also a woman with a racial identity. One of her operatives was Bronze Tiger, who was bronze-colored. When he was brainwashed, she helped him out of it, worrying that the situation was racially charged.

Ostrander writes that Waller was a "consequentialist," which means roughly that "she lets the consequences of her acts define them ethically." Comic-book critic Jamaal Thomas, who sees Waller as a complicated character, wrote that her anger arises from the complexities of being misunderstood and wedged between two cultures:

> Amanda Waller is the reincarnation of the African American leaders.... No matter how much was achieved, no matter how many degrees obtained, or promotions received, successful African Americans at that time had to deal with a community that accused them of abandoning their principles, and institutions that believed them to be inferior. This is where her anger comes from. She was the first to make the Suicide Squad work, and the first to make the hard decisions that leaders have to make. And what does she get for it? Public disapproval. . . . But I can't stop myself from thinking that if she existed in the real world, I'd be the first one to protest against her.

The world of Amanda Waller was never simple. Through her character, like the Dark Sacred Feminine, the audience faced the terrible with a trusted guide. She worked in the abyss, between absolute innocence and absolute sin. She knew the nasty underside of life that ordinary people did not want to see, much less consider, and because she was there they did not have to. She raised important questions. Are ruthless measures necessary to defeat ruthless evil? Can good people employ awful methods? At the end of the *Justice League Unlimited* cartoon, an older Amanda Waller reflected on her life with no regrets. The cartoon revealed her to be a Christian, but she sought no forgiveness. She faced evil. When she could, she killed it. Somebody had to.

Amanda Waller helped to explain why the Dark Feminine has been most popular as an agent of repair and transformation during times of social upheaval—after the Civil War, the Great Depression, and post-Vietnam eras. The Western traditional feminine stance, "Please, don't," will not change anything. When carefully considered, the Angry Black Woman is not a sputtering out-of-control maniacal stereotype. She is resilient, resourceful, and strategic, a much more powerful operator, which is why some people have so much trouble with her and try to use the label as a weapon against black women. But the black writers and bloggers know that anger plays a role in the emotional life of a whole person.

This is where black women and white women get played against one another. Traditionally, white women were not supposed to show anger, and an important mission of feminism was the right to be angry and to act upon anger. As a black woman, I have always had that right. The caricature and condemnation of the Angry Black Woman is meant as a cautionary tale to all women—a way of saying, "You don't want to be like her." Because black women's anger—the real kind—is often depicted as a changemaker.

Because, as the saying goes, when Mama ain't happy, ain't nobody happy.

6

Becoming Coretta:
A Cautionary Tale

IN 1968, MARTIN Luther King spoke to the protesters in Memphis of what would come to be known as the Sanitation Workers' Strike. "We are tired of our men being emasculated so that our wives and daughters have to go out and work in the white lady's kitchen." He was not speaking of his own wife. Coretta Scott was a graduate of Antioch College and the New England Conservatory of Music, a trained violinist and singer, and she had left a budding career as a concert musician when they married. But there were other black women in that crowd of protesters, and until recently they have been overlooked in the histories of those last days in Memphis. The women were not protesting because they wanted to stop working; most worked because they needed to work. They wanted better, more professional, and more "feminine" jobs.

A few days later, King would be dead. But the culturally ensconced idea that black manhood was dependent upon men assuming a Western patriarchal position vis-à-vis a specific and projected image of black women would live on. The projected black woman was less accomplished, less visible, and more vulnerable than black men—a figure at odds with the ambitions of the female protesters. In their mourning, many African Americans would project onto Coretta Scott King the image of the quiet and docile helpmeet.

In the twenty-first century, African American women find themselves at a unique place in American history; they are now a race of women more professionally advanced and accomplished than many of the men in their culture. In 2003, 24 percent of black women had entered the professional class compared to

17 percent of black men. The Bureau of Labor data shows that more than 2.6 million black women were employed in management and professional jobs in 2008.

They are creating businesses faster than any other demographic—faster than white men and three times faster than black men. According to a count by BlackNews.com, the majority of black entrepreneurs were women, and from 1997 to 2002 the number of self-employed black women in the United States grew 70 percent, compared to 21 percent for black men. In 2002, the US census found that black women accounted for 40 percent of black businesses, compared to 34 percent of white businesses owned by women. Between 2002 and 2008, the number of firms owned by African American women increased by 19 percent—twice as fast as all other firms. They generated 29 billion dollars in sales nationwide. A study by the Center for Women's Business Research found that black women were more likely than other women to start and run their businesses without partners.

Black women are also more likely to be employed than black men, the only racial group of women that has that statistic. The Center for Labor Market Studies at Northeastern University found that during the Great Recession black women had no net job loss because were less likely to lose their jobs and more likely to be reemployed quickly than black men. Quoted in the article, I said, "If you're a black woman, you don't have to convince someone that you're strong and nurturing and able to do almost anything—it's almost a brand."

They still make less per hour than black men, white men, or white women, but the difference in earnings between white women and white men is two and a half times greater than that between black women and black men. Black women make up most of the difference between themselves and white women and black men by working longer hours.

The strength and hard work of black women has paid off for them, but their accomplishments come with the fear of social costs. Some men, like Bill Cosby and journalist Juan Williams, are calling for black women to move up to the cultural and political leadership, to save the entire race, but many black men and women are ambivalent or even hostile about such female power. Some of those men are calling for black women to keep quiet, step back, and make more room for black men. It is both a heady and a treacherous time.

It is an old story. Zora Neale Hurston wrote in 1937 that black women were the mules of the world, that when a white man told a black man to do something, the black man turned around and gave it to the black woman to do. Michelle Wallace wrote that the perception of black women as durable superwomen allowed black men in the student wing of the civil rights movement to leave much of the necessary and unglamorous support work to the women while the men made the public speeches. Black women have been carrying the race since slavery, but it's an elaborate charade; they pretend that the men are in control—a common way to say it is that black women are supposed to "build up the men."

Black women routinely hide, even from themselves. They muffle their accomplishments, diverting the attention to the men. More black women than men enter college; at historically black colleges, it is common to have ratios as high as seven or eight women to each man. A study at a major university discovered that black women entered the university expecting the work to be difficult, even unpleasant. But they also expected to work hard and to graduate. And they did. Women earn about two-thirds of the associate and bachelor's degrees awarded to black students, according to the National Center for Education Statistics; black women graduate twice as often as black men and often at rates comparable to those of white women. Many colleges are reporting that black women's graduation rates have surpassed white men's.

It is a major success story that remains hidden, even from black women. Many colleges divide graduation rates by race but not by race *and* gender. Black women I interviewed said that they believed black female students were not graduating; they thought that they and their friends were the exceptions. Often, black women are particularly reluctant to talk to men about their successes. In a discussion I conducted with black female graduate students, the women said that they routinely disguised that they were in PhD programs, because it made black men uncomfortable. One woman said, "I want to have a date." Some admitted that they had considered leaving graduate school because of the reaction of some black men.

Black women do not see or celebrate their own successes even outside the classroom. In direct contradiction to the public image, black women routinely participate in or even orchestrate their own second-class position, to make their partners feel like men. They do as they are expected to do, as they have been trained to do since they were children.

In some cases, black women are not even talking to one another about their accomplishments. In business, networking is considered key to success, but because black women have protected black men by keeping so quiet about their successes, they may not even know about one another. Columnist Tannette Johnson remarked that black women were surprised to find that there were so many others like them. After a 2004 study by the National Women's Business

Council documented black women's successes, she talked to some and found that "they seem to be unaware that they exist in any significant numbers, and that they have greater rates of survival and job growth than businesses owned by women of other ethnic backgrounds."

They are unaware because they have been taught by their culture to be unaware, to look away from themselves. Hiding their accomplishments is part of the unhealthy bargain that black women have made with black culture. Acknowledging and celebrating one's accomplishments are parts of a balanced, healthy life. Many of the black women I interviewed considered it particularly rude to brag. Some had become so good at hiding that they were not able to acknowledge success even to themselves. A prominent media producer decided to go back to graduate school for a PhD. She already had an MA degree, a Peabody Award, and a national reputation in her field. She sped through her coursework, only to hit a puzzling roadblock while writing her dissertation. When she tried to describe her projects, she left odd, illogical holes. In session after session, she and her adviser worked to fill in the gaps. A breakthrough came when her adviser said, "There is a whole person missing here. Who is it?" The graduate student said she did not know but promised to read through the chapters to see who it could be. The next time they met, she said, "I know who the missing person is. It's me."

But that self-discovery still did not solve her problem. She could fully describe the contributions of other people, but even as the producer, she could not bring herself to take any of the credit. Even when her own descriptions did not make sense without her, she kept unconsciously cutting herself out. She said she had been raised as "a good, Southern black girl" and could not "brag on" herself. In all of her full and exciting life, giving herself credit for her own accomplishments was one of the hardest things that anyone had ever asked of her. In the end, she had to interview other members of her team about her own leadership role in order to document it. There are many "good black women" like her who have learned to hide their successes, even from themselves. They have internalized the culture's call for them to keep their accomplishments hidden.

Other times, the work of black women is hidden by force. One of the most significant black artistic events of the last century was the 1959 Broadway opening of *A Raisin in the Sun* by Lorraine Hansberry. It was the first Broadway play written or directed by an African American, and its breakthrough success opened the way for a stream of successful black productions by Ossie Davis, Langston Hughes, James Baldwin, and August Wilson. The *Washington Post* compared its impact to that of *Brown v. the Board of Education* or Jackie Robinson. But when Hansberry wrote it, it was also a black feminist play that depicted the traditional power of black women and the problems of black men.

The character of Mama was loosely based on Hansberry's own mother. She was "full bodied and strong. She is one of those women of a certain grace and beauty who wear it so unobtrusively that it takes a while to notice. . . . Being a woman who has adjusted to many things in life and overcome many more, her face is full of strength." She was "the black matriarch incarnate . . . who scrubs floors of a nation in order to create black diplomats and university professors. . . . She has, we can see, wit and faith of a kind that keeps her eyes lit and full of interest and expectancy. She is, in a word, a beautiful woman."

Hansberry captured the primary motive for black women: "When the world gets ugly enough—a woman will do anything for her family." She wrote to her own mother: "Mama, it is a play that tells the truth about people, Negroes and life." But the truth was short-lived. By the time it was produced, the female roles had been reduced and the lead male role expanded. When black director Lloyd Richards joined the project, he thought that Mama's part was too big. He worked with Hansberry for a year to whittle down the role and build up the part of her son. The play that started out about Mama ended up about Walter Jr.

Sidney Poitier was cast as Walter Jr. During the out-of-town tryouts, Richards noticed that Claudia McNeil, who played Mama, was getting more applause than Poitier, so he cut her part again. "We had to bring Sidney's part up in the play where it belonged," he said. Parts of the original script that had been deleted from the 1959 Broadway production were restored in a PBS production, in the 2004 Broadway reprisal, and in a 2008 television production starring Sean Combs as Walter Lee Jr., Phylicia Rashad as Mama Lena, and Audra McDonald as Ruth. The depiction of black women's traditional power and their roles in the survival of family and race had been brought back.

Every culture values mothers, but in African American culture, mother love is raised to a new level of devotion. Worship is not too strong a word. Reverence for parents and ancestor worship are central to the traditions of many African cultures, and in the United States, reverence for the mother has been raised to an art form. Niara Sudarkasa has looked at the similarities between African Americans and the West African countries from which many slaves were taken. One of the striking similarities is the centrality of the mother. African slaves brought with them a mother-centered family structure, with her as the hub of the family wheel. Western-style patriarchy is not endemic to African American communities—the much decried matriarchy of black families comes not from the pathologies of slavery and poverty but from West Africa. Strong black women have long been central figures in African and African-descendant cultures.

Attempts to impose Western-style patriarchy have been disastrous for black men and women. Some African postcolonial scholars are arguing that rigid gender divisions of male and female are European impositions that ill fit their cultures and that African culture needs to work its way back to the more fluid arrangements of before. They are recognizing the ways in which Western masculinity is misaligned with their cultures and are working toward reclaiming and updating some aspects of precolonial gender roles, where masculinity was defined by service to the common good. There was also a shared power. In many areas, men have a dominant role in the business of the village, while women have a dominant role in the home. Slavery sliced off the traditional public power of African American men but left largely intact—to the extent that it left any families intact—the family power of women.

Western masculinity is won by employment, wealth, and power, but the means of doing that have been cut off for many men. Western patriarchal culture carries the assumption that the greatest threat comes from men, and so in America, from the time of slavery, the dominant culture has worked to isolate and disenfranchise black men. Traditional Western culture also assumes a subordinated woman, and in that light, powerful black women appear to be in the way. Black women often perform a fragile balancing act, accomplishing a great deal without taking the credit.

Although the majority of black households are headed by women, the family structure has been labeled a crisis in the United States. In 1964, the US Department of Labor issued the Moynihan Report, officially entitled "The Negro Family: The Case for National Action." The report defined the common black family structure against the *Leave It to Beaver* images of white families (which were not as common as the mythology suggested) and simultaneously popularized and pathologized the idea of the black matriarch. Black-female-headed households were regarded as aberrant arrangements that grew out of the abuses of slavery and added blame and national embarrassment. The report did not mention the matrilineal African tradition. So many black women choose to have children and build lives without marriage that the majority of black children live in homes headed by their single mothers. Despite the crisis in the black family, black people consider a woman and her children to be a family.

Although many black women are moving up in terms of affluence and accomplishment, there are circumstances of African American women's lives that are not about to change. Black women are less likely to marry, more likely to divorce, less likely to remarry than other women. The combined forces of high rates of homicide, incarceration for minor crimes, black male interracial marriage, and black women outpacing men have shrunk the pool of black men eligible to marry, and black women have been reluctant to marry outside their race. The relative scarcity of black men—as husbands, brothers, or uncles—means that many women have to do what they can to ensure the survival of their families. Black women are traditionally taught to be self-sufficient, to avoid having to depend on a man, but they are left in a quandary. They must make sure that their families survive, and to do that they must go out into the world. When they succeed, they risk the ire of black men.

Joy Jones wrote in the *Washington Post* about the phases in the lives of black women. She interviewed young women who longed for a black man and marriage, for the romantic-love dream life, but the statistical reality was and is that most of them will not marry—black women are the least married demographic in the country. Some wait for the black men who, statistically, will not come. They are loyal to the *idea* of a black man. A twenty-eight-year-old woman told me that she and her friends hold out for black men, knowing they may not come, because to do otherwise would be a betrayal; they will not leave black men even though black men, in many ways, have left them. "They still need us," she said.

Jones found that many of the middle-aged women who talked to her did not want marriage anymore, that they thought they were better off without black men who could come with a more unstable life than the ones they already had. One woman said that if Jesus himself offered her an engagement ring, she'd tell him to keep it.

Black women go on with their lives, man or no. They have made an art of being romantically alone. They don't stop doing most of the things that other women do: They move into their own homes and have or adopt children. They take care of themselves. Black women are serious about decorating their bodies. A study conducted for *Essence* magazine found that African American women spend 80 percent more on cosmetics annually and nearly twice as much on skin-care products as the general market of women does annually.

The picture that emerges is of a hardworking woman who spends Friday night or Saturday at the salon for her hair and nails, maybe going out for drinks and food with her girlfriends, maybe putting on a beautiful hat and going to church, where the pews are full of other black women. They go on cruises, attend birthday parties, luxuriate in spa weekends, and even go clubbing in all-female groups.

Actually, black women are at the forefront of a larger social trend. More women in general are now marrying later or not at all, and many of those single women with incomes are choosing to have or adopt children. The single mother with children is the fastest-growing type of family, according to Rosanna Hertz, chair of Women's Studies at Wellesley College and author of *Single by Chance, Mothers by Choice*. Hertz also says that black women are out ahead of other women, leading the way for single mothers, providing models for creating whole families without male partners. As more nonblack and affluent single mothers appear, black mothers may be less stigmatized.

But for now black women are often left to carry on, to find their own way. Often they depend on one another. A military counselor found that black women who were also single mothers often formed supportive networks that allowed them to stay in the military longer, while other women were forced to leave to care for their children. I see this as a reflection of a particular helping attitude, one that can be healthy or unhealthy. I asked women in interviews why they did what they did. Most said they had never thought about it. A woman in Charlotte said something I heard often from the women I interviewed: "It is what it is and you do what you do." When I urged them to think about it more, they said they still did not know, that they could not remember a time when they were not helping someone. They learned by watching their mothers, but they could not come up with situation-specific reasons why their mothers did it. When circumstances dictated that they not help, they were in agony.

Black women often allow others to ask too much of them. For a while my husband and I taught at the same college, where I had unwisely agreed to be the director of undergraduate studies for a major with one thousand students. There were other advisers, but the students made it clear that they preferred me. Day after day he would wait for me as our agreed-upon departure time came and went, watching the line—an actual line—of students outside my office. He noticed that each student would go in looking stressed and sad and come out looking relieved or cheered. Then finally I would come out, looking drained.

After a particularly busy time, I asked a student how she came to select me. She told me that a group of Jewish mothers in New Jersey were giving out my name and number to other college mothers, saying that if they could not get their children's problems fixed, there was this great black woman who could.

Black students assumed even more, that I was an automatic other-mother, that I would always go to the mat for them, all of them, no matter what. A few expected me to hurt myself for them—one woman lied and expected me to back her up. More than one has expected me to give passing grades to final assignments that did not merit them and became indignant when I did not.

I have to admit, I took some pride in being the fix-it woman. There is a certain machisma to the role, and black women make similar demands of one another. Black women expect other black women to work hard and suffer in stoic silence. The helping tradition actually hides how gender works in black culture. Although the tradition is fading some, helping is still a highly valued part of the culture; everybody is *supposed* to do it. But women are assumed to do it more. I asked black students to name the people in their lives who helped them most. Some of them mentioned men, but *all* of them mentioned women in their families or communities who they said would do anything for them.

The Strong Black Woman is not a lie. There are black women who regularly manage to do more than could be humanly expected. It is easy to find stories of them, either from the women or the people whose lives they touch. The story of one, Angie, came to me through her daughter, Tasia.

I sat in the train station, trying to grade papers, while two black women were talking. I assumed they were friends, but it soon became clear that they were strangers. The older woman was querying the younger woman, getting pretty deep into her business. Tasia, the young woman, was a student and she was having troubles. The older woman, dressed in professional office clothes, had started giving advice. "I don't know your university, but I know there is somebody there that can help you." I listened for a while. Then I entered their conversation. (I learned long ago that black women can enter almost any conversation, because everyone expects you to help. It's like the Pine-Sol or the Phillips' Milk of Magnesia ladies—nobody ever seems surprised.) When the older woman heard that I was faculty at the same university, she released the student into my care. "All right, then, this professor will take care of you." The unspoken agreement was settled.

It took a few days and some phone calls, but I did take care of her advising and logistical problems with the university. It was a good thing, because when the woman in the train station saw me a week later, she asked for a follow-up progress report. I had learned Tasia's story. She had been awarded a prestigious scholarship, one for students who have managed to keep up their grades despite extreme circumstances. But she was struggling under the weight of continuing family responsibilities. The scholarship paid for a dorm room, but she was often shuttling back and forth to help out at home, where her mother had taken on more responsibility than any person should ever have to carry.

Angie, now a married paralegal at a nonprofit community law center, had had her first child in 1982 at the age of fifteen. By 1988, she was twenty-one and had four children of her own. Her parents were supportive, but she also worked multiple jobs, some under the table. Her sister Diane also had four children, and Angie became the secondary caregiver for Diane's children. Diane moved to California, where she thought life would be easier for her, but there she started to use drugs. Soon Diane had two more children, for a total of six with a variety of fathers. She became ill with AIDS. As Diane's health worsened, Angie moved her family to California to look after her sister, becoming primary caregiver for Diane and her children, one of whom had been born HIV positive.

Angie encountered problems—getting the children into schools, finding racially sensitive support groups—all exacerbated by the sheer number of people for whom she was caring. Tasia told me that her mother described weathering emotional trauma when Diane was in the hospital: "The hospital called a cab for her and sent her out of the hospital in knee-deep snow with one shoe on and a blanket. The only reason she got back into the house was because I heard something clawing at the door." Angie tried to get Diane and her children into a Red Cross shelter. She told Tasia, "A white woman at the front desk told me, 'You really messed up, taking care of a walking virus and a gimp.' That's all I have to say about that."

Diane died of AIDS in 1995, and Angie permanently adopted five of her sister's children. By the time she was twenty-four, she had taken in the two children of her oldest sister as well, who also became ill with AIDS and later died. Angie had become the mother of a family of eleven. Later still, she became the primary caregiver for her mother and a brother who was also ill. From 1998 to 2003, she claimed thirteen exemptions on her taxes.

According to Tasia, her mother was "the one constant. The family structure is dependent on Angie supporting everyone in the family. . . . Angie's family may not have been acceptable to some, but it worked for her, and experiences in her life led her to conclude that she did the right thing every step of the way."

Angie said she did what she had to do and she made the choices she had to make. "Love covers a multitude of sins, so as long as I have it to give, there are no sinners in my book. And when people die, I feel the same way. I also believe in resurrection, which makes it easier to cope with. It's a hard process, but that's life." With everything she has gone through, her greatest fear is losing the children, of someone coming and separating her family. Although the child with HIV went to the parent with the best health insurance (the father), Angie still regrets being unable to keep all the children together.

Angie's story showed how the stereotypes don't work. The father of the child with HIV was a responsible father. And while Angie took Social Security for the children and Temporary Assistance for Needy Families at times, she also worked hard and at multiple jobs the entire time. She earned a professional job as a paralegal and manager. She was married to the father of all her children. He, too, worked multiple jobs and came home every night, although his help, according to his daughter, was primarily financial. And as heroic and self-sacrificing as she was, Angie was different from the stereotypical fictional figure of black women; she also knew how to pace her resources. She had to know when to let go. Angie said, "I am hurt every single time it happens. But you have to know when to toss in your chips, when to let them lie in the beds they make or die in them."

Angie's choices affected her daughter. Tasia's scholarship paid for a dorm room, but she took the train home on many weekends to help out. There was no regret in Tasia's voice or face, though. It was what it was and she could not leave her mother alone to take care of their family. She had long since stopped thinking of the other children as cousins. They were her sisters and brothers, and as the oldest girl, she was as responsible as her mother. Tasia was proud of her mother; she was just as proud of herself for being a college student. She was not the first child in the extended family to go to college, but she said that she would be the first to finish. Tasia wanted to be a doctor, a specialist, and often lugged a large bag of books on the train.

I see many black students, most of them women, going home on weekends or even during the week to help out. The university's statistics reveal that the more they do that, the harder their time at the university. It pulls them psychologically away from their work. It takes them away from the games and parties that ease the stress of college; they miss out on the study groups, extra library time. Like me when I was their age, they also opt out of the types of extracurricular activities that build résumés.

Tasia made me reconsider my own life history. When I was a junior in college, the president of the student body came to me and asked me to run for homecoming queen. At the University of North Carolina, Chapel Hill, the homecoming queen was a campuswide election, although most students either made a joke of it or did not bother to vote at all. I was active in student government and well known after a protracted affair that included the SGA Finance Committee freezing the funds of the Black Student Union when some funds went missing.

I was the only person both sides trusted to investigate. I discovered bad bookkeeping and eventually found all the missing money. The finance committee was slow to unfreeze the funds, though, and the BSU decided to march in protest. The march took a detour and stopped by my dorm. The BSU president called to my open first-floor window, and I looked outside to see a long line of black folks standing there, looking at me. But I had already done my part and I was studying for a test, so I was not happy when they persuaded me to come with them and bring the big book of financial records. The front page of the next day's *Daily Tar Heel* showed the head of a long line of marchers led by the BSU president and—so it appeared—me. I was scowling, thinking of the studying that I still needed to do. I looked like an Angry Black Woman leading a march. (Years later, I found that the Justice Department also had a copy of that photograph, and they thought so too.)

So, the SGA president—blond, idealistic, liberal, and already backed by an impressive political organization—said the homecoming thing was just the first step in his plan. He had decided that the following year was to be the year of the woman. I was the woman. The machine would back me for student body president. Homecoming would "soften" me in the eyes of the student body since they had all seen me looking so angry on the front page of the paper.

Now, I never was the queen type. I was a finalist to be the arts editor of the *Daily Tar Heel*, a route that had taken others directly to the *New York Times*. But he persisted: "All you have to do is to pose for one photograph and show up on homecoming day." It would be a practice run for the SGA election. If it worked, I would be the first woman SGA president *and* the first black. It was civil rights time.

He put together a coalition of his political student machine and black sorority women—AKAs *and* Deltas. It was one of the most amazing campaigns I have ever seen. Sam Fulwood, a journalism student who would later cover US presidential elections, took a photo of me that was printed on a poster and plastered all over campus. It was like living in a fun-house mirror—there were pictures of me everywhere, on every kiosk and bulletin board on campus. It worked and led to another photograph: this time of me and my boyfriend (who was smiling more than I was) waving to the homecoming crowd. The election of the first black homecoming queen at UNC drew the attention of Senator Jesse Helms, who told the Raleigh *News & Observer* that the "Flower of Southern Womanhood" had been spoiled. The statement provoked threats by some crazy-scary people, who took his quote as a call to action. But the coalition had worked. Everything was in place.

Then my sister called and told me that my mother had breast cancer. Our father had died of lung cancer when we were young, so "cancer" triggered overwhelming emotions in our family. All the children rushed home to Asheville, but my older sister and brother had jobs out of state. That left me. I notified the SGA that I would not be running for president. I asked the *Daily Tar Heel* to take me out of consideration. Of course, there were neighbors and church members who helped, but my mother was proud and private—there are some things that only family should do. Every Friday night, I drove the four hours home to her. Cancer has a particular smell, and my new goal was to leave my mother, her house, and her laundry free of it.

My nonblack friends were shocked, suggesting that my family was being unfair, even abusive. When I told them that nobody had asked me to drop out of the race, they looked at me as if I were from Mars. I had changed the course of my life, and they thought I was crazy.

My mother lived, healing so fast that the doctors used her for show-and-tell with other patients. I have no regrets. That is what we do.

The popular-culture image of the helping strong woman is an older woman, and grandmothers are central in many black families. Yet I also found helping black women of all ages, their help taking multi-generational paths. Daughters helped mothers, fathers, grandparents. Cousins helped aunts, uncles, and other cousins. Younger women struggled even more than I did to balance the heavier demands of their friends and families and their own life plans. It was expected of them.

Marie's family had come to the United States from the Caribbean more than twenty years earlier, yet she still carried out business and logistical planning for her family from three states away. When they traveled, she made the reservations; when business decisions were made, she got a deciding vote. When they bought a car, she went home to negotiate. She simultaneously respected and managed her parents. When friends needed her, she expanded her helping to non-family members, lending money she could not afford, taking late-night phone calls for advice. "It is hard, very hard," she said. She eventually began to totter under the load, hitting a wall when a friend who was mentally ill but not yet diagnosed began to increase her demands upon Marie. She cringed when her cell phone rang. Her friends suggested that she simply not answer. "I can't," she said. "What if she harms herself because I did not answer my cell phone?" As the other woman's illness spiraled, Marie lost sleep over her. Her work suffered.

She worried and stretched herself until her own friends forced her to stop, to realize her own limitations when the person she was trying to help was clinically ill. Afterward, she said she was in agony and still had trouble accepting that she had to cut the tie in order to save herself. "I help people. That is what I do. That is who I am," she said. "Because I am supposed to help people. I cannot accept that I can't help them. What does it mean if I have to abandon them? It means failure. It means I have failed. And I don't fail."

Her identity as a giver fits in with research that shows black people and black women in particular as different from mainstream Americans. The United States was born out of enlightenment thinking that emphasized individualism and free will. Most Americans whose families have been here for more than a few generations think of themselves as individuals first, with preservation of the individual self as their paramount concern. Researchers have found that African Americans' identities are often rooted in the "I/we," a sense of the group self rather than the individual "I" self of other Americans. Black children often score off the charts on altruism. While women of all races demonstrate concern for the collective, African American women said that their concern went to the core of their being. When black women told me they had no choice but to help, they meant it in two ways: that it was demanded of them and that they demanded it of themselves. Their very identity was on the line. So for the black women I interviewed, it was always all hands on deck in any capacity. Even when their own lives were comfortable enough for them to live without personal despera-tion, they remained on heightened states of alert; they worried about black men, black children. A young woman told me, "All I want to do is to help people." Every stitch of extra energy came into play or they paid with a guilt that could be paralyzing.

The women I spoke to carried themselves with stoicism, but they were aware when they were overgiving and how it contributed to their own suffering. Marie was able to cut it off because the person she helped was not a close friend or family. Another woman found that cutting off family was much more difficult.

Tania was a thirty-year-old woman from New York who lived alone and was busily working to establish her career. She looked as if she had no family responsibilities, but she had them—lots of them. She continued to take on the problems of her sister, her brother, her parents. Like Marie, she had taken on the problems of her parents at a particularly early age. She was not only the doting aunt, she was the responsible aunt. When she was not with her family, she worried about them, so it was actually less stressful to work to find solutions for their problems.

Tania was the most introspective young woman I interviewed, and so she was able to talk about the psychological costs of helping her family and about her resistance to recognizing and treating her own clinical depression. She said, "There is never a moment when I'm not thinking about someone else. . . . I was always the shoulder—they didn't know about boundaries. I was a walking sofa." The balancing act was hard. It became too much. Her work suffered, as did her emotional well-being, but even for this single black woman, family came first. She said, "I work so hard for other people." Still, she thought, rest was not an option. She considered fatigue to be weakness, an adversary to be conquered. "Don't say you're tired—that gives my fatigue more power. It's not giving air time to your weakness."

Her work also required her to be a professional giver, to be a one-woman human resources department, available to support the people who worked under her. But she noticed that much of her work was taken for granted. She felt that she was "working like a dog and not getting any recognition. . . . I was always the friend to help, to take the extra. That's what I do. I have a feeling of obligation to help people." She recognized that she was not being as kind to herself as she was to other people. "I have a hard time with bouts of being overwhelmed," she acknowledged. She slowly realized that she was depressed. As for many black people, it was not an easy self-discovery. Her self-image as a Strong Black Woman prevented her from recognizing her own depression.

She was afraid of appearing weak or sad, for herself and for others, because they seemed to depend so much on her good cheer. "They don't want you to be sad. . . . You are supposed to dig yourself out of it. You have space to be sad for a moment and then you are supposed to pray about it and move on. If you need to cry, cry. Or use laughter to deflect it. I use humor, I do."

"I want to be strong but not at the expense of my health."

She struggled to learn how to be vulnerable. "It's okay to feel vulnerable, but don't feel vulnerable too long."

She was forced to see her own limitations when one of her employees was killed on-site. She was left to deal with police, the family, and traumatized fellow employees. "As someone who lives by commitment, I can't walk away. . . .

I was so overwhelmed. My supervisor said, 'I know you're taking two days off, right?' I was forced to do it for self-preservation. I went to see a friend who is a chaplain. It was nice to have someone else to listen to me."

Subsequent therapy helped her to talk, but she continued to struggle with the expectations of her family and friends. She struggled most with the expectations she still had for herself.

"You are going down a road to hurt yourself. But it was already ingrained." She described the effort as trying to turn back the tide. "I see this as almost rewriting my DNA. . . . I feel like I was punished for not being selfish. I feel bad saying that. Even now I'm more of a caretaker and giver. . . . I live by obligation and commitment."

Although she had managed to "say no to other people's problems," it was still very hard. "I would feel bad. You see that somebody needs help and you don't help them? Then what kind of person are you? Selfish and unfeeling. It is what you are supposed to do. . . . It is a foreign concept that I am trying to adapt. Helping people is already ingrained in me. . . . It feels like I am trying to redirect the tide. It is really hard." She eventually learned that her friends, rather than her family, will let her lean on *them*. "My friends say that you can lean on us. I don't really have a choice. . . . Otherwise, the result is cracking up."

Black women demand stoicism of one another. A white lesbian moved with her family into Pimlico, a black neighborhood near the famous race course where the second leg of the Triple Crown is run. Determined to be a member of the community, she came to be friends with the black women in the neighborhood. She and her family were accepted because they were approved of and protected by the matriarch of Pimlico.

When the mother of a neighbor died, the woman and her white partner did as the other neighborhood women did, as black women all over the country do. They went to the house, taking food to feed the family. In the kitchen, the grieving woman—already older herself—was surrounded by other black women, who were telling her to be strong, to hold herself together. The two white women sat and ate with the others, and when they rose to leave, the bereaved woman asked them to wait, saying she would walk them out. Several times she asked them to wait. When the three women reached the porch, out of sight of the other black women, the grieving woman fell into the arms of the younger white woman, crying, heaving, finally giving herself over to her sadness. Her neighbor held her and let her cry. We have to ask, why was it so important that she be strong? What did it mean to her and to the other women for her to hold up and hold in?

Can we cry only away from other black women? What does it cost us to hold so much in?

Black women are supposed to be stoic in much the same way that men are traditionally supposed to be stoic, and for precisely the same reasons: If we break down, it is a strong signal that something is very, very wrong. Stoicism can be taken to extremes, as when black women "allow" men to beat them so the men can feel like men at the expense of the women's bodies. The data is mixed about whether black women are more or less likely to experience domestic violence—self-report is often unwieldy—but when they do, they are more likely to die from it, because black women fight back.

Domestic violence can take on a different meaning in black relationships. Black men live in a patriarchal society, surrounded by images of Western male power that still teach them that masculinity should come with power over *somebody*. The lesson is that to be a man they must dominate. The conditions of black men's lives mean that they are less likely to live and work in positions in which they have the kind of power that they see in the larger culture. The men know it and the women know it. Black women say they would "starve" if they depended solely on men. Traditionally, male power has been seized rather than given, but without the economic or political power of white men, black men have not been able to seize power in their families. They look to black women to hand it over. Black women are told that they should "let men be men" and "pretend that they are in charge" rather than admitting to shared power. Some enter into the charade, but the odd patriarchy on the backs of working women ill serves black men and women. The situation of black women has traps, areas that they must navigate in order to survive, emotionally and physically.

When it was widely reported that singer Chris Brown had beaten fellow artist and girlfriend, Rihanna, a young black woman told National Public Radio that "it happens all the time."

Abuse can even follow black women into professional work spaces. In 2007, Isiah Thomas of the New York Knicks said in court that he did not consider black men calling black women "bitches" to be as much of a problem as white men calling them the same name. Knicks former executive Anucha Browne Sanders, a black woman, was suing the Knicks organization because she said she was dismissed after complaining about unwanted sexual advances and name-calling. Thomas said that he was sorry but that he made a distinction; black men got to call black women "bitches." The claim seemed preposterous in the mainstream culture, but not so much in black circles. The court did not agree.

Black women are expected to protect black men from exposure to the justice system. Browne Sanders's expected cultural role *was* to take it. Black women are expected to move past wrongs that have been done to them. "Forgiveness" may be too formal a word for it. They are supposed to either overlook it or get over it. Black women are assumed to do to themselves what the culture has done to them—dismiss their pain and go on. The same expectation arose for Anita Hill with Clarence Thomas and for Desiree Washington with Mike Tyson. When Mike Tyson sexually assaulted Desiree Washington, a young beauty contestant, the response of many callers to black radio was to ask what she was doing with him that late at night. Black women are supposed to be so resilient that they are like the old Timex watch commercials: They take a licking and keep on ticking. It is a strange respect, because often it does not come with better treatment. If black men consider black women to be able to take anything, does that create an invitation to do anything to them?

I know how it feels to be pressured to protect a black man who has harmed you. Flashback to the 1970s, one of the most volatile periods in American life. After the assassination of Martin Luther King, black and white liberal communities longed for a new black male leader, with life-changing implications for black girls. This is my story.

"Oooh!"

Reaction crackled around me before the teacher could finish reading the note: "—to the principal's office."

Sharon, sitting in the next chair, leaned in close, loudly whispering, "Wha'd you do?"

"Nothing."

She leaned back, appraising me. "I believe it."

It was true.

I'd been to the office, many times, but not like this. I was one of the "it" students, the ones who could walk the hall without passes because we were so often on official school business. The school had survived the initial shock of court-ordered integration, but the white administrators still needed black student leaders to explain situations they did not understand, giving us access and influence. Asheville, North Carolina, was one of the most liberal cities in the South, maybe because the city had fewer black people to be liberal about. With its steeply sloped mountains and hard clay soil, there had been few farms big enough to have many slaves. Old Marxists left from the once famous Black

Mountain School and the growing artists' colony added the strong liberal streak. It was a heady time to be one of the black chosen. We were president of this, chosen for that, smiling and waving from the homecoming court. Public organizations and corporations, looking for fresh-faced images of racial progress, had become interested in us. I was a Southern Bell management intern, a Sears Teen Board member, and the first teenage board member of the first integrated YWCA in the South. The mayor's office gave us grants to throw Christmas parties for poor black children. Local education reporters had our telephone numbers. We thought we really were the walking embodiment of W. E. B. Du Bois's Talented Tenth.

Our own principal leaned on us for help, and we knew him better than we might have otherwise. So why was he pulling me out of class like a criminal?

Mr. B. was sitting not in the big chair behind his desk but in a regular chair against the wall. The furniture had been rearranged. He motioned that I should sit in another chair against the other wall. I knew what it was meant to say. Casual but distant.

"I suppose you're wondering why I sent for you." I nodded. He continued, "Well, I understand that you and X. broke up." News traveled fast. The principal of a high school with fifteen hundred students was asking about my boyfriend troubles. I guess I should have been surprised, but I wasn't. The boy was valuable: class president, football and baseball captain. *Parade* magazine All Star Team; accelerated classes. Closing in on two hundred pounds, he was both literally and figuratively the biggest black man on campus. He had adult fans. White businessmen followed his stats. Behind our backs they called us Beauty and the Beast.

Mr. B. went on: "Well, he's very unhappy, and we need him to be happy just now. Not only for the game but, you know, he's got the Morehead interview coming up."

"I had my reasons," I said.

"Yes, I know, I understand."

What did he know? How had my business gotten all the way to the principal's office so quickly? It was Monday. We had just returned from Chapel Hill and the University of North Carolina's Merit Scholars Weekend, where the college tried to recruit the state's top black students, urging us to apply early decision before other schools knew who we were. Most of us were planning to go there anyway, but it didn't hurt to be courted. Five of us went down for a taste of college life, staying in the dorms and going to our first party at the Black Student Union. X. and I were the only couple among the five, so the others were looking forward to the party more than I was because I wouldn't be looking at any college men.

But some of the college men looked at me, and that was when the trouble started. X. rode up in the elevator of the high-rise dorm with two upperclassmen who had already scoped out the potential incoming class of women, mentally sorting through them. They got to me. "That one from Asheville, with the long hair and the body, is going to be talking to an upperclassman." X. interrupted them; "But she's my girlfriend." The two college men didn't see him as much of an obstacle and laughed. "I don't care who she is with now; when she comes here, she's going to be talking to an upperclassman." In their eyes, he was an incoming freshman, a nobody who had just been told that he was about to lose his girlfriend.

It was more than he could bear. When he saw me, he told me what the college men had said. I could see that he was scared. I told him it didn't matter what other people said I was going to do, that I would decide. I meant it to be reassuring, but his tone turned hard. He told me that I wasn't going to the party that night. I looked at him, tossed my head, and said, "What do you mean? I'm going to the party." He answered by slapping me, only once, but hard enough to propel me clear across the room, and it left a well-defined, hand-shaped bruise on my cheek. It worked. I ran to the room where my friend was and stayed there, too embarrassed to go out.

The next day we drove the four hours back home, everyone in a tense and embarrassed silence. As soon as I got safely back to my own house, I broke up with him. Still harboring some protectiveness for him, I did not tell my mother why.

Black mothers tell their daughters what to do if a man ever hits them: Wait until he is asleep and try your best to kill him. The methods change according to the region. In the South, you're supposed to throw grits or hit him in the head with a cast-iron pan. My mother would laugh as she told us, so I knew she was partly kidding, but I also knew she was partly serious. If nothing else, the joke emotionally rehearses the possibility of abuse. I would not have to retaliate; my mother had taught in a school up the street from the projects. The little boys she had cradled and taught to read had grown up, but they remembered her. The community saint had dangerous and loyal friends. She would not even have to ask. So I kept quiet and covered the bruise with makeup. Black women protect even those who hurt them.

Now I was in the principal's office. He seemed to know the whole story already.

The Morehead scholarship was the most prestigious in the state, at the time open to men only. The standards were both high and wide—in addition to grades and scores, the man had to letter in several varsity sports and be a high-level student officer and team leader. X. had it all, plus a sweet black-man charm, and already the word was that he was going to be one of the first black boys to get it. It would be a step in racial uplift, a civil-rights jewel, and excitement was building across the city. He had only the interview to go.

But now he was unhappy, and I was supposed to fix it.

"We would very much appreciate it if you would go back with him." There was a trace of an awkward smile. He was getting nervous. It was clear, even to me, that the principal was on an errand, under pressure to get me back with the program. I already knew who "we" were. The black middle class and the white liberals were already writing the press releases. The publisher of the newspaper, members of the school board, black teachers, ministers, doctors, and undertakers, all waiting. My bruised cheek was standing between them and their fondest wish.

"You know, we think he is going to be the next Martin Luther King." That, of course, would make me Coretta. Second, devoted to him and to the cause, because they were one and the same. Nobody had asked me how I felt about my part. Everybody involved knew that I had better grades, better scores, more awards, but that didn't matter. I was a female, and the next Martin Luther King had to be a man.

The principal began to lecture me on my duty to my people. Even then, the spectacle of a white man pushing me to sacrifice myself for the betterment of my people was not lost on me. I was the companion horse. In racing, the thoroughbred is fast but skittish. To keep the racer calm, he is paired with a companion horse, one who is steadier, stronger. The two horses usually move to the starting gate together, side by side; often, the thoroughbred walks with his head tucked into the other horse's neck. But only the thoroughbred runs the race and gets the glory. X. was the project. Everyone assumed that I would be OK no matter what.

There are limits to power, and the principal could not actually force me go back with X. But it also was clear I was not going to be excused until he got something out of me, so I negotiated a deal. I would keep quiet about the violence and the breakup, allowing everyone to save face, until after the interview. Mr. B. did not like it, but it was all he was going to get.

It didn't work.

X. was still distracted, more focused on getting back with me than he was on the scholarship. His own family life was chaotic and unreliable. His father was a distant memory, and his mother lived in Charlotte, two hours away, leaving him with his grandmother and step-grandfather. Their relationship was volatile, sometimes violent. When X. would have to step in to defend his grandmother, his grandfather would throw him out for being disrespectful.

I had taken responsibility for him; I gave him lunch money and got my mother to buy his class ring to keep up appearances. I had bought into the romantic idea of the man as a project, but sometimes it felt too close, too much. I had broken up with him twice before because I felt crowded. Each time I was persuaded to take him back, by friends and once by a black female guidance counselor. He had grown dependent on me, and when I was no longer there, he lost his footing. He appeared at my door, saying that his grandfather had put him out again and he had no place to go. My mother still didn't know about the slap. We put some sheets in my brother's bedroom. I told him that this was one last favor; the next day, he would have to find somewhere else.

That night he came into my room. I awoke to see him standing over me. A little light filtered into the room from a streetlamp, and I could see his expression. It was an odd, determined look, as if he had a job to do. I told him to leave. "I'll call my mama."

"You don't want to do that," he said, slipping into the bed. "I don't want to hurt her, but I will if you call for her or scream." Because he had already hurt me, I believed him. I understood that this was an act of violence, that he intended to conquer me, to break my spirit. If he couldn't have love, submission would do, just as long as I did not leave him.

I turned my face away, toward the window, and I found that was something I could do, even in that awful moment. I heard a train whistle, miles away, as the train crawled across a street intersection. I willed my spirit away with it, hopping a car as the train sped up and into the darkness, leaving only a shell of me to him. That night, I learned how dangerous a desperate person could be, even one who says he loves you.

When he was finished, he seemed to expect me to be different, subdued, obedient, conquered. Of course I was different, irrevocably different, but not in the way he expected or in any way I was about to let him see. Instead, a strength I did not know I had began to gather up in me.

"Are you done?" I asked, as sarcastically as I could muster. He looked a bit confused.

"Then leave," I said. He left.

And again I did not tell my mother, this time in order to protect her.

In the days after, X. continued to press for a reunion, and as I continued to refuse, he played his trump card. He found my best friend. He seemed distraught and told her before I did that he had raped me, and seemed ready to harm himself. Then he disappeared.

After he disappeared, his supporters started searching for him, quietly, without notifying the police, without doing anything that might attract attention or reach the Morehead committee. The blame fell on me. He was missing and it was my fault. He was messing up the Morehead scholarship and it was my fault. He was somewhere dead in a ditch and it was my fault. The whole of this boy's life had become my responsibility. I lay on my bed, my legs folded to my chest, listening to my mother on the phone, telling people to leave me alone. She still didn't know everything, but she knew that she had to defend me against her friends and the community.

Then suddenly he appeared on my doorstep, angry and demanding to see me. I wanted to stay by her, but my mother locked me in my room. She told him he would have to go through her first. I was afraid for her. I knew my mother was strong, but I also knew he was crazy. I heard a long moment of standoff. She held her ground. He backed down and went away.

The next morning Mama and I had to figure out where I would be safe. Home was out. All the neighbors worked, and the middle-class street was too quiet. We decided that I should be out in the crowded openness of school; she drove me there.

It was a good plan but not good enough. X. was already there. He jacked me up against my locker. A black woman looked out from my nearby homeroom and shut the door. His hand wrapped around my neck. "I'm going to kill you."

Fortunately some people heard us. A friend—one of the boys who had gone to UNC with us—tried to distract him. A white male teacher came out of his classroom, and the two of them tried to pull me away. X. twisted my arm behind my back like a pretzel, holding my wrist and my neck in one hand, still choking me. The two sides played tug of war with my body until I blacked out. Witnesses later told me that X. stepped back and said, "My God, I've killed her." When I came to, someone pulled me to my feet and made me run as they restrained him. The dean of girls locked me in her office.

There would be no police, no charges, even though there was an officer assigned to the school. Nobody called my mother or would let me call her. X. spent the rest of the day in the protection of the principal's office as they attempted damage control. I spent the rest of the day in the library, out in the open and on display. "Your mother would be upset. You don't want to ruin his life," a female faculty member told me.

When we looked into pressing charges, a neighbor—a police detective—said that nobody would believe that I had been raped. "The whole town saw you and him smiling and waving on that homecoming float." When we reminded them that there had been a very public attempted murder, we also met resistance, told over and over again not to make too big a thing of it.

We realized that we had no official help and bargained for psychiatric treatment in lieu of charges. But that compromise was not even the end of it. The therapist called and said that he needed me to come to the appointments if X. was to get better. This time, I finally stepped completely out of my assigned role. "I guess he won't get better," I said. We got a restraining order.

As it turned out, he lost the scholarship anyway. Someone leaked the story to the Morehead committee, which quickly withdrew its interest. That was my fault too. The full force of the town's disappointment was directed toward me. Although hope in him was fading, it was not dead, incredibly. More than once I was reminded, "We are still hoping that he will be the next Martin Luther King, you know." He left town when some of my mother's former students suggested that would be best.

It was not the last time I would be asked to sacrifice my self-respect in order to support a black man with great potential. In college, I broke up with my medical-school-student boyfriend (who had been told *he* was the next MLK) after he cheated on me and lied about it. I was summoned to the medical-school offices by the only black faculty member there, a physical therapist. She said he was a "blue chipper"—valuable stock—and that the medical-school dean had high hopes for him. When he failed an exam for the first time, they asked him what was wrong and he told them that I had left him. She asked me to go back with him as a favor to the dean. I asked her respectfully to convey to the dean that the "blue chipper" would have to succeed on his own. She looked taken aback at my answer. She could not know how long I had practiced it.

When they are mistreated, black women are supposed to forgive. Theirs is to be the forgiveness of mothers toward their children: It does not have to be requested, it is just given.

Coretta King reportedly forgave James Earl Ray, who had been convicted of murdering her husband, and spoke out against the death penalty for him and others. Audiences remember her dignified mourning face and think that she was quiet and docile. But they do a disservice to Coretta if they leave her memory as the docile and faithful wife of a great leader, if the woman she was remains hidden behind her veil of widowhood.

In the decades after his assassination, black and white people in towns and cities across America groomed a legion of new Martin Luther Kings. I am married to one from Dallas. I have met black women from coast to coast who were also cast as the next Coretta, often with stories eerily similar to mine, in which they were taught to underplay their own ambitions and accomplishments, to excuse inexcusable behavior, to hide abuses. We were smart, we were leadership material ourselves, but we were all expected to step back and to take on the responsibility for whatever young black men did around us or to us, to sacrifice ourselves to the dream of the next Black Male Leader.

Actually, even Coretta was more than the myth about her. As a child, Coretta already hoped to help the cause of racial justice. The details of her life expose a tension between the life of the woman and the icon. She won a scholarship in voice and violin to the New England Conservatory of Music in Boston, where she met Martin. To perform at that level demands more than docility, and she gave up a promising career to work for civil rights. The Kings, both Coretta and Martin, operated in the ways that were most strategic for their time. Coretta was herself very concerned with the movement—she was not just supporting her husband.

She showed a strength that we do not focus on. She persevered through the death threats and brought her children along so that they could spend time with their father, because they did not know how much time he had left. She was the first woman to deliver the Class Day address at Harvard University and the first woman to preach during a service at St. Paul's Cathedral in London.

Four days after her husband's assassination, she led a march through the streets of Memphis and later that year took his place as a leader of the Poor People's March on Washington. She was founder, president, chair, and chief executive of the million-dollar MLK Jr. Center for Nonviolent Social Change and pushed successfully for MLK Jr. Day to be signed into law during the conservative Reagan administration. The British *Guardian* called the battle to establish the holiday "ugly," with conservatives bringing up FBI evidence of King's infidelities. Coretta King also expanded the message of civil justice to include gay, lesbian, bisexual, and transgender people and AIDS awareness, and she responded forcefully against black ministers who promoted a homophobic message invoking her husband.

Coretta King was a black feminist. In June 1968, she made a speech on Solidarity Day calling for a "solid block of woman power" to fight racism, poverty, and war. In 1974 she formed a coalition of more than one hundred church, labor, business, and women's organizations to campaign for full employment. She took on big business, criticizing media and game and toy industries for promoting violence, and called for regulation of their ability to advertise. In other words, even Coretta was not the public Coretta, the docile and subordinate wife. We have separated her from the brutality and nastiness, the arrests and death threats of that time. She had emotions that we do not associate with her—she could be angry or funny. Her daughters, actress Yolanda and Baptist minister Bernice, have become public figures in their own right, neither silent nor docile. Coretta died in 2006, having never remarried, which, in keeping with the myth, is often interpreted in romantic terms. Maybe by not remarrying she was more ordinary than most would think; most black women never remarry.

The role of the Strong Black Woman as many women live it requires a measure of physical self-abuse. Dr. Angela Neal-Barnett writes that many black women have earned the title of Strong Black Woman because of their ability and determination to rise against daunting odds. "Many women who see themselves as Strong Black Women will keep on keeping on even when they know they should stop."

Black women pay with their health. When they keep responsibility for all that is around them yet place themselves behind black men, they expose themselves to the most dangerous type of stress—responsibility without top-level control. Stress and fatigue exact their tolls. The health problems of black women are well documented, and they are often unknowingly tied to poor health care. Yet, on average, African American women take *more* preventive measures than women of any other race—more tests for high blood pressure, diabetes, more mammograms, according to the Department of Health and Human Services. Yet, they still get sick and die at higher rates. The women I spoke to had taken on overwhelming responsibilities because they felt that they had to, but they did allow themselves to stop long enough to think about it.

Black women handle stress differently than men or white women. Men tend to battle the source of the stress. White women are more likely to "tend and befriend." Black women are likely to "tend, befriend, mend, and keep it in." They double up on roles—the caregiver and the fixer. The role requires a sort of silence, about what they've seen, about whom they've helped, or even about how they feel. But we hold it in, suck it up, and go on.

Dr. Neal-Barnett conducted a study in which self-identified Strong Black Women kept diaries of their activities and emotions for a day while their blood pressures and heart rates were being monitored. She found that almost all the women were unaware of or did not admit to being stressed, even when their physical readings jumped fifteen and twenty points, indicating that their bodies were responding to stress. They told her, "Baby, I don't have time to think about that mess. If I did, I'd be stressed out about everything." But stress does not stop taking its toll on their bodies just because they don't acknowledge it. Refusing to acknowledge stress actually makes them *more* susceptible to stress-related illnesses—chronic upper-respiratory infections, hypertension, heart disease, and obesity. They cannot address what they will not admit in the first place. Many women take better care of their families than they do of themselves—but black women take it further.

Neal-Barnett said, "In the minds of many Blacks and Whites, a weak Black woman simply does not exist. Rather than being seen as less than she is supposed to be, a Strong Black Woman refuses to admit she is stressed and keeps her feelings and emotions bottled up inside while she helps everyone else"—making her more prone to anxiety.

Black women imperil their safety and their lives to protect the people they love. Too many times, a black woman's willingness to "kill or die" for her people results in her own death. It did for Angela Dawson, who lived in a working-class neighborhood in East Baltimore.

Angela was a busy, happy woman, the type who took in other people's children, who helped in any way she could. She had had enough of the drugs. The dealers were selling right in front of her house, and her children had to walk past them to get home. She confronted the dealers, asked them to leave. She called the police, many times—by one report thirty-six times. The police helped, but not enough. The dealers threatened to kill her and her family and vandalized her house over and over. The police offered to relocate the family, but Angela was not moving, even after the first firebombing, which did some damage but hurt no one. Two weeks later, though, on the night of October 16, 2002, a young black man kicked in the door and threw gasoline on the floor and the stairway. The neighbors heard her screaming, "God, please help me. Help me get my children out." The fire that killed Angela, her husband, Carnell, and five children was so hot that all that was left of her house was half of a charred shell. Neighbors whispered that the arsonist was working for the local drug dealers. He firebombed Angela Dawson's house to keep her quiet.

After her death, four hundred neighbors, the same ones who had left her to fight the drug dealers alone, found enough nerve to rally in the street. The

Baltimore Sun and the *Washington Post* wrote articles for months. Politicians scrambled. Mayor Martin O'Malley, who was thinking about a run for governor, told the *Post*, "This is our moment of crisis." A year later, in her name, the city had doubled its drug-treatment program and the state had assigned 150 additional state troopers and 75 more parole officers. Serious crime was dramatically reduced.

But in January 2005, in another Baltimore neighborhood, Edna McAbier's house was firebombed. Same story: She was a community activist who was fighting the drug dealers. She was elderly and highly visible as the president of her community association, but she still became an informant to a policeman she trusted. Neighbors who were afraid to talk passed her notes, which she passed to the policemen. This time it was the Bloods who wanted her dead, a contract that everybody took seriously. She survived, but she could never live in her house again. Michelle Blue, a younger activist, took up the struggle for her and Edna's neighborhood. She and Edna had been loose partners of a sort. Michelle said, "I'm missing that passion. We didn't agree on every issue, but I knew she wasn't going away." But the streets started to fill up again with drug markets, and threats against Michelle began.

Why do black women think they can take on drug dealers on their own? What is it about the women and their culture that puts them on the front lines? So many black women identify with their position on the front lines that the nationally recognized pastor Juanita Bynum calls her popular seminars "Women on the Front Line."

The weight of the role is so onerous that some women are rejecting it. A college professor who blogs under the name Mad Kenyan Woman argues that the Strong Black Woman is a terrifying "scam perpetuated on black women by the rest of the world" and that as long as we believe it "there is no amount of pure nonsense, abuse, overwork, ingratitude, exploitation, underappreciation, and just plain shit that we will not put up with."

She shows the complexity of her feelings because she also admires the women, like her own mother, who are strong and giving. It is not unusual to despise the popular image because it is one-sided, co-opted, but then to praise the dark women who fight, endure, and love. In another blog, she writes of the women of her native Kenya who are brave and resilient enough to organize out in the open despite losing their husbands, sons, and often everything they own to the fighting. But Mad Kenyan Woman believes that black women should resist the call to be always perfectly brave and resilient. She calls on others to stop depending so much on the black women to whom so much is already owed, and she says out loud a heartbreaking truth that maybe even some black women do not want exposed:

> Do you know how much CRAP that woman has had to go through? . . . Have you ever thought that they accomplished them not BECAUSE of some spurious "extra" strength but despite the weaknesses common to us all? I've thought of my own mother, whom I have idolized my whole life, because she did just amazing things. . . . How often do I ask myself if she was ever frightened, insecure, confused, lost? How often do I ask if she ever yearned for opportunities lost, regretted decisions made, missed absent friends? The answer to that would be "once." Today. Because before today, she was just absolutely perfect and pristine. Before today I would have reacted to such a suggestion of human failings and fears in MY mother with snorting and indignant incredulity—except I realized how wrong that would be.

Many black women enjoy the image of the Strong Black Woman. It is a source of pride and strength. Every woman I interviewed said that they felt both responsibility and honor in their association with their roles. Is it possible at this point to admit that they are human? I asked black men what would happen if black women just stopped doing all that they do. Even I was surprised at how disturbing it was for them to seriously consider the suggestion. "They would never do that" was the most common answer. When I pushed, the answer was usually the same. The one man who did give a real answer said, "Then it would be over. It would be all over for us. Black people would not survive it." Then he added, "But they would never do that, would they?" When I asked black women the same question, I was struck by how often they smiled. They answered in the same way, that they would never stop, that they felt they could not stop, but they said it was a nice fantasy, because they were tired.

The images of the Strong Black Woman as Interested Stranger or the Devoted Familiar leaves the power with the person who needs her. Usually, neediness works the other way, to weaken the needy, but black women have traditionally handed over control. Black women deserve to be safe and left to the freedom of our own hearts. It is time for them to save themselves. Black feminist scholar Patricia Hill Collins called on black women to move toward self-determination. The first step is self-recognition, to see themselves as worthy as the world sees them to be. First, black women have to recognize themselves, to admit out loud and in public what they do and who they are. When they hesitate, they leave a void that others fill according to their own needs. They have to *imagine* themselves in the way that Toni Morrison has called for black people to imagine, to envision themselves. She does not mean to make something up that does not exist but to see past all the societal structures that get in the way of something that belongs with them. They will have to figure out a way to be in control of their own lives, their images, and their energies. They will have to belong to themselves. They will have to find a space between bragging and self-recognition.

They will have to address the images that teach people to use them in ways that are unhealthy. The rich image of the Sacred Dark Feminine should be a source of strength, but the co-optation is dangerous. The Dark Feminine has been embraced the world over, and so black women cannot just take it over. But they can and should participate with it.

In a 1971 interview with Alice Walker, Coretta Scott King said, "The black woman has a special role to play. Our heritage of suffering and our experience in having to struggle against all odds to raise our children gives us a greater capacity for understanding both suffering and the need and meaning of compassion. We have, I think, a kind of stamina, a determination which makes us strong."

Angela Dawson and Coretta Scott King and the thousands of women before and after them had something special. Whether it was a gift of the goddess or forged in the suffering of their lives, black women have preserved and practiced a type of female strength that has been true to the lives of women as they lived them, a type of female strength that has kept them and their families alive when everything else was working against them. It has cost them plenty, too much, but now black women have enough hindsight and power to balance their lives, to pace their energies and the demands so they do not die of exhaustion or abuse.

Black women deserve the consideration and care they have been giving to everyone else. At the conclusion of an open letter she wrote during the 2008 presidential campaign, Alice Walker quoted the end of a poem by her friend, the late black female poet June Jordan, whose line she took for the title of her book *We Are the Ones We Have Been Waiting For*. It is time for black women to save themselves.

Making a Way
Out of No Way

"You already know how."
—Eleanor Holmes Norton

MARIA ROACH DID not know Sybrina Fulton before the spring of 2012, before Trayvon Martin was killed. Sybrina was the mother of Trayvon, the seventeen-year-old boy from Miami Gardens, Florida, who was shot while walking down the sidewalk of Sanford, Florida, outside of Orlando. Martin had gone out to buy candy and a drink and was walking to meet his father. He was followed by George Zimmerman, a self-appointed neighborhood watch patrolman with a gun. Trayvon ended up dead but Zimmerman was not arrested, claiming protection from arrest due to Florida's "Stand Your Ground" law. The story was not picked up by the media. Martin's body languished in a morgue.

But the Internet started to buzz, particularly on black websites such as The Root, and that is where Maria Roach, a Maryland mother of a seven-year-old son, felt the connection. She had grown up in the same Florida area. Trayvon looked like a future version of her own young son. She couldn't sleep the morning of Saint Patrick's Day, tossing and turning with frustration. She decided she had to do something, so she logged on to MoveOn.org, where she had been a member since 2008.

She wrote:

Dear MoveOn member,

Seventeen-year-old Trayvon Martin was shot and killed while walking home from a convenience store on the evening of February 26. The shooter, George Zimmerman, was the neighborhood watch captain. Zimmerman, a 200-pound 28-year-old with a history of violence, claimed self-defense, even though Trayvon Martin had no criminal history and nothing more than candy and an iced tea in his hands.

It's a deep injustice that George Zimmerman remains free. That's why I created a petition on SignOn.org to Florida Attorney General Pam Bondi and U.S. Attorney General Eric Holder, which says:

> George Zimmerman's shooting of Trayvon Martin, an African American teenager, reveals a history of racism in Sanford, Florida, that has stubbornly refused to die. Weeks after the shooting, the Sanford police department is slow to release details of the shooting and, more surprisingly, has not arrested George Zimmerman, a man who has a history of violence.

> We urge you to sign this petition to protect private citizens from gun violence and inept law enforcement. Florida's Attorney General Pam Bondi must step in and provide justice for Trayvon Martin, his family, and the community. Will you sign the petition? Click here to add your name, and then pass it along to your friends.

She shared the link with her two hundred followers on Twitter. She thought she'd get a hundred signatures. She got more than half a million.

Rallies and vigils for Trayvon, hundreds of them, were held around the country. Attorney General Eric Holder initiated a Justice Department investigation. NBA players and other celebrities posted photographs of themselves wearing hoodies with the hoods pulled up, the way Trayvon was wearing his in the rain, which Zimmerman had said made him look "suspicious." The media took note. Trayvon's mother, Sybrina Fulton, and his father, Tracy Martin, appeared on the *Today Show* and other national programs. They were remarkably even in their remarks, surviving the media firestorm around them. George Zimmerman went into hiding. He was charged in mid-April and taken into custody. Sybrina Fulton quickly broadened her message to include the mothers of other fallen black boys. She spoke at emotional church services around the country. Her mother, aunt, and sister sometimes joined her. The *Washington Post* reported:

> As Trayvon Martin's mother stood at the altar of Baltimore's Empowerment Temple on Sunday, the Rev. Jamal-Harrison Bryant asked for anyone whose child had also been the victim of "senseless violence" to come forward. At least a dozen women and men assembled at Sybrina Fulton's feet before she stepped down to grab one of them. She squeezed the woman, patted her back and whispered in her ear. Then Fulton moved down the line, tightly embracing each mother, grandmother and father, each of them too familiar with loss, until she'd touched them all.
>
> Congregants erupted into deafening applause and brushed away tears.

Fulton took the dais to a standing ovation. Bryant called her "the mother of the new civil rights movement" and "this generation's Rosa Parks."

"It's so easy for me to cry right now, but I can't because I have work to do," she told the congregation. "I was forced into this position, but I believe God is using me."

Sybrina showed an enormous grace and compassion when she took a moment to say that she knew the Zimmermans were hurting too.

Repeatedly, on rally signs and in the media, Trayvon Martin has been called the Emmett Till of this generation. The story of Emmett Till is well known. The role his mother played in bringing his murder to light is less so. In 1955, Emmett was a fourteen-year-old boy, raised in Chicago, who had gone to visit his great-uncle in Money, Mississippi. He and some friends visited a store and purchased candy, where court witnesses say that Emmett paid for his candy and placed the money in the white woman's hand—rather than the counter, as was the local racial custom. He was also accused of wolf whistling at her, but this part has remained in dispute. Three days later, the woman's male relatives heard the story and kidnapped Emmett, killing him and mutilating his body.

Another three days later, Emmett Till's corpse was pulled from the Tallahatchie River with a seventy-five-pound cotton gin fan tethered to his neck with barbed wire. The sheriff tried to bury his body in Mississippi, without notice to his relatives back home, without witnesses or ceremony. His mother, Mamie Till-Mobley, had been lobbying state officials for days for a writ of court to gain possession of her son's body, and she obtained it just three hours before the planned secret burial. Upon releasing Emmett's body, the sheriff ordered the casket padlocked and sealed with the Mississippi state seal, prohibiting its being opened. Once the body arrived in Chicago, funeral home director A. A. Rayner intended to obey the sheriff's order, but Mamie demanded a hammer. She said, "I need to see my son." She described examining her son's body:

> I decided that I would start with his feet, gathering strength as I went up. I paused at his mid-section, because I knew that he would not want me looking at him. But I saw enough to know that he was intact. I kept on up until I got to his chin. Then I was forced to deal with his face. I saw that his tongue was choked out. The right eye was lying midway of his chest. His nose had been broken like someone took a meat chopper and broke his nose in several places. I kept looking and I saw a hole, which I presumed was a bullet hole, and I could look through that hole and see daylight on the other side. I wondered, "Was it necessary to shoot him"?

> The funeral director advised against an open casket.

> "Mr. Rayner," she said, asked me, "Do you want me to touch the body up?" I said, "No. Let the people see what I have seen. I think everybody needs to know what had happened to Emmett Till."

Reportedly more than fifty thousand people attended the funeral. *Jet* magazine published a picture of the disfigured corpse. The story was picked up by media around the world. Two men were acquitted of Till's murder and kidnapping in less than an hour of deliberation, by an all-white male jury, even though they had admitted to the kidnapping. After the trial, they also admitted to the murder to *Look* magazine. Two photographs of Emmett Till—one taken by his mother the Christmas before, showing a charming child with an innocent smile and beautiful eyes, well-dressed in a suit, tie, and hat, and the one of him dead and mutilated taken by *Jet*—became worldwide symbols of the atrocities of Jim Crow America.

Black women have been presented with extraordinary challenges. They have had to decide whether to meet them or to turn away. Very often, they have chosen to meet them. Their methods and strategies have been their own, different from those their advisors would have chosen for them but carrying echoes of the Sacred Dark Feminine. When we look at their strategies, we learn much about women, leadership, and social change.

Mamie Till-Mobley and Sybrina Fulton faced the terrible circumstances of their lives. I hoped they cried in private because in public they were stoic, self-possessed in their conversations to seek justice for their sons. They were persistent and unrelenting in their campaigns, strategically smart in their cooperation with the needs of the media. It is a model that black women have used in other places too. Maria Roach stepped in, in her own timely and strategic way, because she could see where she was needed and how she could help.

The three women taken together allow us to make some observations about the ways in which black women have taken on positions of social activism. The model is a composite of several elements: situational activism, compassionate intelligence, fierce love, persistence, personal resilience, and nimbleness. The combinations of emotion, what we might usually consider sentimental emotion, with intelligence and fierceness are essential elements, as are the related traits of generosity and spirituality. None of the traits are discrete; each influences all of the others.

All three women were situational activists, not pursuing leadership per se for their own personal power but to rectify a tragic problem. They stared unblinkingly into awful situations, thought strategically, and acted. It is important to note that they acted in response to events rather than their own personal agenda. The strategy was less tied to personal history, style, or training but designed to accomplish the task at hand in the circumstances as they were presented. They understood their roles in the actions and positioned themselves to act as catalytic forces. This is particularly clear with Maria Roach, whose own son was safe. She did not act to change her personal situation or to become a national leader, but to change something bigger. All of the women's actions were highly efficient, in the sense that they garnered the most result for their actions. The results of such strategies have been world-changing.

The women demonstrated a compassionate intelligence. We tend to think of intelligence as rationality, as cold and divorced from emotion. Cognitive research, particularly that concerned with what is called the "social brain," suggests that intelligence is not cold and is continually engaged with other people. Minorities and women, in particular, often demonstrate high levels of altruism, what I call a compassionate intelligence, directed toward fixing the problems in front of them. We also tend to think of sentimental emotions—compassion, love—as somehow stupid. But the accomplished work of women shows that this is not so.

African American women have a long history of working against institutions for the sake of family and community. Cheryl D. Hicks's *Talk with You*

Like a Woman and Nancy Thorton and Faith Pratt Hopp's article "So I Just Took Over" provide post-slavery examples of when compassionate intelligence was an important strategy for black women after other services had failed them.

A trait related to compassionate intelligence is empathy, the ability to sympathize with multiple social positions. This may be the most confusing trait that many black women exhibit and is the root of much misunderstanding of black women. Empathy enables them to see humanity in inhumane situations, to be compassionate with people who are exploiting them while not losing sight of the exploitation. It may be how black women keep on giving to people who are not giving back. It is actually a very sophisticated and nuanced approach, to see the good amongst the bad. It also requires a certain nimbleness to dodge the dangerous parts.

Washington crisis manager Judy Smith is an example of a woman with nimble, intelligent, compassionate empathy. Over two decades, she has very quietly taken on cases for people whom many would have abandoned, people all along the moral continuum who needed help navigating the public trial by media. Though she was a progressive, she worked in the Bush White House during the Clarence Thomas confirmation hearings. Her clients include Monica Lewinsky, the Chandra Levy family, Michael Vick, BP after the Gulf oil spill, former NBA athlete Jayson Williams (who pleaded guilty to aggravated assault in a limo driver's death), ex-Detroit mayor Kwame Kilpatrick, Enron, ex-congressman William Jefferson (convicted of corruption), and former senator Larry Craig after his incident in the Minneapolis airport men's room, all examples of people who the *Washington Post* said "have emerged from the abyss."

"It's difficult to think of many people who have been the confidante of so many in such dire trouble for so long" wrote Neely Tucker, of the *Post*. Hers could easily be considered sleazy work, but she has carried herself in such a way that she is highly respected. "She also has a long reputation—even among reporters—for being honest, straightforward and willing to work marathon hours," according to Tucker.

She managed to retain her professionalism in what her White House boss Marlin Fitzwater called the "blood sport" of national news conferences. During one of the most scandalous moments in American presidential history, she rose above the mess and held to her personal and professional standards. Michael Duffy, executive editor of *Time* magazine, complimented her: "Not everyone representing the interested parties in the Lewinsky impeachment scandal was accurate or fast in getting back to you, but Judy was both. She keeps her word."

She always was a peacemaker, according to longtime friend Michele Welles, and she has empathy for people who find themselves or get themselves into such big messes. Smith's book *Good Self, Bad Self: Transforming Your Worst Qualities into Your Biggest Assets* describes people who have transformed their situation and advises readers how to transform theirs. The transformation from the "abyss" echoes that of the ancient Dark Feminine.

Judy Smith is the model for the central character in the ABC television show *Scandal,* starring Kerry Washington. Smith is also the executive producer of the show, and Shonda Rhimes, creator of *Grey's Anatomy,* is creator/writer. In the 2012 season, *Scandal* was the only show with a black female lead—and this time, she is in charge.

Because black women are willing to work situationally, they can be strategically nimble, jumping from area to area, strategy to strategy. When they form organizations, they tend to be geared to very specific issues such as the Children's Defense Fund or the National Black Women's Health Project, now the Black Women's Health Imperative. The first black woman admitted to the Mississippi bar, Marian Wright Edelman, could have done a lot of things. She chose to work on the problems of children and founded the Children's Defense Fund. Byllye Avery and Lillie Allen were southern health care workers who decided to address the undertreatment of other black women.

When "Mama" Vy Higginsen's daughter told her she wanted to sing, Vy looked for a place to develop her daughter's talent but could not find what she considered to be an appropriate one. So she started one herself and told her daughter to invite some of her friends from the performing arts school. The students came, and came back—more every Saturday morning until she had to find a bigger space. Now she heads the Harlem Gospel Teen's Choir.

We often speak of the unique location of black women—at the crossroads of race, caste, and gender—as a static position, but humans are not static; they are in constant motion. And the black woman's position is really a type of nimbleness, navigating between the three primary divisions of American culture. None of the three categories ever appear alone, so black women are always navigating multiple categories at once.

Racism requires a certain type of nimbleness. Charity Adams was the first African American woman to be an officer in the Women's Army Auxiliary Corps and was the commanding officer of the first battalion of African American women to serve overseas during World War II. In 1942, on the day she was sworn in, she should have been the first woman of either race sworn according to the tradition of taking the candidates alphabetically. But that day, the army broke with tradition and each class was sworn in by platoon. Adams was soon assigned to lead an all-black platoon. Rather than integrate the platoons, the army crowded the white women into other platoons and left a smaller black one. Rather than complain, Adams took the opportunity to train the black women in a wider variety of procedures in a shorter time span than the white women.

Compassionate intelligence and nimbleness affect how black women approach fields as traditional as the military or science. Right now, there is a national push to get more women and minorities of color to go into the sciences, where they tend to be underrepresented. But there is one population that is not underrepresented—black women in biology. Black women who have clustered in biology do so because they want to solve problems. The link to solving problems is so important to black girls and women throughout their lives and educations that it affects how and what they learn. If it is relevant, they excel. This is true for women and it is true for minorities.

Edna Aden Ismail, first lady of Somalia in 1960s, was a midwife. In 1975 she used her position to speak out against female genital mutilation; she was the first in her country to do so. Although she founded a maternity hospital, built and maintained with her own pension money, and worked as the regional director of the World Health Organization, she also continued to deliver babies. She believes all of her work has been nothing more than just living up to her commitment as a midwife.

Coming at science this way means that black women look at science differently and may find different solutions. Black women's accomplishments in biology have already been astounding. Suzanne de la Monte, MD, a professor of pathology and lab medicine at the Warren Alpert Medical School of Brown University, is one of the world's leading Alzheimer's researchers. She and her team found a link between Alzheimer's disease and diabetes, that diabetes of the brain might be the root cause of the brain disease. It was a breakthrough because it was off the beaten path of research for either disease. An increasing criticism of science is that scientists are chasing the grant money and building their own careers, which leads to looking in all the same places rather than going further afield to more innovative and sometimes controversial approaches.

Situational activism and nimbleness helped Peggielene Bartels when she needed it to help her people. She did not know that she knew how to be a king until her phone rang in the middle of the night in 2009. She was a secretary at the Ghanaian embassy in Washington, a naturalized citizen of the United States. And then, as the caller told her, she was the new king of Otuam, a Ghanaian fishing village. Although the country of Ghana is a sovereign state, there are some city-states within its borders that have their own royal families. As the late-night caller said to Peggielene, her uncle, the king, had died. A series of divine messages from the ancestors pointed to her as his successor. But the happily-ever-after was more complicated than in the fairy tales. Otuam was poor, and its finances had been gutted by corrupt village elders who had taken advantage of the king's illness and stolen the tax revenue. Bartels had to take money out of her own savings for her uncle's burial and her own coronation. King Peggy, as she came to be called, has taken on the job of raising funds in the United States for clean water sources, schools, and ambulances in Otuam. She wrote *King Peggy: An American Secretary, Her Royal Destiny, and the Inspiring Story of How She Changed an African Village* with coauthor Eleanor Herman. She made the talk show circuit—NPR, CBS *Sunday Morning, The Tavis Smiley Show, The Colbert Report*. She got on Facebook and formed a partnership with Shiloh Baptist Church in Landover, Maryland, to raise money.

She found that the skills that she used as an office manager transferred to the job of the king. She cleaned up the corruption and set up an accounting system with checks and balances for the village's funds by applying skills she already had.

> If [you] manage an office . . . you have to organize receptions, you have to organize the people coming, and you have to interact with different kinds of people. . . . You have to be really, really professional and be strong. I said to myself, "Maybe God was preparing me for this. That's why I've been a secretary in this embassy for so long—so I can be a good king.

Bartels soon found that the men expected that her gender and her distant life in the United States would make her a weak king. She told them otherwise—that she intended to rule and to be treated as a ruler, demonstrating logistical nimbleness. She told NPR's Rachel Martin, "When I said this, they all stood up—a woman is speaking like this? And I said, 'Yes. I'm serious. Treat me like a man, because—I'm a man. I'm a man. Don't look at me as a woman. . . . If you really understand me as a man, then we can go onward. But if you think I'm a woman, we're not going to work.'"

Several interviewers asked her Why not a queen? "I would have made a lousy queen," she told Tavis Smiley. She explained that there was a queen in place, and that she did not have the power of a king.

Persistence, staying with a problematic situation for years or even indefinitely, like King Peggy, is a common trait. In 1998, Christopher Alder, an honorably discharged black British paratrooper, choked to death at Queen's Gardens police station soon after he was arrested for a fight. His sister, Janet Alder, took on the mission to find out what had happened to her brother, a battle that spanned more than thirteen years. A coroner's jury decided Alder was unlawfully killed, and misconduct and manslaughter charges were later brought against five Humberside Police officers. They were acquitted of all criminal charges in 2002. Janet took her case to the court in Strasbourg, alleging there had been a violation of the substantive aspects of two articles of the European Convention on Human Rights—Article 3, which prohibits torture and inhuman or degrading treatment or punishment, and Article 14, which prohibits discrimination.

She also alleged "a breach of the procedural guarantees" of Article 3 along with Article 2, the right to life, but the court said it had discontinued the case after receiving the government's admission that there had not been an "effective and independent" investigation and that amounted to a human rights violation. The court said that the treatment of Christopher Alder in custody amounted to a violation of Article 3 of the European Convention on Human Rights. The government agreed to pay 26,500 euros (£22,770) to the family, plus 7,500 euros to cover legal costs and expenses. Reacting to the compensation, Janet told the BBC: "I see it as an admission that what we've been fighting for thirteen years was true and that the government had failed to hold them accountable."

Persistence requires the personal trait of resilience, the ability to ride out difficult situations. The Girl Scouts published a 2010 follow-up study of African American and Latina girls entitled "The Resilience Factor" and found that for both African American and Latina girls, unlike for others, culture and ethnic identity were highly significant in the development of resilience. There may also be a biochemical difference in black women that is related to resilience. Researchers have found that black women often do not self-perceive feelings of stress or fatigue, even if their bodies are registering them, and now there is some evidence as to why. Some researchers suggest that estrogen blocks messages of fatigue to the brain, which they say may explain an apparent advantage that women runners have in ultralong marathons, which run as long as a one hundred miles. The effect has been shown in other types of activities as well. Interestingly, black women have higher levels of estrogen than other women have at any point in their menstrual cycle. The effects of higher estrogen on lowered self-perception of fatigue, which aids resilience, may be contributing to persistence in addition to the cultural expectation of black women to be more persistent.

Black women demonstrated an extraordinary level of resilience in the face of being systematically raped as a form of race and gender terrorism in the South. Their individual and group response developed the foundation of the civil rights movement.

In the segregated American South, a white man could rape a black woman with little fear of legal or social recourse, and black women lived in a persistent state of apprehension. Rape was used as a weapon of terror in the subjugation of black women, their families, and whole communities. In *At the Dark End of the Street: Black Women, Rape, and Resistance: A New History of the Civil Rights Movement from Rosa Parks to the Rise of Black Power*, Danielle L. McGuire writes that white men raped black women and girls "with alarming regularity and stunning uniformity," with some victims as young as seven. Affluence was no protection when women were kidnapped off the street and from their own homes. Cases included civil rights workers and a college coed still in her prom dress. The crimes took on an awful sameness: abduction at gun- or knifepoint. Gang rapes and severe beatings were common. Afterward, the rapists often dumped their victims out of cars in remote areas and threatened their lives if they told.

But this is a story of courage. The women did tell, again and again. Many went to police before they went to the hospital and were supported by families and friends who corroborated their stories, at great risk. White control of the justice system meant that relatively few men were ever arrested and even fewer were ever convicted. McGuire reports that between 1940 and 1965, only ten Mississippi white men were convicted of raping black women and girls. Although rape was a capital offense in many Southern states, no white man was ever executed for raping a black woman. Yet black women's resistance grew into a social movement. Years before the Montgomery bus boycott, a coalition of poor and middle-class black women raised money; formed organizations; wrote, mimeographed, and distributed flyers; attended trials; and successfully boycotted the businesses of rapists. These actions created the strategies and alliances that these same women would use again later to extend their rights. In fact, the civil rights movement was a continuation of the anti-rape movement; the early college sit-ins, largely by women, came in response to sexual violence, and Rosa Parks was a central figure well before she refused to give up her seat on the bus.

Black women rallied outside rape trials and faced retaliation by policemen. There are moments in McGuire's book that will make readers cheer. During one Montgomery trial, scores of black domestics arrived to support the victim. When a skittish policeman reached for his gun, one woman told him, "If you hit one of us, you'll not leave here alive." He backed down.

The Achilles heel of the South has always been its concern for public image. The rapes were reported in the black press, and the cases that went to trial became matters of public record. In the 1950s, the national and international press began to pick up the embarrassment. The Southern justice system responded with more indictments and even a few convictions, mostly of poor, uneducated men. They were the first convictions of white rapists since Reconstruction.

Resilience with style is grace, the ability to ride out difficult circumstances with calm. The ability to find joy in difficult work would certainly add to resilience. After a speech, Angela Davis was asked by a student how she had sustained herself in her work over the decades. The famous civil rights activist replied that it had not been difficult because she loved what she was doing. She encouraged the young activist to find causes and people who brought her joy, much like King Peggy, who said, "I love every bit of what I'm doing."

Michelle Obama has grace. Dorothy Height had grace. Height, the grande dame of the civil rights movement, died in 2010 after a long illness. She was ninety-eight. Miss Height, as everyone called her, was a force in the black civil rights movement for sixty years, forty of them as the president of National Council of Negro Women. In life and in death, she has been called the matriarch and the queen of the movement. President Barack Obama called her its godmother. The titles are reverential. She was a tall, stately woman, always perfectly dressed, her voice moderated and mannered. Style was and is an important element in the lives of upwardly moving African Americans—it shows that we can be cultured too.

But behind the image of the grand lady was a woman who was a very active strategist and organizer. That balance, between the mannered lady and the activist, would play out for her entire professional life and says much about the too-often hidden role of black women in the movement.

Many of the articles that immediately followed the announcement of Height's passing noted that she sat on the dais at the most famous moment in civil rights history, as the Rev. Martin Luther King Jr. delivered his "I Have a Dream" speech at the Lincoln Memorial during the 1963 March on Washington for Jobs and Freedom. Indeed, Dorothy Height was among the small group of top African American leaders who strategized and organized the movement into an internationally recognized force, and she was on the dais that day—but she did not speak.

Miss Height was quoted widely as saying that Reverend King spoke longer than expected. She was a particularly gracious woman, and the quote was her way of saying a truth while shielding one of the harsher realities of the movement. She said later that she was disappointed that no one had advocated for women's rights. She would have, had she spoken. There were many that day who did not want her, or any other woman, to speak to the crowd.

Obtaining full manhood status for black men was a focus of the civil rights movement, which meant that black women were often expected to put themselves in the back seat—and historically, African American women have pushed concerns about race ahead of those about gender. Miss Height constantly reminded them that they had to do both. "Dorothy Height deserves credit for helping black women understand that you had to be feminist at the same time you were African," said Washington, DC, delegate Eleanor Holmes Norton.

Indeed, Miss Height's work to improve conditions for women predated the modern women's rights movement. The YWCA was important to the work of black women activists, and Height worked with Mary McLeod Bethune, president of the Harlem YWCA, where Height had first met Eleanor Roosevelt, then moved to direct the Phyllis Wheatley YWCA branch in Washington. Before becoming the fourth president of the National Council of Negro Women, she was the president of Delta Sigma Theta from 1947 to 1955. Although the black sororities held teas and debutante balls, they also built formidable histories as agents of service and change. As black women pushed for the right to be ladies, they also worked hard behind the scenes.

Dorothy Height used the position of the lady as a strategic maneuver. She loved the trappings and manners of being a lady, but she also understood what it allowed her to do and say. She also understood that at other times, it hampered her. Because black women have not pursued power for its own sake, they have often been eclipsed by black men, even in movements started by the women. I, for one, hunger to know what she would have said on the dais at the March on Washington.

When she became the first female ruler of her African village, King Peggy Bartels found that her presence as king began to shift the gender relations in the village culture, and that the other women began to change too.

They are beginning to accept me for who I am, whether I'm strict with them, whether I do or don't see their views. . . . The women are trying to understand me [and that] as a woman you can do a lot. You don't have to sit down and think that you have to wait for a man to succeed in life. If I am a woman and I am doing this, they can also do it. I also talk to the women and say, "If you are being butchered or battered by a man, don't take it because you can do a lot for yourself." The [men] look up to me highly . . . even more than the females. The youth come to me and say, "Nana, with all the male kings we've had, none of them have been so generous and helped us the way you have helped us." . . . The men come to me as a mother, as a sister and as a missionary.

Black women and girls are demonstrating a particularly high investment in leadership. The Girl Scouts conducted a very large survey of girls and their attitudes toward leadership and found that African American girls stood out from girls of other races, and from African American boys, in their attitudes. African American girls were more likely than other girls to want to be leaders. Ninety percent of African American girls said that "no matter who they are, girls can learn to be good leaders" and 72 percent believed that girls can be leaders whether or not they are in positions of authority. The study concluded that for African American girls, "preferred definitions of leadership imply personal principles, ethical behavior and the ability to effect social change." Being a leader was important to 70 percent of African American girls. Primarily, African American girls wanted to be the kind of leader who stands up for her beliefs (87 %) and tries to change the world for the better (83 %).

Eighty-two percent of African American girls said that their mothers encouraged them to be leaders, followed by fathers (59 %) and teachers (59 %), friends (51 %), and older relatives (44 %). More than three-quarters (75 %) have had the opportunity to lead. Yet 60 percent said that they had been discouraged by peers and classmates.

African American girls were more likely to be driven to be leaders by altruistic motives, helping other people, being a role model, sharing skills and knowledge with others, and changing the world for the better. African American boys were more likely to respond that being a leader would help them be their own boss and make more money.

A major key to understanding black women is to recognize their high levels of spirituality. A study by the *Washington Post* and the Kaiser Family Foundation found what other studies have suggested: black women are the most religious group in the country. Further, the study found that in times of turmoil approximately 87 percent of black women say they turn to their faith to get through, much more than any other group. The trend cuts across education and income levels, and the women said that their faith was a higher priority than being married or having children, that it either surpasses or pulls even with having a career.

An earlier study by the Pew Forum found very similar levels of spirituality and also found that African American women weave their faith into every part of their daily lives. African American women go to church more regularly than any other demographic, but even when they are unaffiliated with a place of worship more than three-quarters pray every day. I suspect that if the Pew Forum had phrased the question differently and asked how often black women talk to God, they would have had even higher numbers. A Johns Hopkins medical researcher who was a pioneer in studies on prayer and healing used African American women because they have a more gentle, benevolent image of God and perceive themselves as having a closer, constant relationship.

But as black women say, their faith is a muscular faith—it works wonders. Dawn Carter, a thirty-three-year-old woman interviewed by the *Washington Post*, said that she regularly prayed for her students and that when she heard that their problems had been resolved, she just smiled. When a Georgetown Law School student was nervous before her first time representing a domestic abuse survivor, she looked to her phone and the quote that came up was from Seventh-day Adventist cofounder Ellen G. White: "For what purpose are you seeking an education? Is it not that you may relieve the suffering of humanity?" She was instantly enveloped with a sense of calm and confidence.

King Peggy Bartels talked about the role of her spirituality played in her taking on the role of king:

> I didn't realize I had the strength. The strength that I'm having right now, I tell people, it's not just my own strength, it's a strength from God and from my ancestors. I pray for it. I pray, "God, you have sent me on this mission. And you have to lead me because you have helped me and led me all my life. I left home as a teenager to go to England to go to school. I was by myself and nothing happened to me. . . . I've grown up to be a woman, and you are still leading me. So lead me." My strength is not just me. I have supernatural beings helping me. I feel it. I know it.

But even the religious lives of black women don't rest on too-easy stereo-types. There are signs that black women are interpreting their spiritual beliefs in ways that are just now being detected. On *Midday with Dan Rodricks*, where I am the American Culture critic, we took on the controversial issue of African American churches and same-sex marriage. Maryland was in the middle of a highly contested series of votes on the issue and the assumptions were that black people opposed it. I started with what many heard as an evenhanded academic assessment of the situation: the high levels of religiosity of African Americans, how highly correlated religiosity was with opposition to same-sex marriage, how similar the poll numbers were between black and white religious people but that black ministers had been more outspoken on the issue. We invited two black ministers, Delman Coates, pastor of Mount Ennon Baptist in Prince George's County, Maryland, who had spoken in favor of same-sex civil marriage, and Emmett Burns, a state legislator and a Baptist pastor of Rising Sun Baptist church in Baltimore County, a longtime opponent.

Emmett Burns, obviously not knowing my role on the show and thinking that I was not still sitting in the studio, said, "That lady did not know what she was talking about." He made "lady" sound like a dirty word. Dan responded that I was Professor Sheri Parks and that I was still there. I began to ask Reverend Burns a series of questions, such as, What did he really think would happen if same-sex marriage were legalized? They were the sort of questions that only another black person had license to ask, but it was clear nobody had ever asked him before. He faltered. The phones lit up, mostly with men, which is common on talk radio. Most but not all of the men were religious and conservative, saying that same-sex marriage was wrong. Meanwhile, Twitter was also lighting up, but with things we could not recount over the public airways. Then the e-mail messages began to come in, many of them stating, "I am an African American woman, I am religious, and I support same-sex marriage." When looking at African American women and their religion, we must take into account the ways in which they are different from African American men—more highly educated, more likely to be professional, all consistent with more liberal attitudes toward a host of issues, such as same-sex marriage. And they are beginning to be vocal about the ways in which they are different, to recognize themselves.

A few weeks later, the NAACP board, chaired by a woman, voted in a resolution to support same-sex marriage. Roslyn M. Brock, chairwoman of the sixty-four-member board, said, "We have and will oppose efforts to codify dis-crimination into law."

After President Obama announced his support for same-sex marriage, in part due to the influence of his daughters, a Washington Post-ABC News poll showed an 18 percent increase in support for same-sex marriage among African Americans. The media depicted the the story along gender lines, suggesting that black male ministers were largely still in opposition while religious women, who made up the majority of their congregations, were shifting.

That black women are more invested in their spirituality and the activism through which they show it, may shed light on the particular type of populist feminist activism that is emerging. Women's organizations are beginning to speak with a new tone, in solidarity with other women. National Council of Negro Women executive director Avis Jones-DeWeever highlighted economic perils for women and children, and said that women will stand up for jobs, equal pay, and equal opportunities: "Women will not be silent. We will not be bamboozled. We will not be complacent."

There is a generosity to the way black women act upon the world, a generosity of time, spirit, and money. Black women are operating within a "gift economy." Women, including black women, routinely give without expecting to get anything back. Black women just seem to do it more. The concept is based on abundance. If I have, I give. When you have, you give. A gift economy is very different from the "exchange economy," where the goal is to give as little as possible and to get as much as possible in return. Capitalism is an exchange economy, based on keeping a certain level of scarcity. To keep demand high, an exchange economy will work to create unnecessary, artificial scarcity by disposing of or destroying products or plowing under of crops even while other people are in need. In a gift economy, those who have much of one thing give some to those who have less of it. Elevated to an economic policy, a gift economy calls for spending on nurturing products rather than arms or other weapons of destruction.

Black women inherit their involvement in a gift paradigm in at least two ways: the African American helping tradition and the ways of mothers. The African American helping tradition comes to them from the African tradition of *ubuntu*: I am because I belong; my humanity is inextricably connected to yours; I cannot be happy unless we are all happy. Ubuntu is closely associated with South African archbishop Desmond Tutu, who has called for an African Renaissance through reclaiming this ancient African concept. Actually, similar concepts have been present in other, perhaps all, societies including *unhu* in Zimbabwe ("I am well if you are all right too"), *Khoe!na* in the Kalahari, among

Native Americans, and even in the sixteenth- to seventeenth-century metaphysical poetry of John Donne:

> No man is an island, entire of itself; every man is a piece of the conti-
> nent, a part of the main. . . . Any man's death diminishes me, because
> I am involved in mankind, Therefore never send to know for whom the
> bell tolls; it tolls for thee.

Mothers routinely operate from a gift paradigm. They often give to their
families with no expectation of return. Fathers can and do operate from a gift
paradigm; women seem to do it more often. Microloans are a particularly good
indication of how mothers operate in gift paradigm. While microloans are controversial as a strategy for large-scale social change, the results of years of microloans does tell something about the way women work as small-scale change
agents. It is important to note that there is no doubt that the majority of microloans are made to women. One estimate is that 75 percent are made to women,
and some agencies and banks only extend microloans to women. The rate of
repayment is higher, they are more willing to take out smaller first-time loans
and build up to larger loans, and they are more likely plow the money back into
their businesses and families as opposed to themselves. It is often said in the aid
and development community that changing the lives of women rapidly changes
the lives of the community.

Some scholars have suggested that recognizing the gift economy is a way
of recognizing the macro-level impact of mothers, and that reintroducing it
to other women and men will counter the effects of dominance. Genevieve
Vaughan wrote:

> The gift paradigm has the advantage of restoring mothering to its right-
> ful place in the constitution of the human. What has been wrongly
> proposed in the construction of gender, with devastating effects such
> as the promotion of the values of dominance, competition and hier-
> archy (which are non nurturing values), can be countered by reintro-
> ducing gift giving as a social value and interpretative key. Both male
> and female human beings are basically nurturers. One gender is not
> the binary opposite of the other. If we reintroduce the gift paradigm
> into our interpretation of the world, we will find our "gift giver within"
> which will then be validated. Women, as those who have been socially

designated as the nurturers, will be rightfully restored to their place as the norm, and men can be reinterpreted in this light as those who have been socially dispossessed of that norm-al behavior but who can reacquire it by espousing nurturing values. Institutions are usually organized around the exchange and dominance paradigm, but they can be reorganized to satisfy needs. The rewards which accompany dominance can be eliminated and gift giving can be affirmed and promoted.

A gift economy works better the more people operate within its paradigm. It can be and is devastating if one entity is working in a gift economy when nobody else is, especially if the giver has limited resources. Middle-class black women have actually demonstrated the effect of operating in a gift economy when others around them are not. A recent study found that middle-class black women with good jobs and salaries still had, on average, almost no net worth—their assets after debt were almost nothing. In a study aptly titled "Lifting as We Climb," the researchers found that a major factor was that black women were much more likely to be giving money to friends and relatives:

> In addition to facing discriminatory practices in employment, lending and wealth creation, women of color are more likely to use their own financial resources to help out extended family members. With a history of exclusion from public benefits and economic opportunities afforded to whites, women of color know they are relied on and must rely on others in their families and communities when hard times hit. Unemployment in communities of color at nearly double the rate among whites has put a further strain on women of color who are supporting growing numbers of people.

Black women are the most likely demographic to be employed but they are giving away most of their money. A gift economy within an exchange economy can be devastating. It is a culturally difficult position. The helping tradition in black culture demands that you help if you can, but it appears that black women are helping more than anyone and getting less in return. Although she admires the strength and resilience of women she knows, Melissa Harris-Perry is concerned that the giving tradition is keeping women from making political gains.

Food is a primary example of how exchange economic control of scarcity works and how a gift paradigm can change it. The US Department of

Agriculture has traditionally controlled the supply of certain crops by plowing under the surplus amount or paying subsidies to farmers not to grow them at all in order to keep the prices high, rather than balancing supply by giving the excess to underserved communities. Despite the prominent presence of huge agribusiness, most farmers are women, often on small plots that feed their families and communities. Customary patriarchal legal practices deprive women of control of the land. In particular single, widowed, or divorced women are more likely to be deprived of access to any land at all. Organizations are seeking ways to change these realities. Professional women and farmers in South Africa have demonstrated how a gift paradigm can have a macro-level effect on the world food supply. For instance, in South Africa, communal property associations that formed to redistribute land parcels after the fall of apartheid tended to allocate farmland regardless of gender and family situation.

There is little doubt that women of other cultures exhibit the same motives and strategies as black women. Women still do the job of the Sacred Dark Feminine every day, all day, in their lives; sometimes covertly, sometimes unselfconsciously. Black women have been most closely associated with Her, but hers is the work of anyone who chooses. And while there are differences in circumstances and expectations, the primary difference seems to be what black women expect of themselves and how they carry those expectations. Other groups of women are actively working to find their specific, culturally true way to be loving and fierce, or as the Chicano/Latina Foundation defines it: "Latina Leadership is . . . Walking down the path to find out who we are, making the most of our strengths and speaking our truth."

Native American women also draw from an androgynous model, similar to the Sacred Dark Feminine. The Lenape Program promotes leadership and strength among Native American women. Their website quotes a Sioux Wise Man: "Be strong with the warm, strong heart of the earth. Be strong and sing the strength of the Great Powers within you, all around you." As with other groups, there is a sense of the coming of the Feminine:

> The Elders say the Native American women will lead the healing among the tribes. We need to especially pray for our women, and ask the Creator to bless them and give them strength. Inside them are the powers of love and strength given by the Moon and the Earth. When everyone else gives up, it is the women who sing the songs of strength. She is the backbone of the people. So, to our women we say, sing your

songs of strength; pray for your special powers; keep our people strong; be respectful, gentle and modest. Oh, Great One, bless our women. Make them strong today.

The Native American Women's Health Education Resource Center, which provides direct services to Native women and families in South Dakota and advocates for Native women at the community, national, and international levels to protect reproductive health and rights, uses the fierce motto, "Let no child go hungry in our community!"

Are we in a new era of female compassionate anger? Many women think so. In the early summer of 2012, the Senate prepared to vote on the Blunt Amendment. If passed, this legislation would have allowed any employer to decline to cover contraception health costs for "moral" reasons. A coalition of over fifty women's organizations held a press conference to announce an unprecedented drive to mobilize women voters on the ground and online around Health and Economic Rights—HERvotes—in 2012. Speakers emphasized the power of women voters as a force for change, as well as their collective outrage over the politicization of vital aspects of women's health care, such as birth control and breast cancer services. They outlined strategies to access twenty million women. Lisa Maatz of the American Association of University Women described a $1.5 million campaign being launched to turn out women's votes, particularly Millennial women. Maatz observed. "There is a palpable buzz . . . women are mad. We are fed up. We don't want you to touch our birth control. We're tired of being told what we can do with our bodies. We'll be canvassing, advertising, social media campaigns, and reaching women where they live."

The very name of one organization, MomsRising, suggests a new era. "At MomsRising, here's what we know: Every single one of us can have an impact. And together we are a powerful force." The website reaches over three million women through e-mail, Twitter, Facebook, and other means.

The editors of *Bitch* magazine quoted Rebecca West in defining their mission:

"People call me a feminist whenever I express sentiments that differentiate me from a doormat." We'd argue that the word "bitch" is usually deployed for the same purpose. When it's being used as an insult, "bitch" is an epithet hurled at women who speak their minds, who have opinions and don't shy away from expressing them, and who don't sit by and smile uncomfortably if they're bothered or offended. If being an outspoken woman means being a bitch, we'll take that as a compliment.

After the first edition of *Fierce Angels* came out in 2010, an audience that the publishers had not counted on emerged: progressive women and men of other races. *Ms.*, *Bitch*, and a progressive feminist radio show ran positive reviews. I spoke at the venerable Red Emma's bookstore and filled the big Radical Book Tent at the Baltimore Book Festival. While the audiences were interested in black women, they were seeking two other things: inspiration and strategy. Could the model work for other people?

So the question remains, if other women are approaching activism in ways that are similar to black women, why do they need black women as models for inspiration and strategy? In a sense, that is not a question for me to answer. But women of other races are looking to black women because of the centuries of extreme circumstances, not of their making, to which black women continue to respond. Because of those circumstances and the brave and intelligent ways that black women have faced them, women do look to them. A Japanese scholar, Yuri Kubota, translated the works of black women writers, she said to me, "to show Japanese women how to be strong." From other women, black women can learn ways to care for themselves. And indeed, some black women, Fierce Angels, have already raised the role to a sustainable art form by surrounding themselves with people who nourish them back.

If ever a true coalition of women, all the strong women, could be formed, we would be formidable.

8

Fierce Angels

ON THE MORNING of April 17, 2007, poet and University Distinguished Professor of English Nikki Giovanni paused and looked out at the mass of Virginia Tech families and staff assembled before her. Just the day before, a student had killed thirty-three people, including himself, and injured fifteen more in the deadliest mass shooting in US history. The campus administration hastily called a convocation, and the president asked Giovanni to speak. The major networks had been covering the story since it broke and aired the convocation live. The most active face of the administration was Dr. Zenobia Hikes, a black woman and the university's vice president for student affairs, who had spent the previous night caring for the dead and the traumatized and was now moving around the stage, carrying out her duties as mistress of ceremony with a fierce dignity.

The Daily Kos, a popular political blog, posted, "There was an emptiness, shock, horror . . . a terrible bewilderment, bereavement, loss, and despair . . . until the poet Nikki Giovanni spoke." Widely known as an activist poet, Nikki Giovanni is often irreverent and provocative. She likes to make joyful mischief, to poke her audience with a sharp stick to puncture their old assumptions, all the while with a smile that says, "I love you, but you needed to hear that." Giovanni's mother, who lived with her near the university, had died not long before, and her sister had died six weeks after their mother. Grief was something she knew too closely. Some of her students were among the dead students. In front of an audience of predominantly white parents and students, she stood out in her black suit, white shirt, and tie, with her white curly hair cropped close. She is a small woman, so the big, blingy rhinestone pin that spelled HOKIES stood out on her lapel.

She read her poem "We Are Virginia Tech" and told her listeners that they would be strong enough to embrace their grief. She told the parents that they did not deserve to lose their children, as children in Africa or Mexico or Appalachia do not deserve to die because of things someone else did. She told them all that they would live, that they would also laugh again, and that they would prevail. She repeated, "We will prevail," and "We are Virginia Tech" again and again, part poem, part chant.

She finished, embraced the president, and walked to the side of the stage, but the audience was not done with her. They stood and clapped for a minute. Then, as if on cue, the energy surged. The clapping swelled, joined by voices that began to cheer and whoop, then slid into another, more rhythmic chant: "Let's Go Hokies," *clap-clap, clap-clap*, over and over, swelling louder and louder. The mood had shifted from numb sadness to a shared spirit of survival and resilience, a communal understanding that no one present would ever forget what happened but would live past the trauma.

Giovanni acknowledged the shift by raising her arms, igniting another crescendo of cheers. Dr. Zenobia Hikes retook the stage, laughing. It was a lilting, joyful laugh. She told the crowd, "Boy, didn't we need that?" The two black women, Hikes and Giovanni, had lifted the convocation with emotion. Giovanni's poem had transformed a solemn ceremony into a call for survival, for persistence in the face of death. The official Virginia Tech remembrance website echoed her words: "We will continue to invent the future through our blood and our tears, through all this sadness. We will prevail."

Giovanni later told NPR radio host Michel Martin that she knew that the grief-stricken would have to "embrace their sadness," that "the only way out of any tragedy is love." And then, she said, she knew that they would have to be inspired to move on, to be strong and brave enough to know that they would be able to laugh again. She was fulfilling the archetypal job of the Dark Feminine, delivering the families back to the realm of the living.

None of the media commentators found it odd that a small black female poet had helped so many white families see that they would live again. The university, the media, and the country needed Giovanni at that moment, and she was gracious enough to oblige them. Zenobia Hikes, whose personality the student newspaper called the "warmest on campus," did not live on much longer. She died from heart complications in the fall after the massacre. Giovanni told Martin that she considered Hikes to be the last victim of the massacre, that the responsibility she took on weighed too heavily on her heart. In Hikes's obituary in the Virginia Tech student paper, colleagues and students recalled her calm during the massacre and convocation. Giovanni and Hikes came to symbolize for Virginia Tech a fierce caring, strong enough to help them meet head-on the horrific elements of life.

Fierce love has long been a specialty of black women. Harriet Tubman is one of the stars of the American storybook and as strong as any person could be. Illiterate and in constant pain, the fugitive slave woman nevertheless returned to the South over and over again to rescue hundreds of others from slavery, under the noses of the slave owners. During the Civil War, she worked behind Confederate lines as a spy for the Union army. A friend of Tubman's, Sarah Bradford, wrote *Scenes in the Life of Harriet Tubman* to document Tubman's life because, even after her service during the war, the US government was slow in awarding her a government pension.

Bradford compared Tubman to Joan of Arc and Florence Nightingale, "for not one of these women has shown more courage and power of endurance in facing danger and death to relieve human suffering, than has this woman in her heroic and successful endeavors to reach and save all whom she might of her oppressed and suffering race, and to pilot them from the land of Bondage to the promised land of Liberty."

Abolitionist John Brown called her "General Tubman" and "one of the best and bravest persons on this continent." Frederick Douglass wrote in a letter to her:

> The midnight sky and the silent stars have been the witnesses of your devotion to freedom and of your heroism. Excepting John Brown—of sacred memory—I know of no one who has willingly encountered more perils and hardships to serve our enslaved people than you have.

Parts of Tubman's story have been told over and over—how she led out men, women, and children; how, if they faltered, she pointed her gun at their heads, pushing them on to "go on or die." Yet though her story is told often, it usually tells of a woman who was only steely and determined, robbing Tubman of the totality of her humanity. When the details of a full emotional life are breathed backed into her story, we can imagine her whole again, strong but fallible. She was a woman who loved strongly and whose very strength came from the love she carried. Her first trip back was to get her husband. He refused to go. It must have been a heartbreaking time; she had risked everything to come back for him, only to find that he was not strong enough, trusting enough, or in love enough to go with her. We can only wonder what she might have said to him. *Man, I risked my safety, my freedom, my* life *to come back for you, and you are not* ready? But she did not have time. She found someone else who *was* ready and took him.

The most famous stories show her as stoic, but she was also compassionate. Her very determination grew out of love. She said, "I have heard their groans and sighs, and seen their tears, and I would give every drop of blood in my veins to free them." As she took slaves to the North, the reward for her capture grew richer, the next trip more dangerous, and yet she kept going back because she cared so much. When her trail got too hot, her friends had to spirit her away to Canada to keep her from going back too soon.

She was funny, able to see humor in the most dangerous of circumstances. Bradford wrote, "Sometimes when she and her party were concealed in the woods, they saw their pursuers pass on their horses down the high road tacking up the advertisements for them on the fences and trees. 'And den how we laughed,' said she. *'We* was de fools, and *dey* was the wise men, but we wasn't fools enough to go down de high road in de broad daylight.'" It takes a certain kind of fierceness to laugh that way.

The myth takes a human life and strips it down to the most culturally useful parts. In the case of black women, the culture does not look inside the tough exterior. It makes them into simple and hard women. Harriet Tubman was tough *and* gentle, hard *and* humorous, fierce when necessary *and* compassionate when called upon. She was emotionally and intellectually brilliant. She strategically did not rescue her parents until the end, knowing that the master would keep them well, as bait for her return. She was prescient. British benefactors mailed checks to a store near her home. The storekeeper did not get a chance to notify her, because she would come knowing the check was there and how big it was. Yet she second-guessed even her relationship with God. While still a slave, she prayed for the Lord to change her cruel master's heart. If God would not change his heart, then she prayed that the master would die. He did die, and she worried about what she had done. A complex and nuanced woman lived under the myth of the hero woman.

A stereotype takes the myth a step further, into a caricature. Stereotypes are by definition greatly oversimplified, boiled down to one seemingly essential trait and so made false by extreme omission and exaggeration. More than myth, stereotype is a bald exercise of power: It is an attempt to apprehend and control. To be black in America is to live a life followed by stereotype, to be pressured by popular culture. Strangers may not see the person standing before them but rather the sum total of jokes and television episodes. According to some stereotypes, black women were either castrating matriarchs, clueless Mammies, pathetic welfare mothers, jezebels, or victims, depending on who was telling the story and what they needed their black women characters to be. Black women have often rejected these types of blanket definitions, reluctant to recognize them as anything more than cheap imitations of a greater mythology. It is natural to try to avoid the stereotypes altogether, but we cannot leave the memories of our foremothers mired in stereotypes created for the purposes of others.

Too rarely do the purveyors of that greater mythology look directly and fully at the women they're idolizing, criticizing, oppressing, or trying to uplift with their overly grandiose Strong Black Woman ideals. Perhaps this is because they do not want to see how much the role costs. Perhaps it's because if they stop to make this consideration, they'll see how hard it is for black women to fulfill this role and will no longer be able ask for help without considering the burdens of their requests. Perhaps they simply don't want to face the elements of the Strong Black Woman myth that *are* false—that black women do not suffer, that they are never afraid, that they do not need to think about or take care of themselves. Although black women can draw strong inspiration from other strong women and the Sacred Dark Feminine, they will need to define their roles in their communities—the levels to which they prescribe to the myth of the Strong Black Woman—for themselves. They will need to factor into the image the complexities of life and realistic expectations.

A long trail of intelligent, strong, and loving black women in American life have accomplished this redefinition, and their tradition is being carried out by a host of women today. These women are a unique lot because their goodness and their love is tough. In modern Western life, love has been sentimentalized—it is often thought to be a tender, soft emotion. The idea of goodness and of good people is also considerably weakened. Good people are thought to be docile, vulnerable. But goodness can be stronger than evil, love stronger than hatred. In popular culture, the strong, loving female is often dark. In everyday life, black women feel free to fight lovingly. Peter Ackerman, founding chair of the International Center on Nonviolent Conflict and lead author of *A Force More Powerful: A Century of Nonviolent Conflict*, told me that black women are the single strongest and underutilized group that the country has and that their collective power and strength could become a major force for all Americans.

This is a crucial time for black women. Perhaps for the first time in American history, the problems of black America come as much from within the culture as from without. The traditional comforts of cultural membership—the smiles and the unspoken "I got your back" supports—are often not there any-more. Social class is cleaving a division in black American culture more than at any time. Black neighborhoods that used to have a mix of social classes no longer do, and social class even more than race is defining the quality or lack of it in the lives of poor black families. Any solution to their communities' real problems of poverty, crime, justice, education, and child welfare will require the inclusion of active leadership by black women.

Women are already responding to the call, bringing a newly inspired brand of leadership to the table. African American women have parlayed their skills and educations to move into top positions of power and influence. In politics, Barbara Lee became chair of the Congressional Black Caucus. Michelle Obama is one of the most popular first ladies in American history and could possibly become the most effective first lady since Eleanor Roosevelt. In education, there are Johnnetta Cole, president of Spelman and Bennett Colleges and director of the National Museum of African Art, and Ruth J. Simmons, president of Smith College and Brown University. In business there are women such as Carla Harris, managing director at Morgan Stanley Investment Management, and Laysha Ward, president of Target Corporation's community relations and foundation. In the nonprofit sector there is Marian Wright Edelman, founder of the Children's Defense Fund. They are but the tip of an iceberg. There are thousands of black female educators, directors, community leaders, and grassroots leaders.

In 2007, the four top posts in Baltimore city government were taken over by black women, with Sheila Dixon as mayor, Stephanie Rawlings-Blake as city council president, Patricia Jessamy as the Baltimore state's attorney, and Joan Pratt as city comptroller. Rawlings-Blake went on to succeed Dixon as mayor.

"People come up and say, 'I'm so excited that women are finally running things in the city,'" Patricia Jessamy said in an interview with Reuters. "They say, 'We've tried all these other things. This is something new.'" African American women bring their cultural knowledge with them to their new platforms. When Mayor Sheila Dixon reintroduced community policing—with police interacting daily with neighborhood leaders and residents—the homicide rate of one of the country's most dangerous cities dropped to a twenty-year low.

In mass media, Michel Martin, host of National Public Radio's *Tell Me More*, incorporated a regular panel of "Mocha Moms" to discuss family issues. Soledad O'Brien brought frank racial coverage to the air with the CNN *Black in America* series, as did correspondent Rehema Ellis with her weeklong 2007 series

African American Women: Where They Stand on *NBC Nightly News with Brian Williams*. Brian Williams later said that the network was flooded with responses.

African American women are being associated with a tradition of excellence. In 1996, while Johnnetta Cole was president of Spelman College, *Money* magazine listed Spelman as the number-one historically black college, the number-one women's college, and the number-seven college of any kind in the United States.

When Faye Wattleton took the helm of Planned Parenthood in 1978, she was the youngest person and first woman to lead the organization, and *Business Week* named her as one of the best managers of nonprofit organizations. When she left in 1995, Planned Parenthood was the seventh-largest charity in the United States. She went on to cofound and lead the Center for the Advancement of Women, a nonpartisan think tank.

In Washington, President Obama appointed more senior-level African American women than any president before him. Seven of them were appointed in the early days of his administration alone, headed by senior adviser Valerie Jarrett. Many took posts never before held by black women, including head of the Domestic Policy Council, head of the EPA, and deputy chief of staff. They called themselves "Obama Women." The *Washington Post* noted it in an article entitled: "The Ties That Align: Administration's Black Women Form a Strong Sisterhood." The women were already part of a strong supportive network that included not only policy concerns but hugs and laughter and talk about church, children, and food. The article stated, "Veterans in town see them as part of the steady evolution of power for black women, not only in the White House but also across the country—in the business world, in academia, in policy circles."

In early 2008, the Urban League dedicated its annual State of Black America to black women and acknowledged that many of the race's advances would have been impossible without the women. Some, like Bill Cosby and Juan Williams, are looking to the future. Cosby told the graduating class of Spelman College that they would have to save the race. Juan Williams, then senior National Public Radio correspondent and author of *Enough: The Phony Leaders, Dead-End Movements, and Culture of Failure That Are Undermining Black America—and What We Can Do About It*, told me that the race could no longer afford for black women to work behind the scenes. But he also said that some of the biggest silences in black culture are by and about black women. He and others are breaking those silences.

Many black women already tell stories of their lives as Strong Black Women. When I asked women how they felt about the labels of Fierce Angels or Strong Black Women, they said they were honored, that the labels fit their lives and their feelings about their lives. They were not labels they would have given themselves, but they were pleased that someone else did. None of them set out to be a leader—they just wanted to solve a problem. They are populist leaders—not made, not ordained or appointed, but leaders who grew up in response to the problems and people around them. They did not take up their work for the glory, because they knew in advance there probably would not be any. They are not interested in amassing personal power. One woman said that it was more efficient to work behind the scenes; she could get more done without worrying about people coming after her. Another said that power was a tool rather than an end in itself, that if power meant that you can pick up a phone and help somebody, then it was good. They were proud of their work.

In the popular image, black women are worried about everyone but themselves, willing to fight for and nurture family, friends, and strangers but never themselves. The women I interviewed were not so foolish. Whereas the image has no self-interest, these women did. They were very self-aware. They worked to exhaustion, but they knew they were tired and they rested. They suffered, but they knew they suffered and they looked for ways to avoid it if they could. They were self-sacrificing, but they also learned self-preservation. Theirs was a different sort of bravery.

The most successful of them took care of their energies; they paced themselves. They found balance in their lives. They made sure that their families were functioning, their children protected. They were supported by family and friends. When necessary, they rescued themselves. But the core of the image also was there. They did look beyond their own self-interests. They did face down enemies. They looked upon the work they did as a responsibility, and they asked for little or nothing in return.

The women had preserved an organic leadership model. An organic leader is one who grows from the ranks of her followers and carries the interests and well-being of those followers with her. They have also carried the spirits and strategies of their mothers and grandmothers into what would seem to be the most unlikely of places, from the mines of West Virginia to the highly polished halls of political power.

The combination of strength and compassion is very difficult to counteract, and the women I interviewed had refined the role into masterful strategic positions. Like queens on chessboards, they moved any way they needed to. Their smiles were blessings, and when they turned their attention to someone who needed them, it was a balm to a wounded soul. Aggressors, however, often had reason for regret. The women with whom I spoke were not often angry, and when they were, it did not look like the stereotype. One woman said, "It's not a fiery angry. It is a subtle, just-under-the-surface angry." She said that she chose not to live her life as an angry woman. Instead, the women to whom I spoke talked of determination, strength, commitment, persistence. Like Harriet Tubman, whose first trip was to rescue someone she loved, the emotion the women spoke most about was love—love of family, love of black people, love of women and children. Their love, though, was not the sentimental fluffy stuff of the mainstream feminine stereotypes. Theirs was a vigorous, protective love. Their love had consequences.

The coal hills of West Virginia would seem to be one of the most unlikely places to find a Strong Black Woman, but Joan Hairston is an unlikely woman. When I asked her how she felt about a college professor calling her up, saying she was a Strong Black Woman, a Fierce Angel, she said it was about right. She figured it was a step up. In the coal mines of West Virginia, black women are rare. "They figured I was stupid." That suited Joan Hairston just fine. "I let 'em. That way they didn't know what was about to hit them."

She started out of love too. Her father was one of the few black men at the mines with any stature. He was a safety man, a mid-level job meant to ensure the safety of the workers, but when he retired, the mine management tried to keep his pension. "He was my first one. They laughed at me. A woman, and a black one at that. We sued them and won." Joan was not a lawyer, but she knew how to build a case.

Her most famous case started with a drug bust. A woman came home to find policemen pinning her husband to the ground in front of their house. They had just put in a new front door, and her husband asked her to get the key to let the police in so they would not break down the door. The woman started toward the house. The police told her to go back. She did, but they tackled her anyway. They knocked her to the ground, cracking open her skull. "They beat her like a dog," Joan told me.

I asked the black ministers for help. They said, "Why you getting involved with people who were selling drugs?" They were scared. I said, "It doesn't matter what they did or did not do; nobody deserves to be beaten like she was beaten." They took her to a hospital out of town, so nobody could see her, and said that nobody could take pictures. I went up to the hospital room, to visit. I said, "Can I take your picture?" She pulled up her sheets and I took pictures. The newspaper wouldn't print them, but the TV station in the next town did. Then the Washington, DC, papers took it up.

Now they are sitting in a big, new pretty house. They never did find any drugs in that house.

As Director of New Empowerment for Women Plus (NEW), Joan went to the mines and asked, "Do you have federal grants?" If they had federal grants, they couldn't keep women out of the mines. Of course, she already knew that they did. One mine official told her, "I don't like you. But I respect you." Fine with her.

The black ministers opposed her getting work in the mines for women. One minister said she was taking jobs away from men. She told him, "If they were going to hire black men, they would have done it by now." But then the husband of that minister's daughter died, leaving her with three children. Joan said, "The only jobs that paid enough to support four people were in the mines. The minister changed his mind."

Now Joan is well tended, surrounded by her second husband and children, but it was not always that way. "Everything that has been done to those women, it has been done to me," she told me. She had a first husband, and the things he did awoke in her a determination that still burns.

She became well known and opponents backed down. In 1996, she started a mentoring program for black girls in the high school. They called it BAP, for Believing All is Possible. Pregnancies stopped cold. Men in prison would write her name and number on the wall with the words "She will help you." But now she is older and sick, and she worries about who will take her place. She wants her work to be her legacy, but she said, "I still don't care if they like me or not."

"Strength" is a word that is used a lot to talk about black women. One of the components of their particular kind of strength is the ability to face trouble with grace and even humor. Dominque Stevenson is a calm, pretty woman, with the knowing stillness of someone who has witnessed much yet managed to find her own peace in a difficult world. Hers is an earned calm. Dominque is area director of the Maryland Peace with Justice Program for the American Friends Service Committee, where she dives into the ugliest possible issues, like organizing opposition to present-day slavery in Africa and the United States. For years she has met with incarcerated men, who have come to trust her and have opened their lives to her, letting her be their friend and their advocate.

First she had to save herself. As a younger woman, she was addicted to drugs. "I decided that that was not who I was," she said. The process of healing herself taught her that focusing on her own well-being was crucial.

She grew up in a middle-class home with her mother and stepfather. Their neighborhood was mixed by class and race, and she went to the neighborhood school. She did not recognize social class until she was bused in to an affluent white neighborhood, where teachers looked at her with disdain that even a third-grader could see. Over time, she saw more. "I saw more inequities—who was on the bottom, who had access to services." By high school she had become disenchanted. Eventually she drifted into drugs and became addicted.

"*The Autobiography of Malcolm X* opened my eyes. I felt I had been blinded all of that time. I had kind of heard of things, but I did not really see until then." She had met a good man in rehab and they decided they wanted to build a life together. "I wanted a domestic situation that was normal."

A similar motivation led to her activism. Becoming a mother made her want a better world for her children to live in. Responsibility for the world came with responsibility for children. "You have fears you never knew you had. Our children are up against a lot."

She has learned to weave the public and private strains into a life that sustains her as well as her family. She has never hidden her work from her children. From the time they were young, her children have been involved. She explained her social-justice work to them early on, and they were proud of her. After she and her husband found that they were having to fill in the scant black history taught at school, they decided to homeschool the youngest of them. She wanted the freedom to travel with her children to show them black history. She integrated activism into their lives, taking them to rallies so that they grew up as social-justice workers, knowing the world.

"All of our children are victimized because they don't know. Homeschooling was talking about our history, instilling that kind of education, taking them a couple of times out of the country, having activist friends come around them." She didn't know if they understood everything, but she had to show them. She has taken them on social-justice trips—to New Orleans after Katrina, to Jena for the demonstrations, and to Southern cotton fields to see the landscape of their ancestors' forced labor.

She worked for the AmeriCorps Theater Collective, writing, editing, and performing plays about African American history and experience, before moving on to the American Friends Service Committee. The Friends—or Quakers, as they are commonly known—quietly fund social activism around the world. They took on present-day slavery before it became widely known, and Dominque spearheaded a speaking tour of a former Mauritanian slave and anti-slavery activist.

"It does not feel like a job. It feels like a responsibility. You must care about this. I don't like it when things are wrong. Part of it is, who best to turn it around? The ones who know what right looks like. We cannot rely on the people who kept you [us] in the situation."

Now she spends much of her time counseling inmates and working with other counselors. The Peace with Justice Program has grown to cover six prisons. It is work that requires a steady hand. She says it takes the same kind of patience that it takes to mother her children. Although she is yet a young woman, she operates at the prisons from the position of a mother. "Working with young men in prison, they could have been my sons. . . . The mother thing—they gravitate toward me, to tell the truth, even when it hurts. I love them even when they do not love themselves. It comes from love. I love black people. They need to know that someone cares."

She sees mothering as a traditional way of working with the men. "The men have an internal battle. Who other than a mother would they come to? Mothering people is being what we used to be. We come from nontraditional feminists. I have embraced what we used to do." She points out that in black and brown indigenous cultures, women are *expected* to be leaders and that it sends the wrong message for a woman leader to compromise who she is as a woman as a way to communicate with men.

"The young men have such fractured relationships with women," she explains. But even if their relationships with their mothers are not ideal, mother reverence is still strong enough in men from black and brown cultures that the men have some reference for it. The men, she says, need to learn to interact with a woman, learn other ways of living, and learn that violence is not the way to live.

Men who may not have respected or trusted anyone before come to respect and trust her. "There needs to be trust on both sides. I work with people who have committed murder, and it never occurred to me that I could be in danger." One day the power went out in the prison and the room she was working in went dark. A guard should have come to get Dominque, but he never came. "I did not feel afraid, and I knew that they would not hurt me. They feed off of love." She adds that women also need to turn some of the love toward themselves. "There's a lot that needs to be done in terms of the women. People have to save themselves."

Congresswoman Eleanor Holmes Norton has made a career out of helping women save themselves, and her work is an example of how black women can bring dramatically different thinking and strategies to the table. She is an attorney, a native of Washington, DC, a law professor at Georgetown Law School, and since 1990 the congressional delegate for Washington, DC. A civil rights veteran, she participated in the Mississippi Freedom Summer and was a founding organizer of the Student Nonviolent Coordinating Committee. As interested as she was in issues of race, she was also an early voice in the distinctive challenges of black women. She was a signer of the 1970 *Black Woman's Manifesto* by the Third World Women's Alliance, which declared that black women were concerned with gender as well as race.

She took her Yale Law School degree to become assistant legal director for the American Civil Liberties Union, where she brought nontraditional cases. She orchestrated a particularly dramatic case on behalf of women writers at *Newsweek* magazine whose jobs had been assigned on the basis of gender. Men were reporters and correspondents; women were relegated to doing background research and supplementing the reporting of men. Yet Norton said that she had to teach, encourage, and shepherd the women involved.

> These women had been at the top of their classes, Phi Beta Kappas and Fulbrights. Women were interested in jobs in journalism of various types, and magazine journalism seemed to be quite appealing. Obviously the magazines were getting the best talent. Women had the credentials, but then when they started, they were not allowed equal positions. I had to gather the women together. They were afraid. Even today, women are often afraid to push for higher positions.

She devised an approach that was novel at the time—she initiated a class-action suit, the first of its kind, and then she called a press conference with all the women, attracting media attention. Norton had to educate the women to see the big-picture implications of their individual job situations and then to give them the confidence they needed to go forward. Norton was a striking figure herself. Katharine Graham, owner of the *Washington Post* and *Newsweek*, later recalled Norton as a dramatic figure—"highly articulate, tough, militant, black—and pregnant"—at a time when most pregnant women stopped working.

Newsweek wanted to negotiate with Norton alone, but she insisted that the group of women be in the room. She considered the hearing to be part of the women's education. Concern for the whole collective inspired a brilliant legal maneuver.

Graham had resisted coming to the hearing, but Norton insisted. "Katharine Graham, owner and sister, was there at the negotiation. I was not going to have a woman publisher in charge and she not be there!" Later, Graham would admit that "the suits were right. We [women] made a lot of progress." Now, Norton told me, she regularly sees the women she represented working in higher positions.

She was appointed to the New York City Commission on Human Rights and became its chair from 1970 to 1977. During that period, Norton held the first hearings in the country on discrimination against women, bringing prominent feminists from around the country to testify, and became a leader in the recognition of women's issues in the law. She made history in women's law when she raised awareness of the applicability of the 1964 Civil Rights Act to women and was a founder of the *Women's Rights Law Reporter*, the first legal journal of women's law.

President Jimmy Carter appointed Norton to chair the Equal Employment Opportunity Commission in 1977; she was the first woman in that position. Under her direction, the EEOC issued the first set of regulations outlining definitions of sexual harassment and declaring it to be a form of discrimination that violated federal civil rights laws. Meanwhile, the fight for congressional representation of the District of Columbia was heating up. Today the District is allowed representation only in the House. Eleanor Holmes Norton won her congressional seat in 1990 with Donna Brazile as her campaign manager. Norton rapidly became a major voice in the House and a formidable proponent of full voting rights for residents of the District. By 2009, Delegate Norton was chair of the House Subcommittee on Economic Development, Emergency Management.

Her signature style is a mix of traditional black middle-class charm with a big stick. At the first White House Super Bowl party of the Obama administration, Norton invited Michelle Obama to lunch. The two women met at B. Smith's, a popular upscale black restaurant in the District. They talked about DC voting rights, but Norton said the two were "like any girlfriends who put no limits on their conversation."

In early 2009, Norton wrote a letter to every single Democrat in Congress, reminding them that full DC voting rights was a civil rights issue and that black Democrats had voted for them. Characteristically, the letter was friendly, almost sweet, but the message made clear that she meant business. She suggested that the movement for DC voting rights was but another chapter of the black Civil Rights Movement and suggested that some in Congress were afraid to give a majority-black city full rights of self-governance. Then she reminded them that African Americans were the most reliable Democratic voting bloc and that she was sure no Democrat wanted to disrupt the long history of Democratic support for civil rights. She reminded them that Democrats, no matter their differences on other issues, had made civil rights a unifying signature issue and to forget that was to risk a racial split that would hurt every one of them. "The consistent support of our Democratic Caucus for equal rights, regardless of our differences on other issues, has been so strong for so long that I have no doubt we can remain a unified party on civil rights and avoid an unprecedented split in our ranks on this civil rights bill." Without the black vote, Democrats would be voted out of office. The "girlfriend" lunch with Michelle Obama was a strategic follow-up, another example of the charm and the stick.

Eleanor Holmes Norton is an example of how the Strong Black Woman style works in the corridors of Congress. She agreed that she often speaks protectively of her constituents and that her congressional style is that of a "warm demander," tough and warm at the same time.

Sheila Johnson has taken her own Strong Black Woman style into other very elite spaces. Her particular blend of strength combines the economic power of her family's fortune with a determination to have a positive impact on the way black women are perceived on television and to improve the quality of life for more women around the world. Sheila Johnson wields a kind of power that is new to African Americans, the kind that comes with being the first black female billionaire. Yet she uses that power in a way that is familiar, demonstrating how far the Strong Black Woman style can go.

The first thing you need to know about Sheila Johnson, cofounder of the Black Entertainment Network cable channel with her former husband, Robert Johnson, is that she fought against sexy music videos. Her pet project was the award-winning *Teen Summit*, where young adult hosts and teen guests discussed topics ranging from teen pregnancy to the effect of videos. Like the other women I interviewed, she said she had been helping people all her life. Sheila Johnson grew up in Chicago, the upper-middle-class child of a neurosurgeon, yet she has a very down-to-earth air, a witty sense of humor, and a ready laugh. She told me that it "makes a lot of sense" to call her a Strong Black Woman and a Fierce Angel. "I actually find it to be an honor. I really admire those qualities in women." She said that it has always been a part of her personality. "There is no question about it. It is just in my DNA. From my early childhood, I have always been a giver. I remember a girl in my school who had very little. I remember bringing her home for lunch and giving her my clothes. People have to restrain me from this. My purpose in life is to reach and give to others. I get enormous pleasure out of being a change agent."

Johnson is also a living example of self-healing. In 1999, the Johnsons sold BET to Viacom for three billion dollars. But eventually the differences between Robert and Sheila Johnson took their toll, as did what she calls "the body count" of other women. In her post-BET life—after a painful divorce—Sheila formed a new company that developed and ran hotels, spas, and catering; she named it Salamander Hospitality because salamanders can regenerate their own body parts, including whole limbs and hearts, after they have been torn off or damaged. Sheila's mother told her that she could see that marriage to the wrong man had held her back. "I was feeling very much repressed and not being able to speak my mind. Our husbands want to put us in a box so that we can only go so far. . . . Now I can see who I really am. So many women lose their way, lose their spirit, their sense of self. I came out of my marriage, my mother said, 'I never worried about you, because you never lost your spirit. You repressed it, but you never lost it.'"

After her divorce and her involvement with BET, she became a woman on a mission—actually, on many missions. She quickly became a major philanthropist. By herself and with organizations such as CARE International, she donated buildings, started programs, established micro-banks to fight poverty, and ran water lines in African villages. "I rediscovered myself, reclaimed my life. My spirit came to the surface, threefold now. I wish I had thirty more years to do all I want to do."

She is the only woman to be an owner or partner in three professional sports franchises: the Washington Wizards of the NBA, the Washington Mystics of the WNBA, and the Washington Capitals of the NHL. She is a member of the Council on Foreign Relations and chairwoman of the board for Parsons the New School for Design in New York City. Johnson sits on the boards of the Whitney Museum, the Centers for Disease Control Foundation, and the National Campaign to Prevent Teen and Unplanned Pregnancy. She also established the Sheila C. Johnson Performing Arts Center at the Hill School in Middleburg, Virginia. She has spent a great deal of her energy fostering social change, which is where, she told me, lies her heart.

For her, strength and giving go together. She said she learned how from her eighty-seven-year-old mother. "I got a lot of this from my mother. . . . I can still see that fierceness, she has not lost one spark. . . . She has been a very strong example. I know that in the early part of my life, I could see the spirit of strength." She repeated the DNA reference, how the impulse to help runs deeply in her, that giving heals her in return. "Now it is almost like an urge." She feels that the money she has made is not so much hers as a vehicle to help others. "I believe that the money was given to me for a reason. Even the suffering and betrayal—it was all worth it to end up where I am now. That is the consoling answer of what I have been through."

It is important to her to work personally with the people she helps. "I never get involved unless I can be there," she said. She told me the story of her connection with a particular child. He was a very little boy but he played a big instrument—the cello. As a young woman, Sheila Johnson was the first black person to be the first-chair violin in the Illinois statewide orchestra; she later authored a series of music-lesson books for children, which is still being used in school systems across the country. Before BET took off, she taught at Sidwell Friends, the same school the Obama daughters enrolled in years later, and gave extra violin lessons on the side. So the boy's playing caught the ear of an accomplished musician. "There was a little ten-year-old student who performed in my market at Palm Beach," she told me. "He took it out and played for me. I looked at his bow and it had very few hairs. But the sound that he was getting out of that cello was just amazing. You could just tell that that cello was his salvation—you could tell that it was the most important thing to him. He was able to produce the most beautiful tones, with natural vibrato. I did some inquiries." The boy came from a very, very low-income family, and he was going to lose his cello that very week. "I said I will take care of this talent that he has. His passion is going to save him."

She decided that he would have a new cello, worthy of his talent, and worried that it wouldn't get to him before his old one was taken away. She had her staff find the best teacher in the area and told them that when the cello arrived, "I will give it to him myself so that he knows that I care. I want to see the look on his face."

Sheila knows that she cannot give indiscriminately, though, because she has so much she wants to get done. Instead, she gives in a targeted way. There are issues that are close to her heart: education, music, quality of life—and people, particularly women and children. Together with instinct, her knowledge in these areas keeps her from getting burned. She has become sanguine about the solicitations for money that she receives.

"I innately can see what is needed. I can feel the person who needs it. I can tell a fraud from someone who really needs it. I think it is a combination of age and experience and the more you are burned. Those people, I give them enough rope to hang themselves."

Her interest in women is much more than sentimental. As global ambassador for CARE, she has seen how "women do carry the problems of the world on their shoulders—education, economic empowerment; women really do hold the society together." She believes that women could and should act much more strategically because "they also have the abilities that are beyond the daily responsibility to really turn things around."

But first women have to value and care for themselves. "They have to take responsibility for their own lives." That means that women have to fight for themselves. One of the biggest battles of Sheila Johnson's life began in her own backyard. Sheila's daughter Paige is an accomplished equestrian, jumping fences on horseback at national and international meets; Sheila needed a home with land to accommodate Paige's horses. There was a three-hundred-acre parcel for sale in Middleburg, Virginia—centuries-old venerable horse country. A developer was interested in the property, and local people were worried that he planned to subdivide the land for houses, permanently changing the landscape and the character of the region. The community approached Sheila to save the land. Fortunately for them, she was interested, and she told them at the time that she was thinking about putting a spa on a small part of the property. Her hospitality-company holdings already included a prepared gourmet-food market in the area, and a Salamander Resort and Spa seemed to be a natural fit.

Maybe the community thought it would never happen or maybe they were blinded by their desire to keep the property in one parcel, but no objections to her resort plans came up before the sale. But when Sheila Johnson started the project a different group of people raised their heads, and things turned ugly, *very* ugly.

"I did not expect this kind of combative reaction. . . . They were upper-class white elite society, old money 'trustifarians,' living off of their inheritances." But it was clear that they did not know with whom they had decided to tangle. The area had not included black people like the Johnsons before. Sheila described a time when she was still married to Robert Johnson. "I had clogged a drain and flooded the stables. My ex-husband was standing there with the man who came to repair it. He looked at my husband and said, 'I guess you know where the mop and pail is to clean this up.' Bob said to him, 'I own this place.'" The startled worker spurted, "How did that happen?"

Sheila Johnson said, "I guess they didn't think I was going to do it. My backbone went up even straighter." She was ready for battle—a very carefully laid out and strategic battle. As the opponents made racial references, the personal conflict took on much larger implications. "I worked through all that. I wanted to break the bigger wall of racism. I remained a woman of grace. I had to do my homework, see what made these people tick. You have to do an investigation."

They said to her face, "We defeated Disney and we are going to defeat you." Their arrogance only made her more determined. "The more they push me, the more I just don't give up. I don't believe that it was the people who originally gave me the go-ahead, but they don't come forward to support you. The press loved the story and they worked it—they made the situation worse. And still I remained who I am. I still give to the community, the community center, the hospital. I resigned from the tennis center—it hit the paper—but it was because I had gotten my own tennis court and I didn't need theirs."

When she began to build the resort, some cars sported bumper stickers that read "Don't BET Middleburg." There were racial threats and anonymous letters. The FBI moved in. "It was quite a tragic undertaking. So then I went back into assessment. I hired a good team of lawyers. Land-use folk. I brought real experts in. They said, 'Let's make it work.' We started putting together a strategic plan how to get 'round the haters. They were really coming with some off-the-wall arguments." The building was quietly approved with the support of the people who had supported her in the first place. In other words, the white community broke ranks. Sheila Johnson broke ground.

She said, "I won the battle *and* I won the war."

How did she do it? "First," she said, "you have to take stock of yourself. I think one thing you have to understand is who you really are inside and out and how you project yourself into the community. If you are harsh, aggressive, if you are questionable or the type of person who does not follow through on promises, it is almost impossible to move into a new area." She said that she has been told by men not to be so aggressive, not to speak her mind, but she believes every woman must come to know the difference between superfluous harshness and strength and how to keep their eyes on the prize. She told me there are times when it's more emotionally gratifying to say what is on your mind, but it is important to learn to "bite your tongue sometimes. What is it you really want? Play the game. You've got to learn to be flexible. You have to do what you have to do. Even if it is a temporary moment."

At the same time, she said, it is important not to lose your own identity. Johnson told me that sometimes her children have accused her of selling out, but she said she avoids that trap by "stepping back" out of the game to remind herself who she is. "I have not lost sight of who I am. I don't think there is any job that is too small for anybody. I will be cleaning up a spot and my staff will say, 'Dr. J., you shouldn't be doing that.' If I have to clean up my own step if I have tracked in mud and we've got a meeting coming in here, I'll do it." Stepping back out of the game, remembering who she is, "reconnecting so they could see me in a different way," has the additional benefit of disarming your opponents, because they cannot presume to understand everything about you.

She sees affluent black people who have forgotten how to connect with people, and she views that as a mistake. "I am a woman that likes to give of myself. If I see an employee who is in need, then I am going to be there for them. That is my spirit. They will never say, 'She thought she was above us.' I see people who have gotten to a status in their lives, financially or socially, and they become different people. I hate that more than anything in the world. I could be right back there tomorrow. I keep this all in perspective. I know who I am and I know the gifts that God has given me, and He could easily take them away if I don't take care of them."

She wants women to be, in her words, "fully human and fully powerful," and so she approaches villages holistically, addressing maternal health, building schools, and providing small-business loans. "Women are really the bearers to keep their families alive." In villages in Africa, she and CARE International built water lines. She went to one village to talk with the women. She did not let her staff tell them she was the person responsible for the water. The women saw her as another woman, like them. They asked about her life. They asked how she managed to travel and still do her chores. Her husband, Judge Newman, was with her, and they asked, didn't he mind? He told them that he supported his wife's work. Sheila said, "They straightened up after that. They were different for my having been there."

Clean water is vital to any village, but there was another reason to build water lines to this one; they were particularly important to the survival of the women. Carrying water was considered to be the work of women, and the two-to three-mile trip was dangerous. Two of them had already been raped and killed.

On the very day that the water lines were becoming operational, Sheila Johnson was there. "The women were standing in line waiting for the water to come. They started to cheer." But some other women had left to get water, anyway. Sheila's voice wavered with emotion: "I don't know if they didn't know about the water lines coming on that day or what, but some of the women went out and some of them did not come back."

Women are disproportionately victims of poverty and oppression, and so Johnson has chosen to focus on "building solidarity and empowering women and girls to become catalysts for social change." Women are pivotal in families, and helping them is the best way to help families and communities. International organizations most often give microloans to mothers because they are the fastest path to widespread social change. Johnson is the executive producer of *A Powerful Noise*, also a project with CARE. The film was described as "a meditation on the inherent potential of women to change the world."

Artist and activist Rha Goddess fully intends to change the world. She has a brown china-doll face that slips fluidly from a dead-on serious stare to a wide-open smile and back again in a way that disarms her audiences. She is a "hip-hop baby" and spirit woman who is developing what she calls the "new wave of black feminist artistry." She has long been working on issues of art, political consciousness, and women. As international spokesperson for the Universal Zulu Nation—a hip-hop awareness group founded and led by hip-hop pioneer Afrika Bambaataa—and one of the widely known Nuyorican Poets, she has been central to the spoken-word wing of hip-hop. She is cofounder of the Sista II Sista Freedom School of Young Women of Color and cocreator and co-executive producer of the performance movement *We Got Issues!* and the Next Wave of Women and Power international leadership network for young women. In 2000, *Essence* magazine named her one of thirty women to watch in the new millennium.

Rha Goddess grew up in Brooklyn, New York, and worked for a while in corporate America, but, she says, "The universe had other plans for me." Her moment of transformation came after the deaths of five people close to her in five months—including her mother—and after she faced her own mortality when a loaded gun was aimed point-blank at her head. When she survived, she knew that she had been spared for a reason. In 1998, after a twelve-week cleansing fast, she was given a sacred name by her mentor, Queen Afua, a khemic healer in the African-Egyptian tradition. She has since simplified that name into Rha Goddess. She discovered in herself what she calls "a new trinity of creativity, wisdom, and intuition, the energy of the Great Mother," and now she operates from a "Light Supreme."

Years later, when tragedy once again touched her life and a close friend committed suicide, Rha Goddess wrote, "How Do You Spell Relief?" a poem that would become the genesis of *Low*, a performance piece and the first part of a trilogy called *Meditations*. The series brought to the forefront the multitude of issues surrounding black people and mental illness and the ways that those issues are exacerbated by systemic poverty and challenging cultural attitudes.

The reviews often called the play "raw" because it forced the audience members to see and care about a woman who would otherwise go unnoticed, a commentary on what Rha calls "a society that would rather drug and confine than love." The play jolts its audience on purpose, in part by violating their expectations for a black woman. There are times when you expect the character Low to buck up, take a deep breath, and save herself. You realize that you expect it because you have been trained to expect it and that it has been a long, long time since you spent an evening feeling *with* a black woman in any other way.

Rha Goddess believes that women represent the goddess, and so she also believes what black culture and the larger culture only flirt with—that black women carry the energy of the Black Goddess, the Sacred Dark Feminine. She believes that women's neglect of themselves in favor of caring for other people is dangerous for the person and collective. "I trust in a very deep place that when I fortify my soul and my spirit, when we fortify our souls and our spirits, that the universe will line up beside us and we will have everything we need to go the distance."

In her programs with young women she is working toward a "feminine-centered leadership with energy harnessed from the goddess, based in love and in perfect alignment with who I really am . . . a match between our spirit and soul. Often our girls and women feel that they have to be hard like the fellows, or sexual. I've brought another alternative." The *Meditations* series is designed to embed larger cultural, political, and spiritual concerns in a quest for wholeness. How do young women act as true citizens to begin to shift the political landscape of this society? Rha Goddess answers, "We cannot take our womanhood for granted. . . . We have a responsibility to ourselves to honor who we are and bringing what we have been called to bring."

In 2006, in a speech to the Bioneers conference called "Who's Got Next: Cultivating Feminine-Centered Leadership in a Hip-Hop Era," she explained the connection between women saving themselves and the planet. She told the large audience that the Next Wave was the "celebration of the empowerment, healing, and transformation of humanity through the uplifting of the hearts, minds and souls of young women. . . . Who's got next?" she asked. She looked around the room. "We do."

She is, of course, not alone. New Age writers like Andrew Harvey and Daniel Pinchbeck have been saying that the way of the Dark Feminine will transform the next age. Often, the Dark Feminine is an internal presence of the soul, seen in dreams. China Galland, one of the first writers to call for a renewed recognition of the Dark Feminine, wrote *Longing for Darkness: Tara and the Black Madonna*, which traced her personal journey to the internal recognition of the Dark Feminine.

Women in other cultures have drawn from the Dark Feminine for social justice too. Lillian Comas-Diaz is executive director of the Transcultural Mental Health Institute, a clinical professor at the George Washington University department of psychiatry and behavioral sciences, and a private practitioner in Washington, DC. In an invited address to the American Psychological Association after winning a national award, Dr. Comas-Diaz outlined the role of the Dark Feminine in fights for social justice by women of color and said that many Latina womanist activists preferred a dark feminine divinity that reflected the color of their skin. The goddesses are emblems of international resistance and liberation, such as the South American Christian Virgin of Guadalupe, who is an icon of global liberation. Through her and other forms of womanist spirituality, or "Spirita," the women reconnect with grace, with "the spiritual energy for seeking harmony and beauty." "Womanism" is a term popularized in the 1980s by Alice Walker in *In Search of Our Mothers' Gardens: Womanist Prose*. It refers to a feminism that addresses the lives and concerns of women of color.

Women in Africa who are social-justice workers are also drawing strength and inspiration from their own dark goddesses. Ifi Amadiume, Dartmouth College professor of religion and African and African American studies, predicted that Africa would have to reinvent itself after the ravages of colonialism and that women would be central activists. Important roles have been taken on by African women such as Ellen Johnson-Sirleaf, Liberian president; Baleka Mbete, South African interim president, parliamentary speaker, and African National Congress chairwoman; and the nine female Nigerian senators. African women have a long tradition of being strong. The only thoroughly researched Amazons were the fighting women of Dahomey, elite eighteenth- and nineteenth-century female troops in the Western African kingdom of the Fon tribe, now Benin.

The women were fiercely independent and physically strong, disciplined fighters. French soldiers considered them to be equal warriors.

African culture has retained its own goddesses, and women activists are drawing inspiration from them. In 2000, Ifi Amadiume wrote *Daughters of the Goddess, Daughters of Imperialism: African Women Struggle for Culture, Power and Democracy.* In it, she called the grassroots female leaders who were working to restore African culture and better the lives of ordinary people the "Daughters of the Goddess," contrasted with elite women who were working to enrich and Europeanize themselves and their families.

African women have been effective at the grassroots level. At an Initiative for Inclusive Security conference on Women Waging Peace in 2007, Donald Steinberg, the former ambassador to Angola, told a story: The powerful Angolan rebels had gone into the bush. Male negotiators went in to try to talk with them. They did not survive. A woman went in. She was in there a long time and was feared dead. Then she emerged with a message that the leader was listening and wanted to speak with his own mother. When his mother came, he, too, emerged from the bush.

If black women can celebrate themselves, they break the cycle of struggle, self-sacrifice, and miserable silence. They can draw straight and strong lines from historical black women to themselves. They can talk about their accomplishments and their mistakes. Delegate Eleanor Holmes Norton said that women should bring their whole selves to the table, knowing that the lessons they have already learned will serve them well. "I think that women should bring the confidence that they have built up over their lives and understand that it is transferable. They can't remake themselves for each and every position. In fact, you will be seen as inauthentic if you remake yourself for each and every new role you are playing."

When Delegate Norton says to bring your whole self to the table, when Sheila Johnson says to step back and remember who you are, when Rha Goddess says to reach deep down and listen, they are telling black women to value who they are. When Joan Hairston and Dominque Stevenson talk about having to respond to the problems around them, they are following in a tradition that is honorable and effective.

In the United States, black women have been more defined than defining. Their ability to define themselves has been impeded by history, race, poverty, and gender. The women I spoke to had all taken the time to think deeply about themselves and how they wanted to fit within black people and women. Eleanor

Holmes Norton was instrumental at several important steps in the empowerment of women. Joan Hairston worked to get jobs in the mines for women of several races. Even Dominque Stevenson, who worked primarily with male inmates,
consciously approached them from a woman's perspective. Black women have
historically been hesitant to speak much about gender issues, but by 2003, aca-
demics Johnnetta Cole and Beverly Guy Sheftall broke through with their book,
Gender Talk: The Struggle for Women's Equality in African American Communities.

In several ways the 2008 presidential campaign was an important step for
black women in defining themselves. Hillary Clinton enjoyed early support
from African Americans, particularly women. In an October 2007 CNN poll,
Clinton led Obama in black votes, 57 percent to his 33 percent. Black women
made up most of her lead with black people and a good percentage of her overall
lead. Although black men were more evenly spread between the two candidates,
68 percent of the black females favored Clinton, a 26 percent difference with
black men. The gender gap between white women and men was only 11 percent.
For the first time, black women were breaking the black voting bloc, signaling
with their early support for Hillary Clinton that they were ready to consider
themselves as people of gender as well as race.

CNN political analyst Bill Schneider said that the difference "underscores
the fact that the nation's vote is divided not only by race but also by gender.
Black women don't just vote their black identity. They also vote their identity
as women." The black female vote was the Clinton campaign's to lose, and they
did. In the heat of the race, the Clintons lobbed racialized insults at Obama,
creating several of what are commonly called "black moments" when they suggested that a black man could not win and when they appealed to "hardworking
white" people. Obama might have been biracial, but he was black enough to be
the target of what seemed like racism. The majority of the black vote, including
those of black women, moved to Obama.

Black women recognized the ways in which they were like other women
and needed to form alliances with them. In a letter to white feminists during the
2008 presidential primary season, Alice Walker called for alliances. "We have
come a long way, sisters, and we are up to the challenges of our time. One of
which is to build alliances based not on race, ethnicity, color, nationality, sexual
preference, or gender, but on Truth."

Black women will have to figure out how to honor other black women,
how to speak up and work together as women. Sheila Johnson told the 2008
graduating class at historically black Spelman College to "embrace each other

with strength, dignity, and loyalty." In order to embrace other black women, to network and support, black women will need to stop hiding their accomplishments and work together in new ways.

African American women must figure out how they feel about the Sacred Dark Feminine as the image becomes more prominent in the United States. Rha Goddess overtly draws strength and wisdom from the Dark Feminine and sees in herself a reflection of the strength and love of the Sacred Dark Divine. Dominque Stevenson follows in the traditions of aboriginal female leaders, who often draw from Sacred Dark Feminine divinities. Whether they choose to make use of the Sacred Dark Feminine for themselves, black women will come face-to-face with a rapidly growing use by people of other races around them. Black women around the world live with the knowledge of the Sacred Dark Feminine, the goddesses, orishas, and Madonnas. The newest waves of immigrants from Africa, South and Central America, and the Caribbean are bringing their dark goddesses with them to the United States, where they join up with a centuries-long tradition of secularized images in books, films, advertisements, and television shows. New Age and Jungian writers, therapists, and practitioners are reflecting escalating references to the Sacred Dark Feminine, using images of contemporary black women.

The mythology permeates the secular culture, and black women have to wrestle with a mythology that arrived before them and will linger long after. With it comes some freedoms from the mainstream constraints of Western femininity, but those freedoms also bring a heavy load of responsibility. Even the most wonderful and rich stories will never equal a life. The myth is always an exaggeration, punched up for dramatic effect. It has survived in part because the culture has needed it but also because it makes for good stories. That does not mean that the myth does not carry some truths or connections to the lives of living black women. It matters who controls the myth.

The *idea* of the Strong Black Woman is so big and so wonderful that it would seem too good to be true. The image is just that, an image. But like any other image, it is a combination of social reality and fantasy. The image of Strong Black Women is so strong, so perfectly giving, that it is difficult to imagine an actual human being doing all that she is supposed to do. Could anyone be so selfless, so self-sacrificing as the women in the myths? Would anyone dedicate herself so fully to the causes of other people?

Comparing the image to the actual women I interviewed, I have found the image to be too good to be true, but mainly because it is incomplete. The women identified themselves as cultural and gender workers. Although they spoke modestly, their life stories are woven with the strands of the mythological stories. They are more than willing to face the terrible parts of life; they feel that they *must* face them and fix them. It is easy to see how they could fit into the larger American mythology, because they are strong, giving, and fierce when necessary. They are in the business of redemption, and redemption is the primary American story. Yet—and there is a yet—they have real lives. They care about themselves, and they resist the characterization that fierce is all they get to be.

The Dark Goddesses have long been associated with rivers; the Strong Black Woman and the Sacred Dark Feminine are like rivers on parallel paths, flowing along beside each other but, at least in the United States, rarely joining together. But whether or not a black woman identifies closely with the Dark Feminine, the two figures are quite similar. Some women, like Rha Goddess, draw strength from their relationship with a Dark Female Divine. Others have learned from women in their lives, and many consider their compassionate strength to be innate—as they said, in their DNA. In some ways, the black woman is the most emotionally free adult in American society: freer to show love than many men, particularly black men; freer to show anger, even ferocity, than middle-class white women; freer to tell the blunt truth than just about any adult in polite society. She really is like the queen on the chessboard, able to move in any direction, depending on the game.

In the ancient myths, the role of the Dark Feminine was to help one face the terrible inevitabilities of life; the women with whom I spoke saw it as their mission to enter and address the terrible. Black women, much like many other women, have been taught to be other-oriented. The difference is that, for black women in America, it is often impossible to walk away. Regardless of social class, racially related trouble is never far away. They know of need so great that it is, for many of them, impossible not to answer it all the time.

Many women marked a moment in their lives when they determined that they had no choice but to take on the problems around them. They faced trouble in the same spirit as the black female college students who thought college would be difficult and unpleasant yet expected to and did graduate. The women waded into trouble. Joan Hairston walked straight up to the mines and challenged trouble at its source. They intended to fix trouble, to heal people. And they did.

Of course, black women still face discrimination and there is yet much work to do. In a study reported by the League of Black Women, 80 percent of

professional black women reported racial workplace bias, but the study recom-
mended networking, mentorship, and other support mechanisms as potential
remedies. That is what a discussion of the Sacred Dark Feminine can do for
black women. Black women are faced with a choice: to engage with the Dark
Feminine image or not. The choice is not whether to be associated with the
image in the eyes of the public—that was decided centuries ago and cannot be
readily changed. The Dark Feminine is deeply embedded in Western and other
cultures, and the fierce femininity is so inextricably associated with the black
female body that black women could not divorce themselves from it in the eyes
of others if they wanted to. The choice is how black women respond to the association that still does and will probably continue to affect their lives.

Fierce energy, deep compassion, and often a connection to a holy spirit
create a very powerful combination. Black women need to face the image and
decide if and how to make use of it. They need to engage in the discourse about
the image as full members or recognize that their avoidance of the image will
not stop others from making use of it. Some women will decide that the image
and strategies of the Strong Black Woman are too powerful to run away from.
The power and resonance in American culture can be used in ways that protect
and nurture black women too.

For most of the Western world, the Sacred Dark Feminine is an internal
presence, something that people feel, and it gives them hope and spiritual ref-
uge. For many black women, the Strong Black Woman is only active; the role
becomes their never-ending to-do list. These women run the risk of undernour-
ishing themselves, of mistreating their bodies and draining their spirits. If black
women can reconcile the two, the healing and the doing, they can value and
nourish themselves in a new way. They can give themselves permission to be
still, to go within and learn to listen to themselves. Rha Goddess said, "There
is not a day when I do not get tired thinking of how much work we have to do,"
but because she has learned to nourish herself, she can live a life of joy while
addressing the problems around her.

Other women have been calling for black women to save themselves, to see
themselves as worthy of saving. Susan Taylor has been telling black women for
years to love themselves, to take care of themselves, and to surround themselves
with other people who will care for them. As editor in chief and columnist of
Essence magazine, she told how she had learned to love herself as well as she
loved other people. It is not an easy lesson for women who have been taking
care of a race for centuries. The need for self-care may seem self-evident and

simple, but it can be difficult for women who have been taught to take care of everybody else.

The women leaders to whom I spoke have learned to take care of themselves. For Dominque, bringing balance to her life is important. She has learned that in order to keep going, she has to take care of herself. She makes sure that she gets as much rest as she can. Because her children know and see so much of the world's suffering, she makes sure to balance out their lives with pleasant experiences. Playing keeps her energy up so she can do the work she does. As much as possible, she tries to save the weekends for her family. "I have fun. We hang out as a family. We ran through Borders and played hide and seek. They travel with me too."

She makes time for her relationship with her husband and for vacations. Like many African Americans, even middle-class ones, she did not grow up taking vacations in the way they are generally thought of. Vacations have historically been complicated for black people—public accommodations were difficult or even dangerous. Racist rudeness could spoil the best-planned vacation, and many hotels and restaurants did not serve African Americans at all. Making a mistake could be deadly. For generations, many black families "vacationed" by driving to visit extended family—with whatever family tensions came with that too—and many black women did not grow up with family traditions of getting totally away. Dominque found that she had to create new traditions and make vacations a priority. They did not always have to be expensive, but they allowed her to provide family-only time.

"Grace" is a word that comes up often in discussions of black women. It connotes an inner calmness amid trouble, the ability to survive with one's dignity intact. When the "trustifarians" were attacking her, Sheila Johnson said with pride that "I remained a woman of grace." Grace is a characteristic that has been used often in discussions of Michelle Obama and one that black women have said leads them to both admire and identify with her. A *Washington Post* article ran with the title "The Very Image of Affirmation: In Michelle Obama, Black Women See a Familiar Grace & Strength Writ Large." The article mentioned fifty-four-year-old Aziza Gibson-Hunter, a conceptual artist and mother of four who lives in northwest Washington, DC. Gibson-Hunter said that Michelle Obama would transcend the usual stereotypes, that what she sees in Michelle Obama is strength:

> I saw it in my mother. When I was a kid, I saw it in the women in the church, this dignified strength. Now, I see it in the younger women

of my extended family, who weather their personal tragedies with a resilience that is remarkable for such young women. I think that is real. I think Michelle Obama is her own woman. I think people with the stereotype thing need to get over it. She is forcing people who have never taken the time to know who we are as black women to take a second look. To actually see, for once in their life, that there are black women that are brilliant and graceful, intelligent, well spoken and have their own sense of themselves. And it doesn't have to be measured up to anyone else.

African American women combine traits that are often perceived as separate; they are whole, nurturing and fierce, caring and commanding. It is an organic feminism, an organic leadership. The women to whom I spoke were not interested in a return. They had confronted trouble to remedy it, not for self-aggrandizement. They helped for the sake of helping, and because they were not building reputations or personal brands, they were willing to take risks that more ambitious people may not have. Joan Hairston could afford to not care who liked her.

In films and stories, African American women are often shown as interested strangers, as fiercely compassionate helpers to other people. But in living, breathing black women, compassion becomes bolder, stronger, less serendipitous. The word the women I interviewed use is "love." Theirs is a particularly active love, and they use it in ways that move away from the sentimental passivity commonly associated with womanly love. Dominque Stevenson spoke of prison inmates "feeding on love." Sheila Johnson wielded her fortune as a mighty force that evokes dramatic changes in people's lives. Hers is not an anonymous, gentle philanthropy—the money is only part of her message. She means for the people she helps to know that she cares deeply about them and that her caring means that something dramatic is going to happen to them. For the women to whom I spoke, love was more than a feeling; it was an action verb. It was a process by which a person or group of people became the focus of an intervention. It is fierce.

The women I interviewed considered themselves to be Strong Black Women and Fierce Angels. They willingly shouldered all the commitment and responsibility that came with the job, but they were not self-sacrificial. They were careful to maintain a balance between selflessness and self-care. When they were exhausted, they rested or went on vacations or looked to their spiritual resources.

They were neither lonely nor miserable. They found joy and humor as well as self-meaning in their work.

Although all of the women were educated, most of them found themselves to be working in fields different from their educations. They followed the need and learned, just as Eleanor Holmes Norton said, that they had the skills, the strategies, and the quick studies to do what needed to be done. Although none went looking for the spotlight, when there was a void, they filled it. The Strong Black Woman role and style seems to be particularly flexible as a strategy—it can be combative, smooth, serious, or funny. It appears to work with groups across race, gender, and social class, from the streets, coal mines, and prisons to corporate boardrooms, Congress, and the United Nations, with poor young women and wealthy, powerful men. The combination of strong love and fierce energy is powerful too.

When black women move out of the suppressed, loyal helper role into the lead, they turn the traditional hero story on its head. In American stories—indeed, in heroic stories around the world—the strong (and male) hero is usually alone, unhampered by emotional distractions. Love, in American discourse, is often seen as a passive emotion. It is a feeling, a good feeling but one without muscle. Evil, on the other hand, is often seen as strong and threatening. It is a rather odd way to think about good and evil because it suggests that evil always has the upper hand. But for the African American women as they think of themselves, the battle is not so uneven. They mean for their Strong Black Woman love to threaten evil. They fully intend to save people, and often they do. Their strong love has consequences, delivered with attitude and grace. They remind us that strong love, intelligently and energetically applied, can evoke great change. They are the worthy daughters of Harriet Tubman, these Fierce Angels.

ACKNOWLEDGMENTS

FIERCE ANGELS HAS been a work of love in many ways. Some people worried that a book that unmasked cultural secrets such as this one should never be written, while others, the ones to whom I listened, insisted that it must be written. The insisters are people who have been wonderful to me. The first mentioned must be Craig Seymour, author, photographer, professor, and former student, who is the godfather of this book. He urged me to write the way I needed to write and took steps to guide the project in the right direction, toward Sarah Lazin, the super agent who took an interest in an academic and has been there every time I needed her. Sarah believed in this book from the start and has fought for it all along the way. This paperback edition exists because of her persistence and support. She is *Fierce Angels'* Fierce Angel.

I owe much thanks to the editors at Chicago Review Press, Cynthia Sherry and Susan Betz, who welcomed and championed this edition, and Michelle Schoob, who gently guided it to publication. There are other people to whom I am very grateful, particularly my amazing daughter, Kelsey, who really should be listed as the coauthor for all of the research, article retrieval, printing, photocopying, videotaping, and computer repair that she did and for her constant love and support.

My other family members, Loretta and Khalila Nobles, James, Laurice, and Chris and Mekia Parks, brought to me numerous examples and insights. Freeman, Richa, and Shelia Smith told me their own stories. Three holy women, Rev. Pat Bacon of Calvary Presbyterian Church in Asheville, NC; Sister Mary Aquin O'Neill, RSM, PhD; and Diane Caplin, PhD, of the Mount Saint Agnes Theological Center for Women in Baltimore, provided critical and enthusiastic

262   Acknowledgments

Former and current graduate students, Jesse Scott, Kenyatta Graves, Tamara
Wilds-Lawson, Tyrone Stewart, Chyann Oliver, Lisa Gill, and Patrick Grzanka
took as much care of me as I did of them. Stephanie Stevenson and Mike Casiano
insprired me. Valerie Brown, Ashley Richerson, and Julia Newton provided
essential office help and encouragement. Vernonica McDougal tracked down
Ernest Varner, who graciously lent his beautiful painting *Good Morning Lord* for
the cover of this edition and became an enthusiastic partner. My departmen-
tal chairs, Nancy Struna and John Caughey, gave their blessings for an unusual
project. Michael Robinson and Stanford Carpenter were my knowing guides
to the complex world of comics. Chris Watkins and Jon Boon of the College of
Arts and Humanities Technical Services unit cheerfully disentangled my computer snafus, and Jennifer Patterson uploaded images that were too big for my
computer.

Others who went well beyond the call of their everyday duty to help me
included Jennifer Marsh of the Museum of Fine Arts in Boston; Eliza Mar-
quez of the Associated Press; Gary Gillespie of the American Friends Service
Committee; Joseph Sciorra of the John D. Calandra Italian American Institute
at Queens College, CUNY; Tim Thomas of the *Baltimore Sun* Group; John
O'Brien of Trinity Stores; Elizabeth Bell of the Asia Society; Michael Loren-
zini of the New York Municipal Archives; Jed Sundwall; the folks at DC Comics Rights and Permissions; and photographer Joshua McKerrow, who brought
intelligence and sensitivity to his pictures.

Most of all, I wish to express how deeply honored I am by the women who
trusted me with their stories.

NOTES

Abbreviations: The *New York Times*, www.nytimes.com, is abbreviated as *NYT.* The *Washington Post*, www.washingtonpost.com, is abbreviated as *WP.* The *National Catholic Reporter*, www.ncronline.org, is abbreviated as *NCR.*

Chapter 1: The Sacred Dark Feminine

In the science of particle physics   Physics Nobel Prize laureate Leon Lederman wrote that in the field of quantum physics, it is theorized that a vast darkness existed prior to the big bang, that it held potential matter, and that suddenly, in a trillionth of a second, that potential became everything. But Lederman notes that because there is no data, only God knows how it happened. Leon Lederman with Dick Teresi, *The God Particle: If the Universe Is the Answer, What Is the Question?* (New York: Mariner Books, 2006).

Most mammals are born at night   Karen Fulton, former mammal curator, Baltimore Zoo, personal communication, July 5, 2007.

Creation stories are extremely important   Mircea Eliade, *Myth and Reality*, trans. W. R. Trask (New York: Harper & Row, 1963).

The first statues that humans carved   Stephen R. Berlant, "The Origin and Significance of Anthropomorphic Goddess Figurines with Particular Emphasis on The Venus of Willendorf," *Journal of Prehistoric Religion*, Vol. XIII (1999), 22–29; Marija Gimbutas, *The Living Goddess*, ed. Miriam Robbins Dexter (Berkeley: University of California, 2001).

The oldest known written story   Edward Chiera, *Sumerian Epics and Myths* (Chicago: Oriental Institute Publications, 1934); Samuel Noah Kramer, *Sumerian Mythology: A Study of Spiritual and Literary Achievement in the Third Millennium B.C.* (Philadelphia: American Philosophical Society, 1944); Diane Wolkstein and Samuel Noah Kramer, *Inanna, Queen of Heaven and Earth: Her Stories and Hymns from Sumer* (New York: Harper & Row, 1983).

She was "the womb . . . "   Joseph Campbell, *The Masks of God: Occidental Mythology* (New York: Penguin, 1976), 25.

In pre-Homeric Greece   Jane Ellen Harrison, *Prolegomena to the Study of Greek Religion* (Cambridge, UK: Cambridge University, 1903), 7.

"First of all, then, Khaos came to be" Hesiod, *Theogony*, trans. Robert Lamberton (New Haven: Yale University, 1983), line 116.

Night gave birth to the heavens and day Hesiod, *Theogony*, lines 123–124.

In Greek myth, Rhea Edward Tripp, *The Meridian Handbook of Classical Mythology* (New York: Penguin, 1970).

The Angles—the future English Campbell, *Masks of God*.

Plutarch wrote that Celtic women Peter Berresford Ellis, *The Ancient World of the Celts: An Illustrated Account* (London: Constable, 1998), 8.

Cerridwen (Cauldron, or Fortress of Wisdom) Cerridwen appeared in the work of sixteenth-century Welsh author Elis Gruffudd, who relied upon oral traditions and earlier texts, *Elis Gruffudd's Chronicle*. Available through the website of Llyfrgell Genedlaethol Cymru, the National Library of Wales. www.llgc.org.uk.

In the Hebrew Book of Wisdom *New Jerusalem Bible* in *The New Oxford Annotated Bible with the Apocrypha*, indexed by Michael D. Coogan, Marc Z. Brettler, Carol A. Newsom, and Pheme Perkins (New York: Oxford University Press, 2007).

Hokhmah, translated as "Wisdom" The Hebrew Book of Wisdom may have been written by Solomon, although there is evidence of outside influence. I quote from the *New Jerusalem Bible* and the *Apocrypha*, both included in Michael Coogan et al., *The New Oxford Annotated Bible with the Apocrypha* (New York: Oxford University Press, 2007).

"She enhances her noble birth . . . " *New Jerusalem Bible*, 8:6.

"I loved her more . . . " *New Jerusalem Bible*, 7:10.

"Compared with light . . . " *New Jerusalem Bible*, 7:29–30.

Wisdom was the creative force *Oxford Annotated Bible*, 7:22.

"She reaches mightily from one end . . . " *Oxford Annotated Bible*, 8:1.

"Though she is but one . . . " *Oxford Annotated Bible*, 7:27.

She was "intelligent, holy, unique . . . " *New Jerusalem Bible*, 7:22–23.

"Although she is alone . . . " *New Jerusalem Bible*, 7:27.

"She knows the past . . . " *New Jerusalem Bible*, 8:8–16.

She protected, taught, and saved humans *New Jerusalem Bible*, 10:1–14.

"Wisdom is brilliant, she never fades . . . " *New Jerusalem Bible*, pp. 6–12.

She manifested herself *New Jerusalem Bible*, p. 1065.

She was dark but brilliant *New Jerusalem Bible*, 7:26.

Genesis referred to goddess earth Genesis 3:13–19, *The Holy Bible: New King James Version* (Nashville: Thomas Nelson, 1993).

The dust was the goddess earth Campbell, *Masks of God*, 29.

(Some theologians have questioned) Leonardo Boff, *The Maternal Face of God: The Feminine and Its Religious Expressions*, trans. Robert R. Barr and John W. Diercksmeier (San Franscisco: Harper & Row, 1987).

In 431 AD, Theodosius II summoned Campbell, *Masks of God*, 410.

Along with diminishment Edward C. Whitmont, *Return of the Goddess* (New York: Crossroad, 1982).

Women came to be seen   In the fifteenth century, the *Malleus Maleficarum* was compiled by two Dominican friars and authorized by Pope Innocent VII as the judiciary standard. It defined women as unholy and dangerous, to be tolerated but kept at a distance from holy men. Heinrich Kramer and James Sprenger, *Malleus Maleficarum*, ed. and trans. P. G. Maxwell-Stuart (Manchester: Manchester University Press, 1487, 2008).

Some scholars believe   Monica Sjoo and Barbara Mor, *The Great Cosmic Mother: Rediscovering the Religion of the Earth* (New York: HarperOne, 1987).

Other researchers concluded   Leonard Moss and Stephen Cappannari, "In Quest of the Black Virgin: She Is Black Because She Is Black," *Mother Worship—Themes & Variations*, ed. James J. Preston (Chapel Hill: University of North Carolina Press, 1982), 53–74.

Leonard Moss and Stephen Cappannari   Moss and Cappannari, "In Quest of the Black Virgin."

The most familiar quote is this one   The Song of Solomon 1:5, *The Holy Bible: New King James Version* (Nashville: Thomas Nelson, 1993).

However, the Ethiopian version   *The Queen of Sheba and Her Only Son Menyelek* or *The Kebra Negast*, trans. E. A. Wallis Budge (London: 1932), www.sacred-texts.com. The "and" instead of the "but" is also supported by other early authoritative translations of the Old Testament, from the Hebrew to the Greek (Symmachus, who published his around 200 AD, and the Hebrew Septuagint, sometimes referred to as LXX, which had been begun around 285 BC). The Septuagint is believed to be the oldest translation from the Hebrew to the Greek and is often used by scholars to correct subsequent omissions. Symmachus was an Ebionite, one of the early Jewish-Christian groups, whose translation is important because scholars feel that he worked to capture the meaning rather than the literal translation. Thomas Harwell, *An Introduction to the Critical Study and Knowledge of the Holy Scriptures* (London: Longman, Brown, Green & Longmans, 1846); Thomas Kelly Cheyne and John Sutherland Black, *Encyclopaedia Biblica* (New York: Macmillan, 1902), 5018.

For others, the black bride symbolizes   Linda Van Norden, *The Black Feet of the Peacock: The Color-Concept "Black" from the Greeks through the Renaissance* (New York: University Press of America, 1985).

"Blessed blackness! . . . " St. Bernard of Clairvaux, Sermon 25: "Why the Bride Is Black but Beautiful," *St. Bernard on the Song of Songs*, www.archive.org/details/. St. Bernard is considered to have been one of the most powerful Christians of his day, called the "conscience of all Europe" by Katherine Gill of Yale Divinity School. http://people.bu.edu/dklepper /RN413/bernard_sermons.html.

"Who is the bride?" St. Bernard of Clairvaux, "The Ardent Love of the Soul for Christ," *The Love of God and Spiritual Friendship*, abridged, ed. James M. Houston (Portland, OR: Multnomah, 1983), 172.

In Hawkins's **Partheneia Sacra**   Henry Hawkins, *Partheneia Sacra* (Yorkshire, England: Scolar Press, 1633, 1993), 48–55.

St. Augustine and St. Bernard   Rosemary R. Ruether, *Religion and Sexism: Images of Woman in the Jewish and Christian Traditions* (New York: Simon & Schuster, 1974).

Linda Van Norden studied sixteen English   Van Norden, *Black Feet*, 63–64.

Centuries later, African American Nobel   Toni Morrison, *Beloved* (New York: Knopf, 1987).

Teresa Washington called Nana Buruku "transgeographic"   Teresa Washington, *Our Mothers, Our Powers, Our Texts: Manifestations of Ájé in Africana Literature* (Bloomington: Indiana University Press, 2005).

There are many other African goddesses   John S. Mbiti, *African Religions and Philosophy* (Garden City, NY: Anchor Books/Doubleday, 1970); Wole Soyinka, *Myth, Literature and the African World* (Cambridge, U.K.: Cambridge University Press, 2008).

More-wealthy Haitians revere   Malgorzata Oleszkiewicz-Peralba, *The Black Madonna in Latin America and Europe: Tradition and Transformation* (Albuquerque: University of New Mexico Press, 2009); Terry Rey, *Our Lady of Class Struggle: The Cult of the Virgin Mary in Haiti* (Trenton, NJ: Africa World Press, 1999).

When Winfrey mentioned   The Angel Museum, Beloit, WI, www.angelmuseum.com.

"The various aspects . . . "   Joseph Sciorra, "The Black Madonna of East Thirteenth Street," *Voices*, Journal of New York Folklore Society, Vol. 30 (2004 Spring–Summer), www .nyfolklore.org.

In 1751, Abbot Spitaleri wrote   Cited by Sciorra, "The Black Madonna."

At some point in time,   Peter Duffy, "Neighborhood Report: East Village; Showering a Madonna with Affection, Not Devotion," *NYT*, September 5, 2004.

the Madonna is housed   Margo Nash, "ON THE MAP: Retaining Devotion to a Saint and Her Private Chapel," *NYT*, August 27, 2000.

In 2004 Ernest Davis   Duffy, "Showering a Madonna."

She wrote of her reaction   Bonnie Greer, "Midnight Mass," *New Statesman*, December 25, 2000, www.newstatesman.com.

"Oh, it was horrendous,"   David Barstow, "A Catholic Parish Finds Its Black Voice," *NYT*, February 6, 2000.

Editor Michael Farrell said   Michael Farrell, "Jesus 2000," *NCR*, December 24, 1999.

"This is a haunting image . . . "   Pamela Schaeffer and John L. Allen, "Jesus 2000," *NCR*, December 24, 1999.

"The resulting image is masculine . . . "   Schaeffer and Allen, "Jesus 2000."

McKenzie explained   Schaeffer and Allen, "Jesus 2000."

One of the earliest was   www.shrinebookstore.com/church.aspx.

Due to the rediscovery   Karen King, *The Gospel of Mary of Magdala: Jesus and the First Woman Apostle* (Santa Rosa, CA: Polebridge Press, 2003).

When the Brooklyn Museum of Art   Elisabeth Bumiller, "Political Memo; For Giuliani, Making Most of Artful War with Elite," *NYT*, October 16, 1999.

Much of the early discussion   Michael Kimmelman, "Critic's Notebook: A Madonna's Many Meanings in the Art World," *NYT*, October 5, 1999.

Giuliani said, "You don't have . . ."   Dan Barry and Carol Vogel, "Giuliani Vows to Cut Subsidy Over 'Sick Art,'" *NYT*, September 23, 1999.

The next day he said   Abby Goodnough, "Giuliani Threatens to Evict Museum Over Art Exhibit," *NYT*, September 24, 1999.

William Donohue   Barry and Vogel, "Giuliani Vows to Cut Subsidy."

Bishop Thomas V. Daily   Goodnough, "Giuliani Threatens to Evict Museum."

Newark Archbishop Theodore McCarrick Ronald Smothers, "Newark Archbishop Joins Brooklyn Art Dispute," *NYT*, October 16, 1999.

After viewing the exhibit, Kit Roane, "Buchanan Visits Art Exhibit in Brooklyn and Doesn't Like It," *NYT*, November 6, 1999.

In the US Congress Steven Henry Madoff, "Shock for Shock's Sake?" *CNN*, October 4, 1999, www.cnn.com.

He specifically mentioned Yoruba Carol Vogel, "Holding Fast to His Inspiration; An Artist Tries to Keep His Cool in the Face of Angry Criticism," *NYT*, September 28, 1999.

Ofili said that the genitalia Michael Kimmelman, "Critic's Notebook: Cutting Through Cynicism in Art Furor," *NYT*, September 24, 1999.

American and European spiritual feminists Cynthia Eller, "White Women and the Dark Mother," *Religion*, Vol. 30, No. 4 (2000): 367–378.

Usually, these women described Marion Woodman and Elinor Dickson, *Dancing in the Flames: The Dark Goddess in the Transformation of Consciousness* (Boston: Shambhala Publications, 1997).

China Galland published the first China Galland, *Longing for Darkness: Tara and the Black Madonna* (New York: Penguin, 2007).

Karlyn M. Ward, Jungian therapist Karlyn M. Ward, *Anchored in the Heart: Redeeming the Dark Feminine*, DVD (2006).

Fred Gustafson Fred Gustafson, *The Black Madonna* (Boston: Sigo Press, 1990).

Jungian therapy has become widely popular Thomas Kirsch, *The Jungians: A Comparative and Historical Perspective* (New York: Routledge, 2001); personal communication, May 28, 2009.

Jungian therapy holds Cedrus Monte, "The Dark Feminine," *The Jung Page*, May 23, 2004, www.cgjungpage.org.

Americans believe in redemption Dan McAdams, *The Redemptive Self: Stories Americans Live By* (New York: Oxford University Press, 2005).

Bill Wilson, who cofounded Alcoholics Anonymous Francis Hartigan, *Bill W.: A Biography of Alcoholics Anonymous Cofounder Bill Wilson* (New York: St. Martin's Griffin, 2001).

As the basis of AA Jan Parker and Diana Guest, *The Clinician's Guide to 12-Step Programs: How, When, and Why to Refer a Client* (Santa Barbara, CA: Greenwood Publishing Group, 1999), 30.

Jungian therapists are reporting Daniel Pinchbeck, *2012: The Return of Quetzalcoatl* (New York: Tarcher/Penguin, 2006).

To "live in the lap" Cynthia Eller, *Living in the Lap of the Goddess: The Feminist Spirituality Movement in America* (Boston: Beacon, 1995).

Black, Native American, and Latina Cynthia Eller, "White Women and the Dark Mother," *Religion*, Vol. 30, No. 4 (2000): 367–378.

Black women in Nigeria Ifi Amadiume, *Daughters of the Goddess, Daughters of Imperialism: African Women Struggle for Culture, Power and Democracy* (London: Zed Books, 2000).

Max Dashu The Suppressed Histories Archives: www.suppressedhistories.net /womenspowerdvd.html and www.suppressedhistories.net/womenspowerclips.html.

Lucia Chiavola Birnbaum   Lucia Chiavola Birnbaum, *Black Madonnas: Feminism, Religion & Politics in Italy*, English trans. (Boston: Northeastern University Press, 1993).

In Haiti, where the working classes   Terry Rey, *Our Lady of Class Struggle: The Cult of the Virgin Mary in Haiti* (Trenton, NJ: Africa World Press, 1999), 270.

Most well known   Daniel Pinchbeck, *2012: The Return of Quetzalcoatl* (New York: Tarcher, 2006).

Oxford-trained activist Andrew Harvey   Louise Danielle Palmer, "Empowered by the Sacred," *Spirituality and Health* (September/October 2006): 40–48.

Luisah Teish, a black priestess   www.luisahteish.com

"Spirita" is a female-centered spirituality   Lillian Comas-Diaz, 2007 Carolyn Sherif Award Address: "*Spirita:* Reclaiming Womanist Sacredness into Feminism," *Psychology of Women Quarterly*, Vol. 32, No. 1 (2008): 13–21.

Chapter 2: The Alchemical Mistress of the Dazzling Darkness

As the central figure of the creation stories   Carl Jung, *Archetypes and the Collective Unconscious* (New York: Bollingen Foundation , 1959).

"Every mythical account of the origin . . ."   Eliade, *Myth and Reality*, 21.

Goethe called myth the realm   Johann Wolfgang von Gothe, *Faust: A Tragedy* (New York: Hurst & Co.,1888).

Ferne and Legh, among others   John Ferne, *Blazon of Gentrie* (New York: Capo Books, 1586, 1973); Gerald Legh, "The Accedens of Armorie," in *Workes of Armory*, ed. John Boss-well (New York: Da Capo Press. 1562, 1969).

Newton would write in Opticks   Isaac Newton, *Opticks or a treatise of the reflections, refractions, inflections and colours of light* (London: Royal Society, 1704).

"Light without shadow . . ."   Edmund Bolton, *Elements of Armories* (London: George Eld., 1610).

The color's seemingly paradoxical quality   Bolton, *Elements*; Van Norden, *Black Feet*.

To see black "was to receive . . ."   Lucretius Carus, *On the Nature of Things*, trans. R. E. Latham (New York: Penguin, 1951).

The color black embodied a paradox   Van Norden, *Black Feet*.

Before or outside of life   Ovid, *Metamorphoses*, trans. A. D. Melville (Oxford: Oxford University Press, 1986).

Minor Elizabethan poet Barnabe Barnes   Barnabe Barnes, *Parthenophil and Parthenophe: A Critical Edition*, ed. Victor A. Doyno (Carbondale, IL: Southern Illinois University Press, 1971).

As memory it was experience   Robert Fludd, *Rosicrusians: Their Rites and Mysteries* (London: Hargrave Jennings, 1879); Fulke Greville, "Alaham," *The Works in Verse and Prose Complete of the Right Honorable Fulke Greville Lord Brooke*, vol. 3 (New York: AMS Press, 1966); Cesare Ripa, "Iconologica," in *Baroque and Rococo Imagery: The 1758–60 Hertel Edition of Ripa's Iconologica*, trans. Edward Maser (New York: Dover, 1611, 1971).

"The black, tartareous, cold . . . "   John Milton, *Paradise Lost*, bk 7, lines 238–239, in *The Poems of John Milton*, eds. J. Carey and A. Fowler (New York: Norton. 1968), 419–1060.

Milton and Crashaw recalled black's   John Milton, "Il Penseroso," in *The Poems of John Milton*, 139–146; Richard Crashaw, "Divine Epigrams," in *Steps to the Temple: Delights of the Muses and Other Poems*, ed. A. R. Waller (Cambridge: Cambridge University Press, 1904), 12–19.

developed the culturally held nature of black   H. C. White, *The Metaphysical Poets: A Study in Religious Experience* (New York: Collier,1962).

the "deep but dazzling darkness"   Henry Vaughan, *The Works of Henry Vaughan*, ed. L. C. Martin (Oxford: Clarendon Press, 1957).

"But when he lookes downe   Robert Chester, "Love's Martyr, or, Rosalins Complaint (1601)"

Ethiopians of the poets were mythical   Grace Beardsley, *The Negro in Greek and Roman Civilization: A Study of the Ethiopian Type* (London: Humphrey Milford Oxford University Press, 1929).

their blackness was ascribed a range of features   Van Norden, *Black Feet*.

Being so fair, my Clara   Francis Beaumont and John Fletcher, *The Works of Francis Beaumont and John Fletcher*, ed. A. R. Waller (Cambridge: Cambridge University Press, 1969), Act III, Sc. IV.

C. S. Lewis, writing on allegory   C. S. Lewis, *The Allegory of Love: A Study in Medieval Tradition* (Oxford: Oxford University Press, 1953), 44–45.

"Lust represents an extremity . . . "   Van Norden, *Black Feet*, 96.

Greek figurines and Janiform cups   Beardsley, *The Negro in Greek*.

It would have been widely known   Van Norden, *Black Feet*.

"It can hardly be altered into any other show . . . "   Frederick Edward Hulme, *The History, Principles, and Practice of Symbolism in Christian Art* (New York: MacMillan, 1909), 28n3.

Impossibility, wrote Van Norden   Van Norden, *Black Feet*.

John Lyly wrote in his **Euphues**   John Lyly, *Euphues:The Anatomy of Wit*.

Nicholas Breton in **Pray Be**   Quoted in Van Norden, *Black Feet*.

"When he can wash an AEthiop white . . . "   Modernized spelling. Philip Massinger, *The Bondman: An Antient Storie*, Act. V, Sc. iii, lines 144–146, 155.

Black was the sign   Arthur Edward Waite, "The Sophic Hydrolith," in *The Hermetic Museum* (New York: S. Weiser, 1974), 82. http://www.sacred-texts.com/alc/hm1/hm106.htm.

Chaos and creation of the world   "An Open Entrance to the Closed Palace of the Kind" in Waite, *The Hermetic Museum*, 165.

The raven or vulture   Israel Regardie, *The Middle Pillar*, eds. Chic and Tabatha Cicero (Woodbury, MN: Llewellyn Worldwide, 1938).

"His deadliness produces life . . . "   Van Norden, *Black Feet*, 96–97.

They are opposites, impossibility   Van Norden, *Black Feet*.

In Ben Jonson's Twelfth Night masques   Ben Jonson, *The Complete Masques*, ed. Stephen Orgel (New Haven: Yale University Press, 1969); Rafael Velez Nunez, "Beyond the Emblem: Alchemical Albedo in Ben Jonson's 'The Masque of Blackness,'" http://sederi.org/docs/yearbooks/08/8_31_velez.pdf.

Since Death herself . . .   Jonson, "Masque of Blackness," line 124–129, in *The Complete Masques*, 52.

"that starred Ethiope queen"   Milton, "Il Penseroso," 11.13–20.

"But yet (methinks) my thoughts . . . "   Thomas Randolph, *A Mask for Lydia*, in *Poetical and Dramatic Works of Thomas Randolph*, ed. W. Carew Hazlitt (New York: Benjamin Blom, 1968), 629–630.

"O, let me—"   Randolph, *The Conceited Peddler*, in *Poetical and Dramatic Works*, 48–49.

"I'll rather kiss An Ethiop's . . . "   Thomas Randolph, *Amyntas or the Impossible Dowry* in *Political and Dramatic Works*, 1. 1968), Act II, Scene VII, 310.

Then will I swear beauty   William Shakespeare, "Sonnet 132," in *The Complete Works*, eds. William George Clark and William Aldis Wright, vol. 2 (New York: Nelson Doubleday, 1900).

In the old age black   Shakespeare, Sonnet 127.

 Ovid was a particular favorite   Charles Martindale, ed. *Ovid Renewed: Ovidian Influences on Literature and Art from the Middle Ages to the Twentieth Century* (Cambridge: Cambridge University Press, 1988).

The Bible and Hesiod   Alastair Fowler, *The Poems of John Milton*, ed. John Carey and Alastair Fowler. (New York: Norton, 1972).

God . . . was present from the first   Milton, *Paradise Lost*, Book I, lines 19–20.

"dove-like . . . brooding . . ."   Milton, *Paradise Lost*, Book I, lines 21–22.

"from Chaos sprang Erebus . . . "   Milton, "Prolusion I" (New Haven: Yale University Press, 1953), 233.

As in Virgil, the female Erebus   Milton, *Paradise Lost*, Book II, line 883.

"The secrets of the hoary deep . . . "   Milton, *Paradise Lost*, Book II, lines 891–897.

"cold things strove with hot . . . "   Ovid, *Metamorphosis*, 1, 19f.

Night was described   Milton, *Paradise Lost*, Book II, line 962.

"The dreaded name of Demogorgon"   Milton, *Paradise Lost*, Book II, lines 964–965.

"Into this wild abyss, . . . "   Milton, *Paradise Lost*, Book II, lines 910–916.

"amplifies the fragility . . . "   Fowler, *The Poems of John Milton*, 555.

God's skirts were so bright   Milton, *Paradise Lost*, Book III, lines 375–380.

Light came "from the walls of heaven"   Milton, *Paradise Lost*, Book II, line 1035.

The moon kept the world   Milton, *Paradise Lost*, Book IV, lines 664–666.

"Her garments are old, defiled . . . "   Quoted in Van Norden, *Black Feet*, 55.

African slaves were the largest single group   Peter Wood, *Black Majority: Negroes in Colonial South Carolina from 1670 through the Stono Rebellion* (New York: Norton,1975).

Laws were passed to keep black proportions   Wood, *Black Majority*.

"Slavery informs all our modes of life . . . "   W. H. Trescott. "Oration delivered before the Beaufort Volunteer Artillery, July 4, 1850" (Charleston, SC: South Carolina Historical Society), 14.

"Telling them was what he . . . "   Theodore Rosengarten, *Tombee: Portrait of a Cotton Planter: With the Plantation Journal of Thomas B. Chaplin (1822–1890)* (New York: William Morrow, 1986), 149.

"last days of the holidays..." Rosengarten, *Tombee*, 448.

"he lost his sense..." Rosengarten, *Tombee*, 150.

"a domestic institution..." Willie Lee Rose, *Slavery and Freedom*, ed. William H. Freehling (Oxford: Oxford University Press, 1982).

popular mythology is "unashamed subjectivity" Edward Whitmont, *Return of the Goddess* (New York: Continuum Intl Pub Group, 1982), 52.

extreme social expectations that were contradictory Rose, 1982; Barbara Welter, "The Cult of True Womanhood," in ed. W. Martin, *The American Sisterhood* (New York: Harper and Row, 1972), 243–256.

"Sufficient distinction is also made..." Robert Beverly, who served as clerks of the general court, assembly, and council, and represented Jamestown in the House of Burgesses. http://nationalhumanitiescenter.org/pds/becomingamer/economies/text6/servitude.pdf.

"She is my mother's factotum..." Mary Chestnut, "September, 1863," *Mary Chestnut's Civil War*, ed. C. Vann Woodward (New Haven: Yale University Press, 1981), 463.

"Many a romantic tale was confided..." Anne Marie Broidrick, cited in Nancy Cott and Elizabeth Hafkin Pleck, *A Heritage of Their Own: Toward a New Social History of American Women* (New York: Simon & Schuster. 1979).

using, "very foolishly, my crockery,..." Rosengarten, *Tombee*, 134.

"In the reciprocal dependency of slavery..." Eugene Genovese, *Roll, Jordan, Roll: The World the Slaves Made* (New York: Pantheon, 1974), 344.

"We would not hesitate..." Quoted in Genovese, *Roll, Jordan, Roll*, 357.

"Miss Sarah went to Demopolis..." B.A. Botkin, *Lay My Burden Down: A Folk History of Slavery* (Chicago: University of Chicago, 1945), 173.

"Why I would as soon think..." Jessie Parkhurst, "The role of the mammy in the plantation household," *Journal of Negro History* Vol 23 (3), July 1938, 355.

"He beat my mother til..." Botkin, *Lay My Burden Down*, 174.

"Yes, suh, de Gov'nor..." F.W.P.A. *Texas Narratives*, 5 (3) (1976): 33, 140.

When Susan Dabney Smedes's Mammy died Susan Dabney Smedes, *Memorials of a Southern Planter*, ed. F. M. Green (New York: Knopf, 1965), 47–48.

"It was also the day..." Judith Page Rives to Alfred L. Rives, December 5, 1856, quoted in Genovese, *Roll, Jordan, Roll*, 196.

"had come to love the white family..." Smedes, *Memorials*, 60.

The old woman then died Smedes, *Memorials*, 334.

"I hope and prays..." F.W.P.A. *South Carolina Narratives*, 3 (3) (1976): 38–39.

Genovese argued "willful neglect..." Genovese, *Roll, Jordan, Roll*, 356.

"My mammy she work..." Norman Yetman, *Life Under the "Peculiar Institution: Selections from the Slave Narrative Collection* (Huntington, NY: Robert E. Krieger Publishing Co., 1976), 227.

"Cause I was really only ole Mis' housekeeper..." Fisk University Social Science Institute, *Unwritten History of Slavery: Autobiographical Accounts of Negro Ex-Slaves* (Nashville: Fisk University, 1945), 7.

for her "worth and reliability"   N. W. Eppes, *The Negro of the Old South* (Chicago: Jospeh G. Branch, 1925), 74.

"disloyal" acts such as escape   D. G. White , *Ar'n't I a Woman? Female Slaves in the Plantation South* (New York: Norton, 1985).

"We could talk and do anything . . . "   Fisk University, Unwritten History, 103.

"Those were days of trial and perplexity . . . "   Smedes, *Memorials*, 180.

"I should not offer my services . . . "   M. Cain to Minerva R. Cain, April 14, 1833. Tod R. Caldwell Papers. Emphasis original.

the driver who insisted   H. T. Catterall, ed. *Judicial Cases Concerning American Slavery and the Negro* (Washington, DC: Carnegie Institution, 1926), 200–201.

"The Negroes here have certainly . . . "   Sir Charles Lyell, *A Second Visit to the United States of North America* vol. 1 (London: John Murray, 1849), 224.

"Yes, I belong to them . . . "   Lyell, *Second Visit*, 135.

Genia Woodbury, a former South Carolina Mammy   F.W.P.A. South Carolina Narratives, 3 (4) (1976): 218.

"Our childish associations . . . "   Smedes, *Memorials*, 48.

On formal occasions they were   Smedes, *Memorials*, 71.

They did, however, divide   Herbert Aptheker, *Nat Turner's Slave Rebellion* (New York: Grove, 1966).

Poisoning of food by cooks   Chestnut, *Civil War*; Paula Giddings, *When and Where I Enter: The Impact of Black Women on Race and Sex in America* (New York: Bantam, 1984).

"The place that she made . . . "   Genovese, *Roll, Jordan, Roll*, 360.

"You needn't look that scared . . . " Chestnut, "January 4, 1864," *Civil War*, 526.

Mary allowed Molly   Chestnut, "September 1863," *Civil War*, 481.

"Molly all in tears . . . "   Chestnut, "June 1862," *Civil War*, 376.

"Then when I was so tired . . . "   Chestnut, "August 29, 1864," *Civil War*, 641–642.

When Molly spoke of "our own people"   Chestnut, "January 9, 1864," *Civil War*, 535.

"White mens, which of you . . . "   Chestnut, "November 1863," *Civil War*, 491.

"You had better go yonder . . . "   Chestnut, *Civil War*, 457.

"I felt uncomfortable and wondered . . . "   Chestnut, "June 12, 1862," *Civil War*, 382.

Molly stayed with Mary   Chestnut, "September 1863," *Civil War*, 432.

James Boykin, whom they had met   Chestnut, "September 1863," *Civil War*, 462.

As the trip progressed   Chestnut, *Civil War*, 462, 496.

"I am sure Molly believes . . . "   Chestnut, "November 1863," *Civil War*, 489.

"Shall I ever forget . . . "   Chestnut, "September 1863," *Civil War*, 462.

"perusing the street"   Chestnut, "June 1865," *Civil War*, 829.

"I felt Molly give me . . . "   Chestnut, "November 1863," *Civil War*, 490.

she piled fried oysters on top   Chestnut, "January 18, 1964," *Civil War*, 543.

"We sent for Molly to order . . . "   Chestnut, "January 7, 1965," *Civil War*, 699.

Chapter 3: She Made It Paradise

The propagandistic happy slave Robert Lamberton, *Hesiod* (New Haven: Yale University Press, 1988); Edward Tripp, *The Meridian Handbook of Classical Mythology* (New York: Penguin, 1970).

There were historical black women Deborah Gray White, *Ar'n't I a Woman?: Female Slaves in the Plantation South* (New York: W. W. Norton & Co., 1999); Elizabeth Fox-Genovese, *Within the Plantation Household: Black and White Women of the Old South* (Chapel Hill: University of North Carolina Press, 1988); Jacqueline Jones, *Labor of Love, Labor of Sorrow* (New York: Vintage, 1986).

As in other aspects of the European Alfred Nutt, *The Influence of Celtic Upon Medieval Romance* (New York: AMS Press, 1904, 1972).

An observer writing A South Carolinian, "South Carolina Morals," *Atlantic Monthly*, April 1877, 470.

Henry Watson Jr., explained Henry Watson Jr. to Sarah Carrington, January 28, 1861. Henry Watson Jr. papers, Special Collections, Duke University.

Susan Smedes's father consulted Granny Harriet Susan Dabney Smedes, *Memorials of a Southern Planter*, ed. F. M. Green (New York: Knopf, 1965); Giddings, *When and Where I Enter*.

As cooks and caregivers Chestnut, *Civil War*; Giddings, *When and Where I Enter*.

The proslavery ideology James L. Roark, *Masters without Slaves: Southern Planters in the Civil War and Reconstruction* (New York: Norton, 1977), xi.

Alfred Huger wrote in 1858 Alfred Huger to William Porcher Miles, January 23, 1858. Alfred Huger Papers, Duke University.

Black Diamonds E. A. Pollard, *Black Diamonds Gathered in the Darkey Homes of the South* (New York: Pudney and Russell, 1859).

"At this moment my eyes . . . " Pollard, *Black Diamonds*, 36–37.

But the head cloth Carol Tulloch, "That Little Magic Touch: The Head Tie," *Defining Dress: Dress as Object, Meaning and Identity*, ed. Amy de la Haye and Elizabeth Wilson (Manchester: Manchester University Press, 2000).

Alfred Huger wrote Alfred Huger to John Preston, December 11, 1856. Alfred Huger Papers, Duke University.

By 1862, Catherine Ann Edmonston Catherine Ann Edmonston diaries, "September 28, 1862." North Carolina State Department of Archives and History.

Confederate wealth declined Roark, *Masters without Slaves*, 77.

Ella Clanton Thomas Ella Gertrude Clanton Thomas, "January 2, 1868"; "December 31, 1863"; "May 23, 1864"; "June 28, 1864"; "July 12, 1864"; and "March 29, 1865," *Journal of Ella Gertrude Clanton Thomas*, 13 Vols, Manuscript department, Duke University.

Thomas wrote Journal of Ella Gertrude Clanton Thomas, 1860.

David Gaven wrote David Gaven diary entry, July 8, 1863. David Gaven diaries, Upper Dorchester County Historical Society.

Henry L. Graves wrote Henry Graves to Aunt Sibbie, September 4, 1861. Graves Family Papers, Southern Historical Collection, University of North Carolina, Chapel Hill.

Catherine Edmonston said Catherine Ann Edmonston diaries, May 2, 1862.

In the behavior of blacks   Lewis H. Blair, *A Southern Prophecy: The Prosperity of the South Dependent upon the Elevation of the Negro* (Richmond, VA: E. Waddey, 1889).

People do not alter their worldview   A. Wallace, *Culture and Personality* (New York: Random House, 1970).

As James Roark wrote   Roark, *Masters without Slaves.*

"All those people who . . . "   Virginian C. D. Whittle to "My Beloved Boy," on December 29, 1867. Lewis Neal Whittle Papers, Southern Historical Collection, University of North Carolina, Chapel Hill.

In 1867, William H. Heyward   William Heyward to James Gregorie, June 4, 1868. Gregorie and Elliott Family Papers, Southern Historical Collection, University of North Carolina, Chapel Hill.

Major Joseph Abney, a former slave owner   Lawrence Hill, "The Confederate Exodus to Latin America," *Southwestern Historical Quarterly Online*, Vol. 39, No. 2 (1935).

House servants were usually   Roark, *Masters without Slaves.*

The quick withdrawal of black   Jones, *Labor of Love, Labor of Sorrow.*

Louisiana and Texas mandated   Eric Foner, *Reconstruction: America's Unfinished Revolution, 1863–1877* (New York: Harper & Row, 1988), 200.

Black women were ridiculed   Foner, *Reconstruction.*

"Can you imagine a scene . . . " Originally published on its own in 1858 by the American Tract and Book Society and republished in *The Child's Anti Slavery Book* (New York: Carton and Porter, 1859). Author's collection.

Thomas Nelson Page was primarily responsible   Thomas Nelson Page, *Social Life in Old Virginia Before the War* (New York: Charles Scribners' Sons, 1897); Thomas Nelson Page, *In Old Virginia or Marse Chan and Other Stories* (New York: Charles Scribner's Sons, 1895), http://docsouth.unc.edu/southlit.

The stories romanticized the Old South   Eli Ginzberg and Alfred Eichner, *The Troublesome Presence: American Democracy and the Negro* (New York: Free Press, 1964).

"The women seemed very much pleased . . . " Letters from a hospital written to Mary Lawrence in 1864 and published in *Atlantic Monthly*, May 1876, 585.

In the June 1877 **Atlantic Monthly**   A South Carolinian, "South Carolina Society," *Atlantic Monthly*, June 1877, 671–684.

In another **Atlantic Monthly**   A South Carolinian, "South Carolina Morals."

In "Queen's Good Work,"   Helen Wall Pierson, "Queen's Good Work," *Harper's Monthly*, May 1866, 776.

"It came to the sick man's ears . . . " Pierson, "Queen's Good Work," 775.

"Some sudden hunger for the affection . . . " Pierson, "Queen's Good Work," 777.

"How horrible it all was!"   Pierson, "Queen's Good Work," 777.

"She was nurse . . . "   Olive Wadsworth, "Aunt Rosy's Chest," *Atlantic Monthly*, September 1872, 322–323.

She seemed to have magical powers   Wadsworth, "Aunt Rosy's Chest," 322.

"In fact, there was hardly anything . . . "   Wadsworth, "Aunt Rosy's Chest," 323.

"As for the woes of older children . . . "   Wadsworth, "Aunt Rosy's Chest," 322.

"More than once it happened that . . . "   Wadsworth, "Aunt Rosy's Chest," 322.

In the short story "My Debut,"   Susan P. King, "My Debut," *Harper's Monthly*, September 1868, 531–546.

Mary Chestnut described   Chestnut, *Civil War.*

Thomas Nelson Page   Thomas Nelson Page, "The Old-Time Negro," *Scribner's Magazine*, Vol. 36, 1904, 525.

The rape of young black girls   Diane Miller Sommerville, *Rape and Race in the Nineteenth-Century South* (Chapel Hill: University of North Carolina Press, 2004), 65.

The former slave woman   Harriet Jacobs, *Incidents in the Life of a Slave Girl* (Clayton, DE: Prestwick House, 1861, 2006).

She wasn't a pleasant corpse to look at   Lucy Ellen Guernsey, "Miss Georgine's Husband," *Atlantic Monthly*, November 1874, 576.

The doctor, he talked learnedly   Guernsey, "Miss Georgine's Husband," 576.

This story rests upon a better   Guernsey, "Miss Georgine's Husband," 576.

"That nigh broke me down,"   Maggie D. Hammond, "Derrick Halsey," *Harper's Monthly*, February 1868, 359.

But the sore festered   Hammond, "Derrick Halsey," 359.

"You don't 'preciate life . . . "   Hammond, "Derrick Halsey," 359–360.

"Yes, I do b'lieve . . . " Hammond, "Derrick Halsey," 360.

His sister had escaped   Hammond, "Derrick Halsey," 361–362.

Paule Marshall wrote   Paule Marshall, "The Negro Woman in Literature," *Freedomways* 6 (1966): 21.

Rayford Logan called   Rayford Logan, *The Betrayal of the Negro* (Cambridge, MA: Da Capo Press, 1954, 1997).

Most of us above thirty years   Blair, *A Southern Prophecy.*

The stories were those   Martha S. Gielow, *Mammy's Reminiscences and Other Sketches* (New York: A. S. Barnes and Company, 1898), vii.

Gielow wrote in the foreword   Gielow, *Mammy's Reminiscences*, viii.

"You know young folks . . . "   Gielow, *Mammy's Reminiscences*, 15.

"Dis gittin' mar'ied . . . "   Gielow, *Mammy's Reminiscences*, 13.

"I done tole you befo' . . . "   Gielow, *Mammy's Reminiscences*, 13.

"Cum 'long now an' let . . . "   Gielow, *Mammy's Reminiscences*, 85.

"Cum long ter Mammy . . . "   Gielow, *Mammy's Reminiscences*, 85.

She sang "Blow, Li'l' Breezes Blow"   Gielow, *Mammy's Reminiscences*, 86.

Mrs. Gielow's book   Gielow, *Mammy's Reminiscences*, unpaginated letters.

In 1894, the Bow-Knot   William Lightfoot Visscher, *Harp of the South* (Chicago: Bow-Knot Publishing Company, 1894).

In 1897, Visscher   William Lightfoot Visscher, *Black Mammy: A Southern Romance* (Chicago: H. C. Smith Publishing Company, 1897).

In "The Spinning Wheel"   Visscher, *Black Mammy*, 10.

An illustration later in the book   Visscher, *Black Mammy*, 38.

In great authority she's grown,   Visscher, *Black Mammy*, 21.

"A Memory"   Visscher, *Black Mammy*, 16.

Another poem, "Mammy's Story"   Visscher, *Black Mammy*, 46.

In "A Picture,"   Visscher, *Black Mammy*, 84.

In 1922, in a conciliatory move   Micki McElya, *Clinging to Mammy: The Faithful Slave in Twentieth-Century America* (Cambridge, MA: Harvard University Press, 2007).

An advertisement that appeared   Author's collection.

Green went on to portray   M. M. Manring, *Slave in a Box: The Strange Career of Aunt Jemima* (Charlottesville: University of Virginia Press, 1998); William H. Young and Nancy K. Young, *The Great Depression in America: A Cultural Encyclopedia* (Santa Barbara, CA: Greenwood, 2007).

A large array of premiums   Jean Williams Turner, *Collectible Aunt Jemima: Handbook and Value Guide* (Atglen, PA: Schiffer, 1994).

Aunt Jemima was not a singular   Jackie Young, *Mammy and Her Friends* (Atglen, PA: Schiffer, 1988). Author's collection.

The myth fulfilled their need   Kimberly Wallace-Sanders, *Mammy: A Century of Race, Gender, and Southern Memory* (Ann Arbor: University of Michigan Press, 2008).

South Carolina Senator Ben "Pitchfork" Tillman   "Tillman tells North to Leave South Alone, The South Carolina Senator on the Race Problem," *NYT*, February 15, 1903.

Elizabeth Botume lamented   Elizabeth Botume, *First Days Amongst the Contrabands* (New York: Arno Press and *NYT*, 1893, 1968), 273.

W. E. B. Du Bois wrote   W. E. B. DuBois, "Votes for Women," *Crisis*, 15, November 1918, 8.

As he considered the black vote   Christie Farnham, *Women of the American South* (New York: New York University Press, 1997), 212.

South Carolina Senator   *Maryland Suffrage News*, November 1914. Maryland Historical Society, Baltimore.

Chapter 4: Pop Goddesses

Entertainment and even news   Jack Lule, *Daily News, Eternal Stories: The Mythological Role of Journalism* (New York: Guilford Press, 2001). Psychoanalytic media criticism has established the ability of media to pick up concepts that hover just below the collective consciousness, and media audience research has established the ability of audience members to pick up those concepts and embed them into memory. Jere Paul Surber, *Culture and Critique: An Introduction to the Critical Discourses of Cultural Studies* (New York: Westview Press, 1997); *Media Audiences (Understanding Media)*, ed. Marie Gillespie, Vol. 2 (New York: Open University Press, 2005).

According to the local media, Franklin   On April 3, 2008, Bob Batz of the *Pittsburgh Post-Gazette* wrote that Big Mama's food was "slap-your-face good." www.post-gazette.com. Also www.pittsburghcitypaper.ws/gyrobase and www.urbanspoon.com.

After seeing one, she said, www.cbs.com.

Franklin renamed her restaurant "Big Trouble For Big Mama's Restaurant," June 1, 2010, www.wpxi.com/news/news/big-trouble-for-big-mamas-restaurant/nGrtQ.

The restaurant closed "Throw Mama from the Strip," August 26, 2010, http://pitteats .blogspot.com/2010/08/local-foodie-news_26.html.

Historical Mammies were a varied Deborah Gray, *Black and White Women of the Old South* (Chapel Hill: University of North Carolina Press, 1988); White, *"Ar'n't I a Woman?"*; Fox-Genovese, *Within the Plantation Household;* Jones, *Labor of Love, Labor of Sorrow.*

A 2008 survey found that "The Bible Is America's Favorite Book," *The Harns Poll,* April 8, 2008; "Frankly My Dear, The Force Is with Them as *Gone with the Wind* and *Star Wars* Are the Top Two All Time Favorite Movies," February 21, 2008, www.reuters.com; www.reuters.com/article/lifestyle.

The women were well dressed Jill Watts, *Hattie McDaniel: Black Ambition, White Hollywood* (New York: Amistad, 2005), 38.

In what would have been Watts, *Hattie McDaniel.*

Angela Davis wrote Angela Davis, *Blues Legacies and Black Feminism: Gertrude "Ma" Rainey, Bessie Smith, and Billie Holiday* (New York: Vintage, 1999).

In "I Thought I'd Do It" www.itunes.com and www.mp3.com.

Hattie McDaniel said Dana Stevens, "Caricature Acting," *NYT,* November 27, 2005.

In one of her films, **Alice Adams** Carlton Jackson, *Hattie: The Life of Hattie McDaniel* (New York: Madison Books, 1993).

The response of the black Leonard Leff, *"Gone with the Wind* and Hollywood's Racial Politics," *Atlantic,* December 1999, www.theatlantic.com, 106–114.

Named by **Time** "Hollywood on Race: The 25 Most Important Films on Race." *Time,* 2007, www.time.com/time/specials.

In **Post Traumatic Slave Syndrome** Joy Degruy Leary, *Post Traumatic Slave Syndrome: America's Legacy of Enduring Injury and Healing* (Milwaukee: Uptone Press, 2005).

Ruth Brown Rock and Roll Hall of Fame, www.rockhall.com/inductee/ruth-brown.

Television situation comedy Darrell Y. Hamamoto, *Nervous Laughter: Television Situation Comedy and Liberal Ideology* (Santa Barbara, CA: Greenwood, 1989).

According to Stanis Personal communication, March 8, 2008.

Robert Thompson of Syracuse University Robert Thompson, *Television's Second Golden Age* (Syracuse, NY: Syracuse University, 1997).

White working-class men Richard Butsch, "Class and Gender in Four Decades of Television Situation Comedies," *Critical Studies in Mass Communication* (December 1992): 387–399.

By 1999, the percentage African American Television Report, "Quantity and Content of African Americans on Television Carefully Examined," *Market Wire,* 2005.

Essence *magazine, the first mainstream* www.essence.com/mediakit.

Maya Angelou said www.fundinguniverse.com/company/histories-Essence-Communications-inc-history.

In 1995, editor in chief Deirdre Carmody, "The Media Business: An Enduring Voice for Black Women," *NYT,* January 23, 1995.

The casting directors for **Ghost** Personal communication. *Clear Reception with Sheri Parks*, WTMD-FM, January 2006.

According to the show's official website www.turner.com/planet/gaia.html.

On **The Young and the Restless** www.soapopera.com.

Omarosa Manigault–Stallworth became **The Apprentice** "Omigod, It's Omarosa as No. 1 Reality-TV Villain," *New York Daily News*, June 17, 2008.

In several talks to college students Kevin Foley, "Spike Lee Speaks to Spring Fest," *The View from the University of Vermont*, April 24, 2002, www.uvm.edu/theview/; Matt Huntley, "Spike Lee Criticizes Media Stereotypes," *Accent*, February 12, 2004, www.ithaca.edu /ithacan/articles.

Greg Braxton of the **Los Angeles Times** Greg Braxton, "Buddy System," *Los Angeles Times*, August 29, 2007, http://articles.latimes/2007/aug/29.

"It's not only insulting . . . " http://abellinbrooklyn.blogspot.com/2008/10/20/magical -negroes-on-film.html, accessed October 20, 2008.

Some actresses resisted Braxton, "Buddy System."

She told a Las Vegas rally http://abcnews.go.com.

In a **New York Times** *article* Jeremy Peters, "An Image Popular in Films Raises Some Eyebrows in Ads," *NYT*, August 1, 2006.

Writer and critic Nnedi Okorafor-Mbachu Nnedi Okorafor-Mbachu, "The Magical Negro," in *Dark Matter: Reading the Bones* (New York: Aspect, 2004), 91–94.

She has noted that Nnedi Okorafor-Mbachu, "The Brown Bookshelf: United in Story," http://thebrownbookshelf.com.

Her short story Nnedi Okorafor-Mbachu, "How Inyang Got Her Wings," *Gallery Seven Books Anthology* (Colonial Heights, VA: Gallery Seven Books, 2008).

In **Ivan and Adolf: The Last Man in Hell** Stephen Vicchio, *Ivan & Adolf: The Last Man in Hell* (Pikesville, MD: Woodholme House Publishers, 1997).

"God is not the God . . . " Vicchio, *Ivan & Adolf*, 56.

He busses her on the cheek Vicchio, *Ivan & Adolf*, 40.

He tells her, "I have you . . . " Vicchio, *Ivan & Adolf*, 44.

When Ivan asks Hitler Vicchio, *Ivan & Adolf*, 50.

Sophie schools him Vicchio, *Ivan & Adolf*, 57.

In the popular novel William P. Young, *The Shack* (Newbury Park, CA: Windblown Media, 2008).

The first edition was published privately *NYT*; Windblown Media; Personal communication, July 7, 2009; http://articles.latimes.com/2010/jul/13/entertainment/la-et-the -shack-20100713

"I again finally nod . . ." www.theshackbook.com.

The Secret Life of Bees Sue Monk Kidd, *The Secret Life of Bees* (New York: Penguin, 2002).

"For a number of years I studied . . . " www.bookbrowse.com.

Kidd said, "I knew Lily . . . " www.suemonkkidd.com/Reflections.aspx.

"I felt that any image . . . " www.suemonkkidd.com/Reflections.aspx.

Kidd researched the Black Madonna   www.bookbrowse.com.

She found stories   www.suemonkkidd.com/Reflections.aspx.

Kidd thought at first   www.suemonkkidd.com/Reflections.aspx; www.bookbrowse.com.

"I imagined a masthead washed ... " www.suemonkkidd.com/Reflections.aspx.

Just like that, the Black Madonna   www.bookbrowse.com.

"As I wrote about Rosaleen ... "   www.bookbrowse.com.

"The inspiration for August ... "   www.bookbrowse.com.

Kidd said, "I had a dream ... "   www.bookbrowse.com.

"In South Carolina in 1964 ... "   *NYT Book Review*, August 24, 2008, 24.

The Secret Life of Bees *sold*   www.suemonkkidd.com.

Filming began in eastern   North Carolina Film Office, www.ncfilm.com.

North Carolina native   Anne Thompson, "Trailer Watch: *Secret Life of Bees* Debuts in Toronto," *Thompson on Hollywood*, August 22, 2008, www.variety.com.

Rita Williams wrote   Rita Williams, "On the Set: The Real Bee Movie," *O, The Oprah Magazine*, October 2008, www.oprah.com.

The Associated Press   Allison Hoffman, "Winfrey Holds Fundraiser for Obama," Associated Press, September 8, 2007, www.associatedpress.com.

Forbes *magazine*   July 2, 2007, http://blogs.suntimes.com/oprah.

But, more to the point, she has been   www.beliefnet.com.

The Oprah Winfrey Show   www.oprah.com.

Twelve million people   Dumenco, Simon. "Now Oprah Has 1 Million Followers Too. OMG, Run for Your Lives!" *Advertising Age*, May 14, 2009.

When she endorsed KFC's   www.thebigmoney.com.

A study at the University of Maryland   Craig Garthwaite and Timothy Moore, "The Role of Celebrity Endorsements in Politics: Oprah, Obama, and the 2008 Democratic Primary," September 2008, www.econ.umd.edu.

Access Hollywood   *Access Hollywood*, January 11, 2007.

The Why Black Women Are Angry   www.whyblackwomenareangry.blogspot.com.

Even conservative Fox News   www.deborahkingcenter.com/media/video.

Critics have called it the "Oprahfication"   Trystan Cotton and Kimberly Springer, *Stories of Oprah: The Oprahfication of American Culture* (Jackson, MS: University Press of Mississippi, 2010).

Lisa Marie Presley   www.oprah.com.

"The two principal maid ... "   Janet Maslin, "Racial Insults and Quiet Bravery in 1960s Mississippi," *NYT*, February 18, 2009, www.nytimes.com/2009/02/19/books/19masl.html?_r=1.

By the time the film opened   Martin Chilton, "*The Help* Tops US Box Office but Hits Controversy," *Telegraph*, August 22, 2011, www.telegraph.co.uk/culture/film/film-news/8716498/The-Help-tops-US-box-office-but-hits-controversy.html.

A white female caller   "Brian-Lehrer—Context and a Movie/Play/TV Show," http://tunein.com/radio/Brian-Lehrer---Context-and-a-MoviePlayTV-Show-p412660/.

The film was an immediate hit   Daniel Frankel, "Box Office: 'The Help' Has Strong $25.5M 1st Weekend, But Can't Hold Off 'Apes,'" *The Wrap*, August 14, 2011, www.thewrap .com/movies/article/box-office-help-has-strong-255m-1st-weekend-cant-hold-apes-30085.

CNN asked "Is The Help   Lisa Respers France, "Cover Story: Is 'The Help' Heroic or Stereotyping?" CNN Entertainment, August 10, 2011, http://articles.cnn.com /2011-08-10/entertainment/the.help.movie_1_eugenia-skeeter-phelan-black-maids-octavia -spencer?_s=PM:SHOWBIZ.

In a series of tweets   Chilton, "*The Help* Tops."

I believe it was because   http://movies.nytimes.com/movie/461233/The-Help/details.

Their pleasure trumped history   *Midday with Dan Rodricks*, "'The Help'—As Film, as Historic and Cultural Narrative," August 17, 2011, www.wypr.org/podcast /wednesday-august-17-12-1-pm-help-film-historic-and-cultural-narrative.

Chapter 5: "You Say 'Angry Black Woman' Like It's a Bad Thing"

She liked to call her husband   Rebecca Traister, "Michelle Obama Gets Real," Salon .com, November 27, 2007.

Richard Wolffe of Newsweek   Richard Wolffe, "Barack's Rock," *Newsweek*, February 16, 2008.

When Michelle Obama told   Tonya Lewis Lee, "Your Next First Lady?" *Glamour*, September 3, 2007, www.glamour.com/magazine/2007/09/michelle-obama.

Maureen Dowd   Maureen Dowd, "She's Not Buttering Him Up," *NYT*, April 25, 2007.

Judy Keen wrote in USA Today   Judy Keen, "Michelle Obama: Campaigning Her Way," *USA Today*, May 12, 2007, www.usatoday.com.

"She is vivid, engaging . . . "   Nancy Gibbs, "The War Over Michelle Obama," *Time*, May 22, 2008.

"If his loftiness . . . "   Wolffe, "Barack's Rock."

A Time *reporter wrote*   Gibbs, "Michelle Obama."

"She can be tough . . . "   Wolffe, "Barack's Rock."

Aides called her   Gibbs, "Michelle Obama."

After the surprise loss   Wolffe, "Barack's Rock."

Conservative host Bill O'Reilly   O'Reilly, February 20, 2008, www.foxnews.com.

O'Reilly may have known   "Michelle Obama: Angry Black Woman," Western Voices World News, web division of European Americans United, www.wvwnews.net.

One blogger wrote   www.wvwnews.net.

John Hendren of ABC News   John Hendren, "Michelle Obama in for 'Very Ugly Stuff,'" *ABC News*, June 15, 2008, www.abcnews.com.

A commentator quoted by Time   Gibbs, "Michelle Obama."

The conservative site VDARE   Steve Sailer, www.vdare.com, February 25, 2008. The author may have referenced the phrase "The Rage of a Privileged Class" from *Time* magazine, in which editor Ellis Cose, a black man, wrote of the lingering effects of racism among privileged African Americans.

Maureen Dowd called it "Round two Maureen Dowd, "Mincing Up Michelle," *NYT*, June 11, 2008.

Barack went on the national media *Today*, June 4, 2008, www.msnbc.com.

Lee Walker, senior fellow Mary Mitchell, "Michelle Obama Bitter? Not Likely," *Chicago Sun-Times*, June 19, 2008, www.suntimes.com.

Fox News erroneously called Fox News, June 16, 2008, www.foxnews.com.

Mary Curtis, columnist Mary Curtis, "The Loud Silence of Feminists," *WP*, June 21, 2008.

"I think one way . . . " Fox News, June 16, 2008.

Donna Brazile described Donna Brazile, *Cooking with Grease: Stirring the Pots in American Politics* (New York: Simon & Schuster, 2004), 255.

Barack Obama quipped Obama speech, played on MSNBC, June 23, 2008.

The Dangerous and Angry *New Yorker*, June 21, 2008.

Barack later told NBC's Huffington Post, October 21, 2008, www.huffingtonpost.com.

According to the magazine's Huffington Post, October 21, 2008.

Editor David Remnick Huffington Post, October 21, 2008.

"We need to be here . . . " Leslie Bennetts, "First Lady in Waiting," *Vanity Fair*, December 2007, www.vanityfair.com.

"Even if it's inconvenient" Traister, "Michelle Obama Gets Real."

Mary Mitchell of the Chicago Sun-Times Mitchell, "Michelle Obama Bitter?"

That Black Girl www.thatblackgirlsite.com/author/corynne-corbett.

Communication researchers Geneva Smitherman, *Talkin and Testifyin: The Language of Black America* (Detroit: Wayne State University Press, 1986); Geneva Smitherman, *Word from the Mother: Language and African Americans* (New York: Routledge, 2006); Thomas Kochman, *Black and White Styles in Conflict* (Chicago: University of Chicago Press, 1983).

"I'm a national hero. . . . " Piers Morgan, www.theinsider.com.

Maureen Dowd suggested Dowd, "Mincing Up Michelle."

"In America, . . . " Curtis, "The Loud Silence."

Mrs. Obama told CBS CBS, *This Morning*, January 11, 2012, www.cbsnews.com/8301-505270_162-57356770/michelle-obama-no-tension-with-husbands-aides.

When Alexander *Keeping It Real*, www.npr.org.

According to the New York Times David Herszenhorn, "The Same Old Song on High Gas Prices," *NYT*, May 23, 2008.

Waters "brazenly" suggested Herszenhorn, "Same Old Song."

"I told the kids to sleep . . . " Brazile, *Cooking with Grease*, 132.

When Brazile worked Brazile, *Cooking with Grease*, 36.

"If our opponents were willing . . . " Brazile, *Cooking with Grease*, 176, 199–200.

One read, "Donna . . . " Nia on Wheels, www.niaonwheels.daily.kos.com, May 7, 2008.

CNN's Anderson Cooper. www.cnn.com, June 4, 2008.

"My mama taught me . . . " www.msnbc.com, May 31, 2008.

"The struggle for inclusion..." Brazile, *Cooking with Grease*, 316.

"It's hard..." Brazile, *Cooking with Grease*, 184.

"My American gum, candy..." Brazile, *Cooking with Grease*, 188.

In the wake of the Michelle Obama http://theangryblackwoman.wordpress.com, June 18, 2008.

Theangryblackwoman.com http://theangryblackwoman.libsyn.com.

It was dedicated, in part Denene Millner, Angela Burt-Murray, and Mitzi Miller, *The Angry Black Woman's Guide to Life* (New York: Plume, 2004).

"It wasn't until Rosa Parks..." Millner, Burt-Muray, and Miller, *Angry*, 4.

Tamara Nikuradse wrote Tamara Nikuradse, *My Mother Had a Dream: African American Women Share Their Mothers' Words of Wisdom* (New York: Dutton Adult, 1996).

The Anchored Nomad portuguesa nova, www.theanchorednomad.blogspot.com.

A study of black female classroom Jacqueline Jordan Irvine and James W. Fraser, "Warm Demanders," *Education Week* 17, Issue 35 (May 13, 1998).

The AngryBlackWoman.com blogger http://theangryblackwoman.wordpress.com, January 16, 2008.

At the Angry Black Bitch website Pamela Merritt, "$160 a month," http://angryblack bitch.blogspot.com.

Comic scholar Michael Robinson Michael Robinson, Personal communication, December 28, 2008.

Ostrander wrote in an e-mail Personal communication, April 21, 2009.

Comic scholar Michael Robinson Robinson, December 28, 2008.

A fan wrote, "White Queen..." Anthony, response to Goodcomics, "Comics Should be Good!" www.goodcomics.comicbookresources.com.

According to critic Pedro Tejeda Pedro Tejeda, "4thletter!" www.4thletter.net.

She could outtalk, outcurse The DC Database Project, www.dc.wikia.com/wiki/AmandaWaller.

Tejeda wrote Tejeda, "4thletter!"

A white male hero Kirbydotter, "Comics Should be Good."

"Waller has a strong sense..." Robinson, December 28, 2008.

"Most of the team's criminal..." The DC Database Project.

I still remember one Jamaal Thomas, www.funnybookbabylon.com.

"If you were to ask her..." Tejeda, "4thletter!"

"Waller's response?..." Gavok, "4thletter!"

Another reader wrote Kirbydotter, "Comics Should be Good!"

"Not only was this Amanda..." Tejeda, "4thletter!"

When Waller is done Tejeda, "4thletter!"

One of her operatives The DC Database Project.

Ostrander writes that Waller *Supervillains and Philosophy: Sometimes Evil Is Its Own Reward*, ed. Ben Dyer (Chicago: Open Court Publishing, 2009).

"Amanda Waller is the reincarnation..." Thomas, www.funnybookbabylon.com.

Chapter 6: Becoming Coretta: A Cautionary Tale

In 1968, Martin Luther King   Michael Honey Keith, *Black Workers Remember: An Oral History of Segregation, Unionism, and the Freedom Struggle* (Berkeley: University of California Press, 2000), 287.

Coretta Scott was a graduate   www.antiochne.edu/news; www.newenglandconserva tory.edu/alumni/alumni_profiles/index.

But there were other black women   Laurie Green, "Where Would the Negro Women Apply for Work? Gender, Race, and Labor in Wartime Memphis," *Labor*, Vol. 3, No. 3 (2006): 95–117.

But the culturally ensconced idea   Tyrone Stewart, "What Is a Black Man Without His Paranoia?" Doctoral dissertation, University of Maryland, 2009.

In 2003, 24 percent   Bureau of Labor Statistics, www.bls.gov.

According to a count   www.blacknews.com.

In 2002, the US census   www.census.gov/econ/sbo.

Between 2002 and 2008   "Black Women Business Owners Gain Market," CBS News, June 17, 2008, www.cbsnews.com.

A study by the Center   Center for Women's Business Research, www.nfwbo.org.

Black women are also   Patrik Jonsson and Yvonne Zipp, "Rebuilding the Economy: Job Losses Hit Black Men Hardest," *Christian Science Monitor*, March 15, 2009, http://features.csmonitor.com/economy rebuild.

"If you're a black woman . . . "   Jonsson and Zipp, "Job Losses."

They still make less per hour   "Usual Weekly Earnings, Wage and Salary Workers," www.bls.gov.

Zora Neale Hurston wrote   Zora Neale Hurston, *Their Eyes Were Watching God* (New York: Harper, 1937, 2006).

Michelle Wallace wrote   Michelle Wallace, *Black Macho and the Myth of the Superwoman* (New York: Verso, 1979, 1999), 142.

A study at a major university   University of Maryland Counseling Center, University of Maryland, College Park.

Women earn about two-thirds   Katharin Peter and Laura Horn, "Gender Differences in Participation and Completion of Undergraduate Education and How They Have Changed Over Time," National Center for Education Statistics, http://nces.ed.gov/das /epubs/2005169.

Many colleges   Editorial, "How to Turn Obama's Success into Gains for Black Boys," *USA Today*, January 6, 2009, www.usatoday.com.

Columnist Tannette Johnson   Tannette Johnson-Elie, "African American Women Entrepreneurs Are Alone Together in Milwaukee," *Milwaukee Journal Sentinel*, September 8, 2004.

It was the first Broadway play   Sheri Parks, "In My Mother's House: Black Feminist Aesthetics, Television, and *A Raisin in the Sun*," in *Black Feminist Cultural Criticism*, ed. Jacqueline Bobo (Malden, MA: Blackwell, 2001), 106–122.

The character of Mama   Lorraine Hansberry, *A Raisin in the Sun*, cited by Parks, "In My Mother's House."

Hansberry captured the primary   Parks, "In My Mother's House."

When black director   Wil Haygood, "45 Years Ago, A 'Raisin' to Cheer; Revival of Hansberry Play Stirs Memories of a Racial Milestone," *WP*, March 28, 2004.

"We had to bring Sidney's . . . "   Haygood, "45 Years Ago."

Niara Sudarkasa   Niara Sudarkasa, "Interpreting the African Heritage in Afro-American Family Organization," in *Black Families*, ed. Harriette McAdoo (Beverly Hills, CA: Sage, 2006).

Some African postcolonial   Jamaine Abidogun, "Western Education's Impact on Northern Igbo Gender Roles in Nsukka, Nigeria," *Africa Today*, Vol. 54, No. 1 (Fall 2007): 29–51.

Although the majority   Historical Income Tables: Race of Head of Household, 1980–2007, www.census.gov.

In 1964, the US Department of Labor   "The Negro Family: The Case for National Action," Office of Policy Planning and Research United States Department of Labor.

So many black women   "The State of Black America 2008: In the Black Woman's Voice," The National Urban League, www.nul.org.

Black women are less likely   "Marriage and African Americans," Joint Center for Political and Economic Studies, DataBank 2001, jointcenter.org; Alison Clarke-Stewart and Cornelia Brentano, *Divorce: Causes and Consequences* (New Haven: Yale University Press, 2006).

Joy Jones wrote   Joy Jones, "Marriage Is for White People," *WP*, March 26, 2006.

A study conducted for Essence   "*Essence* Unveils Fourth Installment in Its Smart Beauty Series of Research Findings," *Target Market News*, May 13, 2009, www.targetmarketnews .com.

The single mother with children   Rosanna Hertz, *Single by Chance, Mothers by Choice* (New York: Oxford University Press, 2008); *Clear Reception with Sheri Parks* interview, September, 2006.

Researchers have found that   Leslie Carson, "'I Am Because We Are': Collectivism as a Foundational Characteristic of African American College Student Identity and Academic Achievement," *Social Psychology of Education*, January 29, 2009.

Black children often   James Vasquez, "Teaching to the Distinctive Traits of Minority Students," *The Clearing House*, Vol. 63, Issue 7 (March 1990): 299–304.

The data is mixed about   Institute of Domestic Violence in the African American Community, University of Minnesota, www.dvinstitute.org.

When it was widely reported   "Teens Closely Watching Chris Brown, Rihanna," www.npr.org, February 24, 2009.

In 2007, Isiah Thomas   Thomas Zambito, "Isiah Explains Double Standard on Slurs in Garden Trial," *New York Daily News*, September 18, 2007, www.nydailynews.com.

The British Guardian   Godfrey Hodgson, "Coretta Scott King," www.guardian .co.uk, February 1, 2006.

In June 1968   Peter Applebome, "Coretta Scott King, a Civil Rights Icon, Dies at 78," *NYT*, February 1, 2006.

The role of the Strong Black Woman   Angela Neal-Barnett, *Soothe Your Nerves: The Black Woman's Guide to Understanding and Overcoming Anxiety, Panic, and Fear* (New York: Simon & Schuster, 2003).

Yet, on average, African American   "Health Care for Minority Women: Recent Findings," Agency for Healthcare Research and Quality, Department of Health and Human Services, April 2009, www.ahrq.gov/research/minority.

"In the minds of many Blacks . . . "   Neal-Barnett, *Soothe Your Nerves*.

Mayor Martin O'Malley   David Montgomery, "Remember the Dawsons," *WP*, November 17, 2002.

But in January 2005   Jeremy Kahn, "The Story of a Snitch," *Atlantic*, April 2007, www.theatlantic.com.

Michelle Blue   Matthew Dolan, "A Life Exiled," *Baltimore Sun*, September 19, 2006, www.baltsun.com.

A college professor who blogs   Mad Kenyan Woman, "Sister at Heart," February 25, 2008, www.madkenyanwoman.blogspot.com.

Do you know how much   Mad Kenyan Woman, "Black Women's Mythology Revisited or 'Loving My Inner Conwoman,'" January 31, 2006.

Patricia Hill Collins   Patricia Hill Collins, *Black Feminist Thought: Knowledge, Consciousness, and the Politics of Empowerment* (New York: Routledge, 2000).

They have to imagine   Toni Morrison, *Beloved* (New York: Penquin, 2000), 88.

In a 1971 interview with Alice Walker   Alice Walker, "Coretta King, Revisited," in *In Search of Our Mothers' Gardens: Womanist Prose* (New York: Harcourt Brace Jovanovich, 1983), 146–157.

At the conclusion of an open letter   Alice Walker, "An Open Letter to Barack Obama," *The Root*, November 5, 2008, www.theroot.com.

Alice Walker quoted the end   Alice Walker, *We Are the Ones We Have Been Waiting For: Inner Light in a Time of Darkness: Meditations* (New York: The New Press, 2006).

Chapter 7: Making a Way Out of No Way

She got more than half   Madison Gray, "Social Media: The Muscle Behind the Trayvon Martin Movement," *Time*, March 26, 2012, http://newsfeed.time.com/2012/03/26/social-media-the-muscle-behind-the-trayvon-martin-movement/#ixzz1xga1Fn4q; moveon.org.

As Trayvon Martin's mother stood   Jill Rosen, "Trayvon Martin's Mother Gets an Ovation at Baltimore Church," *WP*, May 21, 2012, www.washingtonpost.com/local/trayvon-martins-mother-gets-an-ovation-at-baltimore-church/2012/05/21/gIQAnPHBfU_story.html.

Sybrina showed an enormous grace   Scott Stump, "Trayvon Martin's Mom: The Zimmermans Are Hurting, But We Lost Our Son," *Today*, April 12, 2012, http://today.msnbc.msn.com/id/47027524/ns/today-today_news/t/trayvon-martins-mom-zimmermans-are-hurting-we-lost-our-son/#.T9iyv1L4LT4.

The story of Emmett Till   Keith A. Beauchamp, "The Murder of Emmett Louis Till: The Spark that Started the Civil Rights Movement," www.black-collegian.com/african/till2005-2nd.shtml.

intelligence is not cold R. Michael Alvarez, "The Amygdala and the Social Brain," *Psychology Today*, February 3, 2011, www.psychologytoday.com/blog/the-psychology-behind-political-debate/201102/the-amygdala-and-the-social-brain.

Minorities and women, in particular Eddy S. Ng and Greg J. Sears, "What Women and Ethnic Minorities Want: Work Values and Labor Market Confidence: A Self-Determination Perspective," *International Journal of Human Resource Management*, 21: 5 (2010): 676–698, http://dal.academia.edu/EddyNg/Papers/1458459/What_women_and_ethnic_minorities_want._Work_values_and_labor_market_confidence_a_self-determination_perspective.

Cheryl D. Hicks's Talk with You Cheryl D. Hicks, *Talk with You Like a Woman: African American Women, Justice, and Reform in New York, 1890–1935* (Chapel Hill: University of North Carolina Press, 2010).

Nancy Thorton and Faith Pratt Hopp's article Nancy Thorton and Faith Pratt Hopp, "'So I Just Took Over': African American Daughters Caregiving for Parents with Heart Failure," *Families in Society* Vol. 92, Issue 2 (Apr–Jun 2011): 211–217.

Her clients include Monica Lewinsky Neely Tucker, "The (Almost) Invisible Woman," *WP*, April 1, 2012.

"It's difficult to think of many people . . . " Tucker, "The (Almost) Invisible Woman."

Michael Duffy, executive editor of Time Tucker, "The (Almost) Invisible Woman."

When "Mama" Vy Higginsen's daughter "The Mama Foundation," *The Nate Berkus Show*, www.nateshow.com.

Charity Adams was the first African American woman Carol Sears Botsch, "Charity Edna Adams Earley," June 10, 2002, www.usca.edu/aasc/earley.htm.

The link to solving problems S. L. Fries-Britt and K. M. Holmes, "Prepared and Progressing: Black Women in Physics," in C. R. Chambers and R. V. Sharpe (ed.) *Black Female Undergraduates on Campus: Successes and Challenges*, Diversity in Higher Education, Volume 12 (Emerald Group Publishing Limited, 2012), 199–218; A. Johnson, "Unintended Consequences: How Science Professors Discourage Women of Color," *Science Education* 10, (2007): 805–821; E. Seymour and N. Hewitt, *Talking About Leaving* (Boulder, CO: Westview Press, 1997).

Edna Aden Ismail, first lady of Somalia Salma A. Sheik, "Somaliland's Most Prominent Woman: Edna Aden Ismail," *Somalilandpress*, February 27, 2010, http://somaliland press.com/somaliland%E2%80%99s-most-prominent-woman-edna-aden-ismail-11973.

If [you] manage an office NPR, "King Peggy: A Cinderella Story—With a Twist," February 19, 2012, www.npr.org/2012/02/19/146879460/king-peggy-a-cinderella-story-with-a-twist.

"When I said this, they all stood up . . . " NPR, "King Peggy."

"I would have made . . . " "King of Otuam Peggielene Bartles," *Tavis Smiley*, February 23, 2012, http://video.pbs.org/video/2201281211.

"I see it as an admission . . . " www.bbc.co.uk/news/uk-england-humber-17132288; Janet Alder speech: www.youtube.com/watch?v=Rsa71hc0Rr; BBC, *Look North*, November 7, 2011, www.youtube.com/watch?v=e-ps6FVRfew&feature=related.

The Girl Scouts published a 2010 "The Resilience Factor: A Key to Leadership in African American and Hispanic Girls," Girl Scout Research Institute, 2010, www.girlscouts.org.

black women have higher levels of estrogen www.unm.edu/~lkravitz/Article%20 folder/fatigueUNM.html; E. E. Marsh et al., "Estrogen Levels Are Higher Across the Menstrual Cycle in African-American Women Compared with Caucasian Women," *Journal of Clinical Endocrinology & Metabolism* (August 17, 2011) jc.2011-1314.

Danielle L. McGuire writes that white men raped Sheri Parks, "Danielle McGuire's Civil Rights History," *WP*, November 19, 2010, www.washingtonpost.com/wp-dyn /content/article/2010/11/19/AR2010111903125.html; Danielle L. McGuire, *At the Dark End of the Street: Black Women, Rape, and Resistance: A New History of the Civil Rights Movement from Rosa Parks to the Rise of Black Power* (New York: Knopf, 2010).

She encouraged the young activist Angela Davis, Speech, University of Maryland, 2012; NPR, "King Peggy."

Miss Height's work to improve conditions Sheri Parks, "Height Fused Struggles of Blacks, Women," *Baltimore Sun*, April 26, 2010, http://articles.baltimoresun.com/2010-04 -26/news/bs-ed-dorothy-height-20100426_1_dorothy-height-black-women-women-s-rights.

"They are beginning to accept me ... " NPR, "King Peggy."

In 2008, the Girl Scouts conducted "Change It Up! What Girls Say About Redefining Leadership," Girls Scout Research Institute, 2008, www.girlscouts.org.

A Johns Hopkins medical researcher *Clear Reception with Sheri Parks*, 2005; www.pew forum.org/A-Religious-Portrait-of-African-Americans.aspx.

When a Georgetown Law School student Theola Labbe'-DeBose, "Black Women in America: Their Faith Is Their Bedrock," *WP*, July 7, 2012.

"I didn't realize I had ... " NPR, "King Peggy."

A few weeks later, the NAACP board Michael Barbaro, "In Largely Symbolic Move, N.A.A.C.P. Votes to Endorse Same-Sex Marriage," *NYT*, May 19, 2012, www.nytimes .com/2012/05/20/us/politics/naacp-endorses-same-sex-marriage.html.

After President Obama announced Scott Clement and Sandhya Somashekhar, "After President Obama's Announcement, Opposition to Same-Sex Marriage Hits Record Low," *WP*, May 22, 2012, www.washingtonpost.com/politics/after-president-obamas -announcement-opposition-to-gay-marriage-hits-record-low/2012/05/22/gIQA1AYRjU _story.html.

Avis Jones-DeWeever highlighted economic perils Bahadur, Gaiutra. "'The Lady' Takes Office in Burma." *Ms.* Winter 2012, www.msmagazine.com/winter2012/thelady takesofficeinburma.asp.

Black women are operating www.gift-economy.com.

No man is an island John Donne, Meditation XVII.

The gift paradigm has the advantage Genevieve Vaughan, "Introduction to the Gift Economy," April 2004, www.gift-economy.com/theory.html.

similar concepts have been present in other, perhaps all Bernadette Muthien, www .engender.org.za.

In addition to facing discriminatory Mariko Chang, "Lifting as We Climb: Women of Color, Wealth, and America's Future," The Insight Center for Community Economic Development, March 2010, www.insightcced.org/publications/assetpubs.html.

Although she admires the strength Melissa V. Harris-Perry, *Sister Citizen: Shame, Stereotypes, and Black Women in America* (New Haven: Yale University Press, 2011).

in South Africa, communal property associations   Debbie Budlender, Sibongile Mgweba, Ketleetso Motsepe, and Leilanie Williams, "Women, Land and Customary Law Community Agency for Social Enquiry," Commission for Gender Equality, Johannesburg, South Africa, February 2011, www.cge.org.za/index.php?option=com _docman&task=doc_details&gid=195&Itemid=.

"Latina Leadership is . . . "   Chicana/Latina Foundation, www.chicanalatina.org /aboutus.html.

The Lenape Program   www.lenapeprograms.info/Women/women1.htm.

"The Elders say the Native American women . . . "   Journal #962 from sdc 11.05-.

The Native American Women's Health Education   www.nativeshop.org.

"At MomsRising . . . "   www.momsrising.org/page/moms/aboutmomsrising.

"People call me a feminist . . . "   www.bitchmagazine.org/about-us.

Chapter 8: Fierce Angels

The Daily Kos   dgr, "We Are Virginia Tech—Nikki Giovanni," April 17, 2007, www .dailykos.com.

The official Virginia Tech   www.weremember.vt.edu.

Giovanni later told NPR   NPR, "Tell Me More," January 15, 2009, www.npr.org.

She died from heart complications   T. Rees Shapiro and Ashley Oliver, "Remembering Zenobia," *Collegiate Times*, www.collegiatetimes.com.

Giovanni told Martin   NPR, "Tell Me More," January 15, 2009, www.npr.org.

In Hikes's obituary   Rees and Oliver, "Remembering Zenobia."

A friend of Tubman   Sarah Bradford (Sarah Hopkins), *Scenes in the Life of Harriet Tubman* (Auburn, NY: W. J. Moses, printer, 1869), http://docsouth.unc.edu/neh/Bradford /menu.html.

Bradford compared Tubman   Bradford, *Scenes*, Preface.

Abolitionist John Brown   Bradford, *Scenes*, "Letter to abolitionist Wendell Phillips, June 16, 1868," 5–6.

Frederick Douglass   Bradford, *Scenes*, "Frederick Douglass letter to Harriet Tubman, August 29, 1868," 7–8.

Parts of Tubman's story   Bradford, *Scenes*, 36.

She said, "I have . . . "   Bradford, *Scenes*, 12–13.

Bradford wrote   Bradford, *Scenes*, 37.

Peter Ackerman   Peter Ackerman and Jack Duvall, *A Force More Powerful: A Century of Nonviolent Conflict* (New York: Palgrave, 2000); *Clear Reception with Sheri Parks* interview, February 2006.

Black neighborhoods   Patrick Sharkey, "Neighborhoods and the Black–White Mobility Gap," www.pewtrusts.org.

"People come up . . . "   Ellen Wulfhorst, "Black, Female Leaders Battle Baltimore Urban Woes," October 30, 2007, www.reuters.com.

When Mayor Sheila Dixon   Ben Nuckols, "Baltimore Not as Bloody in '08 with Fewer Killings," January 1, 2009, http://abcnews.com/TheLaw/wirestory?id=6559935.

In 1996, while Johnnetta Cole   Johnnetta Cole Biography, www.achievement.org /autodoc/page/col0bio-1.

When Faye Wattleton   Faye Wattleton, http://secretary.columbia.edu/trustees-columbia -university/faye-wattleton.

"Veterans in town ... "   Krissah Thompson, "The Ties That Align: Administration's Black Women Form a Strong Sisterhood," *WP*, March 18, 2009.

In early 2008   "The State of Black America: In the Black Woman's Voice," National Urban League, 2008, www.nul.org.

Juan Williams   Juan Williams, *Enough: The Phony Leaders, Dead-End Movements, and Culture of Failure That Are Undermining Black America—and What We Can Do About It* (New York: Three Rivers Press, 2007); *Clear Reception with Sheri Parks*, September 2006 interview.

An organic leader   Antonio Gramsci, *Selections from the Prison Notebooks*, ed. Geoffrey Nowell-Smith (New York: International Publishers, 1971).

She was a signer of the 1970   *Black Woman's Manifesto*, http://scriptorium.lib.duke .edu/wlm/blkmanif.

These women had been   Eleanor Holmes Norton, telephone interview, June 2, 2008.

Katharine Graham   Robin Gerber, *Katharine Graham: The Leadership Journey of an American Icon* (New York: Portfolio, 2005), 78.

Later, Graham   Joan Steinau Lester, *Fire in My Soul: The Life of Eleanor Holmes Norton* (New York: Atria, 2004), 150.

At the first White House   "Congress: Lunch between 'Two Girlfriends.'" District Briefing, *WP*, March 18, 2009.

In early 2009, Norton wrote a letter to every single Democrat   Mary Beth Sheridan, "More Strategizing on D.C. Vote, Norton Sends Letter," D.C. Wire, *WP*, March 11, 2009, http://voices.washingtonpost.com/dc/2009/text_of_nortons_letter_may.

Johnson is the executive   www.apowerfulnoise.org.

The reviews often called   Rha Goddess, *Low*, Pillsbury House Theatre, Minneapolis, June 13, 2007.

"I trust in a very deep place ... "   Rha Goddess, "The Next Wave of Women and Power," Omega Institute, May 27, 2002.

China Galland   China Galland, *Longing for Darkness: Tara and the Black Madonna* (New York: Viking, 1990).

Lillian Comas-Diaz   Lillian Comas-Diaz, The 2007 Carolyn Sherif Award Address: "'Spirita—Reclaiming Womanist Sacredness into Feminism," *Psychology of Women Quarterly* Vol. 32, No. 1 (2008: 13–21.

"Womanism" is a term   Alice Walker, *In Search of Our Mothers' Gardens: Womanist Prose* (New York: Harcourt Brace Jovanovich, 1983).

Women in Africa   Ifi Amadiume, *Re-inventing Africa: Matriarchy, Religion and Culture* (London: Zed Books, 1998).

The only thoroughly researched   Robert Edgerton, *Warrior Women: The Amazons of Dahomey and the Nature of War* (New York: Basic Books, 2000); Stanley B. Alpern, *Amazons of Black Sparta: The Women Warriors of Dahomey* (New York: New York University Press,

1998); Edna G. Bay, *Wives of the Leopard: Gender, Politics, and Culture in the Kingdom of Dahomey* (Charlottesville: University of Virginia Press, 1998).

In 2000, Ifi Amadiume   Ifi Amadiume, *Daughters of the Goddess, Daughters of Imperialism: African Women Struggle for Culture, Power and Democracy* (London: Zed Books, 2000).

"I think that women . . . "   Eleanor Holmes Norton, telephone interview, June 2, 2008.

Black women have historically   Johnnetta Cole and Beverly Guy-Sheftall, *Gender Talk: The Struggle for Women's Equality in African American Communities* (New York: One World, 2003).

Black women don't just   "Poll: Black Support Helps Clinton Extend Lead," www.cnn.com, October 17, 2007.

Sheila Johnson told   "Business Mogul Sheila Johnson Tells Grads to Prepare for Global Competition," *Inside Spelman*, Summer 2008, www.spelman.edu.

In a study reported   League of Black Women, "Survey: Effects of a Dearth of Black Women in U.S. Companies," *Black PR Wire*, August 21, 2007.

"I saw it in my mother . . . "   DeNeen L. Brown and Richard Leiby. "The Very Image of Affirmation; In Michelle Obama, Black Women See a Familiar Grace & Strength Writ Large," *WP*, November 21, 2008.

PHOTOGRAPH AND
ILLUSTRATION CREDITS

1. Maurice Gordon-Bey Sr. and an unidentified man. STAFF/PHOTO BY MONICA LOPOSSAY, JUNE 14, 2007. COURTESY OF *BALTIMORE SUN*

2. Jill Jenkins. STAFF/PHOTOGRAPH BY MONICA LOPOSSAY, JUNE 14, 2007. COURTESY OF *BALTIMORE SUN*

3. Head of Buddha. Thailand. Mon style, late eighth to ninth century. ASIA SOCIETY, NEW YORK: MR. AND MRS. JOHN D. ROCKEFELLER, 3RD COLLECTION, 1979.78. COURTESY OF ASIA SOCIETY, NEW YORK

4. Statuette of Isis and Horus, Egyptian, Third Intermediate Period, Dynasty 21–25, 1070–656 BC. BRONZE MUSEUM OF FINE ARTS, BOSTON, GIFT OF MRS. HORACE L. MAYER 1971.749. PHOTOGRAPH © 2010 MUSEUM OF FINE ARTS, BOSTON

5. St. Mary Magdalene. ARTIST BR. ROBERT LENTZ, OFM. COURTESY OF TRINITY STORES (WWW.TRINITYSTORES.COM)

6. Nana Buruku. Purchased in an antique store in Salvador, Brazil. ARTIST DAVI NASCIMENTO. COURTESY OF OWNER, JED SUNDWALL

7. Members of the Societá di Mutuo Soccorso Santa Febronia Patti e Circondario. FROM ANNE PALERMO CARROCCIO'S FAMILY ALBUM. COURTESY OF JOSEPH SCIORRA

8. Italian Black Madonna. FROM ANNE PALERMO CARROCCIO'S FAMILY ALBUM. COURTESY OF JOSEPH SCIORRA

9. Pope John Paul II. COURTESY OF THE ASSOCIATED PRESS

10. Jesus of the People, selected to be the face of Jesus 2000 by the *National Catholic Reporter*. ARTIST JANET MCKENZIE

11. Confederate Monument. Confederate section of Arlington Cemetery. PHOTOGRAPH BY JOSHUA MCKERROW

12. Close-up of relief at base of Confederate Monument. PHOTOGRAPH BY JOSHUA MCKERROW

13. Amanda Waller with Batman. Cover of *Suicide Squad*, issue 10. COURTESY OF DC COMICS

14. Donna Brazile talking with Rep. Robert Wexler, May 31, 2008.

15. Nikki Giovanni. PHOTOGRAPH BY WHITE HOUSE PHOTOGRAPHER, ERIC DRAPER. COURTESY OF GEORGE BUSH PRESIDENTIAL LIBRARY, SOUTHERN METHODIST UNIVERSITY

16. Joan Hairston; West Virginia Governor, Joe Manchin; and members of Hairston's Logan High School mentoring group. COURTESY OF THE OFFICE OF THE GOVERNOR, WEST VIRGINIA

17. From left: Dominque Stevenson with volunteer Bashi Rose and Ronald Thomas-Bey. COURTESY OF THE AMERICAN FRIENDS SERVICE COMMITTEE

18. Sheila Johnson with a child in Rwanda. COURTESY OF CARE INTERNATIONAL

19. Rha Goddess. PHOTOGRAPH BY JEAN-CLAUDE TIZIOU (WWW.JJTIZIOU .NET). COURTESY OF RHA GODDESS

20. New York City mayor Abraham Beame swears in Eleanor Holmes Norton as Chairman of the Human Rights Commission. COURTESY OF THE NEW YORK CITY MUNICIPAL ARCHIVES

INDEX